Martin Brackett
March 29, 1965

Set up and printed, January, 1956

Reprinted, April, 1960

PRINTED IN THE UNITED STATES OF AMERICA

Outline Studies in the Acts of the Apostles

by

W. H. GRIFFITH THOMAS, D.D.

Edited by his daughter

WM. B. EERDMANS PUBLISHING CO.

Grand Rapids, Michigan

Books by

W. H. GRIFFITH THOMAS

GENESIS — A DEVOTIONAL COMMENTARY
ROMANS — A DEVOTIONAL COMMENTARY
THE APOSTLE PETER
THE APOSTLE JOHN
GRACE AND POWER
SERMON OUTLINES
OUTLINE STUDIES IN THE GOSPEL OF LUKE
OUTLINE STUDIES IN THE ACTS OF THE APOSTLES
CHRISTIANITY IS CHRIST
THE HOLY SPIRIT OF GOD

Outline Studies in the ACTS OF THE APOSTLES

IN LOVING MEMORY OF

ALICE GRIFFITH THOMAS

(1864-1953)

DEVOTED WIFE AND MOTHER

THIS VOLUME, THE FIRST IN ALL THE YEARS TO BE COMPLETED
WITHOUT THE CRITICISM OF HER KEEN MIND AND THE
SYMPATHY OF HER ZEALOUS HEART, IS DEDICATED
WITH EVER-DEEPENING APPRECIATION
ON BEHALF OF THE AUTHOR
AND
BY THE EDITOR

O Almighty God, who by Thy Son Jesus Christ didst give to Thy Apostle Saint Peter many excellent gifts, and commandest him earnestly to feed Thy flock; Make, we beseech Thee, all Bishops and Pastors diligently to preach Thy holy Word, and the people obediently to follow the same, that they may receive the crown of everlasting glory; through Jesus Christ our Lord. Amen.

— Collect for St. Peter's Day
Book of Common Prayer

O God, who, through the preaching of the Apostle Saint Paul, hast caused the light of the blessed Gospel to shine throughout the world; Grant, we beseech Thee, that we, having his wonderful conversion in remembrance, may shew forth our thankfulness unto Thee for the same, by following the holy doctrine which he taught; through Jesus Christ our Lord. Amen.

— Collect for the Day of the Conversion of St. Paul
Book of Common Prayer

EDITOR'S PREFACE

As noted of a former volume, this one, also, contains but a small part of the voluminous notes on Bible passages left by my father. It is not intended as a commentary and the notes do not necessarily cover exhaustively every verse of the Book of Acts. There are passages, however, that are outlined in more than one way, for the notes represent the author's study at various times and for many different occasions. At the risk of some repetition in the book as a whole, each outline study is intended to be complete in itself.

Use of material already published, during my father's lifetime and since his death, notably in the small handbook, *The Acts of the Apostles: Studies in Primitive Christianity,* and also in *Methods of Bible Study, The Christian Life and How to Live It, The Apostle Peter,* and *Christianity Is Christ,* is for the reason that it happens to be based on some of the same notes that I have tried to reproduce and expand here. For kind permission to use the first two of these volumes in comparing and interpreting, I am indebted to Moody Press, of Chicago, and for the third to The Church Book Room Press, Ltd., of London. The two books named last, as also *Sermon Outlines,* from which two sections are taken bodily and adapted in order to make the present volume more complete, are issued by our present publisher. For further and most valuable assistance, I am glad to express once more my deep appreciation to the Editors of *The Sunday School Times,* of Philadelphia, for their kindness in furnishing me with several sets of my father's lesson helps on The Acts written for the paper at different periods. Where the original notes were lacking or too fragmentary, I have often found it expedient to reduce the lesson helps and other printed material back to note form, so as to maintain consistency and completeness. Again, some of the outlines are taken from privately published meditations and word studies dating back to my father's pastoral days, for these have seemed to me too valuable not to be fitted into the scheme of a posthumous book.

These acknowledgments would not be in any sense adequate without a deeply grateful reference to the inspiration of my late beloved mother's life and her encouragement through the years as I have tried to carry on a little of my father's work. It was one of her dearest wishes that these and other notes entrusted to her by the husband she so revered should be made available to fellow-Christians, and thus it is fitting that this volume be dedicated to her memory. I am very grateful too, as always, for the valued co-operation and useful criticism that is still mine from my husband, himself a Bible student and teacher.

Again, if these studies bring to others a blessing such as they have left with me, they will fulfil my purpose as I prayerfully send them forth.

WINIFRED G. T. GILLESPIE

Lafayette, Louisiana
January, 1956

CONTENTS

Outline Studies
in the
ACTS OF THE APOSTLES

INTRODUCTION

1. Composition of Book

a. Author — Luke the Physician (cf. Col. 4:14; 2 Tim. 4:11; Philemon 24), clearly connected with earlier work, as author of "former treatise" (1:1) addressed also to Theophilus — our Third Gospel (cf. Luke 1:1-4) — eye-witness of much (cf. 16:10-17; 20:5 to 21:25; 27:1 to 28:16, where he writes in first person). Medical phraseology additional testimony (cf. 3:7; 12:23; 13:11; 28:8).

N.B. Sir William Ramsay called Luke writer of exceptional genius and versatility, extraordinarily accurate and well-informed, and said Acts invaluable not only as religious, but also as historical document. Was remarkable literary feat to catch evangelical language of other Synoptists in his Gospel and then to turn to narrative style characterizing Acts; needed no ordinary perception of different natures of Peter and Paul to put into mouth of each speeches appropriate to audience and occasion and, even when subject virtually same, to show individuality of either, but seems as natural to Luke as to Shakespeare! Skill of epitomizing letter of Lysias and speech of Tertullus evidence of literary art of highest rank.

b. Scope — covers about 30 years, A.D. 33 to 63 — extending from Jerusalem, through Antioch, to Rome.

2. Relation of Book to other Bible Books

a. Bridge connecting Gospels and Epistles — outcome of former and explanation of latter, sequel of one and introduction to other.

b. Cf. last chapter of each Gospel with first chapter of Acts:
   (1) Matthew refers to Resurrection; Mark to Ascension; Luke to Promise of Spirit; John to Second Coming; all four facts included in introduction to Acts (1:1-11);

(2) Each Evangelist recounts Great Commission of Christ; repeated and confirmed in Acts (1:8).

c. Cf. Epistles of Paul with Acts 13 to 28, which chapters at once introduce and illustrate them.

d. Cf., in O.T., Pentateuch with Gospels, Historical Books with Acts — also Wisdom Books with Epistles and Prophets with Revelation.

3. **Importance of Book**

Consider loss to Christian worker if without it, for its use is —

a. Doctrinal — record of facts — example of results of Christian teaching;

b. Practical — textbook of evangelism and missions — pattern of church government — first chapters of Church history.

THE BOOK AS A WHOLE

I. **The Purpose**

To give the record of —

1. **The Activity of a Divine Worker** — "Jesus" (1:1)

a. *The Real Agent*

(1) Preface (1:1,2) shows connection between Acts and Luke's Gospel and purpose of both: one deals with what Jesus "began both to do and teach, until the day in which He was taken up"; other with what Jesus continued to do, after He was taken up, through the Holy Spirit in lives of apostles as instruments (cf. 1:24; 2:33,47; 3:16; 7:59; 9:5, and many more). Book might be called "The Acts of the Ascended Lord."

(2) We, like them, are to be instruments, not agents — not workmen so much as tools — work is not ours, but His. This book a *"sursum corda"* — "Lift up your hearts!" — "We lift them up unto the Lord!"

b. *The True Power*
   (1) The Holy Spirit (cf. 1:2, and at least 70 other references);
   (2) Book might also be called "The Acts of the Holy Spirit," emphasizing predominance of Divine element over human in life and work of Christian Church;
   (3) But Book called "Acts" — not resolutions, which for most part have not come down to us, but actions, which have.

2. The Description of a Great Mission — "to do and to teach" (1:1)

These words sum up all activity of book:

a. Note the two — Work and Word — not one only;

b. Note the order — conduct before precept (cf. Luke 24:19);

c. Note the Work — doing:
   (1) Equipping believers (1:8);
   (2) Extending Kingdom (1:8);
   (3) Establishing Church (2:41-47);
   This threefold work is being continued by Christ today.

d. Note the Word — teaching:
   Person of Christ substance and center of message (cf. 8:5, 35; 9:20; 11:20), to Jews on basis of O. T. revelation, to Gentiles, of natural revelation. Out of this come three great subjects of book, practically summing up Gospel:
   (1) Resurrection of Christ — involved Divine position and authority of Jesus of Nazareth (cf., e.g., 1:22; 2:24-32; 4:2, 33; 17:18; 23:6; 24:15; 26:23) — Godhead of Christ;
   (2) Reign of Christ — followed naturally — He must be King (cf., e.g., 1:3; 2:33; 8:12; 14:22; 17:7; 19:8; 20:25; 28:23, 31) — Lordship of Christ;
   (3) Remission of Sins — consequence of two foregoing — man as rebel must surrender to God and King

and receive forgiveness (c.f., e.g., 2:38; 5:31; 10:43; 13:38; 26:18) — Atonement of Christ.

3. **The Suggestion of a Particular Aspect — "began" (1:1)**
   Word emphatic — Book of Acts only beginning of Christian Church:
   a. In relation to certain places — Jerusalem (chap. 2), Judaea and Samaria (chap. 8), Syria (chap. 11), Asia Minor (chap. 13), Greece (chap. 16), Rome (chap. 28);
   b. In relation to typical features — first Christian sermon, prayer meeting, church organization, problems, persecution, martyrdom, personal work, foreign missions, conflict with world, inter-communication of churches, etc.
   c. We are to study, ponder, imitate, and see effects in church life and work of first examples of what have become very familiar since that time.

II. The Plan (1:8)

1. **The Purpose accomplished through a special class of People**
   "Ye shall be witnesses unto Me"
   a. Disciples as witnesses now, having been learners hitherto;
   b. Method simple yet sufficient;
   c. Used sometimes with individuals (chaps. 8, 10, 11), and sometimes with crowds (chap. 2, etc.).
2. **The Purpose realized through a special pathway of Progress**
   "In Jerusalem and . . . the earth"
   Three extending circles in two aspects:
   a. Historical aspect:
      (1) Church in Jerusalem (chaps. 1-7);
      (2) Church in Judaea and Samaria (chaps. 8, 9);
      (3) Church of Gentile world leading to Rome (chaps 10-28);
   b. Spiritual aspect:

(1) Witnessing "in Jerusalem, and in all Judaea" — where pure religion falsely held;

(a) Now, as then, home comes first, following naturally from conversion and continuing;

(b) Next, our own nationality, also Jews and other groups in home missions;

(2) Witnessing "in Samaria" — where was mixed religion, partly true and partly false;
N.B. Now, may be thought of as missions to Roman Catholics and to Mohammedans;

(3) Witnessing "unto the uttermost part of the earth" — where was no religion at all, or at best false heathen worship.
N.B. Now, may stand for foreign missions all over the world.

3. The Purpose fulfilled through a special adoption of Policy

a. Taking as centers for work large cities, with dense populations and throbbing life, in order to reach surrounding neighborhoods:

(1) Cf. Peter in Jerusalem and result of Pentecost (chap. 2);

(2) Cf. Philip in Samaria and Azotus (chap. 8);

(3) Cf. Paul in Antioch, Ephesus, Philippi, Thessalonica, Corinth, Rome (chaps. 13ff.);

(4) Cf. Paul's two years and three months in Ephesus (chap. 19);

b. Christianity thus birthright of city which needs strongest life and best workers;
N.B. So today — London, Paris, New York, Calcutta, Shanghai, etc. — great cities attacked for Gospel and then attacking.

III. The Principles

The Acts of the Apostles may be viewed as handbook for Christian workers. In all Christian work there are three indispensable elements, which in this book are brought before reader in order and in proportion:

1. **The Spirit of God — the Might** (chaps. 1 to 11 are full of Him)
   a. Five occasions of bestowal — for all: to Jews (chap. 2), to Samaritans (chap. 8), to persecutor (chap. 9), to Gentiles (chap. 10), to semi-ignorant ones (chap. 19) — all specimens of need and possibility;
   b. What He is in Himself — promise, baptism, gift, fulness, witness, anointing, commander, Godhead;
   c. What He may be to us — power, testimony, boldness, obedience, wisdom, faith, comfort, joy.

2. **The Word of God — the Message** (chaps. 12 to 20 have less of Spirit and more of Word)
   a. Revelation from God to world:
      (1) What Scriptures are: Divinely inspired, powerful, profitable;
      (2) What they do: Save, guide, equip;
      (3) What they require: Knowledge, trust, continuance;
   b. Its titles are varied and significant: "Word" (16:6), "Word of God" (17:13), "Word of the Lord" (15:35), "Gospel" (15:7), "Word of this salvation" (13:26), "Word of His grace" (14:3; 20:32), "Words of this life" (5:20);
   c. Its results are manifest: "Increased" (6:7), "grew and multiplied" (12:24), "grew . . . and prevailed" (19:20).

3. **The Man of God — the Medium** (chaps. 21-28 have little about Spirit and Word, but much about Man)
   a. He is to be Witness to unconverted;
   b. He is to be Workman for the Church;
   c. He is to be Warrior against evil;

   N.B. Eleven chapters emphasize Spirit, nine Word, eight Man (in person of Paul) — that is order and proportion:

Spirit first, Word second, Man third; Spirit greatest and foremost, then Word also very important, and only last of all, Man. But union of all three gives complete *modus operandi* of Acts, and is secret of all blessing in Christian work.

IV. The Outlines

A. A simple outline of the Book of Acts is as follows:

1. *The Gospel in the Jewish World* (chaps. 1 to 12)
   a. Beginnings at Jerusalem (1:1 to 6:7);
   b. Extension into Samaria and Judaea (6:8 to 9:31);
   c. Commencement among the Gentiles — transition (9:32 to 12:25);
2. *The Gospel in the Gentile World* (chaps. 13 to 28)
   a. The work in Asia Minor (13:1 to 16:5);
   b. The development into Greece (16:6 to 19:20);
   c. The journey to and arrival at Rome (19:21 to 28:31);

   N.B. Each section is closed with summary (see last verse). Two main divisions deal respectively with Peter and Paul, each closing with imprisonment. Book is thus fine unity, showing how Peter faced Jews and Paul Gentiles.

B. A more detailed outline is as follows:

1. *The Preface* (1:1-11)
   a. To whom written, and why (vs. 1, 2);
   b. The Risen Lord (vs. 3-9);
   c. The Ascending Lord (v. 10);
   d. The Returning Lord (v. 11).
2. *The Church Empowered* (1:12 to 2:47)
   a. Waiting (1:12-26);
   b. Receiving (2:1-13);
   c. Witnessing (2:14-47).
3. *The Church Established in Jerusalem* (chaps. 3 to 7)
   a. Peter — from Power to Prison (3:1 to 5:42);
   b. Organization (6:1-7);

c. Stephen — from Spirit to Stoning (6:8 to 7:60).

4. *The Church Extended to Samaria and Judaea* (8:1 to 9:43)
   a. New Fields:
      (1) Samaria (8:1-25);
      (2) Lydda and Joppa (9:32-43)
      (3) Caesarea (8:40; 10:1-48);
   b. New Foes:
      (1) Saul and Simon (8:1-25);
      (2) Disease and Death (9:32-43);
   c. New Forces:
      (1) Philip (8:5-40);
      (2) Paul (9:1-31).
5. *The Church Enlightened Concerning the Gentiles* (chaps. 10 to 12)
   a. Peter and the Vision (chap. 10);
   b. Peter and the Council (chap. 11);
   c. Peter and Herod (chap. 12).
6. *The Church Enlarged to the Uttermost Parts of the Earth* (chaps. 13 to 28)
   a. The New Center: Antioch (13:1);
   b. The New Leader: Paul (13:2);
   c. The New Method: Foreign Missions (13:3 to 21:19):
      (1) First Missionary Journey (13:3 to 14:28);
      (2) Second Missionary Journey (15:36 to 18:22);
      (3) Third Missionary Journey (18:23 to 21:19).
   d. The New Difficulties (21:20 to 26:32)
      (1) Ceremonial (21:20 to 22:29);
      (2) Council (22:30 to 23:11);
      (3) Civil Rulers (23:12 to 26:32).
   e. The New Objective — Rome (27:1 to 28:31)

V. The Analysis

1. *According to historical extension* (outwardly)
   a. The church of Jerusalem (1:1 to 7:60);
   b. The church of Palestine (8:1 to 12:25);
   c. The church of the Gentiles (13:1 to 28:31).

2. *According to spiritual expansion* (inwardly)
   a. Definite commencement (1:1 to 6:7);
   b. Deepening experiences (6:8 to 12:25);
   c. Great progress (13:1 to 19:20);
   d. Apparent check (19:21 to 28:31).
3. *According to personal effort* (individually)
   It has been pointed out that St. Luke mentions by name only those persons whose acts directly affected great missionary purpose of God, since Christian workers of no real value unless engaged in preaching Living Word from Written Word; thus we see—
   a. The Apostle Peter (chaps. 1 to 12), closing with his imprisonment and release:
      (1) This section is mainly concerned with Peter's—
         (a) Actions and discourses;
         (b) Relation to other Apostles;
         (c) Personal characteristics;
      (2) But there are other personal factors to note and study:
         (a) Stephen — character, defense, martyrdom;
         (b) Philip — work, limitation, discipline;
         (c) Saul — antecedents, conversion, discipleship;
         (d) Barnabas (i) — consecration, sympathy, service.
   b. The Apostle Paul (chaps. 13 to 28), closing with his imprisonment (and implied release?):*
      (1) This section is mainly concerned with Paul's—
         (a) Life and ministry;
         (b) Preaching and pastoral work;
         (c) Consecration and power;
      (2) But here, again, there are other personal factors to note and study:
         (a) James — position, character, epistle;
         (b) Barnabas (ii) — relation to Paul in journeying and council, part in contention;

*See Study No. 130, p. 537.

(c) Other companions of Paul: Mark, Timothy, Silas, Luke himself, Aquila and Priscilla, Apollos, etc.

As we approach the Book of Acts in detail, we shall do well to keep uppermost the thought of the living Christ: Christ as Lord, Christ as Life, and Christ as Law. We shall find the Gospel of the Resurrection, the Gospel of the Kingdom, and the Gospel of Divine forgiveness. The Apostles proclaimed the Resurrection to prove that Christ was God, and in obedience to Him as their Master they proclaimed the Kingdom; but inasmuch as all men are rebels and therefore not in the Kingdom, it was necessary also to proclaim the forgiveness of sins. This, then, is the threefold message of the Acts of the Apostles: Christ as Saviour, Christ as Lord, Christ as God.

Study No. 1 — "Many Infallible Proofs"

ACTS 1:1-14

THROUGHOUT this inspired textbook for Christian workers we may trace the workings of the Spirit of God through the Word of God and by the men of God whom the Lord Jesus had chosen to carry on His work on earth. The whole volume is illustrative of Mark 16:20: "And *they* went forth, and preached every where, *the Lord* working with them, and confirming *the Word* with signs following."

The true spiritual perspective is apparent in these verses, from the death and resurrection of Christ, through the promise of the Spirit, the ascension, and the prophecy of the second coming, to the prayerful waiting upon God which preceded Pentecost and still precedes every effective effort for God.

I. The Earthly Ministry (vs. 1-3)

1. *Preparatory* (v.1)
   - a. Jesus *began* to do and to teach during His life on earth;
   - b. This doing and teaching was *continued* by Him (cf. Mark 16:20, "the Lord working") from heaven;
2. *Continuous* (v.2)
   - a. To chosen apostles;
   - b. Up until very day of ascension;
3. *Thorough* (v.3)
   - a. By strong evidences;
   - b. By painstaking instructions.

II. The Parting Words (vs. 4-8)

1. *Command* (vs. 4,5)
   - a Promise — the Father's gift of the Holy Spirit to come soon;

b. Instruction — apostles were to wait, both for testing and for preparation;

2. *Inquiry* (v. 6)
   a. Ignorance — cf. "kingdom to Israel" (v. 6) with "kingdom of God" (v. 3) — preoccupation with materialistic concept;
   b. Curiosity — as to its time when they should have been concerned with its nature;

3. *Teaching* (vs. 7,8)
   a. Check — time still God's secret (cf. Matt. 24:36; Mark 13:32; 1 Thess. 5:1);
   b. Encouragement — they were to witness, not speculate; to trust, not argue.

III. The Glorious Ascension (vs. 9-14)

1. *The Fact* (v. 9)
   a. Upward movement of Christ;
   b. Receiving cloud from the Father;

2. *The Reminder* (vs. 10,11)
   a. Gentle rebuke — "Why stand ye gazing . . . ?"
   b. Strong reasoning — "This same Jesus . . . taken . . . into heaven, shall so come . . . "

He is coming, "this same Jesus,"
Sweet the thought that soon the day
With its beams of light shall banish
Earth's dark shadows far away.
"This same Jesus" — He is coming;
I shall see Him face to face;
In the saint-thronged courts of heaven
He has given me a place.

3. *The Outcome* (vs. 12-14)
   a. Return — to Jerusalem and to upper room (Gr., "the" upper room, perhaps same as in Luke 22:12). Cf. feelings of disciples then, and after resurrection (John 20:19), and now, after ascension: they have access, protection, and hope;

b. Occupation — "all continued with one accord in prayer" — here is nucleus of Christian Church.

Conclusion

1. *The Ascended Christ — our Peace*
   a. Perfect — because all barriers removed;
   b. Perpetual — because He ever lives.
2. *The Living Christ — our Power*
   a. For character — joy, trust, holiness;
   b. For conduct — witness, work, warfare.
3. *The Coming Christ — our Prospect*
   a. Personal reunion — with loved ones;
   b. Perfect satisfaction — with Him.

Fair Olivet! thou spot most sweet,
The last trod by those sacred feet;
Upon thy brow, they'll stand again
When He, as King, shall come to reign.

—T.R.

Study No. 2 —

The Holy Spirit in the Acts of the Apostles

ACTS 1:5

THERE ARE many and obvious differences between the methods of God's revelation of Himself in the old Testament and in the New Testament. The Old Testament speaks of Christ as coming, the New Testament of Christ as come; the Old Testament speaks of God as transcendent, supreme; the New Testament of God as immanent, dwelling in the believer and in the Church; or, God over us, and God in us. The Old Testament is concerned with God as Almighty, the New Testament with God as Father. Someone has said that the conception of God in the Old Testament is holiness, and the conception of God in the New

Testament is love; so that, taking the two together, we have the Biblical revelation of God as holy love.

But the most important and far-reaching contrast between the old and the new dispensations as represented by the two Testaments is associated with the revelation of the Holy Spirit of God. There are singularly few references to the Spirit in the Old Testament. The term "Holy Spirit" occurs but three times; and the general teaching about Him in the Old Testament is almost impressive by its rareness. There is much more, of course, in the Gospels, but it is especially in the latter part of the New Testament that we find the teaching so striking. While there was, of course, a genuinely spiritual life before Pentecost, this was nothing in comparison to what Christian life became after the gift of the Holy Spirit.

Yet there are Christians today whose experience is still on the level of the Old Testament and of the Gospels. They may know these things intellectually, but they are really living on a plane of spiritual experience the other side of Pentecost, for although the former dispensations are historically past they unfortunately can be experimentally present. We can see this most clearly in the story of the men in Ephesus (19:1-7) who had not heard about the gift of Pentecost although they were living many years after that event.* Nowadays, people similarly know about the Holy Spirit but have never entered fully into their inheritance in Him. Let us describe briefly, with special reference to the Holy Spirit, the three dispensations, in order to see what our Christian life is intended to be, and then pass to the three ways in which He is delineated in the Book of Acts.

I. The Three Dispensations

1. *The Dispensation of the Father* — Abel to John the Baptist
   What were marks of believer's life then?
   a. Fear of God — word "fear" found 600 times in O. T. and "faith" twice (cf. concordance!) though of course it is frequently implied in word "faithful" — God far off, great, holy, mighty, but nothing more, not fully known.

---

*See Studies Nos. 96 and 97, pp. 371ff.

Jewish people moved by fear rather than by love, though not to exclusion of love (cf., e.g., Psa. 116:1);

b. Sense of sin — sin real and with it came sorrow, powerlessness and hopelessness;

c. Belief in Messiah — Jews looked forward to coming of Christ — thoroughly orthodox;

d. Consciousness of immortality — belief in future life, though limited knowledge of it;

e. Spirit of separateness — Jews exclusive — little diffusion of religion — monotheistic but not missionary;

N.B. Many Christians today dominated by fear of God, oppressed by sin, thoroughly orthodox in belief, expecting to go to heaven, and very exclusive. They are living as though Pentecost had never taken place.

2. *The Dispensation of the Son* — Period of our Lord's earthly Ministry

Represents distinct advance, but what about life of disciples?

a. It was a time of great power in the Word. The Lord Jesus as Teacher very impressive, and Word, as taught by Him, very real and true, but still partial due to nature of case (cf. John 7:39 and chaps. 14 to 16) — sin repressed rather than overcome;

b. There was much variableness of experience. Note contrast between Peter on Mount of Transfiguration and Peter at time of cock-crowing — mountain and valley;

c. There was much domination of tradition. Things had been and still were — bonds of tradition felt to very end, including expectation of immediate earthly kingdom;

d. There was much contention. Even at time of Last Supper disciples still contending as to place, their strife based on ignorance;

e. There was promise, but not presence, of Holy Spirit. As Comforter, Spirit of Truth, Witness — but all looking forward to "that day," day of the Holy Ghost;

N.B. This, too, represents spiritual experience of many Christians today. Word is power and reality to them, but their experience is variable, tradition dominates them, spirit of contention is present; there is expectation of something rather than experience of it. They, also, live almost as though Pentecost had never taken place.

3. *The Dispensation of the Spirit** — The Day of Pentecost on— This seen in Book of Acts which begins with events leading up to Pentecost. Yet all good elements of first two dispensations found united and included in third; everything right and true in Old Testament and Gospels found here, with wonderful additions and amplifications. Acts book of realism — "acts," actions, not resolutions nor ideals — record of Christian life as lived. What was it?
   a. *A life of rich personal experience*:
      (1) Fulness of faith — e.g., Stephen (6:5), Barnabas (11:24);
      (2) Fulness of wisdom — "they could not resist the wisdom" (6:10; cf. also 6:3; 15:28; 20:23; 21:4);
      (3) Fulness of joy — "the disciples were filled with joy and the Holy Ghost" (13:52):
         (a) Blessedness is element of Christian joy that comes from relation to God — cf. beatitudes in Psalms and Gospels and Revelation — blessedness dependent on what we are, not on what we have;
         (b) Joy always mark of real Christian life — came with Gospel; later, in Dark Ages, was absent from religious experience, then burst out in Reformation; receded during 16th and 17th centuries, then came back in Evangelical and Methodist revivals — has been seen and experienced at home and on mission fields all through recent centuries — "joy of the Holy Ghost";
      (4) Fulness of hope — "Stephen looked up and saw the Lord Jesus" (7:55) because "full of the Holy Ghost."

---

*See Study No. 14, page 67.

b. *A life of great personal courage*:

First, experience — then, courage:

(1) Boldness of speech

(a) Cf. Peter, man frightened six weeks before by servant maid, now speaks out with complete frankness (2:23);

(b) Cf. also apostles in 4:31 — result of prayer after trial, not to be kept silent and well-behaved, but "boldness";

(c) Cf. also story of Stephen in chap. 7 — bold speech — called spade spade and not instrument of husbandry!

(2) Boldness of action

(a) Cf. again 4:31, not only speech but action;

(b) Cf. 13:9, Paul and Elymas the sorcerer;

(c) Cf. 8:27, Philip and the great foreign official;

(3) Yes, first, experience, then courage, but also tact, which means primarily "getting in touch" with others.

Illus.: Clergyman wanting graveyard enlarged, and not knowing how to convince officers of church, decided to use tact; so he said, "Don't you see how nicely our cemetery is filling up?"

(4) But, again, tactfulness should not cause nervousness and lack of certainty; boldness or tact alone can hinder cause of Christ; so we need both.

c. *A life of splendid personal service*

Experience and courage expressing themselves in—

(1) Service of speech — "all filled . . . and began to speak" (2:4; 4:31) — better not to "speak" until "filled";

(2) Service of living — "filled" (9:31; 4:31, 32) — Peter (4:8); Stephen (7:55); Paul (9:17, 18; 13:4). Connected with wisdom (6:5), comfort (9:31), power (10:38), faith (11:24), and joy (13:52).

N.B. What about "baptism of Holy Ghost"? Phrase not found in Scripture. People were baptized *with* the Holy Ghost but exactly as with water — once for all, never repeated, or ought not to be. Thus, baptism with Spirit is elementary and initial act, never associated in N.T. with anything except beginning of Christian experience. "Ye shall be baptized with the Holy Ghost" (1:5) referred to Day of Pentecost "not many days" thence; and when Holy Ghost fell on Cornelius (11:15, 16), Peter remembered this word and how "tongues of fire . . . sat upon each of them" (2:3) — that is, falling of Spirit reminded him of baptism (10:44-48). Conversely, baptism is always connected with Spirit falling (cf. 1 Cor. 12:13) — that is to say, when we first accepted Christ as Saviour the Holy Ghost baptized us — not water baptism, but Holy Ghost baptism put us into Body of Christ, the Church. Thus water baptism is symbol connected with God the Holy Spirit, just as other sacrament, the Lord's Supper, is symbol connected with God the Son — not both symbolic of same truth, death of Christ, which would contribute to very neglect and ignorance of Holy Spirit we are here discussing. But — "one baptism, many fillings," as has truly been said — variety of wonderful experiences shown in four Greek words used in connection with Holy Ghost filling: (1) Apostles at Pentecost and after were "filled" (2:4; 4:8); (2) disciples "kept on being filled" (13:52); (3) deacons were "full" (6:3), meaning normal Christian condition; but, most wonderful of all, (4) Stephen was "permanently full" (7:55). Never, therefore, "second blessing" unless prepared to go on to third. in fact, to second hundred, second thousand, second million! Experience often right, but expression of it wrong — experience sometimes orthodox and expression hopelessly heretical. Let us get theology straightened out, but meanwhile enjoy experience to our full capacity.

II. The Three Delineations

A personal experience of the Holy Spirit is thus shown to be—

1. *God's Purpose*

   a. *He is necessary;*

      (1) Not mere luxury to have fulness of Spirit — no luxuries in N.T. in sense of anything in spiritual life we can do without — but, also, "luxury" in sense that we are to "luxuriate" — "enjoy Him for ever," in the well-known phrase of St. Augustine;

      (2) Not only for Christian character, but for good reputation — "full of Holy Ghost and wisdom," so "of honest report" (6:3) — wisdom needed to deal, not only with widows, but with all other people as well!— "Look after your character, and God will take care of your reputation!"

   b. *He is to be universal;*

      (1) Not for favored few, as in O.T., upon special men and women, but for all believers; cf. 5 typical bestowments:

         (a) To Jews (2:38);
         (b) To Samaritans (8:17);
         (c) To newly converted persecutor (9:17);
         (d) To Gentiles (10:44);
         (e) To untaught believers (19:6);

      (2) Not for special times and circumstances, as in O.T., or for special work, but for all work, all times, all circumstances;

         (a) We read of promise of the Spirit, being baptized with the Spirit, gift of the Spirit, fulness of the Spirit, witness of the Spirit, anointing of the Spirit;

         (b) We find the Spirit connected with boldness, obedience, wisdom, faith, comfort, joy, and even with business (6:3);

         (c) All of these we need at various times and in various places; so that we must not draw too hard and fast a line in distinguishing between sacred and secular for, as has been said, "Nothing is secular but what is sinful."

Teach me, my God, in all things Thee to see;
And what I do, to do it as to Thee.
— George Hurlburt

2. *God's Plan*
 a. *Faith obtains His presence* — "Resist not the Spirit" (cf. 7:51)
  (1) This involves entire surrender to God — e.g., Barnabas, significantly described as "a good man, full of the Holy Ghost and faith" (11:24):
   (a) His character — "a good man";
   (b) His secret — "full of the Holy Ghost and of faith";

   Faith was means by which he received Holy Spirit who was source of his goodness (cf. Eph. 3:14);
   N.B. Has been said this description sounds like epitaph! But no need to wait for that, as man who remarked, "A penny's worth of 'taffy' is better than a shilling's worth of 'epitaphy'!"
  (2) This does not necessarily involve feeling, but it does deal with fact — Holy Spirit often associated with great tides of emotion, but emotion largely temperamental — Welsh Revival wonderful but failed in England — Holy Spirit had to deal differently with two peoples, enthusiastic Celts, phlegmatic Saxons; but all may exert faith in fact, and faith is as necessary for Celt as for Saxon or for any other race.
 b. *Faithfulness maintains His presence* — "Grieve not the Spirit" (Eph. 4:30)
  (1) What we have by faith obtained we maintain by faithfulness — yieldedness to Holy Spirit;
  (2) Act becomes attitude, and life of Spirit, without tides of emotion, is simply lived, day by day.
 c. *Fellowship retains His presence* — "Quench not the Spirit" (1 Thess. 5:19)

(1) This admonition followed by another — "Despise not prophesyings" (v. 20), or, Keep close to Bible, listen to what God says; and in fellowship with Him you will retain what you have obtained and maintained;

(2) Thus secret of presence of Holy Ghost only possible when we are faithful to Bible study, for God's Spirit uses God's Word.

So, in regard to faith, we are to resist not; as regards faithfulness, we are to grieve not; as regards fellowship, we are to quench not, the Spirit. This is God's plan — very simple, and yet very satisfying.

3. *God's Power*

a. *The substance*:

In 28 chapters of Acts:

(1) Chapters 1 to 11 — Spirit of God predominant — 38 times mentioned;

(2) Chapters 12 to 20 — Word of God predominant — 23 times mentioned;

(3) Chapters 21 to 28 — Man of God (typified by Paul) — with Spirit mentioned only 3 times;

b. *The relation*:

Note meaning: Spirit of God to be the power, Word of God the message, man of God the channel;

c. *The preparation*:

Note order: Spirit always first, Word second, man last. Spirit is power by means of which God, through Word, uses man; so that each time we receive or transmit man's message from Word which is illumined by Spirit, we may realize more fully God's purpose and plan.

Conclusion

For all this we must appropriate the Holy Spirit Himself. How? It is very simple:

1. Our Lord "the same night in which He was betrayed . . . said, Take——" (1 Cor. 11:23, 24);

2. Our Lord the same night on which He rose from the dead breathed on His disciples and said, "Take——" (John 20:22, "receive");
3. Exactly the same word: "Take, eat——" — "Take (receive) ye the Holy Ghost" — so we may believe that as they had taken the bread on the one night they also took the Holy Spirit on the other;
4. When *we* are willing to take the Holy Spirit in the same way as we take the bread at the Lord's Supper, that is the taking, the receiving, the appropriating of faith;
5. Then does the Holy Ghost come into our lives and fill us with wisdom, power, blessing, joy, faith, courage, and everything we need for life, for character, and for service.

Thus we may repeat in our heart's experiences and our life's energies the power of Pentecost and the vigor of the early Church; thus we may fulfil God's purpose for us and live up to our privileges in Him; and thus we may glorify Him as the God of all grace in a life "full of the Holy Ghost."

**Prayer*: Now, our loving Father, in this moment of silence we want to "take." We rejoice to think that Thou didst use so familiar a word, and that if we "take" Thou wilt undertake. All that we have to do is to receive, and this moment we do it. We do not feel anything very much; perhaps we have no emotional experience at all at this time. But by simple, quiet faith, resting upon Thy Word, we believe now that Thy Holy Ghost is coming into our hearts. We take Him now!

May the grace of the Lord Jesus Christ, the love of God, and the fellowship of the Holy Ghost be with you all, now and forevermore. Amen.

---

*One of my father's few recorded prayers. Ed.

Study No. 3 — Christian Witness

ACTS 1:8

THESE, the last earthly words of the Lord Jesus, provide the key-plan of the Book of Acts, the first volume of Church history ever written. They indicate the first missionary planning and the outline of geographical expansion for Christianity, but also, and chiefly, the secret and model of all Christian witness in every age.

I. The Subject of Witness — "witnesses unto Me"

1. *Personal Testimony*
   a. Christian worker is to be witness — not originator, not discoverer, not philosopher, or even theologian, primarily;
   b. First, personal experience, and then, personal expression of it — no true ministry without these;
   c. Personal, not delegated (cf. Acts 4:20).
2. *Testimony to a Person*
   a. Person of Jesus Christ sums up essential Christianity, and conversely —
   b. Christianity is devotion to Person of Christ — not to a Church, or even to a Book or a philosophy;
   c. Person of Christ includes what He is and what He does:
      (1) His life for righteousness;
      (2) His death for atonement;
      (3) His resurrection for power;
      (4) His ascension for acceptance.
      N.B. What Christ is, and all Christ is, to us, we must show to others.
3. *Methods of Testimony*
   a. By word — confession of lip;
   b. By work — consistency of life;
   c. By writing — circulation of literature;

N.B. We must use all three, and all must be definite, clear, full.

II. The Sphere of Witness — "in Jerusalem, and in all Judaea, and in Samaria, and unto the uttermost part of the earth"

Three extending circles, standing for great principles as well as for geographical locations:

1. *The First Circle* — "in Jerusalem, and in all Judaea"
   a. Home — natural place of commencement;
   b. Also, where true religion is falsely or imperfectly held;
   c. Homeland, neighborhood, city, and country — or sphere of nominal Christianity;
   d. To children, young people, under-privileged, sceptics, etc.;
2. *The Second Circle* — "in Samaria"
   a. Missions to neighboring states;
   b. Also, where is mixture of true and false religions, e.g., Roman Church, Greek Church, Mohammedanism;
   c. On every continent, in every country, we must have "dealings" (cf. John 4:4, 9) with followers of such, in effort to evangelize them;
3. *The Third Circle* — "unto the uttermost part of the earth"
   a. Foreign missions, or "unoccupied fields";
   b. Also, where religion is utterly false, or there is no religion at all;
   c. Written word especially needed there — in all languages.

III. The Source of Witness — "ye shall receive power, after that the Holy Ghost is come upon you"

1. *The Holy Spirit needed*
   a. Only so is any Christian work done;
   b. Even Word without Him is dead;
2. *The Holy Spirit provided*
   a. He is Divine — "Holy Ghost"
   b. He is gift of Christ (cf. John 14:26; 15:26; 16:7);
3. *The Holy Spirit received*
   a. He is to "come upon" believers;
   b. He is to be manifested in their lives — by glow, force, unction.

Conclusion

To bear a true, strong witness —

1. *Realize what Christ is to you;*
2. *Remember those to whom He is nothing, or very little;*
3. *Receive the Holy Spirit's power for service;*
4. *Respond to His claim and call.*

Away with a faithless plea that cannot abide the light,
Be wholly for Christ, and He will teach you to speak aright;
His love will supply the power, the measure, the mode, the theme;
You have but the present hour. O, spend every breath for Him!

Study No. 4 — The Life of the Ascended Christ

ACTS 1:9

MOST MODERN Lives of Christ begin with Bethlehem and end with Olivet, but the New Testament account begins earlier and continues later. In Luke's preface to the Book of Acts he says that in his Gospel he treated "of all that Jesus *began* both to do and teach until the day in which He was taken up" (1:1, 2). Implicit in the following verses is the idea of continuation. In the Acts we are shown what, through His Apostles, Jesus continued to "do," and in the Epistles (in general), what He continued to "teach"; while in Hebrews and Revelation we are given wondrous glimpses of His life in heaven. Thus, the Book of the Acts of the Apostles is really the Book of the Acts of the Ascended Christ. It is not too much to say that Christ's life was never fully lived until the Ascension had taken place. Let us look at His ascended life. It was —

I. A Life of Completed Achievement

1. We are told that, His work done, He "sat down" (Heb. 1:3; 10:12). Cf. Passover eaten "in haste" (Exod. 12:11) with the Lord's Supper eaten sitting down (cf. Matt. 26:20, etc.);
2. We are told that He said of His work "It is finished" (John 19:30). Cf. "once" (Heb. 9:12, 26, 28; 10:10) and "one"

(Heb. 10:12, 14); "His one oblation of Himself once offered" (Book of Common Prayer) — i.e., once for all.

II. A Life of Kingly Dignity

1. God's thought of risen, ascended Christ — set at His "right hand" (2:33-35; Heb. 1-3; 10:12) — honor for what He was and reward for what He did;
2. Man's thought of Him — worship (cf. Phil. 2:9-11; Rev. 3:21; 4:10).

III. A Life of Personal Satisfaction

1. The Son had looked on during earlier dispensations and yearned to do His Father's will in redemption (cf. Psa. 40:8; Luke 24:26; Heb. 10:5, 9);
2. He did it with joy (Luke 10:21), and sat down, satisfied (cf. Isa. 53:11; Heb. 12:2).

IV. A Life of Priestly Service

1. It is still not spent for Himself — not self-gratification, but accessibility (cf. Heb. 4:16; 10:19-22);
2. It is spent for us — He is——
   a. Hearing prayer (1:24; 7:59, etc.);
   b. Bestowing the Holy Spirit (2:33; 4:31, etc.);
   c. Converting wanderers (9:5);
   d. Overseeing Church:
      (1) Individually (9:10; 18:9);
      (2) Collectively (cf. epistles to Seven Churches, Rev. 2 & 3);
   e. Helping workers (Mark 16:20);
   f. Sympathizing with sufferers (Heb. 4:14 to 5:10);
   g. Interceding for believers (Heb. 7:25);
   h. Welcoming overcomers (7:56):
      N.B. Cf. "sat" twenty times with this one "standing."

V. A Life of Eternal Unchangeableness

1. The true ground for our hope — unchangeable priesthood of Christ:
   a. Cf. Him with earthly priests (Heb. 7:11-28; 13:8);
   b. See why one undying Priest better than line even if con-

tinuous — "power of an endless life" (Heb. 7:16) — **i.e.,** endless life means power, and power needed to save.

2. The true meaning of Christ's intercession:
   a. Not representation of Calvary (cf. Heb. 9:24, 25; also 1 John 2:2, "*He is* the propitiation" — not "His death was —");
   b. Not merely prayer — cf. Jewish ritual on Day of Atonement (Lev. 16):
      (1) High Priest in Court of Tabernacle represented Christ on Cross; but —
      (2) High Priest in Holy of holies represented Christ in heaven for us;
   c. Not only deeds, but presence — as High Priest then, so Christ now: not only His death, but more particularly His life, though inseparably connected (cf. Rom. 8:34);
3. The true value of Christ's priestly life:
   a. It is assurance of our complete salvation (cf. Heb. 7:25);
   b. It is pledge of our glorious future (cf. John 14:19) — "a Man in the Glory"

VI. A Life of Blessed Promise

1. Christ is Captain of our salvation (cf. Heb. 2:10; Josh. 5:13-15);
2. He is our great Forerunner (cf. Heb. 6:19, 20);
3. He is our firstfruits in resurrection (1 Cor. 15:20-23); and we are His firstfruits in redemption (James 1:18; Rev. 14:4);
4. He is our hope of reunion (cf. 1 Thess. 4:14).

VII. A Life of Glorious Expectation

1. Christ's ultimate victory is potential — He is not yet in full possession (cf. Heb. 2:8; 10:13);
2. God's promise is sure (cf. Psa. 2:8; 110:1; Heb. 1:13);
3. Satan's short cut was repudiated (cf. Matt. 4:8-10; 16:22, 23);
4. The Cross came first, but victory is certain by-and-by (cf. Phil. 2:8-11).

Conclusion

The life of our Lord in heaven is the true revelation of His "perpetual presence." Let us see in it —

1. *A Warning*
   a. When once risen up from His seat at right hand of His Father, Christ will usher in "day of vengeance of our God" (Isa. 61:2);
   b. Then "He must reign" (1 Cor. 15:25), and "every knee" bow (Phil. 2:10).

   Therefore, Yield and Accept!

2. *An Encouragement*
   a. Identity of gaze — as Christ looks forward (cf. Heb. 10:13), we look up (cf. Heb. 9:28) — same Greek word;
   b. Identification of grace — as Christ is seated at His Father's right hand, we "sit together in heavenly places" in Him (cf. Eph. 2:5, 6);
   c. Identification of glory — as Christ is God's Son and Heir, we are "joint-heirs" with Him (Rom. 8:17).

   Therefore, Lift up your hearts!

Come ye who stood at Calvary 'neath the cross,
And there beheld the penalty of sin
Inflicted on the spotless Son of God,
Who heard His cry, "'Tis finished!" Justice laid
Your sins on Him and now is satisfied.
Come leave the cross a-while and follow on
And view the place wherein His body lay.
He is not there; death hath no power with Him;
He triumphed o'er it, like a conqueror rose;
But His blest presence in the grave has left
A sacred influence there, an angel form,
Which to believers takes the sting away.
The gloomy portal's but the entrance-hall
To all the blissful mansions in the skies,
For since the King of glory entered in
The everlasting doors are lifted up.
His sacrifice accepted, wrath appeased,
He now sits down at the right hand of God
And ever lives to intercede and plead
For all whose names He bears upon His breast.

With joy He sees the travail of His soul
And gathers one by one His loved ones home;
Nor will He rest content till all are brought
To sit with Him and share the Marriage-feast.
(Dedicated to the Author in 1916, by K.E.T.)

Study No. 5 — Before Pentecost

ACTS 1:15-26

WE KNOW that the time between the Resurrection and Ascension had a profound influence on the life of the Apostle Peter. The appearances of our Lord enabled him to understand what had been strange and mysterious, and to enter more fully into the Master's purpose for him. But then came the ten days after the Lord's departure into heaven, when the disciples were waiting for the promise of the Spirit to commence their ministry; and this section of the chapter raises several questions in the present-day reader's mind.

I. The Position (v. 15)

1. As always, Peter mentioned first in list of names of those present (cf. v. 14 with Matt. 10:2-4, etc.);
2. As before, Apostle characterized by prompt, energetic decision — "stood up . . . and said" — consistent with Peter of Gospels;
   N.B. But was it quite wise or right? He had been told to "wait" (v. 4).

II. The Statement (vs. 16-20)

1. Peter's speech probably recorded in vs. 16, 17 only — "Judas . . . was numbered with *us*";
2. Luke's explanatory comment would be interpolated in vs. 18-20 — "Now this man . . . known unto all the dwellers at Jerusalem . . . *their* language" (A.S.V.);
   N.B. Cf. idea of necessity — "must" (vs. 16, 22); had Peter been instructed as to this?

III. The Counsel (vs. 21, 22)

1. Quotation from Peter resumed — "these men . . . companied with *us*";
2. Urged substitute for Judas must have qualifications of an apostle:
   a. Personal experience of Christ's earthly ministry;
   b. Personal knowledge of Christ's resurrection;
   N.B. These unique and therefore impossible after that generation; would they have disqualified Paul from being numbered among the Twelve in view of his own words in Gal. 1:11-24 and 1 Cor. 15:5-11?

IV. The Action (vs. 23-26)

1. Appointed "two" candidates only (v. 23), both otherwise unknown; why so limited? Were there only two out of 120 (cf. v. 15) who fulfilled qualifications?
2. Prayer offered only after two chosen (vs. 24, 25); was this quite right? Why restrict God's leading thus?
3. Casting lot seems strange for companions of Jesus:
   a. Old-time method (cf. Lev. 16:8; Josh. 14:2; 1 Sam. 14:41, 42; Neh. 10:31; 11:1; Prov. 16:33), appearing to show lower plane of spirituality than we might have expected;
   b. But "the Holy Ghost was not yet given" (John 7:39), and Apostles still in "Dispensation of the Son" (see Study No. 2, p. 27) and bonds of O. T. tradition still understandably strong;
   c. It was after Pentecost (chap. 2) that Holy Spirit led Apostles by perception and insight;
   N.B. We never hear of lot-casting again. Is this not strong argument against Christians "taking chances," or talking about "luck"?

V. The Result (v. 26)

1. Vagueness of expression — "the lot fell" — no reference to any action of God;
2. Unknown disciple chosen — "upon Matthias" — no previous or subsequent reference to him, but he must have "companied

with" apostles "all the time that the Lord Jesus went in and out among" them (cf. v. 21) and therefore had adequate experience in spite of obscurity;
Illus.: The monument to Virginia's unknown Confederate dead bears this inscription: "Who they were none knows — what they were all know."

3. Record closed — "he was numbered with the eleven apostles";

   N.B. (1) Was Peter right in this procedure? May not God have had His own way and time for filling gap by choice of Paul? There are only "twelve foundations" of the heavenly city, "and in them the names of the twelve apostles of the Lamb" (Rev. 21:14). It seems almost as though Peter had once again acted impulsively instead of simply waiting as his Master had told him;

   (2) *Contra*: — It has been urged, however, that these two candidates, though obscure, had right of faith and character to stand for membership in apostolate, and that legitimate human part in momentous decision may well be to reduce possibilities to two and ask God's blessing on final choice; and that thus effect on apostolate wrought by Judas' sinful human nature and fatal choice of conduct was counteracted through human method of choosing his successor.

Conclusion

As noted previously, several questions have been raised, to which no final answers seem possible. For our own spiritual experience, however, we may well emphasize the fact that, since the events recorded in this passage, the Christian Church has been given —

1. *A Great Gift* — the Holy Spirit of God, to teach us all things (cf. John 14:26); and also that we still have —
2. *A Great Need* — humility and repose of soul, so that our life and service are dependent on —
3. *A Great Rule* — waiting on God, receiving from God, standing still and seeing His salvation (cf. Exod. 14:13).

Then will come —

4. *A Great Attitude* — simple faith and loving obedience for —
5. *A Great Work* — that of witnessing through personal experience to the Risen Saviour whom the Holy Spirit has made so blessedly real to our hearts.

Study No. 6 — The Day of Pentecost (1)

ACTS 2:1-47

ONE OF THE most interesting places in Jerusalem is the site of the house in which the Upper Room is said to have been. This was a spot well known as the center of the early Church. It was the scene of the Last Supper (cf. Mark 14:15), of Pentecost (cf. 1:13; 2:1), and it is likely to have been part of the house belonging to John Mark's mother (12:12). There is record of such a room in connection with the Jerusalem Church in about the year 117 A.D., during the reign of the Emperor Hadrian. Those who stand on its reputed site cannot but feel impressed with the thought that here on the Day of Pentecost the Christian Church began, and here were first seen the essential characteristics of Christianity.

Here is an outline of the chapter: (1) The waiting disciples (v. 1) in a unity of place, time, purpose, prayer; (2) The descending Spirit (vs. 2-4) in three symbols — wind, fire, tongues, suggesting energy, enthusiasm, expression; (3) The witnessing people (vs. 5-13) in attendance on one of Scripture's best-attested events — Jews present from all over the world; (4) The faithful preacher (vs. 14-36) in a sermon textual and expository — his delivery powerful, his declarations refuting error and appealing to sinners — a type of preaching proceeding only from the Holy Spirit; and (5) The wonderful results (vs. 37-47) in the birthday of the Church and the commencement of a new dispensation. As G. Campbell Morgan said: "There was born the Christian Church, not by sprinkling of water, not by votes and resolutions, not by creeds formulated and signed, but by the baptism of the wind and fire of God."

I. When Was Pentecost?

The Holy Spirit was first given on a special occasion:

1. *Day of Pentecost Jewish Feast*:
   a. Appointed 50 days after Passover (corresponds to our Whit-Sunday):
   b. Appropriate for commencement of Christian Church since Christianity crown and culmination of God's dealings with Jews;
   c. Book of Acts far more Jewish in character than Epistles of Paul — Jews mentioned often:
      (1) No Gentiles evident in crowd on Pentecost — all Jews of Dispersion, gathered in Jerusalem from almost every part of known world; some born in foreign lands, and many Roman citizens; some may have been proselytes, but none, in direct sense of word, appear to have been Gentiles;
      (2) Same limitation seen in Peter's address (vs. 14, 22, 23, 29, 36) — development of Christianity among Gentiles very gradual;
      N.B. All events up to then preparatory — cf. three dispensations:*
         (a) That of Father (Old Testament);
         (b) That of Son (Gospels); and now —
         (c) That of Holy Spirit (Acts, Epistles, Revelation, and to present).
2. *Day of Pentecost Feast of Harvest*:
   a. Instituted as part of Law from Sinai (Lev. 23:15-22) — all Jewish males required to appear before God in Jerusalem — hence so many strangers;
   b. Christianity to be life of fruit-bearing — from God and to God;
   c. Christianity new law for world made possible by Spirit (cf. Rom. 8:1-4);

*See Study No. 2, page 27.

d. Pentecost firstfruits of great harvest of souls from many nations down through ages.

II. What Was Pentecost?

The characteristics of Pentecost are also those of Christianity itself:

1. *Revelation of Truth*:
   a. Vindicating Christ —showed Him in new position, glorified, as Holy Spirit still does;
   b. Illuminating minds of Apostles — now, Holy Spirit who directly enabled them to understand what they never could grasp before does this for present-day believers through His inspired Scriptures;
   c. Convicting unbelievers of sin — today, He does this also through Holy Scriptures, and by instrumentality of Church.
2. *Manifestation of Power*:
   a. In speech — for propagating Gospel (v. 4);
   b. In courage — for confronting world (v. 14);
   c. In influence — for impressing others (v. 43);
   d. In holiness — for exemplifying Christ (v. 47).
3. *Expression of Love*:
   a. In fellowship (vs. 42, 44);
   b. In unselfishness (v. 45).
4. *Demonstration of Joy*:
   a. Of reconciliation with God (v. 41);
   b. Of consecration to God (v. 46).

III. How Was Pentecost Experienced?

The secret of Pentecost is in three words four times repeated — "with one accord":

1. *In prayer* (1:14);
2. *In expectation* (2:1);
3. *In life* (2:46, 47);
4. *In praise and purpose* (4:24-31);

N.B. George Matheson, author of "O Love that wilt not let me go," prayed as follows: "I thank Thee, O Lord, that Thou hast placed so many lights in the upper chamber — so many and so varied . . . Thou wouldst have me, not merely to keep my own glow, but to get from others the color which in me is dim. Thou hast put Peter beside John that the impulsiveness of Peter may be moderated; Thou hast put John beside Peter that the slowness of John may be quickened. Illuminate me by my brother's light. Give to my love the quality in which it is not strong. Let me catch the impress of the opposite star . . . Reveal to me that my song of praise is not complete till it blends with a counterpart in the great symphony. I shall know the meaning of the many voices when I learn the need of Thy manifold grace."

Conclusion

1. As on Pentecost, the blessing of the Holy Spirit is given to all believers (cf. vs. 1, 4, 7, 17, 32, 44), and not to a privileged few. We today are not called on to "wait" for the Spirit, but since, as Christians, we have received Him at conversion, we are to yield ourselves more and more as He requires entire possession of hearts and lives.
2. Thus, the Day of Pentecost is not to be repeated historically, but its experience is to be re-appropriated spiritually.
3. Pentecost marked the first of five bestowals of the Holy Spirit, all initial: 2:4; 8:17; 9:17; 10:44; 19:6; for, just as baptism with water speaks of initial gift of salvation never to be repeated, so baptism with the Holy Spirit refers to initial gift of the Spirit when we are united to Christ (cf. 1 Cor. 12:13; Eph. 1:13, A.S.V.).
4. But, from time of conversion to end of life, it is possible to be filled with the Spirit again and again. Truth of N.T. teaching seems to be "one baptism, many fillings" (cf. vs. 4; 4:18; 6:5; 7:55, Gr.; 13:52).
5. The Holy Spirit is for the Church and not for the world — given only to believers — makes His home in Church. Thus, awful responsibility rests on us because if world is to know about Christ it must be by the Spirit through our human instrumentality. If we are "filled" with the Spirit we shall

witness by lip and life to those not in Christ; and the Holy Spirit will be —

a. In us as presence of God in our life;

b. On us as power of God in our work; and —

c. Through us as manifestation of God in our testimony.

Let me be Thine forever,
My gracious God and Lord;
May I forsake Thee never,
Nor wander from Thy Word.
Preserve me from the mazes
Of error and distrust,
And I shall sing Thy praises
For ever with the just.

Lord Jesus, bounteous Giver
Of light and life Divine,
Thou didst my soul deliver;
To Thee I all resign.
Thou hast in mercy bought me,
With blood and bitter pain;
Let me, since Thou hast sought me,
Eternal life obtain.

O Holy Ghost, who pourest
Sweet peace into my heart,
And all my soul restorest,
Let not Thy grace depart;
And while His Name confessing
Whom I by faith have known,
Grant me Thy constant blessing,
Make me for aye Thine own.

Study No. 7 — The Day of Pentecost (2)

ACTS 2:1-11

THE WORD "began" of 1:1 applies here; only when the Spirit came did the Church begin to expand. In Old Testament times, it is true, the Holy Ghost had been in the world — striving with the antediluvians, leading Israel, inspiring the prophets, and dwelling with men, as a Power rather than as a Person (e.g., Isa. 48:16; 63:10-14; Zech. 4:6). Now, in a new and unique way, He was revealed as the Spirit of Jesus Himself, coming to be *in* men instead of merely with them. The Old Testament saints had had a spiritual life but this was not commonly associated with the Holy Spirit, only with God the Father and Creator. This is particularly true of the Psalms. Now He is shown to be a Person in activity instead of merely an influence from God. He is made not so much more real as more universal.

I. Pentecost Then

1. *On Them* (vs. 1-3) — "upon each of them" (v. 3) — Symbol
   a. Sound — as wind: Life — purifying, vitalizing (cf. Ezek. 37:1-14; John 3:8);
   b. Sight — as fire: Power — energizing, warming (cf. Exod. 3:1-5);
   c. Speech — as tongues: Utterance — equipping, teaching:
      (1) Note gift of tongues meant immediate power in language;
      (2) But not continual or permanent — special manifestation for this occasion (cf. 10:46; 19:6);
      (3) Different in some respects from subject in I Cor. 12:10, 30;
      (4) It has been pointed out that Jews believed membership in Messianic kingdom would be confined to

Hebrew nation, so gift of tongues corrected error, indicating all peoples should praise Messiah's Name in own tongues — hence appropriateness of sign during early days of Church;

(5) This and other outward miraculous manifestations ceased when Israel rejected Gospel as preached in Acts period:

N.B. Note references to miraculous gifts in earlier Epistles (e.g., Corinthians, Romans), but not in later ones (e.g., Philippians, Colossians, Ephesians).

2. *In Them* (v. 4) — "filled" — Reality
   a. Soul — Presence of Christ — center of being;
   b. Heart — Love of Christ — feelings;
   c. Life — Truth of Christ — thoughts, words, and deeds;
      (1) Note this fulfilled John 15 and 16;
      (2) Note "all" were filled — 120 — both sexes (cf. 1:14, 15).
3. *Through Them* (vs. 4-11) — "began to speak" (v. 4) — Manifestation
   a. Immediate testimony (v. 6) — only as long as news took to travel;
   b. Impressive testimony (v. 7) — called attention to Christ, greatest Galilean;
   c. Divine testimony (v. 11) — tongues definitely of God — cf. time taken to learn foreign language naturally.

II. Pentecost Now

Cf. v. 4 with Eph. 5:18 — no "tongues" in latter, only "speaking," "singing," and "giving thanks," evidently in one's own language:

1. *The Truth*
   a. "All filled with the Holy Ghost, and began——" — secret of all power in spiritual life;
   b. Intended as specimen and type for all times:
      (1) Not "gifts" nor outward accompaniments, but possession and graces within;

(2) Peter (4:8), "all" (4:31), deacons (6:3), Barnabas (11:24), and Paul (13:9) "filled" on other occasions, but without spectacular effects;

c. For believers only — not for world:

(1) Never was so poured out — never could be;

(2) Because "the natural man receiveth not the things of the Spirit of God" (1 Cor. 2:14), and "the carnal mind is enmity against God" (Rom. 8:7).

2. *The Meaning*

The gift of the Holy Spirit is —

a. Distinct from conversion:

(1) These already converted disciples — yet two experiences may be coincident (cf. chap. 10);

(2) These already received Spirit in some measure (cf. Luke 9:55; John 3:5, 6);

b. Intended for service and equipment:

(1) "Tongue" includes man's voice and speech empowered by God's truth;

(2) Apostles did not attempt any preaching till "Spirit gave them utterance" (v. 4; cf. 1 Cor. 14);

(3) Some one has said Holy Spirit did not distribute pens, but tongues at Pentecost; Gospel to be proclaimed primarily by human lips — witnessing for Christ one form of preaching all may do;

c. Proved by results:

(1) Consciousness of power within believer;

(2) Evidence of blessing through believer — in one word, unction (cf. 1 John 2:20; Acts 6:10).

3. *The Secret*

a. Singleness of aim:

(1) "One accord" — unanimity to God's glory;

(2) Confidence of obtaining — claiming blessing because no longer need for waiting;

b. Preparedness of spirit:

(1) "Continued . . . in prayer" (1:14) — waiting (cf. 1:4) had searched them and made of them cleansed vessels ready for further blessing;

(2) Had found God's way — Holy Spirit coming down on individual men and women, forming them into corporate body, the Church, in which He was to dwell;

c. Willingness of life:

(1) "Began to speak" (v. 4) — doing that which God intended;

(2) Holy Spirit always associated with devoted Christian life, with reality and not mere profession of Christianity (cf. 5:32); His province is to unite us to Christ and to each other in Body of Christ, the invisible Church.

Conclusion

1. *The Church of Pentecost*——
   a. Expressed its life in truth, power, love, joy;
   b. Explained its message as——
      (1) Christ for believers — a Saviour accepted;
      (2) Christ in believers — a Friend experienced;
      (3) Christ through believers — a Master manifested.
2. *The Church of Today*——
   a. Often has a plenitude of organization — a machine;
   b. Sometimes shows a paucity of power — so what value the machine? We must have organization and arrangement, but without Divine power permeating the whole they are useless. God's power is manifested through the Holy Spirit in the Church. If we desire Pentecostal power, we must have Pentecostal preparation, Pentecostal prayer, and Pentecostal praise.

Study No. 8 — Fulness — A Meditation

ACTS 2:4

WE ARE TOLD that "Nature abhors a vacuum." Apparently, therefore, the opposite condition, namely, the state of being full, or fulness, is one of the necessities of life. But full of what? There are right types of fulness and there are wrong types; it is right to be filled with some things, but not with others. This is exemplified by a number of passages in the Book of Acts which will reward careful study:

I. A Right Fulness

Most important "fulness" for believer is with —

1. The Spirit of God (cf. 2:4; 4:8, 31; 6:3, 5; 7:55; 9:17; 11:24; 13:9, 52);

   This leads to fulness with —
2. Wonder (3:10);
3. Doctrine (5:28);
4. Wisdom (6:3);
5. Faith (6:5, 8);
6. Power (6:8);
7. Good words (9:36);
8. Joy (13:52; cf. "gladness," 14:17).

II. A Wrong Fulness

This is sadly possible and may take form of —

1. Lying (5:3);
2. Indignation (5:17);
3. Subtility and Mischief (13:10);
4. Envy (13:45);
5. Confusion (14:29);
6. Wrath (19:28).

Conclusion

Making a right choice in this matter of "fulness" will indeed make us "full with the blessing of the Lord" (Deut. 33:23).

Study No. 9 — The First Christian Sermon

ACTS 2:14-40

The sermon of Peter on the Day of Pentecost is the first instance of Christian preaching and it introduced a new type of religious ministry. The occasion was without parallel, the substance of the sermon was fresh and startling, and the impression made by it was strange and unprecedented. It is a model of homiletics for all Christian preachers and of didactics for all Christian teachers.

I. Assertion (vs. 14-21)

To confute:

1. *Negative Confutation* (vs. 14, 15)

   First necessity laid upon Apostles was to confute charge made against them (v. 13):

   a. Categorical denial — "not drunken"

   b. Groundless charge — "as ye suppose"

   c. Clear improbability — "third hour" — or 9 A.M., earliest of stated hours of prayer and time for offering morning sacrifice — against Jewish law to take drink before this hour.

2. *Positive Confutation* (vs. 16-21)

   a. Fulfilment of Holy Scripture — cf. Joel 2:28-32, with which Jews might be supposed to be familiar;

   b. Meaning of "last days" — days of Messiah, Christian era:

      (1) To be associated with extraordinary manifestations of the Spirit (vs. 17, 18);

      (2) To bring convulsions in natural world (v. 19);

(3) To usher in "great and notable day of the Lord" (v. 20);

c. Literal fulfilment of Joel's words not exhausted on Day of Pentecost, but will still find complete explanation in future "day of the Lord" (cf. 1 Thess. 5:2); meanwhile, men are to heed —

d. Message of Holy Spirit — salvation possible (v. 21); promise has special reference to future, but is also applicable to entire dispensation of Holy Spirit (cf. Rom. 10:13).

II. Argument (vs. 22-36)

To convince:

Peter proceeds to show Jesus of Nazareth is man's Saviour. He describes —

1. *The Work of Christ* (vs. 22-32)
   a. His life (v. 22):
      (1) Approved of God;
      (2) Performed miracles for God;
      (3) Known of men;
   b. His death (v. 23):
      (1) Taken by lawless men;
      (2) Overruled by God (cf. Luke 22:22) for His Divine purpose;
   c. His resurrection (vs. 24-32):
      (1) Emphasized as work of God (v. 24):
         (a) Father thereby vindicated Son and showed acceptance of what He had done;
         (b) All through N.T., resurrection invariably attributed to Father, never to Son — Divine act sealing atonement;
      (2) Shown to be according to Holy Scripture (vs. 25-32), with certain assumptions:
         (a) Authority of O.T. (v. 25);
         (b) Reference to resurrection in Psa. 16:8-11 (vs. 25-28);
         (c) Reference not to David (v. 29);
         (d) Reference to Christ (vs. 30-32).

Then Peter depicts——

2. *The glory of Christ* (vs. 33-36)
   a. Exalted by God (v. 33);
   b. Acknowledged by God (v. 33);
   c. Honored by God (vs. 34-36).

Peter's argument intended to prove Christ's exaltation predicted; prediction could not apply to David, who did not ascend to heaven to be invested with glory and power at right hand of God; i.e., Psalmist does not speak of self, but of Messiah. Note also striking contrast all through between God's action in exalting Christ and action of Jews in putting Him to death. As Bengel said, "There is a sting in the close" (cf. v. 36).

III. Appeal (vs. 37-40)

To constrain:

After argument, personal, practical appeal naturally follows. Peter desires to lead hearers to —

1. *Conviction* (v. 37)
   a. Consciousness of guilt — it was sin;
   b. Consciousness of responsibility — it was personal sin;
   c. Consciousness of powerlessness — it was irreparable sin.

Then he drives home his message — words "pricked in their heart" (v. 37) show how deeply consciences were touched. Then hearers naturally wanted to know what they could do, so he gives them —

2. *Direction* (vs. 38-40)
   a. Blessings offered (vs. 38, 39):
      (1) Pardon for past;
      (2) Presence of Holy Spirit for present and future;
   b. Conditions required (v. 38):
      (1) Repentance — breaking with sin and turning from it;
      (2) Baptism — witnessing to faith in and surrender to Christ — expressive of trustful obedience;
   c. Promises made (vs. 38, 39):
      (1) Certainty — "shall receive";
      (2) Welcome — "unto you, and to your children, and to all that are afar off";

d. Witness continued (v. 40):
    (1) Testimony — "with many other words";
    (2) Exhortation — to separation.

Conclusion

1. *The matter of Pentecostal Preaching*
    a. Simple —
        (1) A powerful Christ;
        (2) A personal salvation;
    b. Complete —
        (1) Three facts as to Person and Work of our Lord:
            (a) Christ's life our pattern;
            (b) Christ's death our pardon;
            (c) Christ's resurrection our power;
        (2) Three conditions of acceptance with God:
            (a) Repentance;
            (b) Faith;
            (c) Obedience;
        (3) Three promises of blessings from God:
            (a) Pardon;
            (b) The Holy Spirit;
            (c) Eternal life.
2. *The Manner of Pentecostal Preaching*
    a. The Man:
        (1) Expositor, unfolding Scripture;
        (2) Reasoner, dealing with arguments;
        (3) Orator, studying effectiveness;
        (4) Pleader, making use of appeal;
    b. The Method:
        (1) Scripture known;
        (2) Christ real;
        (3) Spirit mighty.

Therefore, the Word of God and the Son of God are proclaimed by the Man of God through the Spirit of God, and all to the Glory of God. May this be true of our witness today!

Study No. 10 — Spiritual Vision

ACTS 2:17

OF ALL our faculties that of vision is the most precious and powerful. Hearing, taste, touch, smell — all are of great value, but the greatest of the five senses is sight. This is because it is the surest, fullest method of contact with the world around us. It would seem that Scripture testifies to this fact, for it brings into prominence the faculty of sight in relation to things spiritual. It does indeed speak of tasting, hearing, holding fast, etc., but especially and universally is the faculty of sight mentioned.

In the Old Testament, for instance, we have Balaam and Job saying, "I shall see Him" (Num. 24:17; Job 19:26, 27). In the New Testament we read of Christ declaring that only the pure in heart "shall see God" and only the "born again" can see His kingdom (Matt. 5:8; John 3:3). Said the Greek inquirers, "We would see Jesus" (John 12:21), and two of the last promises in the Bible are "We shall see Him as He is" (1 John 3:2) and "They shall see His face" (Rev. 22:4). We also read of "looking unto Jesus" (Heb. 12:2), and "with open face beholding as in a glass the glory of the Lord" (2 Cor. 3:18). At the same time, we are reminded, "Now we see through a glass, darkly; but then face to face" (1 Cor. 13:12).

Because it is the fullest and surest way of having before us the unseen world, and our relation to it and possession of it, let us consider spiritual vision as one of the characteristics of true Christian life. It implies two things: Reality, or something to see, and Realization, or something by which to see. There is a correspondence between the eye and its object: one implies and demands the other.

I. Reality

1. *What is this Reality? God*:

a. Moses and Ezekiel both saw Him (Exod. 33:11; Ezek. 1:1);
b. Job yearned to see Him (Job 23:3), and David panted after Him (Psa. 42:1);
c. This God is known to us in Christ — "he that hath seen Me hath seen the Father" (John 14:9); all we know of God and all we have from Him comes through His Son;
d. He is also revealed by His Holy Spirit (Joel 2:28; Acts 2:17).

2. *Why does man need this Reality?*
a. Man incomplete: imagine one who has intellect of Shakespeare, learning of Bacon, will of Napoleon, skill of Caesar, position of Alexander, imagination of Turner — if such a one has "no vision" he, too, will "perish" (Prov. 29:18);
b. God gave man capacity to know Him — "Thou hast made us for Thyself, and our hearts are restless till they find their rest in Thee" (Augustine);
c. Sin disturbed relations between God and man — religion and history testify to this in national life, and so with individual life (cf. Matt. 13:13-17);
d. Sight of God energizes whole life: purifies motives and strengthens principles.

II. Realization

1. *In what way does Realization come?*
By at least five visions, as seen in this Book:
a. Of pardon (26:19; 9:18);
b. Of instruction (10:11-16);
c. Of guidance (16:9, 10);
d. Of strength (18:9, 10; 23:11);
e. Of hope (7:56; 23:23-25);
Illus.: Insight of great artist Turner shown when, sunset in picture having been criticized by viewer who said: "*I* never saw such colors in a sunset," he replied, "No? But don't you wish you could?"

2. *How are these spiritual visions obtained?* By —
a. Surrender (cf. 9:6 — "what wilt Thou——?");

b. Sincerity (cf. Matt. 5:8 — "pure in heart");
c. Service (cf. 26:19 — "not disobedient to the heavenly vision");

Illus.: Eye gives itself to telescope in order to see distant star — no other way.

Conclusion

The plea for a prophet in Num. 12:6 is answered in Acts 2. Note also 1 Sam. 9:9:

1. He has power of seeing truth;
2. He has gift of preaching it;
3. He has high spiritual authority in proclaiming it;
4. He and his message are what world wants and needs today.

Only pouring out of the Holy Spirit can make us prophets, seers, men of God.

Study No. 11 — A Divine Impossibility

ACTS 2:24

Several things are stated in Scripture to be impossible. The statement here relates to Christ's death and resurrection. Why was it "not possible that He should be holden" of death? Because the resurrection was —

I. The Divine Vindication of His Character

1. His claim to represent God:
   a. This claim denied, so He was rejected, crucified;
   b. Resurrection was God's answer;
2. His claim to veracity:
   a. Said He would rise, but His power denied;
   b. Resurrection God's answer.

II. The Divine Acceptance of His Atonement

1. The meaning of His death:
   a. Penal;
   b. Redemptive;

2. The power of His resurrection:
   a. Proof of acceptance (cf. Rom. 4:25);
   b. Basis of new birth (cf. 1 Pet. 1:3).

III. The Divine Acknowledgement of His Lordship

1. His purpose includes more than mere deliverance; it brings life, with manifestation of Divine power;
2. His resurrection; His designation as Lord — "with power" (Rom. 1:4).

IV. The Divine Guarantee of our Resurrection

1. His purpose includes future as well as past and present: Salvation, Life, Immortality;
2. His resurrection pledge of ours (cf. John 14:19; 1 Thess. 4:14).

Conclusion

The resurrection is:

1. A solid foundation of faith;
2. A strong inspiration of love;
3. A sure consolation of hope.

Study No. 12 — The Fact of the Resurrection

ACTS 2:32

NO ONE can read the New Testament without seeing the prominence given in it to the resurrection of Christ. It is a fact most essential. Why? But, first of all, let us ask a question not always considered in connection with the resurrection, and yet very vital: How? By whose act, His own or God the Father's, was Christ raised up? This at once leads to a second query: Why? For what purpose was Christ raised up?

I. How?

1. *The Power*
   a. A.S.V. states it thus: "This Jesus did God raise up" — not "could have" or "might have";
   b. Scripture emphatic that deed was done by Father (cf. 2:24; 3:15; 10:40; 13:33-37; 17:31; Rom. 4:24, 25; 6:4, 9; 8:11; 10:9; 1 Cor. 6:14; 15:15; 2 Cor. 4:14; Gal. 1:1; Eph. 1:20; Col. 2:12; 1 Thess. 1:10; Heb. 13:20; 1 Pet. 1:21);
2. *The Importance*
   a. Belief in this essential to salvation (cf. Rom. 10:9);
   b. No quibble provided for.

II. Why.

1. *God's Witness to Person of Christ*:
   a. His Sonship declared (cf. Rom. 1:4);
   b. His claim vindicated — had died because of it (cf. Mark 14:61-64);
   c. Thus His Deity proved (cf. v. 24).
2. *God's Witness to Work of Christ*:
   a. Adequate atonement made and accepted — how else could it have been known that wrath of God was gone?

b. Certain salvation wrought — "faith and hope" (1 Pet. 1:21);
c. Complete redemption provided — body as well as spirit (cf. 1 Cor. 15:35-50).

Conclusion

1. Belief in the Resurrection of the Lord brings salvation (cf. Rom. 10:9);
2. Confession of the Lord of the Resurrection proves salvation (cf. Rom. 10:10).

Study No. 13 — The Witness of the Church to the Resurrection *

ACTS 2:32

FROM the Nore Lightship one may see the River Thames, at its mouth, its very greatest width. In the Cotswold Hills, many miles to the northwest, one may see it at its source, where it is but a narrow rivulet. But it is the same stream and may be traced all along its course. So Christianity covers the world today and is at its widest scope yet; on Pentecost, its first day, it had but come to birth. Yet it is the same body all down the ages, and its very existence has ever raised questions in the minds of men.

I. How Did the Church Begin?

"The Church of Christ was built on an empty grave";

1. Peter preached Resurrection of Jesus six short weeks after Crucifixion — note change in him — no attempt now to deny Master;
2. Three thousand people believed what he said, so that they united in fellowship, especially in relation to Baptism and

*For more complete treatment, see author's volume *Christianity Is Christ*, chap. 9.

the Lord's Supper — must have seemed strange to others — accounted for only by belief in Resurrection.

II. How Did the Church Continue?

1. By preaching of same message — "Jesus and the Resurrection" (17:18);
2. By receiving same message — and Baptism and Lord's Supper solemnized wherever it went.

The great problem, therefore, is —

III. How May We Account for the Christian Church?

Its beginning, its growth, and its continuance may be said to be contained by four links:

1. Proclamation of Christian message;
2. Initiation of rite of Baptism;
3. Fellowship in Lord's Supper;
4. Worship on Lord's Day.

All these, taken together, compose one bond — personal relation to Christ as living — impossible to account for Church except by Resurrection — no compulsion, no worldly advantage; on contrary, persecution, ostracism, death.

IV. Why Is Christianity Stronger Than Ever?

In spite of being opposed, checked, thwarted, its growth continues. Note —

1. Its achievements in past —
   e.g. Effects on children, women, slavery;
2. Its influence today —
   e.g., At home, on mission field;
3. Its power compared with that of other religions —
   e.g., Redemption from sin, inspiration to holiness, incentives to progress.

It is therefore no mere question of something which happened 19 centuries ago as fact of history, but of existence of living and widespread force today, i.e., Christianity itself.

Conclusion

1. Each individual Christian, added to the Church by the same Spirit as at Pentecost, is a witness to the Resurrection

as he —
  a. Experiences new birth;
  b. Receives new life;
  c. Exerts new powers;
  d. Entertains new hopes.

2. The Church, then, both individually and corporately, must witness to the Resurrection by —
  a. Life;
  b. Testimony;
  c. Holiness;
  d. Love.

Then our experience will be like that of Paul in Athens (17:18-34): When we preach Jesus and the Resurrection (v. 18), people will inquire (vs. 19, 20) and, while some will mock or postpone (v. 32), others will cleave unto us and believe (v. 34).

Study No. 14 — The Dispensation of the Spirit

ACTS 2:33

HISTORY is full of landmarks, turning-points, great events upon which everything hinged. The greatest of these was the Day of Pentecost, for then God's grace was made available for the whole world. His relationship with man may be said to be in three stages or dispensations, that of the Father, that of the Son, and that of the Holy Spirit. Note now the third of these, the Dispensation of the Spirit:*

I. Its Preparation in Heaven

1. *The exaltation of Jesus* — "being by the right hand of God exalted"
  a. New phenomenon in heaven — perfect Man;
  b. Never known before that — only "spirits of just men *made* perfect" (Heb. 12:23);

---

*See Study No. 2, page 27.

c. Importance of Ascension Day — God's thought of Christ (cf. John 14:12).

2. *The acknowledgement of His work* — "having received of the Father the promise of the Holy Ghost"
   a. He had finished that work (cf. John 17:4);
   b. Ascension Day substantiated voice of God heard before: "Thou art My Son" (cf. Psa. 2:7; Mark 1:11; Luke 3:22; Acts 15:33; Heb. 1:5; 5:5).

II. Its Manifestation on Earth

1. *A new gift* — "hath shed forth this"
   a. Christ "received" Holy Spirit for us, not for Himself;
   b. "Poured forth" (A.S.V.) — made everything real;
   c. Now Spirit essentially "Spirit of Christ" (Rom. 8:9; Gal. 4:6; Phil. 1:19; 1 Pet. 1:11);
2. *A new glory* — "which ye now see and hear"
   a. Sight:
      (1) Holiness from within;
      (2) Boldness without; — both resulting from force behind;
   b. Sound:
      (1) Witness of personal experience;
      (2) Proclamation of Divine message.

Therefore, there was manifest a new spirit of —
(1) Life;
(2) Light;
(3) Liberty;
(4) Love;
(5) Labor;
(6) Loyalty;
(7) Likeness.

Conclusion

1. *What is Pentecost to us today?*
   Is it mere history, or is it experience? Cf. 19:1-7: — in effect, Were you converted when you thought you were? Many Christians still baptized "unto John's baptism" (v. 3) "of repentance" (v. 4), instead of truly "in the Name of

the Lord Jesus" (v. 5), and so the Holy Ghost has not come "on them" (v. 6).

2. *How may we make Pentecost our own?*
By receiving, retaining, and reproducing the Holy Spirit of God. May this be our experience!

Study No. 15 — The Calling of God — A Meditation

ACTS 2:39

AMONG the outstanding words of the New Testament are those associated with the idea of "calling." They touch at once on some of the deepest and some of the most practical truths connected with the Christian revelation. This thought of "calling" has several aspects, and there seems to be a distinct progress in the meaning of the word. In the Gospels it appears to be limited to the mere invitation to the sinner (cf. Matt. 22:14; Luke 14:7), as here in Acts (cf. also 15:17, quoting Amos 9:11, 12). In the Epistles, however, the word implies also that the invitation has been accepted.

I. The Source of the Calling

1. Primal — "God" (1 Thess. 2:12; 2 Tim. 1:9; 1 Cor. 1:9);
2. Mediate — "Jesus Christ" (Rom. 1:6).

II. The Subjects of the Calling

1. As to destined scope — universality (1 Cor. 1:24);
2. As to spiritual condition — "sinners" (Luke 5:32);
3. As to Divine estimate — "vessels of mercy" (Rom. 9:23, 24);
4. As to actual fact — "not many wise," etc. (1 Cor. 1:26).

III. The Purpose of the Calling

God calls us to "inherit a blessing" (1 Pet. 3:9), which includes —

1. Repentance (Luke 5:32);
2. Salvation (2 Thess. 2:13, 14);

3. Peace (Col. 3:15);
4. Light (1 Pet. 2:9);
5. Fellowship (1 Cor. 1:9);
6. Service (Rom. 1:1);
7. Freedom (Gal. 5:13);
8. Holiness (1 Cor. 1:2);
9. Suffering (1 Pet. 2:20, 21);
10. Eternal life (1 Tim. 6:12);
11. Eternal inheritance (Heb. 9:15);
12. Eternal glory (1 Pet. 5:10; 1 Thess. 2:12; Rev. 19:9).

IV. The Principles of the Calling

1. According to Divine purpose (Rom. 8:28);
2. According to Divine grace (2 Tim. 1:9);
3. Not according to human merit (2 Tim. 1:9).

V. The Sphere of the Calling

1. In the Lord (1 Cor. 7:22; Phil. 3:14);
2. In grace (Gal. 1:6);
3. In holiness (1 Thess. 4:1);
4. In peace (1 Cor. 7:15);
5. In one body (Col. 3:15).

VI. The Means of the Calling

1. Through the Gospel (2 Thess. 2:14);
2. Through God's grace (Gal. 1:15);
3. Through God's glory (2 Pet. 1:3, Gr.);
4. Through God's character (2 Pet. 1:3, Gr.).

VII. The Characteristics of the Calling

1. It is high (Phil. 3:14);
2. It is holy (2 Tim. 1:9);
3. It is heavenly (Heb. 3:1);
4. It is humbling (1 Cor. 1:25).

VIII. The Requirements of the Calling

1. Abide in it (1 Cor. 7:20, 24);
2. Walk according to it (1 Cor. 7:17);
3. Walk worthy of it (Eph. 4:1);

4. Walk worthy of the Source of it (1 Thess. 2:12);
5. Give diligence to realize it (2 Pet. 1:10).

IX. The Incentives of the Calling

1. Its hope (Eph. 1:18; 4:4);
2. Its prize (Phil. 3:14).

X. The Guarantees of the Calling

1. God's character — faithful (1 Cor. 1:9; 1 Thess. 5:24);
2. God's purpose — irrevocable (Rom. 11:29);
3. God's grace — eternal (Rom. 8:30).

Conclusion

Here, then, is —

1. *Our Portion* — we look back and remember the "darkness" out of which we have been called (1 Pet. 2:9);
2. *Our Privilege* — we look around and "see" our calling (1 Cor. 1:26) as it concerns our present life;
3. *Our Prospect* — we look forward and "know what is the hope" of His calling (Eph. 1:18).

In the light of all this wealth of grace we bow before God in adoration, contrition, and consecration, trusting Him for grace to "walk worthy" (Eph. 4:1) of His kingdom on earth, and to be accounted "worthy" (2 Thess. 1:11) of the glory that is to be revealed.

Study No. 16 — The First Christian Church

ACTS 2:41-47

THE FIRST of anything, be it specimen or illustration, is usually of great interest, as, for example, the first book ever printed, or the first newspaper, or the first railroad engine or airplane. These verses are the record of the first Christian Church in its present organized form; and they contain the germ of everything else found in the rest of the New Testament concerning the Christian community. This includes new power, new preaching, and new practice. How did the Christian Church commence, and how did it continue?

I. Commencement (vs. 41-43)

1. *Entrance into the Church* (v. 41)

   The Word of God was —

   a. Preached faithfully — by Peter (cf. vs. 14-36, 38-40);

   b. Heard contritely — by gathering (cf. v. 37);

   c. Received gladly — by "three thousand souls";

   d. Obeyed implicitly — through baptism;

   N.B. Note precise order: Christ preached, accepted, then adds to Church. Between first and second, direct contact of individual penitent with God, by means of faith on man's side and Holy Spirit on God's (cf. 1 Cor. 12:13). It is Christ who places us in Church and not vice versa. Church only instrumental in preaching Christ and accepting men into visible fellowship.

2. *Adherence to the Church* (v. 42)

   Showing true spirit, those early Christians continued in:

   a. Apostles' teaching:

   (1) Divine truth both light for mind and food for heart;

(2) No true church life possible apart from prominence given to Word of God:

N.B. Safeguard for new converts against danger of error;

b. Apostles' fellowship:

(1) Christianity first individual but then social — Christ first attaches soul to Himself, then connection between one and another in Him inevitable;

(2) Church first spiritual organism, then ecclesiastical organization — outward form coming from within, as spiritual body expressed life;

(3) This corporate aspect of supreme importance because unattached Christian life impossible;

(4) Word "saints," so frequently found in N.T., never used in singular;

(5) Holy Spirit always in Christian society and never apart from it;

(6) Various Christian graces, such as kindness, long-suffering, etc., only possible in association with other believers;

(7) Thus, fellowship around our Lord and Saviour to be emphasized, neither overrating nor underrating importance of Church:

(a) Former will mean spiritual loss if Christ is forgotten and Church put between sinner and Saviour;

(b) Latter will also mean spiritual loss, because individual Christian needs Church for fellowship and world needs strong Church for witness;

(c) Exalting Christ will make us value Church aright, and we shall be true stones in God's Temple (cf. 1 Pet. 2:5);

N.B. Safeguard for new converts against danger of coldness.

c. Breaking of bread:

(1) This reference to Lord's Supper as integral part of Christian life is of great and solemn importance:

(a) Means obedience to our Lord's command (cf. 1 Cor. 11:24), "This do";
(b) Suggests remembrance of His redemptive work — "in remembrance of Me";
(c) Indicates fellowship, since we are all one body in Christ — "drink ye all";
(d) Expresses hope for future, as we observe this ordinance "till He come";

(2) Christianity marked by wonderful simplicity in regard to ordinances:
(a) Only two required;
(b) Of these, the Lord's Supper, with regular appeal and blessed associations, is real inspiration in Church life;

N.B. Safeguard for new converts against danger of superficiality.

d. Prayers:

(1) Word used here indicates one of deepest secrets of devotional life — steadfast earnestness;
(2) Supplication to be united;
(3) Then presence of God would be realized; and —
(4) His power would be received.
(5) James Denney says expression "*the* prayers" implies public and stated prayers such as Jews had used in Temple, but they became new when in Name of Jesus. He was their inspiration and also their limit, and it was mark of true Church to cherish communication with God;

N.B. Safeguard for new converts against danger of independence.

3. *Influence of the Church* (v. 43)

Arising out of corporate life came influence exercised on others:

a. Life so real that awe and reverence fell on those around;
b. Life so powerful that miracles were done by Apostles among people, testifying to presence of God.

II. Continuation (vs. 44-47)

1. *Position of the Church*

   True Christian spirit shown among new disciples:

   a. Unity (v. 44)

      They were united by —

      (1) Common faith — "believed" (cf. "unity of the faith," Eph. 4:13);

      (2) Communal fellowship — "were together" (cf. "unity of the Spirit," Eph. 4:3);

      (3) Community of goods — "had all things common" on entirely voluntary basis (cf. 4:32; 5:4);

   b. Unselfishness (v. 45)

      (1) Due to reciprocal love of new community;

      (2) Giving is one of essential marks of true Christian life, and proves reality of profession;

2. *Progress of the Church* (v. 46)

   Development natural and normal — Christian life centering in church and in home:

   a. Public fellowship — "in the temple"

      (1) Natural center of Jewish religious life;

      (2) Connection until, after long time and special Divine revelation, permanent distinction and proper relations would be established betwen Judaism and Christianity;

   b. Domestic fellowship — "from house to house" (Gr., "at home")

      (1) "Breaking bread" — Lord's Supper celebrated in each other's homes;

      (2) "Eat their meat" — shared meals with one another, in joy and simplicity.

3. *Power of the Church* (v. 47)

   a. Gratitude was great — "praising God" — believers full of praise;

   b. Favor was general — "having favor with all the people" — consistent conduct commended them to those around;

   c. Blessing was Divine — "and the Lord——" — Christ Himself doing His part;

d. Growth was constant — "added to the church daily" — community strengthened;
e. Salvation was continual — "those that were being saved" (A.S.V.) — evangelism ever one of truest signs of spiritual power.

Conclusion

What is the secret of a church such as here described? It is twofold:

1. *On the Divine side*:
   a. Christ for us — a Saviour accepted;
   b. Christ in us — a Friend experienced;
   c. Christ among us — a Master honored;
   d. Christ through us — a Lord manifested.
2. *On the Human side*:
   a. Salvation through Christ — perfect; suppression of sin — daily;
   b. Surrender to Christ — absolute; repression of self — continual;
   c. Satisfaction in Christ — real; expression of Him — increasing;
   d. Service for Christ — definite; impression of power — infinite.

Granted these experiences, and the life of the Christian Church will provide an ever-deepening realization among God's people, will bring an ever-widening blessing to those around, and will prove an ever-increasing glory to God.

Study No. 17 — Healing and Preaching

ACTS 3:1-26

THE ACTS is the book of Christian beginnings after the Ascension of our Lord (cf. 1:1, 2). This chapter records the commencement of the quiet, ordinary life of the Church after the wonderful experiences of Pentecost. It and the chapter following are worthy of study also because they record the first collision of the Church with the world and show the true attitude of both Church and individual Christian to "them that are without" (Col. 4:5).

We may note also the association of Peter and John, particularly interesting in view of what has already been seen of them (cf. Luke 5:10; 22:8; John 20:3, 4; 21:20-22). Leaders among the apostles, they are found together on other occasions later on (4:13; 8:14). These two men have been described as "an admirable combination of strenuous activity and thoughtful love." Christianity is not a solitary, individualistic religion. "Friendship in Christ Jesus," says Alexander Smellie, "has an extraordinary value. It does more than double the capabilities of the individual disciple; it multiplies these capabilities fourfold or sevenfold or twentyfold."

It was Peter and John, on their way to worship in the Temple, who met a lame man and recognized —

I. Human Need (vs. 1-5)

1. *Extreme* (vs. 1, 2)
    a. The Man:
        (1) Extent — lame, had never walked — hopeless condition symbolic of sin, which ever prevents true Christian walk;
        (2) Time — all his life, forty years (cf. 4:22) — had lost simple confidence of childhood, ready wonder-

ment of youth, simple love of early manhood; had gained awful familiarity with pain, knowledge of sin's power, and experience of handicapped life. Why had he not come when Christ was in Jerusalem? (Cf. John 5:2-15; chap. 9)

b. The Place:

(1) Man taken day after day to where religion and charity were to be expected, as even now in that and other parts of world beggars are gathered around church doors at hours for services;

(2) Apostles' entrance into temple shows —

(a) As yet no idea or need of break with old religion;

(b) Intention to pray, indicating place and importance of worship, also regularity and punctuality.

2. *Expressed* (vs. 2, 3)

a. Usual hope — first generally (v. 2; cf. John 9:8) — then specifically (v. 3);

b. Having same experience for so long, it is not surprising that he contemplated nothing higher than alms.

3. *Encouraged* (vs. 4, 5)

a. Expectation aroused — to secure attention;

b. Expectation evinced — soon "gave heed" — mind in contact with Apostles'.

II. Healing Power (vs. 6-11)

1. *Claimed* (v. 6)

a. Absence of money — Peter frankly disclaimed its possession — "none"

b. Presence of power — Peter boldly claimed its control — "walk!"

(1) "In the Name" — standing for Christ Himself and His authority;

(2) "Jesus Christ of Nazareth" — place name particularly significant in view of former associations (cf. John 1:46), and all that had happened (cf. Luke 24:19; John 19:19).

2. *Shared* (v. 7)
   a. Through sympathy — taking man by right hand and raising him up — fine gesture that doubtless helped him to believe, for trust usually responds to sympathy;
   Illus.: At battle of Waterloo, Wellington ordered his friend General Picton to take perilous position. Picton replied: "Give me a grasp of your hand, and then I will." So, nerved for dangerous task, he accomplished his commander's mission.
   b. Through help — acting as channel between man's helplessness and Divine power — "immediately . . . strength"
3. *Proved* (vs. 8-11)
   a. Man leaped, stood, "began to walk" (marg.), entered temple, still walking and leaping, and did not forget to praise God;
   b. People saw him walking and praising, knew him as lame beggar, wondered, were amazed, surrounded group, still "greatly wondering";
   c. Peter, natural leader, older and more experienced, yet had associated John with his deed (cf. v. 4), so man clung to both in gratitude.

III. Heavenly Truth (vs. 12-26)

Astonishment of people gave Peter opportunity which he used faithfully and well, speaking plainly regarding Jesus Christ:

1. *Self disclaimed* (v. 12)
   a. The question — "why marvel ye . . . why look ye so earnestly on us?"
   b. The assumption — "as though by our own power or holiness——" (cf. Psa. 115:1).

   What follows is theme of Peter's second sermon:
2. *God honored* (vs. 13-15)
   Two climaxes traced:
   a. Christ exalted by God:
      (1) "His Servant Jesus" (A.S.V.) glorified;
      (2) "The Holy and Righteous One" (A.S.V.) vindicated;
      (3) "The Prince of Life" (cf. 5:31; Gr. also translated

"captain," Heb. 2:10, and "author," Heb. 12:2) raised;

b. Christ rejected by men:
   (1) Delivered up Son (cf. Matt. 27:2, 18);
   (2) Denied Holy One (cf. John 19:15);
   (3) Desired murderer (cf. Matt. 27:21);
   (4) Destroyed Prince of Life (cf. Luke 20:14, 15).

3. *Explanation supplied* (v. 16)
   a. Source of blessing — "His Name" — always means revealed character and power (cf. Psa. 118:10-12; John 16:23, 24);
   b. Channel of blessing — "faith in His Name" — man's need linked to Divine supply through —
      (1) Faith exerted by Peter and John (v. 6);
      (2) Faith exerted by lame man (cf. v. 8; Isa. 35:6).

4. *Exhortation continued* (vs. 17-26)

   Here is appeal of Peter's second sermon, and here also is shown spiritual miracle alongside physical — masterliness of preacher's transformed character. His able address deserves carefully detailed study as remarkable combination of intellectual force, courageous testimony, loving wisdom, and spiritual power:

   a. Generous extenuation (vs. 17, 18)
      (1) Peter was conscious of people's ignorance, but this not innocence;
      (2) Hope lay in God's overruling of sin (cf. v. 13);
   b. Earnest pleading (v. 19)
      (1) To repent;
      (2) To turn to God — Gr. word in active voice, implying, as always, very definite move on part of man towards God;
   c. Gracious promises (vs. 19, 20)
      (1) Blotting out of sin;
      (2) Times of refreshing;
      (3) Coming again of Jesus Christ;

      N.B. Contrast this reference with later ones, made after final rejection of Christ by Jews. Had they been willing to receive him, it seems clear He would have returned soon, so all references to speedy return are to be interpreted in light of offer to Jews of Divine Kingdom. When they finally rejected Christ and Gentile Church became prominent (after 28:28), teaching on Second Coming inevitably changed: e.g., word "*parousia*" found in Paul's earliest Epistles, Thessalonians and Corinthians, but not once in later Epistles, such as Ephesians and Colossians. Opinion on this question differs, but probable reason for change of standpoint, and therefore of teaching, was that Paul in earlier days fully expected Christ's immediate Messianic return for Jews. When offer refused and Apostle led to turn to Gentiles, he would no longer adopt same attitude or give same teaching. Difference doubtless due to leading of Holy Spirit through circumstances brought about by exercise of man's free will. Kingdom never yet set up and still in abeyance during present dispensation of Church;

d. Clear prophecies (vs. 21-24)
   (1) Restitution — "all things" of v. 21 limited by mention of "all things" of v. 22, spoken by Moses and prophets, i.e., restoration of Israel and of theocracy. We must therefore look to O.T. for prophecies concerning glories of future, when new heavens and new earth will be ushered in, and all confusion caused by sin done away. Christ now center of adoration in heaven, by all redeemed and by angels, while waiting for appointed time for His return;
   (2) Destruction — of those who will not listen (v. 23);
e. Personal application (vs. 25, 26)
   (1) To Israel as children of prophets and of Abrahamic covenant, having priority;
   (2) To Gentiles who would be blessed through Israel's turning from sin to Christ.

Conclusion

Let us regard this incident as a parable of the Church:

1. *The Church and the Sinner*
   a. The Sinner:
      (1) Incurably crippled;
      (2) Begging for mercy;
      (3) Debarred from worship;
   b. The Church:
      (1) Fellowship with each other;
      (2) Worship of God;
      (3) Sympathy with sinner;
      (4) Power over evil.
2. *The Church and the World*
   Twofold testimony —
   a. Of life — like lame man healed —
      (1) Showing change in self;
      (2) Showing forth praise to God;
   b. Of lips — like Peter, to show his own changed life, speaking with —
      (1) Humility;
      (2) Faithfulness;
      (3) Candor;
      (4) Love.
3. *The Church and the Master*
   a. Her Life — like Peter's, will show —
      (1) Worship of Him;
      (2) Fellowship with Him;
      (3) Faithfulness to Him;
      (4) Blessing from Him;
   b. Her Power — like Peter's, will result from —
      (1) Christ pre-eminent;
      (2) Self hidden;
      (3) Truth revealed;
      (4) Faith exercised.

It follows that what is true of the Church will be true also of each of her members if the full blessing of God is to be experienced.

Study No. 18 — The First Persecution

ACTS 4:1-31

TEN persecutions are reckoned as directed against Christianity by the Roman Empire during the first three centuries. The interest of the present passage is that it records the first of these. After the account in chapter 2 of the special power of Christianity, and in chapter 3 of its twofold ministry of preaching and practice, here is the commencement of the long chain of worldly opposition. In one way or another, the Christian Church has suffered persecution ever since, and it is therefore especially important to look at this first instance of it, and to try to discover the secret of meeting it.

Peter's sermon (3:12-26) was interrupted towards nightfall by the arrest of the two Apostles (4:3).

I. Opposition Manifested (vs. 1-4)

A. *Power* (vs. 1, 2)

1. *Collision inevitable between new faith and old*:
   a. "Priests" represented religious opposition — men on temple duty at time (cf. 2 Chron. 23:6; Luke 1:5, 8, 9, 23);
   b. "Captain of the temple" stood for political power, in charge of temple guards responsible for order (cf. 5:24-26);
   c. "Sadducees" were priestly family of aristocratic type, small in numbers but very influential:
      (1) Some think them descended from Zadok of 2 Sam. 8:17, while others favor little-known Zadok, president of Sanhedrin during period between Malachi and Matthew, about B.C. 250;
      (2) We do know posterity of former Zadok were

high priests down to Exile, and that main body of priests after Exile were descended from him;

(3) Sadducees conspicuous in Acts because acceptance of Gospel imperiled interests and contradicted rationalistic tenets:

(a) Held only Pentateuch to be authoritative, and —

(b) Disbelieved fact of resurrection or existence of angels and spirits as expressive of future life (cf. 23:8; Mark 12:18).

2. *Reason for opposition threefold*:

a. That Apostles taught people at all, being unofficial and untrained, and had caused commotion by miracle (v. 7);

b. That they proclaimed Resurrection — especially objectionable to Sadducees; and, chiefly —

c. That all this was associated with Jesus, for it represented blow at their authority;

N.B. Christianity ever brings teaching direct to the people!

B. *Punishment* (v. 3)

1. Seizure — two Apostles taken from temple;

2. Detention — put in prison until next day (cf. 5:18);

N.B. True witness often stirs up trouble!

C. *Progress* (v. 4)

1. Blessing — "Howbeit" — no cessation of faith in spite of anxiety over two leaders;

2. Increase — "number of the men came to be (marg.) about five thousand" — not including women and children (cf. Matt. 14:21), and indicating accession over Pentecost (cf. 2:41);

N.B. Persecution always makes for growth!

II. Opposition Met (vs. 5-12)

A. *Attack* (vs. 5, 6)

1. *The Tribunal* (vs. 5, 6)

a. Council of Sanhedrin, some seventy in number, necessary to decide on procedure; perhaps they hoped to prove Apostles guilty of magic and therefore liable to death (cf. Exod. 22:16);

b. Names familiar — we may imagine Peter's feelings facing men who had decreed death of Master:
   (1) "Rulers" probably represented Sadducees (cf. 3:17; 13:27);
   (2) "Elders" seem to mean members of Sanhedrin, or council;
   (3) "Scribes" were teachers of Law, belonging usually to Pharisees;
   (4) "Annas the high priest," appointed and later deposed by Romans, had great influence though not actually in office at time;
   (5) "Caiaphas," his son-in-law, appointed high priest by predecessor of Pilate, and removed from office A.D. 37;
   (6) "John, and Alexander" — nothing known of them except they seem to have belonged to high priest's family.

2. *The Inquiry* (v. 7)
   a. Shows blindness of rulers;
   b. Yet admission of existence of "power" and "name."

B. *Answer* (vs. 8-10)
   1. *Fullness* (v. 8)
      a. For office of spokesman, Peter received fresh filling with Holy Spirit;
      b. Initial baptism with Spirit at Pentecost not repeated — repetition always impossible, but several separate fillings for specific work blessedly possible, as here (cf. 4:31; 13:9);
      c. Peter probably remembered Master's promise of special help for special need (cf. Matt. 10:18-20; Luke 12:11, 12; 21:12-15);
      d. Note also his respectful salutation.
   2. *Boldness* (vs. 9, 10)
      a. Implies strange reason for inquiry — as though leaders

did not approve of "good deed done to the impotent man" (v. 9);

b. Plainly states miracle performed through "Jesus Christ of Nazareth" — again showing disregard of associations — whom they had crucified but God had raised from dead.

C. *Assertion* (vs. 11, 12)

1. *Christ's Vindication Proclaimed* (v. 11)

a. Used their own Scriptures to point his message, stating Christ was Stone despised by those presumably builders of national life (cf. Psa. 118:22);

b. It has been suggested some members of council must have remembered Christ, only few months before, quoting same words and applying them definitely to Himself (cf. Matt. 21:42-44, etc.);

c. Peter cites same passage again in First Epistle (2:6-8);

d. Continues now, with respect for officers but also with unabated boldness, and makes transition to —

2. *Christ's Salvation Preached* (v. 12)

a. Needed by all;

b. Offered to many;

c. Supplied by One.

III. Opposition Matched (vs. 13-18)

A. *Surprise* (v. 13)

1. *Cause* — Peter and John "unlearned and ignorant men," i.e., untrained in official schools; but what a "private education" they had had!

2. *Recognition* — remembered their association with Jesus months before — evidently impression had been made, but how different now in degree of boldness! Power of Holy Spirit was enabling them to maintain fellowship with Christ and to bear strong testimony to His grace;

N.B. Spurgeon once said: "You have read lives of Christ, beautifully and eloquently written, but the best life of Christ is His living biography, written out in the words and actions of His people."

Illus.: Persian parable says lump of clay emitted beautiful odor and, on being asked for explanation, replied, "I have been near a rose."

B. *Silence* (v. 14)
   1. *Proof* — above all, miracle had actually been wrought;
   2. *Presence* — probably man had not been imprisoned with Apostles, but had again taken his stand with them.

C. *Subterfuge* (vs. 15-18)
   1. *Confession* — action necessary, so acknowledged miracle;
   2. *Proposition* — to take refuge in threats, in order that by silence about Christ new religion might no longer spread among people;
   3. *Command* — sign of weakness, in view of all Peter had said.

IV. Opposition Mastered (vs. 19-22)

A. *Reality* (vs. 19, 20)

   Futile effort of foes increases Apostles' sense of reality:
   1. *Of Experience* — "the things which we have seen and heard" — they in flesh, we in spirit — in Christ, in others;
   2. *Of God* — "in the sight of God to hearken . . . unto God" — supreme claim;
   3. *Of Duty* — "we cannot but speak" — strong constraint.

B. *Release* (vs. 21, 22)
   1. *Threatening* — all rulers could do for fear of people;
   2. *Thwarting* — everyone knew of miracle and "glorified God" for it — not necessarily ready to accept His Son, but at least convinced of good deed done;
   3. *Testifying* — man's age mentioned here as additional proof of strength of evidence — perhaps Luke as physician took special note that mature man's limbs had been healed.

V. Opposition Minimized (vs. 23-31)

A. *Report* (v. 23)
   1. *Action* — particularly noteworthy as, on release, with beautiful sense of spiritual affinity "they went to their own company";

2. *Attitude* — told companions all, but showed no change in themselves.

B. *Result* (vs. 24-31)

1. *Prayer* (vs. 24-30)

a. Instead of determining to keep quiet, or showing fear, they lifted voices to God;

b. Gave glory to His Name as Creator;

c. Used O. T. Scripture (Psa. 2:1, 2), showing clear understanding of what had just happened;

d. Recognized foreordained events (cf. 2:23), in which Jew and Gentile had been united in enmity towards God's "holy Servant" (A.S.V.);

e. Full of experience of Christ, reminded God of "threatenings" (vs. 17, 21), but requested not preservation, but renewed courage in utterance;

f. Besought accompanying "signs and wonders" in same Name — "Thy holy Servant Jesus" (A.S.V.).

2. *Response* (v. 31)

Came at once in —

a. Increased power — another filling with Holy Spirit;

b. Further opportunity for testimony — boldness brought blessing.

Nothing could have been finer than this magnificent attitude of unselfish, Scriptural, and definite prayer, with God's instant reply.

Conclusion

Persecution, while the same in fact, often varies in character. Today, the Christian may or may not be called upon to suffer physically, but there are other ways of experiencing persecution. How may he face it?

1. *The Christian's Attitude*

In Peter's example, we see:

a. His testimony to Christ — full statement about Person and power of Master. We, too, should be ready always to bear our witness;

b. His character through Christ. In himself perhaps "unlearned and ignorant," but in Christ bold in speech and bearing because filled with the Spirit;

c. His work for Christ. Like facts connected with miracle that silenced rulers, there is today nothing like consecrated service for Christ to prove reality of Gospel.

2. *The Christian's Ability*

There is threefold secret to enable him to maintain true attitude:

a. For testimony, he must be "filled with the Holy Spirit";
b. For character, he must be always "with Jesus";
c. For work, he must do everything "in the Name," that is, by the authority of Jesus Christ.

Grace can thus transform weak, ordinary people into strong, noble, courageous witnesses and workers for Christ.

Study No. 19 — Salvation

ACTS 4:12

CONSCIOUSLY, or unconsciously, man has always had a sense of great need. Need for what? It may be summed up by the word "salvation," with its different aspects of purification, justification, safe-keeping, approach to God. This verse gives the Christian answer to that great need.

I. The Great Necessity — "we must be saved"

Why "must"? Because —

1. We are lost (cf. sheep, Luke 15:3-7);
2. We are helpless (cf. silver, Luke 15:8-10);
3. We are hopeless (cf. son, Luke 15:11-32).

II. The Great Possibility — "salvation"

What are its characteristics ?

1. Pardon for past ("son");
2. Power for present ("silver");
3. Peace for future ("sheep").

III. The Great Provision — "Name"

Who has supplied salvation, and how? God the Father, by —

1. Christ's death for pardon;
2. Christ's life for power;
3. Christ's presence for peace.

IV. The Great Opportunity — "under heaven"

Who may receive this salvation?

1. It is offered to all;
2. It is available for all;
3. It is sufficient for all.

V. The Great Limitation — "none other"

How is that indicated?

1. Only one source of information — the Bible;
2. Only one plea — the Person of Christ;
3. Only one way — the New Birth through grace;
4. Only one means — faith in Christ.

   N.B. A. P. Gibbs has well summed it up: "There is no room for evasion here. Either the Lord Jesus, by the sacrifice of Himself, did all the work necessary for the salvation of every believing sinner, or He did not. Since Christ is the alone Saviour, it follows that there is no other way to be saved, except through faith in Him. All the sinner's good works, prayers, tears, beliefs, ordinances, good resolves and religious professions will avail him nothing. He must realize that Christ is the only Door and Way into God's acceptance, forgiveness and blessing; and, apart from faith in Christ there is no salvation."

Conclusion

1. No other way (cf. John 10:1; 14:6);
2. No other foundation (cf. 1 Cor. 3:11);
3. No other God (cf. 1 Cor. 8:4; John 3:16);
4. No other message (26: 22; 2 Cor. 1:13).

There is no other Name than Thine,
Jehovah-Jesus! Name Divine!
On which to rest for sins forgiven,
For peace with God, for hope of heaven.

Study No. 20 — The Life of the Early Church

ACTS 4:23-35

THIS PASSAGE gives us the first detailed account of the inner life of the Church. In it the Church is seen both as a body in relation to the outside world and also as an entity in relation to God.

I. The Peace of the Church (v. 23)

After storms of persecution (vs. 1-22), there must inded have been comparative peace for Peter and John in returning to "their own company."

1. *Affinity*
   a. Law of association — naturally tended toward "their own";
   b. Lure of responsiveness — valued open ears and receptive hearts.
2. *Sympathy*
   a. Instinctively craved to report what had been said;
   b. Owned Christ as —
      (1) Object of common affection;
      (2) Subject of common thought;
      (3) Cause of common action;
      (4) Source of common grace.

II. The Prayer of the Church (vs. 24-30)

Answer of early Church to reported threats of world — neither fear, nor counter-measures, but — prayer! This included —

1. *Adoration* (vs. 24-28)
   Realizing God with wonderful fullness, they first ascribed honor to —
   a. His Power — "Lord" (v. 24) — as Supreme Ruler;
   N.B. Gr. word used is one from which comes our word "despot" (cf. 2 Pet. 2:1; Jude 4);

b. His Creatorship — "made" (v. 24) — as Originator of World;
c. His Revelation — "hast said" (vs. 25, 26) — Author of Word;
N.B. In life of early Church, Word of God and prayer always united (cf. 6:4; Eph. 6:17, 18);
d. His Sovereignty — "determined . . . to be done" (vs. 27, 28) — Overruling Providence.

2. *Supplication* (vs. 29, 30)
At this point threats taken definitely to the Lord in prayer:
a. Its Spirit — earnest — "lifted up their voice"; united — "with one accord" (see v. 24);
b. Its Substance — not for protection, but for "boldness"; for usefulness — "to heal"; and for power — "signs and wonders."

III. The Power of the Church (v. 31)

1. *The Result of the Prayer*
It was —
a. Immediate;
b. Palpable;
c. Effectual.

2. *The Signs Granted*
They were —
a. Place of meeting shaken;
b. Holy Spirit filling;
c. Word boldly spoken.

IV. The Prosperity of the Church (vs. 32-35)

1. *Reality Within* (vs. 32, 34, 35)
a. Unity — "multitude . . . of one heart and of one soul" — in spite of great growth since 120 referred to in 1:15;
b. Unselfishness — "had all things common" (see also 2:44, 45):
(1) Not obligation to give up possessions, but voluntary (cf. 5:4); perhaps realized by fund administered first by rich members (cf. 2:45) and then, as Church grew, in common;

(2) Yet distribution would not encourage abuse or unwise dependence on others, because giving was not indiscriminate, but "made unto every man according as he had need";

(3) This practice sometimes called "Christian Socialism," but in any case attitude it represents of readiness to help brethren in need is of essence of Christianity.

2. *Prosperity Without* (v. 33)*
   a. Testimony — shown by words — "great power . . . witness"
   b. Blessing — shown by works — "great grace . . . upon . . . all"

   N.B. First two of six "great greats" in early Church: (3) "great fear" (5:5, 11); (4) "great company . . . obedient" (6:7); (5) "great joy" (8:8); (6) "great number believed" (11:21).

   Illus.: Locomotive magnificent piece of machinery, but must have three things: steam, or no power; rails, or power causes destruction; and good engineer, for only efficient if rightly handled. So Christian — used and powerful and efficient as he is filled with grace, going on in God's ways, in hands of Holy Spirit.

Conclusion

1. *A Picture* — of body of people with love and knowledge of each other:
   a. Repression of self — for glory of God and well-being of others;
   b. Expression of Christ — oneness in love of and faith in Him;
   c. Impression of power — boldness of speech and beauty of life.
2. *A Possibility* — for local church today:
   a. Power requested — heartily, unitedly, intelligently, unselfishly;
   b. Power received — all filled with Spirit for special service;

---

*For fuller treatment, see Study No. 23, p. 103.

c. Power reflected — by willingness to testify to Christ and to deny self.

Does the picture presented by my church today resemble that of the early Church shown here?

Study No. 21 — "Their Own Company"

ACTS 4:23

There is a natural law of affinity, i.e., like attracts like, and it operates in all departments of life. Examples of this operation in the physical realm are chemical affinities, one particle attracting another, and as their power on each other is exercised their very shapes are modified. In human experience the analogy is clear. On the social plane, men and women tend to congregate in levels or classes, giving rise to ancient proverbs such as "Birds of a feather flock together," and "A man is known by the company he keeps." On the intellectual plane, people are united by similar views, ideas, principles; and instances of this fact abound in politics, in literature, and in the arts and sciences. On the spiritual plane, there is indeed a gravitation of the godly, a communion in Christ, and, conversely, a union of the ungodly, an association of anti-Christian forces.

In this verse we read some simple words about Peter and John: "Being let go, they went to their own company." These words are worthy of consideration today because —

I. Everyone Belongs to Some Company

1. Man social, not solitary — must attach himself to others;
2. Man spiritual, and in this aspect he finds only two positions — no middle ground, no twilight, but light and darkness, "hath" and "hath not" (cf. 1 John 5:12).

II. Everyone Ought to Belong to the Best Possible Company

This is Church of Christ, best man has ever known, for it is only society that —

1. Has God as Founder;
2. Has Christ as Saviour;
3. Has as qualification for entrance, to "admit bearer" — blood-bought salvation;
4. Has real human fellowship on all planes;
5. Has reputation for best work done;
6. Has guarantee that it will last forever.

III. Everyone May Know that Supreme Truth is Fact of Belonging — Not Method

1. Cf. conversions, i.e., admissions to this company:
   a. In chap. 16: child, Timothy — no violent change (vs. 1-3); woman, Lydia — quiet change (vs. 14, 15); man, jailer — sudden, revolutionary change (vs. 25-34);
   b. In John 1: Andrew — by preaching (v. 40); Peter — by individual influence (v. 41); Philip — by direct appeal (v. 43); Nathanael — by personal experience (vs. 45-51);
2. All of these different, and yet —
   a. All heard call;
   b. All felt need;
   c. All accepted Christ as Saviour and Lord;
   d. All proved experience in their lives.

IV. Everyone is Sometimes Hindered from Joining His Own Company

1. Worldly influence in Church — self-interest, public opinion, denominationalism, etc.;
2. Christian in world — fear, backsliding, carnality (cf. Gal. 5:7), etc.

V. Everyone, When Hindrance is Removed, Goes to His Own Company

1. Christian to Christians — denominationally or inter-denominationally, congregationally or in small groups (cf. Mal. 3:6);
2. Worldly to worldly — revelation of true self to others — tiger shows itself only at night, when restraints of day lifted; N.B. D. L. Moody once said: "Character is what a man is in the dark!"

VI. Therefore, Our Own Company is a Test of Character

1. Suppose Christian has perfect liberty to go and to do whatever he pleases:
   a. Will he be like Scottish elder on trip to Stockholm, "far frae hame" and therefore "far frae kirk"?
   b. Or like believer described in Isa. 58:13, 14, with principles regarding Sunday amusements, etc.?
2. Thus, there is danger of judging while barriers are up — more accurate estimate of character possible when they are removed — "being let go."

VII. And, Our Own Company Indicates Our Destiny

1. Death, or Second Coming of Christ if that comes first, will be great liberator — nothing left to withstand our desires — cf. Judas, who went "to his own place" (1:25), and "every man in his own order" (1 Cor. 15:23);
2. Life, at its best, means harmony with environment, and so at end, while Christian will gladly go to heaven, sinner neither will go nor will want to go; instead, he will take his own fire to hell — and he is settling his destination now, in this present life.

Conclusion

There are two questions asked in the Old Testament: "Where art thou?" (Gen. 3:9), and "What doest thou here?" (1 Kings 19:9). They indicate —

1. *The Solemnity of Freedom*
   We may each say, I am, I ought, I can, I will!
2. *The Responsibility of Choice*
   Church has no need of "chalk-line" Christians — but of definite, decisive ones who, like Rebekah and Ruth of old, declare, "I will go" (Gen. 24:58; Ruth 1:16).
   Therefore, accept Christ's invitation now, and pass "from death unto life" (John 5:24), "out of darkness into His marvellous light" (1 Pet. 2:9), and "into the kingdom of the Son of His love" (Col. 1:13, A.S.V.). Then, "being let go" you will indeed be in your "own company" until you reach the fulness of joy above — and forever after!

Study No. 22 — Prayer

ACTS 4:31

"WHEN THEY HAD PRAYED," we read of those Jerusalem believers in the first century, "the place was shaken." Today, and for as long as the Lord may tarry, one thought may well be constantly in the mind, one longing deep in the heart, and one determination strong in the soul of each of His followers on earth: it is to continue "instant in prayer" (Rom. 12:12). Surely this is one of our greatest and most urgent needs — more prayer, individual and united supplication and intercession. Thus, and only thus, shall our "place" be "shaken," our lives "filled with the Holy Ghost," and the Word of God be spoken in our generation "with boldness."

I. Prayer in Relation to Spiritual Power — "the place was shaken"

1. *Power against Sin*
   a. Sin is terrible fact because of its awful possibilities — "every man (shall know) the plague of his own heart" (1 Kings 8:38);
   b. Prayer is efficacious act because it brings power over sin:
      (1) Heart purified;
      (2) Conscience made more sensitive;
      (3) Will strengthened; and —
      (4) Soul protected on every side.
2. *Power against Backsliding*
   a. Slipping back is hideously possible through yielding to temptation;
   b. Prayer spells power here, too, for it arms against backsliding by keeping crevices of soul intact against leakage of spiritual strength.
3. *Power against Slackening*

a. Slackening in service is often shown by tendency to regard work as burden;

b. Prayer makes duty light and service delightful — "strengthened with all might" (Col. 1:11), and "ready to every good work" (Tit. 3:1):

(1) "His yoke is easy," and "to serve Him is to reign";

(2) His "service is perfect freedom" when prayer lubricates life.

II. Prayer in Relation to Spiritual Life — "they were all filled with the Holy Ghost"

1. *Prayer is means of maintaining and expressing right attitude to God*:

a. This attitude is complex, combining —

(1) Surrender and submission;

(2) Aspiration and desire;

(3) Dependence and trust;

(4) Communion and fellowship.

b. Prayer enters into every aspect of our hidden life and gives expression to its attitude:

(1) Would we be right with God? "Let us pray";

(2) Would we be true to God? "Let us pray";

(3) Would we be strong for God? "Let us pray."

2. *Prayer leads to constant realization of presence of God* — "His presence is salvation":

a. The peace of His presence, calming;

b. The joy of His presence, cheering;

c. The light of His presence, guiding;

d. The glory of His presence, irradiating.

3. *Prayer makes clear the will of God.*

As we pray, that sure mark of spiritual growth, discernment (cf. Phil. 1:9, A.S.V.), becomes ours in ever-increasing measure:

a. The perceptions of the soul are clarified;

b. The balance of the mind is poised;

c. The determinations of the will are strengthened.

III. Prayer in Relation to Spiritual Work — "they spake the Word of God with boldness"

1. *Prayer will bring constant blessing on our testimony*:
   a. We shall be enveloped in Divine power;
   b. We shall be sealed by God's authority.
2. *Prayer will take us into deeper fellowship with God's purposes for the world*:
   a. We shall realize chief end of Divine revelation is extension of knowledge of redeeming love;
   b. We shall become conscious of our share in its fulfilment and accept our responsibility for other souls.
3. *Prayer will assure us of bounden duty of intercession*:
   a. We shall remember that in great, ascending climax of our Lord's work (cf. Rom. 8:34), His intercession crowns all;
   b. We shall see His continued ability to save completely based on His eternal life of intercession (cf. Heb. 7:25);
   c. We shall devote not small, but prominent part of daily prayer-life to priestly intercession of believer (cf. Rev. 1:6; 5:10; 20:6).

Conclusion

For power, therefore, for life, for service, "let us pray," as did the Apostles of old:

1. For this attitude of prayer, we must have acts of prayer — occasions for accumulation of light, and power, and grace;
2. For these acts of prayer, we must have times of prayer — definite, solitary, regular.

Thus, from the act will come the habit; from the habit, the attitude; from the attitude the character — settled, strong, sure, abiding. Then God's presence will be more and more a delight, and God's power more and more realized.

"When they had prayed"—
"The place was shaken." So too will any place
Where faithful hearts their wills in longing bend;
The Word with boldness will they plainly speak,

In patience serve the man that still is weak,
And wickedness its course will surely end—
When men have prayed!

When men have prayed—
The uttermost of heaven's resources wait
To shield the man beset by sin's recruits.
Up from the fray, though fierce bemauled, his eyes
He lifts to heaven! Again in faith he tries,
And God awards of righteousness the fruits—
When men have prayed!

When men have prayed—
Ah! hard the discipline, taxing oft the task!
For prayer is not the dream of leisure hours;
It has its midnight sweat, its blood-drops red,
Its hand upraised, its wine press lone to tread,
Yet reck we little when the storm-cloud lowers—
If we have prayed!

When men have prayed—
The busy course of life runs smoother on,
The fret of toil, temptation's subtle test,
And all the worries which the soul attack,
Or sense of longing for the things we lack,
Are lost in heaven's benediction best—
When we have prayed!

—Ernest Bourner Allen

Study No. 23 — The Church of God (1)*

ACTS 4:32, 33

THE NEW TESTAMENT has at least two unique features — its revelation of Christ and its revelation of the Church. These stand today, as they have ever stood, unparalleled creations of God. When the two disciples of John the Baptist heard their master proclaim, "Behold the Lamb of God," and left him to follow Jesus of Nazareth, they entered upon a new relationship to a new Master. On that day, a new bond was introduced into the world, a tie of relationship to Christ and to one another in Him. Up to that time, there had been ties of blood, of friendship, of intellectual affinity, of patriotism, of political alliance; and to some extent the tie of our common humanity had been contemplated in theory. But a society in which the one and only bond between members was their relation to their Master, Jesus Christ — this was something entirely novel and unique. This may be seen in the "new commandment" of love (John 13:34, 35), where the newness lay not in the fact or in the standard of the love, but in the object, "one another," a phrase emphatically repeated.

This society was subsequently spoken of as "the Church." Our English word, the translation of the Greek *"ecclesia,"* meaning "assembly," "congregation" (cf. Matt. 26:28; 18:17), is etymologically derived from a word which means "that which belongs to the Lord," so that it may be truly said to represent a Divine society. This Divine society was in due course constituted by the Apostles' witness to the risen Christ and the power of the Holy Ghost on the Day of Pentecost, and in the Book of Acts we have some record of its progress during the first thirty years of its existence.

---

*For another treatment of this general subject, see Study No. 100, p. 397.

The Book of Common Prayer describes the Church thus: "the blessed company of all faithful people," and "the communion of saints." The Church is at once a society of saved sinners and one of sanctified servants of Christ. Let us take the picture of the primitive Church as it appears in these verses, and try to discover some of those elements which ought to characterize the life of the Church today.

I. The Reality of Inward Life

Since Christianity always works from within, life of Church showed two great elements:

1. *Spiritual Unity* — "the multitude of them that believed were of one heart and one soul" (v. 32)
   They were —
   a. A multitude which "believed" — large in number and varied in temperament, capacity, and antecedents, yet characterized by same faith in Christ;
   b. A multitude possessed of "one heart and one soul" — fulfilling prayer of Master for unity (cf. John 17:21); N.B. Cambridge Ms. has very suggestive clause here: "Neither was there any difference between them"; Oxford Codex has: "Neither was there any severance between them." What a picture! One heart, one soul, no difference, no severance!
2. *Striking Unselfishness* — "not even one said that anything he possessed was his own" (v. 32, Gr.)
   a. Out of spiritual relationship to Christ came social relationship to each other — unity and unselfishness, cause and effect;
   b. Here is genuine Christian socialism:
      (1) Spontaneous expression of love of God in hearts;
      (2) Systematic provision for poor instituted:
         (a) Unknown in heathenism, and —
         (b) Largely neglected by Jews, despite Mosaic law;
      (3) Startling contrast with modern non-Christian socialism which says, What is yours is mine; while early Christians said, What is mine is yours.

II. The Prosperity of Outward Life

Spiritual life always expresses itself in power:

1. *The Power of the Apostolic Testimony* — "with great power gave the Apostles witness" (v. 33)
   a. Life of Church acted upon preaching — pew still influences pulpit, and when congregation is right with God it necessarily affects life, preaching, and witness of minister: *Illus.*: When asked reason for church's blessing, Spurgeon pointed to place where prayer meeting was held, and said, "My people pray for me."
   b. Apostles able to proclaim resurrection of Christ because He was center of Church's life and testimony.
2. *The Power of the Christian Life* — "great grace was upon them all" (v. 33)
   a. "Grace" not only in sense of "favour with all the people," as in 2:47; but —
   b. Grace of God so manifestly upon all that blessing abounded in extension of Church and to glory of God.

III. The Spirituality of Upward Life

Outward and inward attitudes are affected by upward attitude, for only as believers were right with God were they right with themselves and with one another. In every true Christian life, individual or corporate, "the length, and the breadth, and the height of it are equal" (Rev. 21:16).

1. *Theirs was a Life lived in Prayer* (cf. vs. 23-30)
   a. Their prayer was immediate — "they reported . . . and when they heard that, they lifted up their voice to God"
   b. Their prayer was united — "with one accord"
   c. Their prayer was unselfish and undaunted — asked not for protection, but for "boldness" to speak and power to work "wonders . . . by the name of . . . Jesus"
   d. Their prayer was Scriptural — quoting and pleading God's Word as spoken by David.
2. *Theirs was a Life lived by the Holy Spirit* (cf. v. 31)
   a. One of the "many fillings" was bestowed on them in view of special need (cf. 2:4; 4:8);

b. This gift of Holy Ghost power was thus special mark of primitive Church.

Conclusion

What has all this to do with the Church of today?

1. In proportion as it produces these elements of Reality, Prosperity, and Spirituality, the cause of the Gospel will be powerful and triumphant; in proportion as they are absent, that cause will be weak and defeated:
   a. Each individual must reproduce this Christian life of co-operation, liberality, testimony, and power through prayer and the Holy Spirit. Let each search his own heart and cry to God that there be no hindrance in it;
   b. Each congregation must reproduce this same life of the primitive Church. Evangelization depends on the spiritual condition of the Church, and missions would never be hindered if it were kept on a high plane;
   c. All bodies of Christians taken together need the same elements, especially that of unity:
      (1) Not as a unit of organization, for this has never existed since the Church left Jerusalem;
      (2) Not unanimity of opinion on everything, for this is manifestly impossible;
      (3) Not uniformity of organization and ceremonial, for this is a mere dream;
      N.B. Westcott says: "External visible unity is not required for the essential invisible unity of the Church";
      (4) But, a fundamental unity of those who are in Christ, with no compromise on essentials, yet with a blessed comprehensiveness for the sake of peace — all on same spiritual level based on evangelical truth, with no terms of fellowship not found in Scripture. We cannot tolerate any Papacy, whether from Rome, Canterbury, Geneva, Plymouth, or anywhere else.
2. Resting upon this wide and firm foundation, there need be no essential difficulty in maintaining a high standard of

Church life. As in our Lord's prayer in John 17, there are four great principles closely associated:

a. Sanctification — in order to —
b. Unification — in order to —
c. Evangelization — in order to —
d. Glorification.

3. How shall we proceed? We must make more of —
   a. Prayer, individual and corporate;
   b. Scripture, to be studied, believed, practised;
   c. The Resurrection, for the living Christ is the secret of perpetual and permanent victory; and —
   d. The Holy Spirit, from whom come light, liberty, blessing.

Then will the words about the Church be fulfilled: she will be seen "fair as the moon, clear as the sun, and terrible as an army with banners" (Song of Sol. 6:10).

Study No. 24 — Barnabas (1)*

ACTS 4:36, 37

WHEN the sun is shining the stars are eclipsed, and even in moonlight they seem relatively insignificant. But view them on a night when the moon is not visible and the sky will be bright with myriad suns. God "made the stars also," not only the "two great lights" (Gen. 1:16). Similarly, in the presence of our Lord and of His great Apostles Peter and Paul, other names in sacred history seem relatively unimportant. Yet a consideration of just such persons is most rewarding to study and strengthening to faith. One of these is Barnabas, who is introduced in these verses.

I. The Man (v. 36)

1. Was from island of Cyprus, between coasts of Syria and Asia Minor — O.T. "Chittim" (cf. Num. 24:24; Isa. 23:1,

---

*For other studies of Barnabas, see Studies Nos. 52, 53, 54, 79, pp. 213-218, 296.

12, etc.) — first stop on Paul's first missionary journey cf. 13:4-12).

2. Name had been Joses, or Joseph, but Apostles had "surnamed" him Barnabas, or "Son of Exhortation" (A.S.V.), because special characteristic was his influence with and encouragement of fellow-Christians (9:27; 11:22-30; 15:37, 39, treatment of which see, pp. 176, 213-218, 296); was first member of early Church to be re-named.
3. Was of tribe of Aaron, and of family of Levi, priestly line.
4. Comes before us later as man of means and of importance in Christian church (cf. 12:25; chaps. 13 to 15, treatment of which see, pp. 225 f.); 1 Cor. 9:6; Gal. 2:1-13; Col. 4:10).

II. The Money (v. 37)

1. Made from sale of Barnabas' land, brought and laid at Apostles' feet — private interests secondary to cause of Christ.
2. Meant self-sacrifice voluntary and complete.
3. Indicated Barnabas not only talker ("said," v. 32 — "exhortation," v. 36, A.S.V.), but doer.

III. The Motive

One of love, as outcome of being —

1. Spirit-filled — cf. 4:31 with 5:3;
2. Surrendered — first, livelihood — then, life (cf. 15:25, 26).

Conclusion

Two sides to the coin:

1. Barnabas —
   a. Looked up — "believed" (v. 32);
   b. Looked around — "distribution" (v. 35).
2. This is true spirit of Calvary, when Christ —
   a. Looked up — "Father' (Luke 23:34) — faith strong;
   b. Looked around — "Finished" (John 19:30) — salvation accomplished.
3. Love is connecting link, for —
   a. "Though I bestow all my goods to feed the poor . . . but have not love, it profiteth me nothing" (1 Cor. 13:3,

A.S.V). and —

b. "Whoso hath this world's goods, and beholdeth his brother in need, and shutteth up his compassion from him, how doth the love of God abide in him?" (1 John 3:17, A.S.V.)

Therefore, "my little children, let us not love in word, neither in tongue; but in deed and in truth," as did Barnabas of old.

Study No. 25 — Sin in the Church

ACTS 5:1-16

IN THE previous chapter (4:23-37) we have a beautiful picture of an entire Church indwelt by the Holy Spirit. Now come the first instances of individual Christian life in relation to the presence of the Spirit. The Apostle Peter must necessarily be given special attention but, at the same time, in marked contrast, we read of the first flagrant sin in the Christian Church. It was a sin against true brotherhood and destructive of the first principles of truth and love.

I. Sinful Pretence (vs. 1-10)

Word "but" (v. 1) indicates awful contrast of this story of Ananias and Sapphira with mention of Barnabas (cf. 4:36, 37). In outward appearance acts were similar, but in reality very different:

1. *Spiritual Perception* (vs. 1-4)

Apostle Peter —

a. Detected sin (v. 3) by supernatural, Spirit-revealed knowledge:

(1) Avarice — desire for selfish gain; hypocrisy — desire to be thought saint, wholly consecrated like Barnabas;

(2) Hypocrisy takes various forms: not only exaggerating gifts or minimizing means of giving, but boasting wrongly of worship, devotion, use of time, etc.;

(3) Word "hypocrite" from Greek, and originally meant masker, or actor — one who pretends to be what he is not;

(4) Worst form of pretense is religious — temptation to galvanize life into spiritual force, through simulated holiness, very great and perilous, especially, e.g., in times of revival or mass evangelism;

b. Traced sin to source (v. 4) — will of man always yields, is never overpowered; Satan, resisted, flees (cf. Jas. 4:7; 1 Pet. 5:9);

c. Revealed awfulness of sin — lie against Holy Spirit (v. 3) and offense against God, not man (cf. Psa. 51:4);

d. Thus taught clearly and simply personality and deity of Spirit, also His immediate superintendence of Church as "executive of Godhead" — lie can be told only to person (v. 3);

e. Reminded Ananias of liberty to retain, or sell, or give only part of proceeds (v. 4), but not to lie;

f. Accused him of premeditated sin (v. 4) and held him personally responsible (note use of singular pronoun), regardless of wife's collusion (v. 1);
N.B. But note use of plural pronoun in vs. 8, 9; cf. Gen. 3:10, 13.

2. *Swift Punishment* (vs. 5, 6)

a. At once Ananias fell dead, with no opportunity for exhortation or repentance;

b. God's swift judgment descended, agreeing with man's conscience smitten by "hearing these words" (v. 5);

c. "Younger men" (v. 6, Gr.) probably servants or minor officials, though perhaps not yet organized; reference to youth may indicate strength suited to task (cf. Exod. 24:5);

d. Sad to think first burial in Christian community was that of hypocrite.

3. *Searching Proof* (vs. 7, 8)

a. About three hours later, when wife Sapphira entered unsuspecting, Peter asked her straight question;

b. Significant inquiry as to price of land — "for so much" — intended to probe her conscience and give her opportunity to tell full truth;
c. Money actually laid at Apostles' feet may have still been there;
d. In any case, answer was shameless — lying, deliberate, and defiant, adding to sin of original deception, for suppression of truth suggests falsehood.

4. *Solemn Prerogative* (v. 9)
a. Peter's rebuke shows clearly Sapphira's co-operation in husband's sin (cf. v. 2);
b. Wife can be either wonderful help or terrible hindrance to husband;
c. Peter again spoke of testing or trying Holy Spirit, but did what he had not done in case of Ananias — declared God's judgment in advance.

5. *Similar Penalty* (v. 10)
a. Judgment at once took effect, and Sapphira fell down dead "at his feet," where deceitful offering had been laid and may still have been lying;
b. She also was carried out, and was buried — "by her husband."

II. Spiritual Progress (vs. 11-16)

God overruled sin to His own glory by permitting:

1. *Great Fear* (vs. 11, 13)
a. Third "great great" of Acts (see Study No. 20, under IV, 2, b. p. 93);
b. Not surprising that solemn awe fell upon whole Church and upon all others who heard;
c. We may wonder why God acted in such swift and terrible judgment; perhaps it was because —
(1) Seriousness of first notable sin in Church needed emphasis, thereby urging complete and all-important sincerity on all; and —
(2) Church's infancy needed profound revelation of nature of sin and of holiness of God. Cf. similar lessons

taught Israel in early days of national life (e.g., Exod. 32:19-28; Lev. 10:1-3; Num. 3:4; 16; Josh. 7; also Psa. 111:9, 10);

N.B. H. J. Horn says: "This iniquity . . . was a gash in the lovely body of the infant Church; a splash of filth on the white raiment of the chosen of God; a rent in the seamless robe of the unity of the saints."

d. "The rest" (v. 13) probably refers to certain outsiders who were so impressed at doings in Church as to fear to join such a body.

2. *Glorious Faith* (vs. 12, 14-16)

Through terrible purging came:

a. Great wonders (vs. 12, 15, 16) — unmistakable blessings came to entire community:

(1) Hands of Apostles wrought signs and wonders — sick persons healed, "even carried out . . . into the streets" (v. 15, A.S.V.);

(2) No virtue in Peter's shadow — Divine power alone, through faith, brought healing, — but even shadow of godly man may bring comfort;

(3) Neighborhood around Jerusalem impressed by news — first notice of expansion of work beyond city — Gospel cannot be hidden;

b. Great development (v. 14) — in part of parenthesis (vs. 12-14), we are told of Church's growth:

(1) Only instance in N.T. where this word for "multitude" found in plural, suggesting exceptionally large additions to numbers;

(2) Women mentioned as well as men (cf. 1:14; 4:4) — perhaps in view of "widows" (6:1), but characteristic of Luke's writings to draw special attention to women believers.

Conclusion

1. It was a sin against the Holy Spirit that marked the life of Ananias and Sapphira; and it included:

a. Avarice — on surface — or, the fruit:

Can be met by Spirit of love, for the more we are filled with that Spirit, the less room there will be for selfish greed;

b. Hypocrisy — deeper — or, the branch:
Can be met by Spirit of truth, for the more His teaching penetrates our inner life, the more genuine we shall be;

c. Unfaithfulness to God — deepest — or, the root:
Can be met by Spirit of holiness, for the more we are ruled by Him, the more He will keep us faithful in every part of life.

2. The virtues emphasized by this sad story are:
   a. Spiritual Perception: Even apart from miraculous gifts, this is possible, coming from fellowship with and growing experience of God — proof of Christian maturity;
   b. Spiritual Purity: Absolute necessity in Church, for one unworthy member may hinder whole community;
   c. Spiritual Power: Fulness of Satan and sin gave place to fulness of Spirit, and love triumphed over avarice, truth over hypocrisy, holiness over sin.

Gracious Spirit, dwell with me!
I myself would gracious be,
And, with words that help and heal,
Would Thy life in mine reveal;
And, with actions bold and meek,
Would for Christ my Saviour speak.

Truthful Spirit, dwell with me!
I myself would truthful be;
And, with wisdom kind and clear,
Let Thy life in mine appear;
And, with actions brotherly,
Speak my Lord's sincerity.

Tender Spirit, dwell with me!
I myself would tender be;
Shut my heart up like a flower
In temptation's darksome hour,
Open it when shines the sun,
And His love by fragrance own.

Mighty Spirit, dwell with me!
I myself would mighty be;
Mighty so as to prevail
Where unaided man must fail;
Ever, by a mighty hope,
Pressing on and bearing up.

Holy Spirit, dwell with me!
I myself would holy be;
Separate from sin, I would
Choose and cherish all things good;
And whatever I can be
Give to Him who gave me Thee.
—Thomas Toke Lynch (1818-71)

Thus the early Church went forward, blessed and made a blessing. What about the Church of God in these latter days?

What kind of a Church would my Church be
If every member were just like me?

Study No. 26 — The Second Persecution

ACTS 5:17-42

The judgment on Ananias and Sapphira caused the Church to be blessed and used more fully; but it had other effects also. The enthusiasm of some it checked, but won the admiration of others, while it gained the active adherence of "multitudes both of men and women." At length the authorities felt impelled to move.

I. The Story

1. *Arrest* (vs. 17, 18)
   a. Anger on part of high priest and his party — "sect of the Sadducees" (v. 17)
   b. Seizure of Apostles — put in "common prison" (v. 18)
2. *Deliverance* (vs. 19, 20)
   a. Rebuke to persecutors — "angel of the Lord . . . brought

them forth" (v. 19)
b. Rousing of people's attention — "speak in the temple" (v. 20)
c. Reason for speaking — "all the words of this life" (v. 20)

3. *Outcome* (vs. 21-25)
a. Obedience — "entered into the temple . . . and taught" (v. 21)
b. Surprise — "found them not" — "found no man within" (vs. 22, 23)
c. Uncertainty — "they doubted . . . whereunto this would grow" (v. 24)
d. Consternation — "in prison . . . in the temple" (v. 25).

4. *Trial* (vs. 26-28)
a. Caution — "without violence: for they feared the people" (v. 26)
b. Accusation (v. 28) of —
(1) Insubordination — "should not teach"
(2) Indoctrination — "filled Jerusalem with your doctrine"
(3) Intention — "intend to bring this man's blood upon us" — i.e., accusing high priest's party in return, or raising insurrection against them (cf. "stoned," v. 26).

5. *Defence* (vs. 29-33)
a. Reply of Apostles (vs. 29-32)
(1) Principle — of obedience to God — "obey God"
(2) Fact — of resurrection of Christ — "raised up Jesus"
(3) Crime — of death of Christ — "whom ye slew"
(4) Truth — of ascension of Christ — "Him hath God exalted" —
(a) "To be a Prince and a Saviour";
(b) "To give repentance . . . and forgiveness"
(5) Witness — to all this:
(a) "We are His witnesses";
(b) "So is also the Holy Ghost."
b. Result (v. 33)
(1) Hearers "cut to the heart";
(2) Counsel taken "to slay" Apostles.

6. *Suggestion* (vs. 34-40)
   a. Recommendation by Gamaliel — caution to be observed in view of former experiences — "if . . . of men" (v. 38) — "if . . . of God" (v. 39)
   b. Agreement — sentence, to be beaten — attempt at silencing — dismissal — "to him they agreed" (v. 40)
7. *Consequence* (vs. 41, 42)
   a. Feeling — rejoicing at shame "for His Name" (v. 41)
   b. Action — daily witnessing in temple and home in spite of edict — "ceased not" (v. 42)

II. The Teaching

There were three forces at work here:

1. *The Spirit of Error*
   Exemplified by the High Priest:
   a. Animosity (vs. 17, 33, 40) — typical of world vs. Church;
   b. Force (v. 18) — might only argument;
   c. Fear (v. 24) — of potential growth of new group;
   d. Insincerity (v. 28):
      (1) Not a word about mysterious release (v. 19) — convenient to ignore reference to supernatural — cf. Sadducees' doctrine (v. 17; 4:1, 2);
      (2) Refusal to name the Name (cf. vs. 28, 40).
2. *The Spirit of Compromise*
   Exemplified by Gamaliel:
   a. Plausibility — argument carried apparent weight — let time test! But not whole truth, for many erroneous systems have lasted centuries, but are not thereby proved to be "of God" (v. 39);
   b. Falsity — success does crown end, but how about course? Impossible to wait for proof when eternal issues at stake;
   c. Indifference — from man morally bound to satisfy himself and others on evidence about Christ there should not be neutrality;
   d. Cowardice — because if of God, Gamaliel should have felt bound to accept, not merely ignore; but seems never to have had intention of taking sides.

3. *The Spirit of Truth*

   Exemplified by Peter:

   a. Fearlessness (v. 20, 29) — obligation to obey command of God through His angel;
   b. Faithfulness (vs. 30-33) — testimony full and strong;
   c. Steadfastness (vs. 41, 42) — exulting and continuing;
   d. Reality — (vs. 20, 41) — living "this life" (cf. Gal. 2:20), and suffering "shame for His Name."

Conclusion

1. *Our Only Safety*
   a. Resoluteness (v. 21) — in speech bold, with no uncertain sound;
   b. Faithfulness (v. 29) — in heart courageous, with no uncertain conviction;
   c. Confidence (v. 32) — in soul trustful, with no uncertain faith;
   d. Persistence (v. 42) — in will determined, with no uncertain force of character.
2. *Our Only Strength*
   a. God powerful (v. 31);
   b. Christ precious (v. 41);
   c. The Spirit possessed (v. 32).

Study No. 27 — What God Thinks of Christ

ACTS 5:31

WE KNOW from the Gospels what God the Father thought of His Son while on earth (cf. Matt. 3:17; 17:5, etc.). Here we are shown something of what God thinks of Jesus Christ since Calvary.

I. The Place

God has exalted His Son (cf. 2:33) —

1. "With His right hand" — expressive of power; or —
2. "To His right hand" (as Gr. allows) — expressive of position.

II. The Person

This is to constitute Him —

1. "A Prince" — Gr. word found three other times only in N.T. (cf. 3:15, which see in Study No. 17, p. 79ff.; Heb. 2:10; 12:2), and means ruler who is also leader.
2. "A Saviour" — one who "is just, and having salvation" (Zech. 9:9), which is one of most inclusive of N.T. words, looking backward, outward, and forward:
   a. In relation to past — deals with deliverance from penalty and guilt of sin, and is complete;
   b. In relation to present — deals with deliverance from power and love of sin, and is process, gradual and continuous, which believer may experience here and now;
   c. In relation to future — deals with deliverance from presence and result of sin, and is certain hope to which believer may look forward;
   Illus.: Hindu woman who had realized her sinfulness and God's holiness declared: "I need some great prince to stand between my soul and God!" When she read in

Matthew 1 of Christ's long line of ancestors, she thought, "What a wonderful prince this must be!" But when she came to the words, "He shall save His people from their sins," she exclaimed, "Ah, this is the Prince I want! This is the Prince I want!"

III. The Purpose

All this is intended to give —

1. Repentance — God's exaltation of Christ as Prince should produce in man humbling of heart and renunciation of sin;
2. Forgiveness — God's exaltation of Christ as Saviour provides remission of sin for repentant sinner.

Conclusion

Since this is God's idea of Christ, it follows that ours should be in exact accordance therewith. It is thus for us to respond as God intends, expects, and desires to the searching question "What think ye of Christ?" (Matt. 22:42). Everything concerning Christ may be summed up in three well-known N.T. phrases:

1. "It is I" — The Person (cf. Matt. 14:27);
2. "It is Finished" — The Work (cf. John 19:30);
3. "It is Written" – The Word (cf. Matt. 26:24; Mark 9:12; Luke 24:46, etc.).

If we are true to God's thought of Christ, we shall attend to what is written about Him, accept His finished work, appropriate all that is in His unique, blessed Person, and abide in Him forever.

Study No. 28 — Settling the First Dissension

ACTS 6:1-8

"CALLING A SPADE A SPADE, and not an instrument of husbandry" is a modern phrase often used to describe candor and downrightness. The Bible uses the plainest of speech and its writers do not hesitate to record everything pertinent, whether bad or good, concerning men and institutions. The Book of Acts is a striking instance of this frankness, for it records the tragedy of Judas Iscariot, the first sin in the Church, and the story of the first dissension. In this treatment of a new problem there is no hiding of weak spots, and yet there is detailed information as to how the crisis was met and the difficulties were overcome. We are thus shown both the importance of the situation and the necessity for a new step in organization.

I. The Problem (v. 1)

1. Caused by growth of Church — success frequently creates serious situations (cf. Deut. 1:9-18);
2. In daily distribution of food (cf. 4:35; 11:29), some widows were being neglected;
3. Care of Church for widows, i.e., those with no natural protector, noteworthy —
    a. Showing thus early what afterwards became recognized part of church life (cf. 9:39, 41; 1 Tim. 5:3-16);
    b. First in long series of organized activities relating Christian philanthropy ("man-lovingness") to human needs; and —
    c. Another instance of concern of Gospel with women and children (cf. Jas. 1:27).
4. Difficulty arose almost entirely out of language differences — Greek-speaking Jews complaining against Palestinian Jews;
5. "Grecians" — Jews from Greek cities who spoke Greek;

Hebrews — Jews of Palestine who spoke Aramaic;
6. But "murmuring" is bad method of raising objections.

II. The Proposal (vs. 2-4)

1. Secular work increasing, but Gospel ministry, primary purpose of Apostles, all-absorbing to them. It has been pointed out that this passage teaches two related truths:
   a. Supremacy of Spiritual — while everything should be done as unto God (cf. 1 Cor. 10:31), there are varying degrees of importance inherent in different actions;
   b. Sanctity of Secular — even common duties to be discharged by spiritual men and in spiritual way.
2. Suggestion to delegate secular work to seven men, with these qualifications (v. 3):
   a. Reputation — "honest report"
   b. Godliness — "full of the Holy Ghost"
   c. Sagacity — "wisdom."
3. Yet even for secular work qualifications were spiritual and moral, and, thus fitted, men were able to meet new emergency (cf. Rom. 12:10-16);
4. Though not spoken of here as "deacons," generally regarded as precursors of later order of deacons mentioned in Epistles (cf. Phil. 1:1; 1 Tim. 3:8-13);
5. Apostles to continue in spiritual work — "to prayer, and to the ministry of the Word" (v. 4);
6. Not that seven were to give up all spiritual work, for Stephen and Philip both continued and even increased their spoken testimony for Christ (v. 8; 6:9 to 7:60; 8:5-40).

III. The Reception (vs. 5, 6)

1. Suggestion met with instant and hearty approval (cf. Jas. 2:14-17);
2. Seven men chosen, about five of whom we know nothing further, and Stephen, and Philip;
3. But all had Greek names, showing conciliatory spirit of Church and evident willingness of Palestinian Jews to avert further trouble;

4. Commissioned by prayer and laying on of hands — benediction and commission (cf. 13:3; Num. 27:18), but never transmission of spiritual authority or position.

IV. The Result (vs. 7, 8)

1. Effect of new action immediate and striking:
   a. Great extension of spiritual work — "the Word of God increased" (cf. similar phrases in 12:24 and 19:20);
   b. Great accession of Jerusalem disciples, including priests "obedient to the faith" — noteworthy in light of previous references to progress (cf. 2:47; 5:14; 6:1).
2. Stephen, best known of Seven, strengthened —
   a. In character — "full of faith and power"
   b. In work — "did great wonders and miracles."

Conclusion

1. *Church difficulties occurring*
   a. Inevitable — large numbers of different natures, with humanity imperfect, even at best and under influence of Gospel;
   b. Not invincible — should be met fairly, and firmly, with conviction that solution is possible.
2. *Church difficulties overcome*
   a. By trust — Apostles called together and consulted whole Church — "multitude of the disciples" (v. 2);
   b. By frankness — people told candidly of necessity of rearrangement;
   c. By willingness — truth of statement recognized and necessity of action agreed to;
   d. By love — setting aside differences, seeking good of all, realizing need for each member, honoring diversities of gifts and division of work.
3. *Church difficulties overruled*
   a. Satan unable to drive in wedge of discord;
   b. Numbers of members increased;
   c. Striking development of spiritual gifts in Christian community.

Thus story reveals beautiful way in which early Christians bore one another's burdens and so fulfilled law of Christ (cf. Gal. 6:2). Do we, in these latter days, do the same?

Study No. 29 — A Christian Leader

ACTS 6:3

A BRIEF description of a Christian leader may be found in this verse, where an ideal is set forth of one we may call an "all-round" man. A study of the qualifications of the Seven Deacons, as we like to think of them, is very important since, as it has been well said, the person of the Christian leader is the life of his work. We may also see how these qualifications apply to the ministry of today, clerical or lay. The ideal Christian leader has —

I. His Relation to Man — "of honest report"

A good reputation is —

1. *Prominent in New Testament*
   a. Examples:
      (1) Our Lord — in favor with . . . man" (Luke 2:52);
      (2) Cornelius — "of good report" (10:22);
      (3) Timothy — "well reported of" (16:2);
      (4) Ananias — "having a good report" (22:12);
   b. Exhortations:
      (1) "Walk circumspectly" (Eph. 5:15);
      N.B. Greek means "accurately" — English suggests looking around carefully while walking;
      (2) "Walk in wisdom" (Col. 4:5);
      (3) "Walk honestly" (1 Thess. 4:12);
      (4) "Provide things honest" (Rom. 12:17; cf. 2 Cor. 8:21; 1 Pet. 2:12);
      (5) "A bishop . . . must have a good report" (1 Tim. 3:2, 7).

2. *Important in Christian life*
   a. Proof of Christianity — "What have they seen in thine house?" (2 Kings 20:15) — e.g., servants, relatives — also contemporaries in church, college, business, etc.;
   b. Profession of Christianity — marred by carelessness, unreliability, unpunctual habits; if our spirituality is not ethical it is not spirituality, i.e., not in accord with Him who is called "the Spirit of holiness" (Rom. 1:4).

II. His Relation to Self — "full of . . . wisdom"

1. *What is wisdom?*
   a. Knowledge applied and used;
   b. Common sense, sagacity, ability to judge.
2. *Why is wisdom necessary?*
   a. Note these seven deacons: they had to distinguish between cases, administer charity, use money with impartiality and integrity;
   b. They could not be weak, nor prejudiced, nor merely shrewd, nor even merely kindly.

III. His Relation to God — "full of the Holy Ghost"

1. *Source of power — "the Holy Ghost"*
   a. Enlightening judgment — natural wisdom illuminated;
   b. Controlling feelings — natural sympathies consecrated;
   c. Directing will — natural determination energized;
   d. Possessing every faculty — natural character glorified.
2. *Measure of power — "full"*
   a. Full capacity normal — virtue as well as enthusiasm;
   b. Full capacity necessary for secular as well as sacred work — in home and office, in church and mission.

Conclusion

1. *The Outcome*

   The "all-round" Christian worker, like Stephen and Philip, will be known by —

   a. "Grace and power" (v. 8, A.S.V.)*;

---

*See author's volume by this title, *Grace and Power,* Wm. B. Eerdmans Publishing Co., 1949.

(1) Not grace without power;
(2) Not power without grace;
N.B. Book of Common Prayer recognizes this — "grant that (Thy people) may . . . know what things they ought to do, and also may have grace and power faithfully to fulfill the same."

b. "Wisdom and the Spirit" (v. 10; cf. Isa. 11:2; Eph. 1:17, 18);
c. Character and appearance (v. 15);
d. Courage and witness (chap. 7);
e. Evangelism and teaching (chap. 8);
N.B. Since the person of the worker is the life of his work, it is the worker who counts in all work, the speaker in all speech; and so everything that enriches personality is to be coveted for the sake of the work.

2. *The Secret*

This "all-roundness" may be obtained through faith;

a. Faith receives grace;
b. Grace gives wisdom;
c. Faith, grace, and wisdom are shown in character, service, and witness.

Study No. 30 —

The Power of Prayer — A Word Study

ACTS 6:6, 7

PROBABLY it is not too much to say that the supreme need of the Church is power, and that therefore the most pressing duty of the Church is prayer, because prayer brings power. In answer to it the Holy Spirit guides and enables as He did in the crisis recounted in this chapter. "When they had prayed —," we read, they took the appropriate action, and two results were seen — "the word of God increased; and the number of the disciples multiplied." The emphasis placed on prayer in the New Testament shows us not only its importance in the life of the Church, but also God's will concerning the reliance of the Church upon it. Let us consider —

I. Aspects of Prayer

1. Sense of need (Eph. 6:18);
2. Expression of desire (Phil. 4:6);
3. Spirit of humility (Heb. 5:7);
4. Act of consecration (Acts 6:6);
5. Privilege of fellowship (Acts 10:9; Rom. 8:27, 34; 11:2; 1 Tim. 2:1; Heb. 7:25);
6. Spirit of inquiry (John 16:24; Acts 1:24; 1 John 5:16);
7. Bond of union (Matt. 18:19).

II. Aspirations in Prayer

1. For spiritual adjustment (2 Cor. 13:8);
2. For spiritual progress (Col. 4:12);
3. For power in service (Mark 9:29; Acts 4:31);
4. For friends in Christ (Jas. 5:16);
5. For Christian ministry (2 Thess. 3:1);
6. For world-wide evangelization (Matt. 9:38);

7. For universal Church (Eph. 6:18).

III. Attitudes in Prayer

1. Unceasing (Rom. 1:9; 1 Thess. 4:17);
2. Steadfast (Rom. 12:12);
3. Active (Col. 4:12; 2:1);
4. Intense (Acts 12:5; Luke 22:44);
5. Submissive (1 John 5:14);
6. In Christ's Name (John 16:24; 15:7);
7. In the Holy Spirit (Eph. 6:18; Jude 20).

IV. Accompaniments of Prayer

1. Confidence (1 John 5:14; Mark 11:24);
2. Fasting (Acts 14:23);
3. Watching (Eph. 6:18; Col. 4:2);
4. Obedience (1 John 3:22);
5. Forgiveness (Mark 11:25);
6. Thanksgiving (Phil. 4:6);
7. Joy (Phil. 1:4).

Conclusion

These are but a few of the indications of God's will concerning prayer, for the Old Testament also, by both precept and example, is full of its value and power. If only the Word of God in this regard is allowed to impress itself on our souls, the immediate and ever-increasing result will be —

1. A life of prayer — and with it, through it, in it —
2. A life of power — peace, purity, progress, praise.

Study No. 31 — The First Martyr — Stephen (1)

ACTS 6:9 to 8:4

HERE IS the first instance of Christian martyrdom, and its detail is very striking compared with the summary account of the later martyrdom of James (cf. 12:1-3). Doubtless this is due to the fact that Stephen's death is to be regarded as a turning-point in the history of the Church. His speech was the first defense of the wider extension of Christianity, and thus it marks an epoch in Church progress and teaching.

Of the seven newly-appointed deacons, Stephen was in particular greatly used, going far beyond the immediate object for which he was appointed (cf. 6:2, 3 with v. 8). Thus it was against him that special enmity was manifested.

I. The Accusation (6:9-14)

1. *Source* (v. 9)

   Different classes of Jews perversely united against Stephen:

   a. Members of "synagogue of the Libertines," or freedmen (A.S.V., marg.), evidently located there in Jerusalem;

   b. Others from various countries — Africa ("Cyrenians, and Alexandrians"), and Asia Minor ("them of Cilicia and of Asia").

2. *Methods* (vs. 9-12)

   a. Dispute — argument, debate, but foes "not able to resist" (v. 10) —

      (1) His "wisdom";

      (2) "The Spirit (A.S.V.) by which he spake";

   b. Craft — "suborned men" (v. 11) — bribed men to stir up people;

   c. Violence — "caught him" (v. 12).

3. *Charge* (vs. 13, 14)

a. While absolutely false in letter, was substantially true in spirit;
b. Stephen first to see inevitable universal destiny of Gospel;
c. Recognized acceptance of Jesus of Nazareth would necessarily affect temple, and law of Moses — argument perhaps echo of John 2:19 and Mark 14:58;
d. Still, accusation as worded was unwarranted by anything said or done.

II. The Appearance (6:15)

1. Members of council impressed by look on Stephen's face (see Study No. 33, p. 137).
2. This perhaps in memory of Saul, having watched and listened (cf. 7:58); but note word "consenting" (8:1), suggesting thought of pleasurable agreement — used also in Paul's own confession of this sinful deed (cf. 22:20).

III. The Answer (7:1-53)

Longest defence recorded — doubtless because first defence of wider extension of Christianity:

1. *Statement* — history of Israel known and valued;
2. *Plan*:
   a. God's dealings always show constant progress — illustrated by Abraham, Moses, David;
   b. God never limited Himself to Palestine and Temple, but was manifested in other countries as well — illustrated from Mesopotamia, Egypt, Midian, and Tabernacle in Wilderness;
   c. God's people had always been perverse in resisting Him and His messengers — illustrated by Abraham, Joseph, Moses, David;
   d. God's people, not Stephen, were opposed to Divine revelation — illustrated by sins of their fathers.
3. *Application* — "the Just One; of whom ye have been now the betrayers and murderers" (v. 52)
   a. Stephen thus brings hearers back to present and shows fearful culmination of their national history;
   b. Having received God's law by ministration of angels (cf.

vs. 20, 25, 28; Gal. 3:19; Heb. 2:2; also Deut. 33:2, Sept.), they still "have not kept it" (v. 53);

c. And here was one speaking to them whose face they saw "as it had been the face of an angel" (6:15).

IV. The Opposition (7:54-60)

1. *Madness* — of anger and action (v. 54) — cut to heart and gnashing with teeth;
2. *Manliness* — in peace and power (vs. 55, 56) — through fullness of Holy Spirit, Stephen —
   a. Gazed up into heaven and saw his Master standing at God's right hand, ready to succor and receive him;
      N.B. A. C. Gaebelein pointed out three aspects of Christ's Second Coming: "First He comes (rises up, so to speak) to welcome His own into His presence . . . and comes into the air to meet (them) there. This is represented by the first appearing to Stephen, receiving him. Then Israel will behold Him; they who pierced will see Him, like Saul of Tarsus beheld the Lord. Then He will appear as John saw Him, the One who judges the earth in righteousness."
   b. Then Stephen testified boldly to what he saw.
3. *Murder* — by consent and cruelty (vs. 57-59a) — nothing could stop enemies, and they —
   a. Illegally (cf. John 18:31) put him to death by stoning;
   b. Accomplished primary object of getting rid of Stephen, but not end of Christian religion as they hoped.
4. *Martyrdom* — with fearlessness and forgiveness (vs. 59b, 60) — confidently, he —
   a. Prayed his Master to —
      (1) Receive him (cf. Luke 23:46), and —
      (2) Pardon murderers (cf. 2 Chron. 24:22; Luke 23:34); and —
   b. "Fell asleep" — because Jesus died, death for Stephen, as for all believers, is only sleep of body (cf. Luke 8:52; John 11:11; 1 Thess. 4:13, 14), and awakening of soul with Christ in glory (cf. Phil. 1:21-23);

Oh, may the grave become to me the bed of peaceful rest,
Whence I shall gladly rise at length, and mingle with the blest.

N.B. As Alexander Maclaren once said of Stephen: "Shaping his death after the pattern showed him on the Cross, he changes its grisly shape into the soft similitude of quiet slumber."

V. The Outcome (8:1-4)

1. *Persecution* (vs. 1, 3)
   a. Saul, entering Church history here, prime mover (cf. 9:1, 2; 22:4, 5; 26:9-12);
   b. Yet even Saul was being impressed, so that Augustine could say: "If Stephen had not prayed, Paul had not preached";
   c. Cf. Saul, the persecutor, "entering into every house" (v. 3) as Satan's instrument, with Paul, the pastor, teaching "from house to house" (20:20) as Christ's servant.
2. *Devotion* (v. 2)
   a. "Devout men," in spite of opposition, bravely determined to render last offices of love for Stephen;
   b. With sorrow and sympathy, he was buried (cf. this second Christian funeral of which we have record with that in 5:6, 10).
3. *Dispersion* (vs. 1, 4)
   a. "All scattered abroad throughout the regions of Judaea and Samaria" (v. 1) — carrying out command of our Lord (cf. 1:8) as far as second extending circle (see The Book as a Whole, under II, 2, p. 18);
   b. "They that were scattered abroad went everywhere preaching the Word" (v. 4) — beginning to carry out command of our Lord (cf. 1:8) as far as third extending circle (cf. 11:19, et supra);
   c. Thus, from this first of "noble army of martyrs" on, "the blood of the martyrs was the seed of the Church" — fuller and wider proclamation of Gospel instead of hindrance foes intended;
   d. Impetus given to evangelization of world;

N.B. It has been said that persecution was a storm permitted to scatter the seed of the Word, disperse the sowers and reapers over many fields — God's way of extending His kingdom, bringing good out of evil, making the wrath of man to praise Him, all things working together for good. There is that scattereth and yet increaseth, we are told. So the Huguenots driven from France, the Protestants from Spain, the Puritans from England. Luke gives prominence to this new departure — this home mission effort of the Church.

Conclusion

1. Stephen's death was an illustration of his witness in life:
   a. Surrender to the fulness of the Holy Spirit;
   b. Realization of heavenly glory;
   c. Consciousness of the presence of Christ;
   d. Testimony for the Lord;
   e. Courage in the face of danger;
   f. Power in prayer;
   g. Love for enemies.
2. Stephen's life and death should be the inspiration of the Church's corporate witness:
   a. Open-eyed and large-hearted attitude when rightful developments are necessary;
   b. Fearless testimony for God in the face of dangerous foes;
   c. Splendid character towards God and man;
   d. Readiness to die, if necessary, for the sake of the truth;
   e. Christlikeness of spirit even when persecuted;
   f. Thorough knowledge of Bible truth and power to impart it;
   g. The fullness of the Divine Spirit.

If only these features characterized all believers and all churches, what wonderful results would follow!

One day in loved Jerusalem
There rushed a shrieking, maddened crowd
Upon a lowly kneeling form,
Before his God and Saviour bowed;

And when with cruel stones they crushed
His beautiful and gentle life,
He prayed the Father to forgive
Their ignorance and raging strife.
This man was Stephen,
Lo, a Jew
Who died for Christ;
Would I? Would you?

Study No. 32 — The First Martyr — Stephen (2)

ACTS 6:9 to 8:4

Stephen is often called the Proto-martyr — first of the long line of "martyrs of Jesus" (Rev. 17:6). The Greek word from which is transliterated our word "martyr" originally meant "witness," and in the New Testament it is almost always thus translated. It means "one who testifies" and includes the evidence of the life as well as that of the death of the testifier. Indeed, the evidence of the life is primary and fundamental and so, while we naturally associate the term "martyr" with death, we must never forget that it has a special reference to life. It is thus that we now look at it in connection with Stephen, for he witnessed first by his life and then by his death.

I. The Splendor of Stephen

1. *He was a Man of Divine Common Sense.*
   Incongruous to speak of common sense as "Divine"? No, because we know "wisdom" was not only special feature of his character, but expressly connected with the Holy Spirit (cf. 6:3, 10).
   a. What is this wisdom?
      (1) Knowledge applied;
      (2) Structure of reason based on faith;
      (3) Not necessarily intellectual ability or capacity, but only "that exercise of reason into which the heart enters";

(4) Can be illustrated by wisdom recorded in O.T. which invariably has moral as well as intellectual element — e.g., in Book of Proverbs;

(5) On contrary, "fool" of O.T. (cf. Psa. 53:1) not man who cannot understand, but one who will not — not case of intellectual incapacity, but of moral wilfulness.

b. Why was this wisdom needed by Stephen?

(1) Condition in Church that brought him to fore called for ability to distinguish one situation from another, to administer charity with impartiality, and to provide system of distribution to satisfy both parties to dispute;

(2) Use of other people's money constitutes fine test of character, showing Stephen to be no weakling, nor merely shrewd, but marked by splendid moral integrity.

2. *He was a Man of Dauntless Courage.*

This clear at every point of Stephen's story:

a. In new post — worked hard and earnestly, bearing such fearless testimony that foes could not dispute him successfully, so resorted to false charges of blasphemy;

b. Before council — no compromise in spite of intense and virulent opposition;

c. At death — bore suffering without fear or complaint, and died as he had lived, noble and brave — crowning proof of courage.

3. *He was a Man of Deep Conviction.*

This seen in two ways:

a. Stephen was well-versed in Scriptures — facts of history:

(1) Before council, reviewed history of his people from time of Abraham to that of Kings in seven distinct, though connected, stages;

(2) Point by point, showed himself thoroughly conversant with record; but still more important —

b. Stephen had marvellous grasp of truth — meaning of facts:

(1) One thing to know facts, still another, their interpretation and correlation;

(2) Had two great truths clearly in mind:

(a) Universality of God — not limited to Palestine, since He had revealed Himself to His servants in different lands at different times;

(b) Perversity of Israel — intense opposition to God, showing sinfulness of nation throughout its history.

4. *He was a Man of Devoted Character.*

Character has been well defined as "what a man is in the dark," and in Stephen's there was —

a. Reality before God:

(1) Council so impressed by him that only possible description of his face was "as it had been the face of an angel" (6:15)*:

(a) Where did they derive their idea of an angel's face? Perhaps reminiscent of Moses on Sinai (cf. Exod. 34:35) — one who had been in presence of God — or of angel who appeared to Manoah with "countenance . . . very terrible" (Judg. 13:6);

(b) Believers must have been reminded of our Lord in transfiguration (cf. Luke 9:29), or of His words about angels beholding (cf. Matt. 18:10) and perhaps reflecting God's face (cf. Heb. 1:7); and women at Christ's tomb had seen "the angel of the Lord" with "his countenance . . . like lightning" (Matt. 28:3);

(2) We may think of Stephen's face as expressing both strength and sweetness, and great thoughts, holy motives, lofty purposes — mirror of his great heart; but there was also —

b. Reality before men:

As he died, Stephen —

(1) Prayed for their forgiveness, showing love of souls;

---

*See following Study No. 33, p. 137.

(2) Committed his own soul to the "Lord Jesus," in true witness to very last.

Thus we see Stephen, as it has been well said, "serving, suffering, and shining."

But how came his life to be thus characterized?

II. The Secret of Stephen

It is fourfold:

1. *Faithfulness before Man*
   a. First feature in original requirement for seven deacons was they were to be "men of honest report"; and this means —
      (1) They were well spoken of by fellows;
      (2) Their reputation was good;
      (3) Their brethren able to trust them because their value known;
   b. This feature very prominent in N.T. (see previous Study, No. 31, p. 126 for fuller treatment); and this shows importance of Christian standing well with those around him, being reliable, punctual, upright, etc.
2. *Faith in God*
   a. Narration of Jewish history shows how real God was to Stephen;
   b. Steadfast look into heaven shows strong faith, rewarded by sight of "glory of God" (7:55; cf. "God of glory," 7:2) — may have been manifestation of old Shekinah glory (cf. Exod. 40:34; 1 Kings 8:11, etc.).
3. *Fellowship with Christ*
   a. He showed reality and power of his communion with the Lord in both His Humanity and His Deity — the Jesus of history and the living Christ:
      (1) He spoke of "the coming of the Just One" (7:52);
      (2) He saw "Jesus standing on the right hand of God" (7:55);
      (3) He reported this sight as "the Son of man standing" (7:56);

(4) He addressed prayer in dying, "Lord Jesus . . . Lord" (7:59, 60);

b. He "looked up" (v. 55) — not, as one-time theological watchword, "back to Christ," but, better, "up to Christ" — i.e., it is not enough to be concerned solely with Christ of Cross, but true spiritual perspective is shown by fellowship with living, exalted, reigning, coming Lord (cf. Rev. 1:18);

It is not looking backward down the list of years,
To see our failures, sins, temptations, follies, fears,
And tears;
Nor is it looking on, with hope all bright and fair,
To meet, so often, bitter disappointment there,
And care.
No, it is looking up, a living Christ to see,
And leaning calmly, Lord, and, oh, so trustingly
On Thee.

—S. T. F.

4. *Fulness of the Spirit*
   a. This another of requirements when appointed (cf. 6:3, 5), and blessing of it continued with Stephen (cf. 6:10);
   b. Original of phrase in 7:55 — "being full of the Holy Spirit" — implies he was permanently possessed of this fulness — his normal experience, regarded as essential for secular as well as for sacred work;
   c. By means of it, his judgment was enlightened, his feelings controlled, his will directed, and his life equipped.

Thus, with faithfulness, faith, fellowship, and the fulness of the Spirit, Stephen lived his life and died his death, glorifying God from beginning to end.

Conclusion

1. *The same life may be ours if the same conditions are fulfilled*:
   a. This is the true life of the believer, one faithful to God and to man;
   b. All of it is the outcome of close and constant contact with God, whose we are and whom we serve.
2. *Thus we may be true "martyrs" or witnesses to Christ* —

"living evidences of Christianity," as it has been said:

a. Not, perhaps, to suffer and die;
b. More probably, to live our lives unnoticed in spheres ot insignificance and contracted influence;
c. Though possibly in a place of prominence, for which our witness must always be ready.

3. *But however and wherever, if only we are true to God and His grace, we shall have the incomparable joy of bearing testimony, as did Stephen —*

   a. By lip "ceaseth not to speak" (6:13); and —
   b. By life — "did great wonders" (6:8).

I do not ask that my life may be
Honored and known of men;
I do not ask a brilliant path
With voice, or with song, or with pen;
But oh, I ask that my human strength
May give place to His power Divine,
That, filled with His wisdom, His goodness, His life,
My life with His glory may shine.

Study No. 33 — The Face of an Angel*

ACTS 6:15

THIS IS a remarkable description. How did Luke know what an angel looked like? Had he heard from the Virgin Mary, or from Peter, both of whom had seen one? Or was this an echo of Paul's eyewitness account of a later experience? In any event, Luke probably could give no truer description of the face of Stephen.

The face of any created being is highly indicative of character; and an angel, then as now, suggested the highest ideal of character and appearance. There is, however, a sense in which a saved sinner in his glorified body will out-shine the most resplendent of the angelic host. He will sing —

A song which even angels
Can never, never sing;
They know not Christ as Saviour,
But worship Him as King.

I. What Characterizes the Face of an Angel?

1. *Light*
   a. This is reflection from above and includes intelligence, moral excellence, glory (cf. Matt. 28: 3; Rev. 10:1);
   b. There is also reflected a true wisdom (cf. vs. 3, 10; Eccles. 8:1) from within;
2. *Warmth*
   a. This includes attractiveness, lovingkindness, gentleness — "spirit" (v. 10) — both human and Divine;
   b. Face with light but no warmth likely to be what poet called "icily regular, splendidly null."

---

*From author's *Sermon Outlines,* p. 131 (Wm. B. Eerdmans Publishing Co., 1947).

3. *Repose*
    a. Only light in face might indicate over-anxious thought; only warmth, too great vivacity;
    b. Repose is balance needed — showing no care or unrest.
4. *Strength*
    a. Light, warmth, and repose alone may be weak;
    b. Strength needed to complete picture (cf. Psa. 103:20; Judg. 13:6);

These four elements of a noble face may also be called: Truth, Love, Peace, Power.

II. Why was Stephen's face like that of an angel?

1. *It was revealing* — light
    a. There is revelation of heaven in good face (cf. Exod. 34:29-35 with 2 Cor. 3:7; Matt. 17:2 with Luke 9:29);
    b. It may be compared with shining of God's own face (cf. Num. 6:25; Psa. 31:16; 67:1; 80:3; 119:135).
2. *It was attractive* — warmth
    a. Face and manner count in God's service, showing sympathy and kindliness, and inspiring trust (cf. Heb. 1:7);
    b. Others see (cf. Exod. 34:30), even if owner does not (v. 29).
3. *It was peaceful* — repose
    a. In spite of persecution, Stephen had air of perfect peace;
    b. Peaceful face reflects beauty and glory of God as did "the face of Jesus Christ" (2 Cor. 4:6-8).
4. *It was reassuring* — strength
    a. Strong face brings courage and reassurance (cf. Ezek. 3:8);
    b. It spells an indefinable power — possible for all, as for Stephen, because it derives from character, and not from position, or possessions, or even intellect.

III. What is the Secret of an Angelic Face?

1. *Privileged Position*
    a. Angels see God (cf. Matt. 18:10), and so did Stephen (v. 55);

b. Shining in heart makes shining out of face (cf. 2 Cor. 4:6);
c. Awareness begets likeness when heart is right (cf. 2 Cor. 3:18; Heb. 12:2).

2. *Personal Purity*
   a. Face often index of nature and occupation (cf. Luke 9:29);
   b. "Pure in heart" (Matt. 5:8) denotes holiness of entire personality;
   c. We grow like those we love — so let us love God.
3. *Perfect Obedience*
   a. Disobedience darkens face (cf. 2 Pet. 2:4; Jude 6) — submission makes for serene countenance, full of light and peace;
   b. Greek word for "angel" means also "messenger" — one sent for purpose.
3. *Perpetual Fellowship*
   a. Human side of abiding fellowship with God indicated by fact that Stephen was "full of faith" (vs. 5, 8) — surrender and trust open avenues of being;
   b. Divine side of abiding in fellowship with God indicated by Stephen's being "full of the Holy Ghost" (vs. 3, 5) — bestowal of God's Holy Spirit fills avenues of being.

Is it any wonder that his face was like the face of an angel?

Satisfied and full of favor
By my King I stand,
Having blessings without number
From His opened hand;
Oh, the richness of His treasure,
Oh, the greatness of His measure,
Oh, the fulness of my pleasure,
As His gifts expand!

—Henry W. Frost

Conclusion

Each child of God has —

1. *A Privilege*
   To reflect God and thus attract others to Him;

2. *A Possibility*

Of developing a surrendered personality through which God may shine.

Therefore, let us —

Think God's thoughts by meditation in His Word;
Receive God's life by trust in His Son;
Live in God's presence by prayer through His Name;
Do God's will by obedience to His will; and thus —
Show forth God's praise "not only in our lips but in our lives"!

Study No. 34 — The Evangelist and the Crowd

ACTS 8:5-8

Among the beginnings recorded in the Book of Acts as specimens or models of important methods in Church life and work, which have since become familiar, is this first instance of mass evangelism, as distinct from sermons primarily in defense of the new faith, such as Peter had preached. In view of the supreme importance of evangelistic endeavor to the growth of the Church, it is necessary that we should study most carefully this first instance of it, with special reference to its essential characteristics.

The life and service of Philip constitute a sort of pivot in the story of the early Church. The persecution following the death of Stephen had led to the scattering of the Jerusalem Christians and thus to the first evangelistic tour, with Philip as the first evangelist.

I. The Preaching (v. 5)

1. *The Preacher* — "Philip"

a. His character:

(1) Philip one of those seven men whose qualifications are described in 6:3 (see Study No. 28, under II, 2, p. 119). They were —

(a) Reputation — "of good (A.S.V.) report" — true that if we take care of our character God will take care of our reputation, but equally true that reputation is important for us to keep in mind too, so that we may remain faithful before men.

(b) Godliness — "full of . . . the Holy Ghost" — obviously such spiritual equipment absolutely essential for spiritual work of evangelism — gospel to be preached "in demonstration of the Spirit and of power" (1 Cor. 2:4; cf. 1 Thess. 1:5);

(c) Sagacity — "full of wisdom" possessed of what has been called "uncommon common sense" — constant occasion for its exercise in evangelistic work;

(2) Although these elements of Philip's character were primarily intended for secular work of serving tables (what we might call business administration of Church), they are equally essential to sacred work of saving souls.

b. His circumstances:

(1) Work as deacon soon set aside;

(2) Work as preacher allotted to him.

2. *The Place* — "Samaria"

Philip's choice of field —

a. Proof of obedience — because in exact line of his Lord's purpose and plan for His Church (cf. 1:8);

b. Test of sympathy — because of Jewish attitude towards Samaritans (cf. 2 Kings 17:24-41; John 4:9);

c. Example of boldness — because Samaritans reciprocated with hostility towards Jews (cf. Ezra 4:1-24);

d. Mark of sagacity — because Christ had been there before him, and had done great work (cf. John 4:39-42) — some think success of Philip in Samaria largely due to influence of his Master, not many years before.

3. *The Subject* — "Christ"

Philip's theme was "the Christ" (Gr.) i.e., Messiah of O.T., substance of Divine promises, foundation of human hopes; and message was —

a. Positive — declaring Scriptural truth, not negative, nor denouncing Samaritan error;

b. Personal — neither creed, nor church, but "Christ" — evangelistic message not merely truth for intellect, nor support for institution, but concerns Person in whom truth becomes vital and institution natural (cf. 2 Cor. 4:5; Col. 1 : 27, 28) ; such preaching will always be accompanied by Divine power and blessing.

4. *The Manner* — "proclaimed" (A.S.V.)

Word indicates —

a. Certitude of conviction — clear and emphatic declaration;

b. Urgency of message — important and conscience-arousing. This always right way of preaching Gospel (cf. 2 Cor. 4:13).

II. The Results (vs. 6-8)

1. *The Reception* (v. 6)

a. Close attention — "the people . . . gave heed";

b. United acceptance — "with one accord."

2. *The Proof* (v. 7)

a. Of Divine source — deeds miraculous and extraordinary;

b. Of Divine character — deeds merciful and practical.

Today, though we may not count on physical miracles, we may confidently look for spiritual ones in transformed lives; and these are equally strong proofs of true evangelism.

3. *The Rejoicing* (v. 8)

No wonder there was "great joy in that city" — immediate, universal result of true Gospel preaching, which will include —

a. Joy of perfect pardon from Christ;

b. Joy of conscious power through Christ;

c. Joy of realized preciousness of Christ.

Same characteristic seen all through ages of Christian Church: in proportion as Gospel proclaimed in purity and fulness,

joy is instinctive, inevitable outcome;
N.B. Cf. Reformation with preceding "Dark Ages" when there had been absence of joy because Gospel not faithfully declared.

Conclusion

Every evangelist needs:

1. *Full Heart*
   Preaching must be spontaneous, cordial, winning — what has been described as "wooing note";
2. *Clear Head*
   Progress must depend on knowledge of God's Word and how to impart its truth — certainty one of essential features of all true testimony to Christ;
   N.B. P. T. Forsyth once said that in old days, "Here am I!" showed prophets perfectly certain of position; today, in hazy lack of certitude, many preachers and teachers apt to ask, "Where am I?"
3. *Clean Hands*
   Power must develop only through sincerity of attitude and consistency of action — channel must be clear.

When these three qualifications are found, we may be sure that evangelistic work will be blessed of God and souls won to Christ. But how are they possible? As in the case of Philip, of Stephen, of Paul: "Be filled with the Spirit!" (Eph. 5:18).

Study No. 35 — The Case of Simon Magus

ACTS 8:9-25

THIS EPISODE, which took place during the early days of the Church in Samaria, has always given rise to speculation. Simon Magus, or the Sorcerer, is mentioned in the New Testament only here, yet tradition gives him a permanent place as a heretic, and certain sects, notably the Gnostics, were reputed to follow his teachings. But was Simon a heretic, or was he a hypocrite, or was he a backslider, or was he perhaps, what Paul later called carnal? This passage is, in any case, worthy of close attention, particularly if we try to put aside accepted interpretations of it and, reading it afresh, discover what impression it makes on our minds.

I. Simon and the Evangelist (vs. 9-13)

1. *Simon's Influence Great* (vs. 9-11)
   a. The claim — "used sorcery . . . giving out that himself was some great one" (v. 9) — evidently no mere trickster, but used some satanic arts;
   N.B. Cf. spiritism today — similar mixture of fraud and demonic power, under guise of religion;
   b. The acceptance — "all gave heed, . . . saying, This man is the great power of God. And to him they had regard" (vs. 10, 11) — people under spell, "bewitched" (Gr., "amazed").
2. *Simon's Influence Weakened* (v. 12)
   a. The greater power — "but when they believed Philip . . . concerning . . . the name of Jesus Christ" — faith in omnipotence, or great power met by greater (cf. Luke 11:21, 22;
   b. The instant result — "they were baptized" — indicating

new allegiance — Simon's influence evidently weakened and neutralized by preaching of Gospel.

2. *Simon's Influence Transformed* (v. 13)

a. The acceptance — "Simon himself believed also: and . . . was baptized";

(1) "Believed" — word, used by historian years afterwards, perhaps derived from evangelist himself, same as in v. 12 — so why read in falsity on part of Simon? On contrary, we have no right whatever to assume insincerity or hypocrisy; taken as it stands, his faith no different from that of other Samaritans;

(2) Simon seems to have fulfilled conditions of Mark 16:16a; if so, must have obtained result;

b. The adherence — "continued with Philip" — this much certainly in Simon's favor, with no mention yet of anything wrong;

N.B. Apostles' rejection of Simon (vs. 20-23) was due to something else that did not arise until after their arrival.

II. The Apostles and the Church (vs. 14-17)

1. *Tidings Received* (v. 14)

a. When news of happenings in Samaria reached Jerusalem, Apostles took immediate action;

b. Indicated importance of event as significant extension of Christianity beyond Judaism by sending two leading men, Peter and John, as deputation; (cf. John's attitude now with his words in Luke 9:52-56);

c. No "supremacy of Peter" here — Twelve acted together as body, and visitation was shared by John;

d. Purpose of it that Samaritan church might receive gifts of Holy Spirit.

2. *Prayers Offered* (vs. 15, 16)

a. Supplication for miraculous gifts, as distinct from common grace of conversion (cf. v. 12; 2:38; 1 Cor. 12:3);

b. Bestowal of these gifts limited mainly to medium of Apostles, and mark of first century — apparently not even within province of evangelist, for Philip's work was only to proclaim Gospel and baptize;

c. Manifestations of this bestowal evidently visible and recognizable (cf. v. 18 and 2:3 with v. 12 and 2:41).

3. *Gifts Bestowed* (v. 17)

a. Instrumentality — laying on of Apostles' hands (cf. 19:6; Deut. 34:9; 1 Tim. 4:14);

b. Recipients — "they" who "received the Holy Ghost" must have included Simon;

c. Source — "the Holy Ghost" — supernatural, special acknowledgment of work in Samaria, recognizing people as part of universal Church;

N.B. Inaccurate and impossible to interpret passage in reference to confirmation, ordination, or other "laying on of hands," because bestowal of Holy Spirit here is associated with special supernatural gifts, mediated through hands of Apostles. All believers have received Holy Spirit (cf. 1 Cor. 12:3), but this great gift may come before baptism or after it, in sovereignty of God. "Sealing" of Spirit takes place on, not after, believing (cf. Eph. 1:13, Gr.). Mechanical view of baptism, and of confirmation and its equivalents, is at root of many errors, a deadly foe of spiritual realities.

III. Simon and the Apostles (vs. 18-24)

1. *Request Proffered* (vs. 18, 19)

a. Simon deeply impressed — feeling doubtless fostered by antecedents, for manifestations appeared to be like own old career — so request seemed natural;

b. Simon suddenly tempted along old lines — sin was due to envy, and nostalgia for past, prompting desire to purchase ability to bestow supernatural gifts;

c. Word "simony," or sin of paying for possession of religious office, comes from this story;

N.B. It is quite clear from v. 19 that it was apostolic prerogative that Simon coveted, not gifts themselves.

2. *Rebuke Given* (vs. 20-23)

Peter horrified and used characteristic vehemence:

a. Denunciation (vs. 20, 21)
   (1) "This matter" — bestowal of Holy Spirit, not salvation itself;
   (2) "Not right" — not straight, not upright — presumptuous, had indulged wrong thought and desire;

b. Exhortation (vs. 22, 23)
   (1) "Repent . . . and pray" — would this be said to unconverted, with no mention of faith in Christ's saving power?
   (2) "Thought" — in singular, implying the one sin of which Simon was guilty;
   (3) "Art in the gall of bitterness" — Gr., "art in the direction of," or, "wilt become" (see A.S.V. marg.) — pointing out danger ahead, rather than that Simon had reached stage already;
      (a) "Gall" suggests wretchedness caused by sin (cf. Deut. 29:18; Psa. 69:21; Lam. 3:19; Heb. 12:15);
      (b) "Bond" suggests dominion of sin leading to misery (cf. Rom. 8:15; Gal. 2:4; 4:9; 5:1).

3. *Repentance Shown* (v. 24)

a. Acknowledgment — "pray ye to the Lord for me"

b. Fear — "that none of these things . . . come upon me"

Neither motive nor form of repentance so important as reality — God hears and forgives even in presence of low or mixed motives, so great is His grace towards us;

N.B. When all these points are carefully studied apart from any preconceived ideas, do they not suggest that Simon was a backslider rather than a hypocrite? Did he not "slide back" into his old mode of life, or into applying his old standards to his new life? The statement about his belief is clear (cf. v. 13); the counsel of Peter is more appropriate to a backslider than to a hypocrite (cf. story of Ananias and Sapphira, 5:1-16 — see Study No. 25, p. 107); the warning of Peter indicates danger and not actual loss; and the contrast of Paul's stern language to a sorcerer who really was a scoundrel (cf. 13:10, 11 — see Study No. 61, under II, 4, p. 247) is significant, suggesting that Peter would have dealt very differently with Simon had he been a hypocrite and never converted at all. The reply of Simon seems to confirm all this and does not sound like that of an utterly base man. Rather, it indicates healthy fear and dawning desire for better things.

IV. The Apostles and Evangelism (v. 25)

1. *Personal Testimony* — "when they had testified"
   a. Situation in Samaria doubtless improved by Peter and John telling own stories of Christian experience;
   b. This always helpful in "follow-up" work with new converts.
2. *Preaching the Word* — "preached the Word of the Lord"
   a. Then Samaritan Christians ready for Bible study and instruction in their new faith;
   b. This always affords deeper knowledge of Christian life after evangelistic effort and is indispensable.
3. *Preaching the Gospel* — "preached the Gospel"
   a. On return journey to Jerusalem, Church leaders themselves became evangelists in Samaritan villages;
   b. This always high privilege, however learned and prominent God's ministers become.*

These activities afford still another illustration of way in which Gospel of Christ was making way outwards.

Conclusion

Returning to Simon Magus and regarding him as a backslider, let us notice:

1. *The Possibility of Backsliding*
   a. Old temptations often transformed — Simon's past led him astray;

---

* Ed. Note: My dear father was sometimes inclined to discount his ministry as a preacher, teacher, and writer when he thought of the comparatively few actual conversions of which he had any knowledge as attributable to that ministry. He was never entirely comforted by a reminder of the thousands of Christian workers whom he must have influenced and equipped to go out and "do the work of an evangelist" (2 Tim. 4:5). This was the measure of the value he placed on evangelism.

b. Old habits often powerful — converted drunkards, etc., have fallen;

c. Old desires often active — such as avarice, lust for power, longing for popularity;

N.B. Regeneration is not necessarily renovation — young Christian only babe in Christ and needs growth in grace in order to withstand temptations;

Illus.: Christian father had daughter with ungovernable temper, and when asked for her hand in marriage told young man she was not worthy of him. "But," he asked in surprise, "she is a Christian, is she not?" "Yes," was the reply, "she is a Christian, but the grace of God can live with some people with whom no one else could ever live."

2. *The Treatment of Backsliding*

There should be —

a. Strong emphasis on God's holiness;

b. Thorough faithfulness in personal dealing;

c. Earnest encouragement to repentance.

3. *The Protection again Backsliding*

a. The Spirit of truth, instructing the young convert;

b. The Spirit of holiness, making sensitive the conscience;

c. The Spirit of power, triumphing over the old nature;

d. The Spirit of love, expelling all else from the heart.

Study No. 36 — The Evangelist and the Individual

ACTS 8:26-40

"HANDPICKED FRUIT is always the best," a familiar saying, contrasts fruit taken from the branch by hand with that which falls when the tree is shaken. So also it may be said that individual work for Christ is often more productive and permanent than a general appeal made by preaching or teaching. In these verses we have the first instance in Church history of individual dealing with a soul, in remarkable contrast with the crowds evangelized on the Day of Pentecost and after, and during Philip's ministry in Samaria. It may well be a model for personal work today.

We naturally wonder why Philip was supernaturally (cf. v. 26) called to leave the work in Samaria where, humanly speaking, he was so greatly needed, and this in order to deal with one individual in the desert. Perhaps Philip, as a Hellenistic Jew, was suited to witness to an Ethiopian; and it is believed that the Coptic and Abyssinian Churches of today are the fruit of the labors of this desert traveller. Also, it has been asked, where is the Church of Samaria today? Certainly the encounter represents another stage in the widening spread of the Gospel and foreshadows the evangelization of the Gentile nations. At any rate, the Divine appointments then were just as appropriate to personalities and circumstances as they are today. The picture of the Ethiopian is of intense interest. He was —

I. An Earnest Enquirer (vs. 27, 28)

1. *His Nationality*
   a. Evidently African Gentile by birth;
   b. Home may have been Abyssinia, or Nubia, or Sudan — some think near modern Khartoum.
2. *His Position*
   a. High in court circles — wielding "great authority" (v. 27);

b. In charge of royal treasury — bearing great responsibility; N.B. Name "Candace," like "Pharaoh," expressive of dynasty, not individual ruler.

3. *His Character*

a. Thoughtful, intellectual — had been able, amid cares of state, to give attention to religion, and had seen sufficient reasons to adopt Jewish faith (cf. Psa. 68:31);

b. Sincere, earnest — had cared enough to come some 1200 miles to worship, and was still intent on learning more of Jewish Scriptures;
N.B. Would almost certainly be using Greek version known as Septuagint, translated from Hebrew during third century before Christ.

II. A Lowly Learner (vs. 29-35)

1. *The Opportunity* (vs. 29, 30)

a. God's Providence:

(1) Philip soon made aware of reason for transfer from busy city to lonely desert, for Holy Spirit guided him to approach Ethiopian traveller;

(2) These two men to meet awhile, then part, probably forever, but great results would come from meeting;

b. Human means:

(1) Beautiful harmony with Divine will, as Philip "ran thither" (v. 30) — to chariot where man, in Eastern fashion, was reading aloud (cf. 1 Tim. 4:13);

(2) No abruptness in inquiry, for original has interrogative particle suggesting something like our "Quite so, but — do you understand what you are reading?"

(3) Shows tactful approach so necessary in personal work — if true that "every man's house is his castle," still truer that every man's soul is a republic, and worker must show due respect for this essential independence in things spiritual.

2. *The Willingness* (v. 31)

a. Ignorance confessed — quick response showed humility in spite of exalted rank;

b. Invitation given — open-minded desire to be taught, even by stranger.

3. *The Question* (vs. 32-34)
   a. The Scripture — this, of course, was Isaiah 53:7, 8;
   b. The meaning:
      (1) Ethiopian in difficulty over what is to us familiar passage;
      (2) In particular, wanted to know if Isaiah referred to himself or to another;
      (3) Jews to this day interpret passage either of Prophet Jeremiah or of their whole nation — but too personal for latter, and no individual but Christ ever fulfilled it;
      (4) Passage omitted from calendar of synagogue lessons, evidently because of Christian association of it with Christ

4. *The Instruction* (v. 35)
   a. The fulfilment of Scripture:
      (1) This gave Philip opportunity, using passage, to show true meaning and exact realization in Person and work of Jesus of Nazareth;
      (2) Not difficult to imagine evangelist telling Ethiopian something of life and death and resurrection of Christ;
   b. The secret of preaching:
      (1) Emphasis on relation between Scripture and Christ, Word of God and Lamb of God, Written Word and Living Word, Record and Person;
      (2) Whether to crowds or to individuals, preaching on such themes owned and blessed by God because very heart of Gospel.

III. A Faithful Follower (vs. 36-40)

1. *The Desire* (v. 36)
   a. Rapid growth — convictions doubtless prepared for long beforehand by reading of Scripture; but perhaps Ethiopian knew of baptism through visit to Jerusalem, or else Philip had included it in his talk;

b. Real satisfaction — Philip's testimony to Christ as fulfilment of prophecy must have had instant appeal.

2. *The Confession* (v. 37)
   a. This verse not found in best manuscripts, being thought to have crept in from marginal note;
   b. But faith always requirement for baptism, so statement true in itself.
3. *The Determination* (v. 38)
   a. Decision immediate, absolute, submissive;
   b. Philip, having authority to baptize (cf. v. 12), performed rite in what must have been either pool or small stream in oasis.
4. *The Joy* (v. 39)
   a. Of sin forgiven, of difficulties removed, of peace enjoyed, of power possessed;
   b. We may imagine Ethiopian bearing witness on return home, perhaps to queen herself, and forming nucleus of new church.
5. *The Parting* (vs. 29, 40)
   a. Philip "caught away" (v. 39) by Holy Spirit — no lingering, or else perhaps gifts offered by Ethiopian;
   b. Work continued at Azotus (or Ashdod, cf. Josh. 15:47; 1 Sam. 5:1; Neh. 4:7), twenty miles north, half way between Gaza and Joppa — and then from place to place, some fifty miles farther, till Philip reached Caesarea, later his home (cf. 21:8, 9).

Conclusion

This story is full of striking and valuable suggestions in regard to the essentials for personal evangelism. The soul-winner must have these qualifications:

1. *Fellowship with the Spirit*
   a. Receptive — ready to receive Divine influences;
   b. Responsive — quick to sense atmosphere of Divine harmony;
   N.B. Worker not called to indiscriminate dealing with all, but should be much in prayer for God's leading to indi-

viduals (cf. Psa. 25:9); for the Holy Ghost works "at both ends," preparing soil as well as sower.

2. *Faithfulness to the Spirit*
   a. Trustful — in spite of feeling needed in one place, to be willing to go to another;
   b. Obedient — to leave many for one, busy city for dreary road, if necessary;
   N.B. This is true spirit of Christian worker (cf. John 2:5; 2 Sam. 15:15).
3. *Fearlessness in the Spirit*
   a. Aggressive — to "run" (cf. v. 30), because so full of Christ it is joy to bring Him to others;
   b. Careful — at the same time, to be tactful, pleasant, attractive, wise — endowed with "sanctified common sense";
   N.B. Danger of blundering is real because of sensitiveness in many souls when approached spiritually.
4. *Forcefulness through the Spirit*
   a. Scriptural — to know Bible so well that Christ may be preached from any passage;
   b. Practical — not only to proclaim, but to apply — concerned not merely with ideas, but with obedience;
   N.B. Ideas will never save a soul and truth is insufficient without man's acceptance.

Therefore, like Philip the Evangelist, let us —

1. Live in the Spirit — for surrender of self;
2. Learn of the Spirit — for knowledge of Scripture;
3. Lean on the Spirit — for strength for service; and be —
4. Led by the Spirit — for salvation of hearers.

Thus, life will be one of true satisfaction to ourselves, perpetual blessing to others, and constant glory to God.

Study No. 37

The Holy Spirit and the Christian Worker

ACTS 8:29

THE UNIQUE feature of Christianity, its last, most characteristic and, in some ways, its greatest fact and factor, is the Holy Spirit of God.* If this is true of Christianity generally it is pre-eminently true of Christian work and witness. Our Lord's ministry began "in the power of the Spirit" (Luke 4:14). He told His disciples to tarry until they were "endued with power from on high" (Luke 24:49). St. Paul said that his ministry was "in demonstration of the Spirit and of power" (1 Cor. 2:4). The Holy Spirit is "the Spirit of truth" (John 14:17); the Word of God is "the sword of the Spirit" (Eph. 6:17); and over all the operations of the Christian Church recorded in the Book of Acts the Holy Spirit exercised constant and complete control.

In the story of Philip and the Ethiopian eunuch, the Holy Spirit is closely connected with Christian service, and we see two elements of the first importance:

I. The Relation of the Holy Spirit to the Christian Worker

1. *The Holy Spirit speaks, disclosing God's will.*
   a. Why should it be incredible for God to speak? Cf. human ability to communicate by means of telephone, telegraph, radio, etc.;
   b. He has spoken through His Word which is itself the work of the Spirit (cf. 2 Tim. 3:16; 2 Pet. 1:21);
   c. He still speaks to soul as He applies Word:
      (1) Word without Spirit dry and useless;
      (2) Spirit without Word has no intelligible message; but —

*See author's volume under this title (Wm. B. Eerdmans Publishing Co., 1955).

(3) Spirit in Word is twofold method that God uses to communicate with man; and especially is this true of believer.

2. *The Holy Spirit needs ready, obedient heart.*
   a. Why must human soul be receptive? Cf. Marconi and wireless — had to have two perfectly attuned stations, one sending and other receiving, or message lost;
   b. So Philip, whose obedience in Samaria (cf. vs. 26, 27) made hearing acute.
3. *The Holy Spirit's word to one agrees with what is said to others.*
   a. Why was Philip sent to desert? Cf. providential meeting with eunuch in vs. 27, 28;
   b. Ethiopian's heart had been prepared for evangelist's message, and over a long period of time.

II. The Work to be Done Through the Holy Spirit

Philip here represents Church preaching Gospel to world. We see —

1. *The Gospel and personal power* — symbolized by eunuch's position — political, financial, etc., but may be influential for good;
2. *The Gospel and material power* — symbolized by eunuch's chariot — formidable, but may be consecrated to God;
3. *The Gospel and intellectual power* — symbolized by eunuch's reading — strong, but may be means to salvation;
4. *The Gospel and spiritual power* — symbolized by eunuch's heart-hunger — this, above all, is to be used in right way in behalf of our greatest work, for there are —
   a. Hungry ones to feed;
   b. Thirsty ones to satisfy;
   c. Empty ones to fill;
   d. Sad ones to cheer; and —
   e. Blind ones to illuminate.

Thus, when man of God has Gospel of God and preaches Christ of God in power of Spirit of God, those in need of salvation of God soon go on their "way rejoicing" (v. 39).

Conclusion

The life of the Christian worker is here in view. There should be in each of us —

1. *Spiritual sensitiveness*
   a. This comes by means of fellowship with God;
   b. Christ said to His disciples, "Ye know Him" — the Father (John 14:7); do we?
   c. Prayer and meditation will provide channels for Spirit's flow through us.
2. *Spiritual responsiveness*
   a. This comes through obedience to the Spirit's voice;
   b. Christ said to His disciples, "Tarry . . . until ye be clothed with power from on high" (Luke 24:49); are we?
   c. Obedience is means of vision and guarantee of power.
3. *Spiritual equipment*
   a. This comes with training in the things of God;
   b. Christ said to His disciples, "The Spirit of truth . . . shall guide you into all truth" (John 16:13); is He guiding us?
   c. Two essentials are Bible knowledge and personal experience: first the Word to bring us to the Lord (cf. v. 35; Rom. 10:17); and then the Lord, the Spirit, to illuminate the Word (1 Cor. 2:10-16).

Study No. 38 — "He Went on His Way Rejoicing"*

ACTS 8:39

A CHILD has discovered that a magnet that someone has given him may be used to pick up needles from his mother's sewing basket. Then he quite naturally tries to pick up some pins that are there; but we know, as he soon will, that the magnet will take not the slightest effect on the pins. Why the difference, the little boy may ask, for it is the same magnet each time. The answer, of course, is in the composition of the pin; made of brass or some such metal, and not of steel as the needle is, there is nothing in its nature to respond to the magnet.

Christ said in John 12:32, "I . . . will draw all men unto Me." It was as though He said that in His death He would exert power, influence, on men, that they might yield themselves and come to Him. But many did not, would not, come. Why? For the same reason that the pin will not come to the magnet. "Ye will not come to Me," Jesus said, "that ye might have life" (John 5:40; cf. Luke 13:34). In these men's natures there is no response. Yet the illustration of the magnet is faulty for, while pin and needle "natures" are changeless, man can exert his will and change his mind; and, though a pin, because inanimate, is motionless, man, if he does not respond to Christ, will not remain static but will drift farther and farther away from the Saviour.

There are in the New Testament two instances of contact with Christ in which the men involved were of the same general type. Both had position and power, and both were characterized by earnestness and thoughtfulness. But one, a young ruler, "went

---

* Ed. Note: This is the outline of a sermon often preached on a Sunday evening when a companion sermon on Matt. 19:22, "He went away sorrowing," had been delivered in the morning. A short treatment of a parallel passage of the latter may be found in *Outline Studies in the Gospel of Luke*, pp. 274-276.

away sorrowing" (Matt. 19:22), and the other, a more mature man of authority and responsibility, "went on his way rejoicing." The Ethiopian eunuch responded to what he read and heard, and we may see, as it were, three pictures of him merging into one:

I. The Man

Encounter between Philip and the Ethiopian was what we might call worth-while contact, for eunuch had —

1. *High Position*:
   a. Was state official with wide influence;
   b. Had confidence of his queen.
2. *Great Responsibility*:
   a. Treasury position one that tested his integrity;
   b. Dealing with money brings out man's powers or lack of them;
3. *Keen Intellect*:
   a. Interest not wholly in state affairs, for he was evidently versed in Jewish religion;
   b. Having worshipped God at Jerusalem, he was still reading Scriptures, examining, inquiring.
4. *Intense Earnestness*:
   a. Not only examining, but had changed his religion, which meant great deal in those days;
   b. To Jerusalem from his Ethiopian home and back at least 1200 miles — did he read Scriptures all the way?
   N.B. But eunuch had one lack — Christ! So have many fine men today.

II. The Man and the Messenger

It was "angel of the Lord" who gave Philip the Evangelist Providential direction "toward the south" (v. 26), and "the Spirit" (v. 29) who commanded him to join traveller in chariot; and there followed —

1. *Pointed Question*
   It was —
   a. Courteous — note Gr. form;
   b. Faithful — not just polite comment, but pressing inquiry;

   c. Practical — not how much, but how well did reader understand — quality, not quantity, of matter grasped.

2. *Frank Admission*

   There was —

   a. Need of more knowledge — "how can I —?"
   b. Lack of human guidance — "except some man shall guide me" (v. 31)
   c. Absence of prejudice — in ignorance, God can work, but in prejudice, even God cannot.

3. *Hearty Invitation*

   It was caused by —

   a. Wishfulness to know;
   b. Willingness to learn;

      N.B. This in spite of difference in race and rank and of presence of servants.

4. *Full Explanation*

   This included —

   a. Text — Scripture: from Isa. 53:7, 8 (vs. 32, 33);
   b. Theme — Person: "Jesus" (v. 35), and doubtless touched upon sin, sacrifice, salvation, satisfaction;

      N.B. Preacher telling, teaching, testifying; hearer listening, learning, longing — so all true preaching.

III. The Man and the Master

It was kind of sermon that brought —

1. *Personal Acceptance*

   a. Immediate — "on their way" (v. 36);
   b. Full — "baptized";

      Illus.: Not like D. L. Moody's sermon in which he postponed invitation till "next week" — and during interval never again would he fail to "draw in net" — and he never did!

2. *Complete Surrender*

   a. Instantaneous — no hesitation;
   b. Courageous — before servants;
   c. Convinced — mind, heart, conscience first — then will.

3. *New Life*
   a. Within — something stirring toward life, light, liberty;
   b. Without — everything different with new convert, either young or mature.
4. *Exultant Joy*
   a. Because of forgiveness — free, full, eternal — burden gone;
   b. Because of fellowship — no longer alone, even forgot about Philip, because had new Friend;
   N.B. The Master — giving power, love, grace;
   The Man — every inch a man, more than ever — surely he testified of Christ at home — may have been church already there, or he may have founded it on return.

Conclusion

1. *Will you become a Christian?*
   a. No satisfaction unless —
      (1) Mind finds truth;
      (2) Heart receives love;
      (3) Conscience enjoys peace;
   b. No strength until —
      (1) Mind resists sin;
      (2) Heart insists on fellowship;
      (3) Conscience persists in well-doing.
2. *How may you become a Christian?*
   a. Surrender to Christ as Saviour;
   b. Serve Christ as Lord;
   c. Submit, admit, permit, commit, transmit.

Then shall you experience reality and restfulness, sanctification and satisfaction, gladness and glory, of life in and for Christ.

Be Thou supreme, Lord Jesus Christ,
Nor creed, nor form, nor word
Nor holy church, nor human love
Compare with Thee, my Lord.

Be Thou supreme, Lord Jesus Christ,
Thy love's constraint I feel;
I see Thy Cross, and mind and heart
Obey its mute appeal.

Be Thou supreme, Lord Jesus Christ,
Live o'er again in me
That, filled with love, I may become
Like Thee in my degree.

Be Thou supreme, Lord Jesus Christ,
My inmost being fill;
So shall I think as Thou dost think,
And will as Thou dost will.

Be Thou supreme, Lord Jesus Christ,
My soul exults in Thee;
To see Thy face, to do Thy will
Is my felicity.

Be Thou supreme, Lord Jesus Christ,
And when this life is o'er
Lead me to yon completer life
With Thee for evermore.

Study No. 39 — The Conversion of Saul

ACTS 9:1-31

SPECIAL DAYS in our lives are often called "red-letter days," the phrase originating in the custom of marking holy days on the Church calendar with a red letter. Surely the day on which Saul the persecutor was changed into a disciple of Christ was one of the greatest red-letter days in the history of the Church. This may be seen by the fact that we have in Acts no fewer than three accounts of Saul's conversion (cf. chaps. 22 and 26), as he himself reverts to this the great event of his life (cf. also 1 Cor. 15:8; Gal. 1:15, 16). It was indeed the pivot on which turned not only his own career, but the future of the Christian Church. It has also been called "a great landmark on the highroad of missionary progress."

The other Apostles had been led through their physical contact with the human Jesus to a belief in His Deity as Christ the Lord. Saul, on the other hand, was led from the Divine to the human — from a supernatural vision of the Risen Lord to a conviction that He and the hitherto despised Jesus of Nazareth were one and the same Person.

It was fitting that Saul should experience a unique conversion because he was a unique person: by birth, a Jew; by citizenship, a Roman; by education, a Greek; and by grace, a Christian. Missionary and theologian, evangelist and pastor, organizer and leader, thinker and statesman, saint and man of affairs — the man who later became known as Paul the Apostle was many-sided and his influence wide and deep, then as now.

I. Saul Persecuting (vs. 1, 2)

Attitude of Saul to Christians impressively described and shows to what extent religious fanaticism may lead (cf. his own accounts in 22:4, 5; 26:9-12; 1 Cor. 15:9; Gal. 1:13, 14; Phil. 3:6; 1 Tim. 1:12-16). It was —

1. Persistent in mistaken zeal — "yet" (v. 1)
2. Intense in vital expression — "breathing out"
3. Fierce in vindictive strength — "threatenings and slaughter"
4. Aggressive in taking of initiative — "went unto the high priest"
5. Extreme in lengths to which he was ready to go — "to Damascus" (v. 2) — 150 miles away — journey of about six days (see Study No. 40, page 170)
6. Cruel in that even tender womanhood not exempted — "whether they were men or women"

   N.B. As Bengel puts it: "In the utmost fervor of sinning was he laid hold of and converted."

II. Saul Penitent (vs. 3-9)

Note what brought about such a revolutionary change:

1. The Light (v. 3) — sudden, startling, supernatural;
2. The Voice (v. 4) — personal, poignant;
   a. Repetition of name indicating earnest appeal;
   b. Use of Hebrew tongue (cf. 26:14) identifying the Lord with His ancient people;
   c. Form of question identifying the Lord with His redeemed people — "why persecutest thou me?"
3. The Revelation (v. 5) — requested and received
   a. Significant that Saul immediately addressed Him as "Lord";
   b. In reply, did Voice pause after "I am —"? In any case, testimony concerning Himself was here given as to Moses (cf. Exod. 3:14), to woman of Samaria (cf. John 4:26), and to scribes and Pharisees (cf. John 8:28).
4. The Surrender (vs. 6-9) — prompt and practical
   a. It has been said that "Lord, what wilt Thou —?" was query of Paul's heart spoken not only on road to Damascus in hour of blind ecstacy, but constantly during his whole life;

b. What a difference between actual and intended entry into Damascus! What became of undelivered letters?

c. What a profound spiritual experience three days' blindness and fasting must have been! Cf. Eph. 3:1-12;

d. It has been said that though afterwards Paul came nearer to justification through works than any man that ever lived, even his eyes were so sinful that he could not look on Divine glory without blindness.

III. Saul Praying (vs. 10-19)

1. A Difficulty (vs. 10-14) — created by new circumstances:
   a. Ananias (see 22:12 for his description), though instructed by supernatural communication (vs. 10-12), was naturally fearful and sceptical, Saul's fury having been directed against just such as himself;
   b. His knowledge of persecutor (vs. 13, 14) striking testimony to Saul's widespread influence (cf. vs. 1, 2; 8:3).
2. A Solution (vs. 15, 16) — soon found:
   a. Because God's command was clear and His explanation sufficient;
   b. Sign would be Saul's attitude of prayer (v. 11) — perhaps ignored thus far by Ananias because totally unexpected;
   c. Christ's words about Saul, "chosen vessel" (v. 15) — Gr., "vessel elected" — striking metaphor used by Jeremiah (18:1-6), and by Paul in his Epistles (cf. Rom. 9:21-23; 2 Cor 4:7; 2 Tim. 2:21);

      N.B. Vessel not self-made, nor self-kept, but made and kept by potter, empty, clean, useful, noiseless, ready to be filled with contents of more value than itself;
   d. Note contrast between "do" (v. 6) and "suffer" (v. 16) — young convert led on one step at a time.
3. A Welcome (v. 17) — from older Christian:
   a. Beautiful contrast between words of Ananias in vs. 13 and 17 — "this man" and "Brother Saul";
   b. Beautiful agreement between "the Lord said, I am Jesus"

(v. 5) and testimony of Ananias, "the Lord, even Jesus" (v. 17);

N.B. Account of Ananias' part fuller in 22:12-16 (see Study No. 106, p. 420).

4. A Blessing (vs. 17-19a) — from God:
   a. Spiritual (v. 17) — this Paul's "Pentecost," showing —
      (1) Gift of Holy Spirit can be bestowed at conversion and through instrumentality of ordinary Christian layman;
      (2) Spiritual gifts in apostolic age not limited to particular class or order, yet given mainly through Apostles (cf. 8:14-17);
   b. Physical (vs. 18, 19a)
      (1) Reference to "scales" (v. 18) medical way of describing blindness;
      (2) Reference to baptism (v. 18) shows Saul united with Church by usual initiatory ordinance and that he who threatened Damascus Christians is now publicly one of their number;
      (3) Reference to food (v. 19a) characteristic of Luke with his medical interest and strong sympathies (cf. 2:46; 14:17), for Saul would naturally need refreshment after his three days' abstinence.

      N.B. While circumstances vary, elements of conversion remain constant: the sinner — convicted, deciding, seeking, receiving; the servant — believing, upright, spiritual, obedient; the Saviour — living, sympathetic, gracious, powerful.

IV. Saul Preaching (vs. 19-22)

1. Preparation (v. 19) — food, strength, fellowship;
2. Proclamation (v. 20) — prompt and practical;

   N.B. Title "Son of God" found only here in Acts, showing Saul had seen His glory so clearly he claimed for Jesus of Nazareth Divine nature;
3. Perplexity (v. 21) — no wonder people of Damascus "amazed" in view of all that had preceded;

N.B. Difficult to know precisely where to place Saul's visit to Arabia (cf. Gal. 1:15-17), which was probably desert near Mount Sinai (cf. Gal. 4:25), but best to insert it between verses 21 and 22, because he tells us (Gal. 1:17) he returned to Damascus after his retirement;

4. Power (v. 22) — increase of strength and of intellectual ability in defense of Christ would thus follow visit to Arabia, being result of deepening spiritual experience.

V. Saul Persecuted (vs. 23-25)

1. Plot (vs. 23, 24) — former persecutor persecuted — Jews would not tolerate his intensified witness, so endeavored to kill him;
2. Preservation (vs. 25) — plan prevented by his own knowledge (vs. 24a) and by action of "his (Gr. and A.S.V.) disciples" — converts won to Christ by his own earnest work; thus his ministry fruitful from very first;
   N.B. Basket of large sort that would easily hold adult — what we might call hamper: and it was let down from window of house built on wall (cf. 2 Cor. 11:33; Josh. 2:15).

VI. Paul Protected (vs. 26-31)

After three years (cf. Gal. 1:18), Saul paid first visit to Jerusalem since leaving on his journey to persecute Damascus Christians. What must have been his thoughts! How different from his departure! When he tried again and again (v. 26, Gr.) to unite with Jerusalem Church he found —

1. Suspicion (v. 26) — painful but natural — disciples sceptical of destroyer turned disciple and persecutor become preacher — also afraid of attempt at fresh persecution under guise of friendship; but finally, there was —
2. Reception (vs. 27, 28) — under sponsorship of Barnabas, true "son of consolation" (4:36), who "took him by the hand" (v. 27, Gr.), and gave full explanation — evidently old friend, possibly fellow-student in Tarsus or Jerusalem:
   a. We may imagine mutual joy of these two with Peter and James (cf. Gal. 1:19) as Saul was "with them" (v. 28) for "fifteen days" (Gal. 1:18);

b. It was there and then he received his commission as Apostle of Gentiles (cf. 22:17-21).

3. Disputation (v. 29) — word "disputed" found in connection with Stephen (cf. 6:9), one of Saul's opponents at that time; but now Saul is great Christian disputant against very men who had withstood Stephen.
4. Decision (v. 30) — to protect Saul as brother in Christ from those who would kill him:
   a. Brethren took him to Caesarea, on coast, and put him on board boat for Tarsus, his own city (cf. 22:3), in Cilicia (cf. Gal. 1:21-24);
   b. There he was at home, and presumably safe, among relatives and friends, who must have been surprised at great change in him — home and quiet doubtless helpful at this stage.
5. Intermission (v. 31) — after Saul's departure — ("so," A.S.V.) — churches of Palestine experienced relief from external difficulties, including persecution, and from internal dissensions; and this resulted in growth —
   a. Upward toward God in edification; and —
   b. Outward toward men in multiplication; and all —

   "Walking in the fear of the Lord, and in the comfort of the Holy Ghost" (see Study No. 43, p. 177).

Conclusion

Every true conversion means a turning to God and a changing of the life. Here are some of the results of the change in Saul's life:

1. *To Saul himself*:

   The change was —
   a. Real — in heart and life;
   b. Lasting — with no reversal, and constant in growth;
   c. Divine — by the grace of God and for the glory of God (cf. Gal. 1:24).
2. *To Christians then*:

   The change in Saul told of —

a. God's care — not indifferent to persecution, but watching over His own;
b. God's power — strength to help in time of need;
c. God's resource — even that great difficulty overruled.

3. *To Christianity now*:
The change in Saul is —
a. An evidential force:
(1) If his testimony for thirty years is true, his conversion was real (cf. 26:16-18);
(2) If his conversion was real, Christianity is Divine, for there is no other way to account for the change in his life, though writers have tried to find other satisfactory explanations (cf. 26:19);
So Saul of Tarsus becomes one of strongest evidences of Christianity;
b. A spiritual force:
(1) Proves Christ living (cf. Gal. 1:16) — Saul himself becomes one of greatest spiritual forces: if life was real, conversion was true; if conversion was true, Jesus Christ rose from dead, for Saul saw Him (cf. 1 Cor. 9:1; 15:8);
(2) Shows Holy Spirit powerful (v. 17) — here, also, is evidence of supernatural in life of Church;
N.B. Baur spoke of conversion of Paul as "psychological mystery," which it will ever be to those who deny supernatural cause;
So we may rejoice in same spiritual realities today.
c. A practical force:
(1) Intended as pattern of God's mercy to others (cf. 1 Tim. 1:16);
(2) Used as means of blessing to all (cf. 22:15; 26:18);
So with every conversion — we are saved for purposes of winning others to Christ and of showing possibility of Divine grace in daily life.

Study No. 40 — Damascus (A Fragment)

ACTS 9:3

DAMASCUS is the oldest city in the world. It was at one time the most important city in Syria, being on the highway of traffic to the East. In New Testament times it gradually became eclipsed by Antioch (cf. 11:19-30), but is now again an important city which includes a large colony of Jews. Lying in a plain of great fertility, measuring about thirty miles in diameter, its beauty has been likened to that of a pearl among emeralds. Seven streams of the River Abana flow through or near it, but Damascus has no defence and it is far from the sea, some sixty miles.

During the seventh century A.D. Damascus was the capital of all the land stretching from the Atlantic Ocean to the Bay of Bengal. Having been the first city connected with the conversion of the Gentiles to Christianity, it was also the first Christian city to be taken by Islam. In 1860, a massacre of 6,000 Christians took place there. The largest place of worship was half church and half mosque, and then the Christians were gradually pushed out, so that the building became wholly Moslem. But still over the south portal were engraved the words — "Thy Kingdom, O Christ, is an everlasting Kingdom, and Thy dominion endureth for ever and ever" (cf. Psa. 145:13) — an unconscious prophecy of the future.

Damascus is mentioned in Scripture a number of times:

1. It was the home of Eliezer, Abraham's servant (Gen. 15:2);
2. It was conquered by David (2 Sam. 8:6);
3. It was the capital of Syria (1 Kings 11:24, 25, etc.);
4. It was the home of Naaman (2 Kings 5:12) and center of the worship of the god Rimmon (2 Kings 5:18);
5. It was mentioned by several of the prophets (e.g., Isa. 17:1-3; Jer. 49:23-27; Ezek. 27:18; Amos 1:3-5);

6. It was closely associated with the conversion of Saul (Acts 9:22; 26);
7. It was mentioned by St. Paul as the scene of his first ministry (Gal. 1:17; cf. Acts 9:19-22);
8. It was included in the prophecy of the future land for Israel (Ezek. 47:16-18).

Conclusion

Yes, Christ's Kingdom is everlasting — and all will yet be for Christ, and Christ for all.

Jesus shall reign where'er the sun
Doth his successive journeys run;
His Kingdom stretch from shore to shore,
Till moons shall wax and wane no more.

—Isaac Watts

Study No. 41 — Salvation and Service

ACTS 9:5, 6

"What is your life?" asks St. James (Jas. 4:14). We may well echo his question, seeking to know the object of life, the reason for existence. To awake to consciousness is to awake to mystery — this ego, whence, what, why, whither? We know it is not self-caused, and so we know it must have some object not of our choosing. We can find the true answer only in the Gospel of Christ. In these verses there is a message for the individual life, whatever there is elsewhere for humanity as a whole. Not "the survival of the fittest" — that is no message for me or for any other sinner, for I know I am not "fit."

Saul of Tarsus asked two questions: "Who art Thou?" and "What wilt Thou?" These and their answers epitomize his and every other Christian life: First, conversion, for the answer provides the all-important identification of the Saviour — "I am Jesus" — and goes on to mention conviction of sin — "it is hard for thee to kick against the pricks" (cf. 7:58; 8:1, 3; 9:1, 2). Then comes the second question, which follows conversion and has to do with Christian service:

I. The Purpose of Christian Service

1. *The Fact of it*
   a. It is based on Divine revelation and on personal experience;
   b. It is God's intention that converted man becomes spiritually alive, in order to live Christ and to bring men to Him.
2. *The Extent of it*
   a. It begins with start of new life and goes on to very end;
   b. It goes step by step — cf. "arise . . . go . . . do" (vs. 6) and later "suffer" (v. 16).

II. The Possibility of Christian Service

1. *The Glory of it*
   a. It is inspiring to realize God has distinct plan for each believer — not just any niche in life on which chance falls;
   b. It lends dignity to humblest office, for there is neither "small" nor "great" with God.
2. *The Blessing of it*
   a. It is something that comes only through Gospel of grace;
   b. It is not to be missed if believer expects deepest joy.

III. The Preparation for Christian Service

1. *The Willingness for it*
   a. It involves realization that convert is no longer independent;
   b. It places him at the disposal of his Saviour and Lord, with no reservations.
2. *The Readiness for it*
   a. It should be complete, so far as in him lies, in order that he may go anywhere and do anything;
   b. It includes perfect trust which will lead to perfect obedience, since he is persuaded that God knows best.

IV. The Practice of Christian Service

1. *The Claim of it.*
   a. It owns Christ as Master through His purchase made long ago;
   b. It recognizes that only now has He entered into possession of heart and soul and mind.
2. *The Consecration to it*
   a. It owns Christ as Master through His conquest;
   b. It recognizes Him as Lord through soul's surrender.

My Master and my Lord!
I long to do some work, some work for Thee;
I long to bring some lowly gift of love
For all Thy love to me!

The harvest fields are white;
Send me to gather there some scattered ears;
I have no sickle bright; but I can glean
And bind them in with tears.

I would not choose my work;
The field is Thine, my Father and my Guide;
Send Thou me forth; oh, send me where Thou wilt,
So Thou be glorified!

I need Thy strength, O Lord;
I need the quiet heart, the subject will;
I need the patient faith that makes no haste,
The love that follows still.

And if Thou wilt not send,
Then take my will and bend it to Thine own
Till, in the peace no restless thought can break,
I wait with Thee alone.

It is not hard to wait,
To lean my weariness on Thee for rest,
To feel in suffering or in service still
My Father's choice is best.

Conclusion

1. What are the steps to conversion and, afterwards, to service?
   a. *Submit*: Essence of sin is independence and rebellion — we must cease all opposition;
   b. *Admit*: Christ must be invited to come into the life as Saviour;
   c. *Permit*: We must allow Him to be our Lord and Master, working in and through us;
   d. *Commit*: We must place all we are and have in His hands — life, will, talents — for protection, provision, power;
   e. *Transmit*: We shall do as Saul did, pass on grace and blessing to others.
2. Why take these steps?
   Because there is no real peace, no full satisfaction, no true service, until we have taken them.
3. When shall we take them?
   Now!
   As vassals of a feudal baron would kneel before him and place their hands between his hands in token of submission, let us now say:

   My glorious Victor, King Divine,
   Shut these surrendered hands in Thine;
   At length my will is all Thine own,
   Glad vassal of a Saviour's Throne!

Study No. 42 — Saul and the Church

ACTS 9:26-30

THE CHRISTIAN LIFE is both individual and social, having an individual relationship with Christ and a social relationship with Christians. In the first section of this chapter (vs. 1-9), we read of Saul's personal relation to Christ, and in the second section (vs. 10-19), we read of his first contact with fellow-Christians, Ananias and the other Damascus disciples. After his return to Jerusalem he attempts to establish similar Christian contacts there.

I. Church Membership Sought (v. 26)

1. *Natural* — Saul assumed that, being changed man, he would find congenial company among other changed people;
2. *Necessary* — individual life impossible and imperfect — "with all saints" (Eph. 3:18) Christian way of life.

II. Church Membership Hindered (v. 26)

1. *Fear*
   a. Not to be wondered at, though three years had elapsed (cf. Gal. 1:18);
   b. Some Jerusalem Christians still ignorant or sceptical of great change in persecutor;
   c. Perhaps quarrel between Herod and Archelaus had cut off communications between cities; and perhaps some knew but were irreconcilable.
2. *Test*
   a. Severe and painful, yet just;
   b. Suspicion, in some respects, hardest experience of all — yet natural result of Saul's doing of "many things contrary to the Name of Jesus of Nazareth" (26:9).

III. Church Membership Obtained (v. 27)

1. *A Friend's Sympathy* — Barnabas grasped hand (Gr.) and led Saul to Apostles (cf. v. 8);
2. *A friend's testimony* — "declared"
   a. How did he know details of Saul's conversion? Perhaps two were old friends, fellow-students, or had met for first time in Arabia or Damascus and had compared notes;
   b. Qualifications mentioned by Barnabas were:
      (1) Saul had seen the Lord;
      (2) Saul had spoken to Him;
      (3) Saul had spoken boldly in the Name of Jesus.

Hast thou seen Him, heard Him, known Him?
Is not thine a ravished heart?
Chief among ten thousand own Him,
Gladly choose the better part!

— F. Bevan

IV. Church Membership Enjoyed (vs. 28-30)

1. *Fellowship with other disciples* — "with them" (v. 28);
2. *Freedom of their homes* — "coming in and going out" (v. 28);
3. *Fearlessness in mutual testimony* — "spake boldly" (v. 29);
4. *Fraternal protection* — "the brethren brought him . . . and sent him" (v. 30).

Conclusion

Qualifications for church membership today should be the same as in Saul's time; and their lack or neglect is cause of much internal difficulty:

1. *Conversion*
   a. Sight of Christ as Saviour — personal experience of Him;
   b. Sight of Christ as Master — definite commitment to Him.
2. *Communion*
   a. Listening to Christ — personal reading of Scripture;
   b. Speaking with Christ — definite engaging in prayer.
3. *Confession*
   a. Verbal and courageous — personal testimony of lips;
   b. Consistent and strong — definite witness of life.

Study No. 43 — The State of the Church

ACTS 9:31

GOD has many ways of working and blessing. Secular historians tell us that, at about the time of Stephen's death and Saul's conversion, the Emperor Caligula attempted to force the Jews to worship him as God. Such universal horror gripped the scattered Hebrew race that the attention of the Jerusalem authorities was distracted from the new Christian sect which their arch-persecutor Saul had tried in vain to stamp out. The result was a cessation of persecution and a breathing-spell for the Church. Progress was made, spiritually and materially, intensively and extensively, "throughout all Judaea and Galilee and Samaria," until the time mentioned in 12:1. Then, after Caligula had been replaced by Claudius, and the pressure on Palestine lifted, Herod Agrippa I renewed the persecution of the Christians "because he saw it pleased the Jews" (12:3; cf. Mark 15:15). But meanwhile we may note —

I. The Condition of the Church — "had peace" (A.S.V.)

1. *Peace from External Difficulties*
   a. Peace in nations develops resources;
   b. Peace in nature develops seed;
   c. Peace in church develops strong evangelism — disseminates "the seed" which is "the Word of God" (Luke 8:11).
2. *Peace from Internal Dissensions*
   a. Jewish Christians and Gentile Christians in brotherly intercourse;
   b. Satan's divisive power thwarted.

II. The Attitude of the Church — "walking"

1. *Conduct — practical purity*

Walking is —

a. Expression of life — part of young child's normal development;

b. Proof of life — tests health and strength;
So also is Christian walk.

2. *Direction — spiritual power*

a. "In the fear of the Lord" — cf. 2 Cor. 5:11, and O.T. Proverbs (e.g., 1:7; 8:13; 14:26; 15:33, etc.);

b. "In the comfort of the Holy Spirit" — or "exhortation," according to best authorities — rendered by Weymouth as "receiving encouragement."

III. The Progress of the Church — "were edified: and . . . were multiplied"

1. *Progress Upward* — "were edified" — or built up (cf. Eph. 2:20-22);

a. Foundation — faith;

b. Cement — love;

c. Cornice — hope;
N.B. Result of having "peace" (see I.).

2. *Progress Outward* — "were multiplied" — branching out (cf. John 15:5; Rom. 11:16):

a. Not merely gathering together of crowds, but gathering in of souls for Christ;

b. Not only gathering in, but going out;
N.B. Result of "walking in the fear of the Lord" (see II.).

Conclusion

Thus we see the four stages of experience for congregations as well as for individuals:

1. *Peace*
Only a peaceful church can give attention to purity of conduct and doctrine;

2. Purity
Only a pure church can become powerful against evil;

3. *Power*
Only a powerful church can make progress in this world under Satan's sway;

4. *Progress*
   Only a progressive church can attract sinners and serve saints.

Study No. 44 — Peter at Lydda and Joppa

ACTS 9:32-43

PETER speaks of "the manifold grace of God" (1 Pet. 4:10), meaning, thereby that Divine grace shows itself in a remarkable variety of ways. Few things in this Book of Acts are more interesting than the illustrations given of the different methods used in the supernatural work of redemption.

Luke's narrative returns to Peter after recording the experiences of Stephen, Philip, and Saul. It is important because it traces the steps leading up to the official entrance of the Gentiles into the Christian Church as recorded in chapter 10. Saul is in retirement at Tarsus, and Peter meanwhile is being led on very gradually to the next great stage in Christian experience.

This passage may also be considered in itself as a record of Christian progress; and it gives us three different pictures of what the Gospel can do.

I. Sickness and the Gospel (vs. 32-35)

1. *Visitation* (v. 32)
   a. Journey of Peter illustration of quiet state of Church (cf. v. 31) — probably inspection tour (cf. 8:14-25) of some scope and length, extending through villages and cities even to Antioch;
   N.B. Ramsay: "A process of world-wide extent and importance is summed up" and "never was a big piece of work mentioned in words so few";
   b. Lydda (Lod of 1 Chron. 8:12 and Ezra 2:33, and present-day Ludd) in fertile plain of Sharon (v. 35), some ten miles southeast of Joppa; town of some importance, on caravan route between Babylon and Egypt;

c. Group of Christians found, perhaps unexpectedly, by Peter, doubtless originated through Philip's preaching tour (cf. 8:40);
d. Term "saints" (v. 32) as designation for Christians first found in this chapter (vs. 13, 32, 41), and in only one other place in Acts (26:10), but frequently in Epistles of Paul:
   (1) Means "consecrated," or "belonging to God" (cf. Rom. 1:7);
   (2) Refers primarily to spiritual position, entered upon at conversion, never to spiritual condition;
   (3) But sanctification by the Spirit is term used of gradual process by which we may realize and actually become what we are already in God's sight through Christ's atonement (cf. Eph. 5:26; 1 Pet. 1:2).

2. *Infirmity* (v. 33)
   a. At Lydda Peter found paralytic called Aeneas — name Greek, so probably Greek-speaking Jew;
   b. Case of real need, involving prolonged, incurable disease; mention suggests Luke's professional interest (cf. 3:2; 4:22; 8:7; 9:18; 14:8;
   c. Was Aeneas a believer? Possibly, because —
      (1) He seems to have been among the "saints" (v. 32);
      (2) No questions or conditions of healing are recorded;
      (3) Name of Christ appears to be familiar to him;
   d. But silence as to his status, in contrast to designation of Dorcas as "a certain disciple" (v. 26), suggests to some that Aeneas was not believer; if true, Peter must have seen in him beginnings of faith (cf. 3:16; 14:9).

3. *Blessing* (v. 34)
   a. Came direct from our Lord — Peter lays emphasis on fact that Christ Himself is Healer — note his own humility;
   N.B. Maclaren: "Let us hide ourselves behind our Lord. The prop that holds up some great trophy to the eyes of the world is behind the trophy, and hidden by it. The herald is not to blow his own name or praises through his trumpet, but his King's; and be forgotten when the

royal progress has come."

b. Was both immediate and complete — Peter commands Aeneas, "Arise and make thy bed," that is, roll up mat on which he "had kept his bed eight years" (v. 33);
c. This he did "immediately," doing for himself at last what others must have done for him all that time (cf. Mark 2:1-12).

4. *Influence* (v. 35)
   a. Influence of miracle was impressive and widespread — not only at Lydda, but through well-known maritime plain of Sharon (cf. Isa. 35:2), stretching from Carmel to Joppa;
   b. "All saw" — knowledge and conviction — and "turned to the Lord" — conversion and change of heart.

II. Sorrow and the Gospel (vs. 36-39a)

1. *A Worthy Woman* (v. 36)
   a. Name — Tabitha, in Aramaic, meaning "gazelle" — Dorcas, Greek equivalent; perhaps she was marked by gracefulness and gentleness associated with that animal;
   b. Nature — "disciple . . . full of good works and almsdeeds which she did" —not just talked about doing! Perhaps had means — certainly showed ability and influence blessedly possible for godly woman; cf. other records of Christian womanhood in Acts (6:1; 8:3; 9:2; 12:12-15; 16:14-19; 18:2, 3, 26; 17:34); interesting that gatherings of Christian women today to make garments for poor and carry on other good works are often called "Dorcas Societies";
   c. Home — Joppa — modern Jaffa, port of Jerusalem, and only harbor for shipping between Egypt and Mount Carmel; Philip probably preached there on way to Caesarea (cf. 8:40) — was and still is important place (cf. 2 Chron. 2:16; Ezra 3:7; Jonah 1:3).
2. *A Sad Loss* (v. 37)
   a. Sickness and death — Dorcas became ill and died in midst of usefulness and influence — often so;

b. Love and care — lovely soul gathered love by giving love, and so loss felt and love shown to body.

3. *A Great Hope* (v. 38)

a. Pressing appeal — natural for sorrowing Christians of Joppa to send to Lydda, about ten miles away, for Peter — shows what they thought of Dorcas;

b. Basis of call — hope that he would be able to do what his Master had done, raise the dead — shows what they thought both of Peter and of the power of God.

4. *A Ready Response* (v. 39a)

a. Man of faith — good to have him near at time like that;

b. Prompt departure — Peter went with messengers without question, though not known whether previously acquainted with Dorcas — perhaps knew her by repute.

III. Death and the Gospel (vs. 39b-43)

1. *Sorrow* (v. 39b)

a. Splendid testimony — widows for whom Dorcas had worked so faithfully stood weeping and showing, as they wore them (Gr.), clothes she had made: "coats" would be close-fitting tunics, and "garments" loose cloaks;

b. Good example — another instance of care of widows by Christian Church (cf. 6:1; 1 Tim. 5:16);

N.B. We treasure mementoes of dead, e.g., handiwork, garments, toys, etc. — better still not to fail to express appreciation to living:

It isn't the thing you do,
It's the thing you leave undone,
Which gives you a bit of heartache
At the setting of the sun.
The tender word forgotten,
The letter you did not write,
The flower you might have sent,
Are your haunting ghosts tonight.

2. *Solitude* (v. 40a)

a. The need — to be alone; so Peter, in "the upper chamber" (v. 37), "put them all forth" (cf. Matt. 9:24, 25);

b. The example — acted very much as His Master had done at house of Jairus (cf. Mark 5:41);

c. The difference — marked by Peter's prayer, in recognition that power must come from above (cf. 1 Kings 17:20, 21; 2 Kings 4:33);

d. The command — if Peter spoke in Aramaic, words would be, "Tabitha, cumi"! — Thus wonderfully like "Talitha, cumi" of Mark 5:41 ("Talitha" said to mean, "my little lamb").

3. *Sequel* (vs. 40b-43)

a. The restoration — at once Dorcas "opened her eyes," "saw Peter," then "sat up" (v. 40b), reminding us of Christ's raising of widow's son near Nain (cf. Luke 7:15);

b. The action — included —

(1) Courtesy — "gave her his hand";

(2) Strength — "raised her up" (cf. 3:7); and —

(3) Satisfaction — "presented her alive" to "saints and widows" (v. 41);

b. The result — miracle became "known" (v. 42), so that —

(1) "Many believed in the Lord" because of it — it being for their benefit chiefly, for Dorcas herself had been "with Christ; which is far better" (Phil. 1:23):

(2) Peter stayed on in Joppa in fellowship with Christians, lodging with another Simon, a tanner (v. 43);

(a) Word occurs only in this instance (cf. 10:6, 32);

(b) Trade of skin-dressing regarded as unclean by Jews because it involved contact with dead animals, so Peter's association with it shows he was already losing some of racial prejudices in preparation for new revelations and further developments;

N.B. Attention has been called to contrast between miracles at Lydda and at Joppa. If miracles are signs of spiritual things, as we believe, such points as these are suggestive:

(1) One performed on man; other on woman;

(2) In one, Peter was present of own accord; in other, was sent for;
(3) In one, recovery immediate; in other, more gradual;
(4) In one, life present but infirm; in other, wholly absent;
— but in both, results were strickingly complete, and led men to Christ (cf. vs. 35, 42).

Conclusion

This passage presents two pictures for meditation:

1. *A Picture of the Visible Church*
   a. Power — over sickness and death, as seen in work of Christ through Peter;
   b. Holiness — as expressed in two references to "saints," meaning consecration, dedication, purity;
   c. Humility — as indicated by description of Dorcas as "disciple," learner in school of Christ;
   d. Usefulness — as revealed by good deeds of Dorcas, fruit and proof of faith;
   e. Sympathy — as shown by attitude of other Christians at time of her death;
   f. Progress — due to these miracles, showing unmistakable results in belief on the Lord, and conversion to Him.
2. *Picture of the Invisible Christ*
   We cannot fail to attribute all these results to the Lord Jesus Christ Himself. He, and He alone, is source of all good character and conduct. We find Him —
   a. In the Home of Aeneas (v. 34);
   b. In the Heart of Dorcas (v. 36);
   c. In the Hope of the disciples (v. 38);
   d. In the Hand of Peter (v. 40);
   e. In the Harvest of converts (vs. 35, 42).

Thus, it is seen, it is only possible to have reality in the Church when Christ is realized in the Christian.

Study No. 45 — Peter and Cornelius

ACTS 10:1-11:18

This passage ushers in a new epoch in Church history. So far, the members of the Church have been Jews only, though even so there have been difficulties. Now comes a fresh development which we today take as a matter of course, but which, to those first Christians, was a subject for special revelation. It had reference to the admission of Gentiles into the Christian Church. There was no real difficulty as to the *fact* of their entrance into the Church, because Christ, having died for "the world" (John 3:16), had spoken of teaching, baptizing, and preaching to "all nations" (Matt. 28:19; Luke 24:47). Further, He had told His disciples that they were to be His witnesses "unto the uttermost part of the earth" (Acts 1:8). Even earlier, Simeon, had spoken of the Infant Jesus as "a light to lighten the Gentiles" (Luke 2:32). But the serious question was as to the precise *terms* on which the Gentiles were to enter the Church: through the gateway of Judaism, by first becoming Jews, or direct, on exactly the same terms as the Jews.

This problem, which was to involve new lessons for the Apostle Peter, was solved by means of his experience with Cornelius, but the situation was very acute for several years during the early ministry of St. Paul (see Gal. 2:1-16; Eph. 2:11 to 3:12). However, Dr. Still of Edinburgh thinks it difficult to believe Peter could have acted towards Gentiles as he did in Antioch (cf. Gal. 2:11-14) *after* his vision at Joppa, and that therefore Paul's opposition to Peter must have taken place *before* the incident regarding Cornelius. In any case, it has been pointed out by Sir William Ramsay that the space given to this story, the great detail, and the repetition of parts of it indicate its importance, as in the case of Paul's conversion.

Let us trace the steps whereby, in the providence of God, this important matter was decided:

I. The Double Preparation (10:1-16)

1. *Of the Gentile* (vs. 1-8)

a. The Place — "in Caesarea" (v. 1)
   (1) City of great importance, on sea-coast, about 30 miles north of Joppa;
   (2) Built by Herod the Great in honor of Emperor Caesar Augustus, and was political capital where Roman governor lived;
   (3) Where Philip had preached (cf. 8:40), and which became his permanent home (cf. 21:8).

b. The Man — "Cornelius, a centurion" (vs. 1, 2)
   (1) His Position:
      (a) Was Roman centurion, in command of one hundred men of troops stationed in Caesarea to maintain authority of Rome — somewhat corresponding to modern captain in rank;
      (b) All centurions mentioned in N.T. seem to have been men of sterling character (cf. 22:25, 26; 27:1, 3, 42; Matt. 8:5-13; 27:54);
   (2) His Character:
      (a) No exception — man of piety, good practice, and prayer;
      (b) Exerted fine influence on his own household and soldiers (v. 7), and on Jews (v. 22);
      (c) Not Jewish proselyte, though worshipped the one true God — perhaps knew something of Philip's preaching;
      (d) In view of circumstances, one of finest characters in N.T. — as natural man, has few superiors.

c. The Vision (vs. 3-6)
   (1) Came at one of Jewish hours of prayer, 3 P.M. (cf. 3:1);
   (2) Spiritual revelation from God by angel who —

(a) Assured Cornelius his prayers and alms had not been forgotten;

(b) Told him to send to Joppa for Simon Peter; and —

(c) Prepared him for what was to come.

d. The Response (vs. 7, 8)

(1) Prompt obedience noteworthy, in view of strangeness of information;

(2) Sent two "household servants" and one soldier whom we should call an orderly, one who gives officer personal service.

2. *Of the Jew* (vs. 9-16)

a. The Man (vs. 9, 10)

(1) Simon Peter, same Apostle who had been permitted to open kingdom of heaven to Jews on Day of Pentecost (cf. 2:36-41; Matt. 16:19);

(2) Was on flat roof of tanner's house "by the sea side" (v. 6) at about midday "on the morrow" (v. 9), while waiting for meal to be served;

(3) Like Cornelius the day before, received new revelation while at prayer;

(4) Threefold condition, of soul (prayer), body (hunger), and mind (trance), was occasion used by God.

b. The Vision (vs. 11, 12)

(1) Corresponded with Peter's physical needs — hunger used as medium for teaching;

(2) Carried beyond ordinary action of his senses (cf. 2 Cor. 12:2-4), for he saw heavens opened and sheet let down containing all manner of animals, birds, and creeping things.

c. The Command (vs. 13, 14)

(1) Voice told him to satisfy hunger by killing and eating;

(2) Refusal natural to Jewish scruples and very like old temperament of Peter of Gospels (cf. Matt. 16:22, 23; John 18:10, 11);

(3) Evidently horrified at suggestion because opposed to all religious rules;

(a) Law of Moses had prescribed certain animals as fit for food and declared others unfit (cf. Lev. 11; 20:25; Deut. 14:3-21);

(b) Jews particularly careful to observe distinctions — one of main reasons why they refused to associate with Gentiles, who did not observe Mosaic dietary laws.

d. The Lesson (vs. 15, 16)

(1) God was teaching Peter that —

(a) All things had Divine source and real value;

(b) Old distinctions of clean and unclean no longer valid for ceremonial and religious purposes (cf. Rom. 14:14; 1 Cor. 10:23-33; 1 Tim. 4:4, 5; Tit. 1:15); and —

(c) Now sin to "make common" (v. 15, A.S.V.) what God had cleansed;

(d) When did God do this cleansing? Either then, or at some time before — perhaps reminder of Mark 7:1-23, leading to Christ's healing of Gentile child (vs. 24-30); note especially A.S.V. of v. 19.

(2) Lesson repeated twice, for emphasis, before vision came to end by vessel's being received up into heaven.

II. The Divine Providence (10:17-29)

1. *The Messengers* (vs. 17-20)

As Peter pondered what he had seen —

a. With exact coincidence of timing, messengers from Cornelius arrived and inquired for him;

b. The Holy Spirit definitely told him of them, and directed him to meet and accompany them since He had sent them.

2. *The Message* (vs. 21, 22)

a. On inquiry, Peter found whence and why men had come;

b. They bore testimony to their master and told of his vision and resulting request.

3. *The Meeting* (vs. 23-29)

a. After receiving messengers and giving them overnight lodging, Peter set out with them for Caesarea;

b. Took wise precaution of having six Jewish Christians accompany him as witnesses of what might follow (cf. 10:45; 11:12);

c. Arrived next day, and found not only Cornelius waiting, but kinsmen and friends;

d. Peter's character finely revealed here, showing grace of God at work:

(1) Humility (v. 26);

(2) Fearlessness (v. 28);

(3) Directness (v. 29);

e. Necessary to know precise meaning of Cornelius' summons, for it was against custom to have such association with Gentiles:

(1) By this time Jews had elaborated system of exclusiveness far beyond simple requirements and safeguards of Mosiac law;

(2) Judaism, which had helped Cornelius to think about God but had hindered Peter from immediately enlarging his sympathies, now taken up into wider and deeper idea of Gospel for both Jew and Gentile;

f. Peter also tells company what God had been teaching him, realizing connection between vision and visit.

III. The Difficult Problem (10:30-33)

Cornelius tells his story:

1. *The Vision* (vs. 30, 31)

a. His circumstances (v. 30);

b. God's acceptance (v. 31).

2. *The Command* (vs. 32, 33a)

a. Clearly given (vs. 32);

b. Promptly obeyed (v. 33a).

3. *The Attitude* (v. 33b, c)

a. Approbation (v. 33b);

b. Readiness (v. 33c);

N.B. Cornelius' expectation fixed on God Himself, even

though Peter was mouthpiece (cf. Psa. 62:5; 1 Thess. 2:13).

IV. The Direct Proclamation (10:34-43)

Peter responds, emphasizing three special points:

1. *God's impartial character realized* (vs. 34, 35)
   a. Scripture clear about "respect of persons" (cf. Deut. 10:17; 2 Chron. 19:7; Luke 20:21; Rom. 2:11; Gal. 2:6; Eph. 6:9; Jas. 2:1-9; 1 Pet. 1:17);
   b. Cornelius already worshipper of true God, so accepted in order to obtain further blessing in Christ;
   c. All apparent partiality to be done away with, since God looked with no distinctive favor on any race or class.
2. *God's immeasurable love recounted* (vs. 36-41)
   a. In Christ's life (vs. 36-39a);
   b. In Christ's death (v. 39b);
   c. In Christ's resurrection (vs. 40, 41).
3. *God's incomparable Gospel revealed* (vs. 42, 43)
   a. Christ as Master of disciples (v. 42);
   b. Christ as Judge of living and dead (v. 42);
   c. Christ as Fulfiller of prophecy (v. 43);
   d. Christ as Saviour of believers (v. 43):
      (1) The strong confirmation — "to Him give all the prophets witness"
      (2) The one way — "that through His Name"
      (3) The simple means — "whosoever believeth in Him"
      (4) The definite statement — "shall receive remission of sins."

V. The Definite Proof (10:44-48)

Peter still speaking when Holy Spirit descended:

1. *Witnessing to the truth* — full, uncompromising (v. 44)
   a. Sign from heaven equal to that when Jewish believers admitted (cf. 2:2, 3);
   b. This was Pentecost of Gentiles;
2. *Bestowing power* — immediate, definite (vs. 45, 46)
   a. Proof beyond all question that Gentiles no longer to be regarded as "common and unclean" (v. 14);

b. Jewish Christians naturally astonished;

3. *Warranting discipleship* — unhesitating, complete (vs. 47, 48a)
   a. Peter's response all the more striking since as yet Gentiles had not professed faith through public baptism (cf. 8:36-38);
   b. But inevitable that Gentiles should not be refused admission to visible Church of Christ;
   c. They having received Holy Spirit as well as Jews, all were to be equal in Gospel dispensation, with no national or social distinctions;
4. *Creating fellowship* — desired, granted (v. 48b)
   a. As further proof of brotherly love, Peter stayed in Caesarea and lived with Gentiles, which obviously included eating with them (cf. 11:3; Gal. 2:12);
   b. Doubtless used opportunity to instruct new converts further in Gospel truth.

VI. The Defensive Presentation (11:1-18)

1. *The Objection* (vs. 1-3)
   a. Made by narrow party in Jerusalem Church as soon as tidings reached there;
   b. Not to Gentiles coming in, but to terms of equality so evident in Peter's brotherly intercourse.
2. *The Explanation* (vs. 4-16)
   a. Stated in conciliatory way, without arguing;
   b. Striking contrast to former impulsiveness (cf. 2 Tim. 2:24-26).
3. *The Challenge* (vs. 17, 18)
   a. Given, throwing burden on objectors;
   b. Accepted, with no dissenting voice, resulting in glory to God for granting "to the Gentiles . . . repentance unto life";

   N.B. Word "also" used at beginning (v. 1) and at end (v. 18).

Conclusion

In this passage we see a remarkable manifestation of God's working in the affairs of men:

1. *The Purpose of God*
   Striking in its intention:
   a. Breaking down temporary barriers;
   b. Bringing in eternal blessings.
2. *The Plan of God*
   Simple in its process:
   a. Preparing Peter and Cornelius naturally yet supernaturally, separately yet simultaneously;
   b. Leading gradually on, through Samaria experience, and through contacts such as those with Ethiopian eunuch and Simon the tanner, to Cornelius and to Gentiles in general.
3. *The Power of God*
   Sufficient in its scope:
   a. Arranging all circumstances to coincide;
   b. Accomplishing all results according to Divine fore-ordination.

That we may be in harmony with this Purpose, Plan, and Power, let us, like Peter —

1. Abide in Christ — keeping soul close to Him by prayer;
2. Attend to Christ — keeping mind open to Him by meditation;
3. Act for Christ — keeping will obedient to Him by action.

Study No. 46 — Cornelius (1)

ACTS 10:1-8, 22, 24, 25, 30-48

IN THE STUDY of history, a consideration of the lives that make it is interesting and instructive from two viewpoints, distinct yet connected. We may consider the characters of history as men and women, studying their weakness and strength, their power and influence; and note both what they were, and how they were what they were. Or, we may contemplate such men and women as factors in history, influencing and being influenced by their periods, as creators or mere products. Napoleon, for example, may be studied as a man or as a historical force; so also the men of the Bible, viz., Moses, David, Isaiah, Paul, may be considered in themselves or in relation to their times and to Church history; or the two aspects may be blended. So now Cornelius is before us: for young men, as a man; for students of foreign missions, as a representative convert. There is but one thread running through both, which we may easily see in outline:

I. A Good Man's Life

1. *Official Position* (v. 1)
   a. Of centurion, placed over one-sixth of cohort, or 100 men — not very distinguished, yet calling for ability and capable of influence;
   b. Over Roman troops necessary to uphold authority and reputation of Empire;
   c. Stationed at Caesarea, residence of Roman procurator.
2. *Sterling Character* (v. 2)
   Cornelius man of —
   a. Piety — not joined to Judaism as proselyte, but doubtless influenced by it for worship of true God;
   b. Practice — like other centurions of N.T. (cf. 27:3; Matt. 8:5-15; Luke 7:1-10; 23:47);

c. Prayer — constant and regular.

3. *Real Influence* (vs. 2, 7, 22)
Like circles from stone thrown into water, ever enlarging:
a. With family (v. 2);
b. With soldiers (v. 7);
c. With Jews (v. 22).

II. A Good Man's Incompleteness

1. *Goodness Recognized* (vs. 3, 4, 22)
   a. God's notice (vs. 3, 4) — looking down and delighting — no thought or action overlooked (cf. vs. 34, 35);
   b. Messengers' witness (v. 22) — human approval corroboration of Divine acknowledgment; yet —
2. *Life Unsatisfied* (v. 4)
   Continual prayer (v. 2) showed continual need and longing for —
   a. Definite leading (cf. v. 6, "what . . . to do");
   b. Increased knowledge (cf. v. 22, "to hear words");
   c. Complete salvation (cf. 11:14, "whereby . . . saved").
3. *Earnestness Rewarded* (vs. 5, 6)
   a. The way (v. 5) — very simple and satisfying;
   b. The instrument (vs. 5, 6) — Simon Peter, lodged with Simon the tanner;
   c. The result (v. 6) — God, who knew void, was about to fill it.

III. A Good Man's Spirit

1. *Instant Obedience* (vs. 7, 8)
   a. Immediate action (v. 7) proving reality of motive (cf. John 7:17, "If any man will do . . . he shall know");
   b. Reliable messengers (v. 7) given full instructions (v. 8).
2. *Genuine Humility* (vs. 24, 25)
   a. Sought presence of friends (v. 24) — though he knew not what involved;
   b. Welcomed and acknowledged Jew (v. 25) — though he knew how exclusive Jews were and how despised were Gentiles;

c. Proved that true man is humble — humility not humiliation — "stoop to conquer."

3. *Manly Simplicity* (vs. 30-33)
   a. Full statement;
   b. Perfect satisfaction;
   c. Complete readiness.

This spirit sure of blessing.

IV. A Good Man's Reward

1. *A Just God Proved* (vs. 34, 35)
   a. No respecter of persons (v. 34; cf. Deut. 10:17; Rom. 2:11, etc.);
   b. No respecter of nations (v. 35; cf. Rom. 2:27-29).
2. *A Mighty Saviour Proclaimed* (vs. 36-42)
   a. The life of Christ (vs. 36-38) — a Person, central and powerful;
   b. The death and resurrection of Christ (vs. 39-41) — foundation facts (cf. 1 Cor. 15:3, 4);
   c. The second coming of Christ (v. 42) — He to be Judge and therefore all men responsible to Him.
3. *An Earnest Welcome Given* (v. 43)
   a. Immediate — no more waiting or proving — "receive"
   b. Full — complete — "whosoever";
   c. Free — nothing required but faith — "believeth."

   This was climax for Cornelius — "remission of sins," salvation at last.
3. *A Marvelous Blessing Received* (vs. 44-48)
   a. Immediate (v. 44) — not only while Peter "yet spake," but as he "began to speak" (11:15) — sermon never finished;
   b. Universal (v. 45) — Gentiles included now and ever after;
   c. Real (v. 46) — accompanied by "gifts for men" (Psa. 68:8);
   d. Divine (vs. 44, 45, 47, 48a);
      (1) In connection with the Word, the Spirit fell (cf. 11:15);

(2) In connection with falling of the Spirit, came thought of baptism (cf. 11:16; Matt. 3:16; John 1:32, 33);

e. Human (v. 48b) — desire for fellowship and instruction. N.B. Picture Cornelius then, echoing words of Philip the Apostle, "We have found Him" (John 1:45); picture joy in his household as members spent those days with Peter, receiving deeper knowledge, greater blessing, more power, in order to spread Good News far and wide.

Conclusion

Thus Cornelius, the Man and the Gentile: one thread running through both concepts of him. What is it? The need of Christ:

1. *The Man — Christ for the Good*
   - a. The Need
     - (1) Surely, if any deserved to know Christ, Cornelius did — piety splendid — yet insufficient;
     - (2) Today, many young men, moral, well-disciplined, praying, church-going, surely have all necessary? No, there must be salvation, spiritual power.
   - b. The Supply
     - (1) A personal Christ — preached and received;
     - (2) A powerful Holy Ghost — blessing and energizing;
     - (3) A true conversion — repentance and faith.
2. *The Gentile — Christ for All Nations*
   - a. The Need
     - (1) Cornelius representative of highest type of mankind, yet insufficient — men need Christ and justification;
     - (2) Today, religions, old and new, may have good points, yet they are as insufficient as character of adherents — average then and now not even as fine as Cornelius;
     - (3) No satisfaction till there is pardon, power, peace.
   - b. The Supply
     - (1) Pardon in Christ — immediate, full, free;
     - (2) Power through Christ — over bondage, defilement, evil;
     - (3) Peace of Christ — satisfying, complete, eternal.

Hence, Christ realized in souls of men and nations will bring practical and personal sympathy in helping and sharing. So tide of Gospel rolls on to every shore, light to every heart, warmth to every life:

Till o'er our ransomed nature
The Lamb for sinners slain,
Redeemer, King, Creator,
In bliss returns to reign.
— Reginald Heber

Study No. 47 — Cornelius (2)

ACTS 10:1-8; 34-38

ONE OF THE highest testimonies to Christianity is found in Luke 15:2: "This Man receiveth sinners." The solution of the sin problem is the glory of the Gospel. But some, like the Pharisees and scribes of old, are not impressed; they think they have no experience of sin. But Christianity is for "good" people as well as for "sinners," since *all* have "come short of the glory of God" (Rom. 3:23).

There are several notable examples of "good" men in the New Testament. The Elder Brother in the parable was no less in need of his father's love and forbearance because he had sown no wild oats; and the Rich Young Ruler recognized his need of eternal life even though he did not care to meet the conditions. The Ethiopian Eunuch is another example of one of the "not many noble" (1 Cor. 1:26) who, while in the minority among Christ's followers, are none the less a vital part of the Church of God. Here is another such, Cornelius, the Roman centurion, who is described at the very outset as "devout." Let us see him in the two stages of his spiritual experience:

I. A Religious Man

1. *Cornelius Exemplifying —*
   a. Piety — had embraced pure theism of O.T., yet not full

proselyte, for was classed as Gentile, "one of another nation" (v. 28);

b. Reverence — was seeker after God in awe and seriousness;

c. Influence — on household, on soldiers under him, and on Jews;

d. Liberality — unlike usual Roman officials who plundered wherever possible;

e. Prayerfulness — had great sense of need;

f. Receptivity — was able to apprehend vision when it came;

g. Obedience — ready, as true soldier, to comply immediately with instructions.

2. *Cornelius Practising*

a. Living up to light he had — had stepped out of paganism into monotheism, but there was further step to be taken;

b. Was judged by light he possessed — because all such men have power to make progress but all do not exert it;

c. Yet all this not enough — religion and Christianity not synonymous.

II. A Christian Man

1. *What did Cornelius do after Peter's arrival?*

a. He heard the Truth of Christ:

(1) Christ the specific message of Christianity;

(2) Christianity *is* Christ in His Person and work;*

b. He accepted the Salvation of Christ:

(1) Knew sin had to be dealt with;

(2) Found Christ was God's Mediator;

(3) Made contact with Christ;

c. He received the Spirit of Christ:

(1) As Fount of holiness;

(2) As Source of satisfaction;

(3) As Channel of power.

2. *What more did Cornelius obtain?*

a. Assurance of forgiven sin, leading to —

b. Fuller revelation of God's love;

---

*See author's volume, *Christianity Is Christ* (Wm. B. Eerdmans Publishing Co., 1955).

   c. Larger vision of truth;
   d. Secret of holy living.

Conclusion

1. *Christ is for all*
   a. He is necessary — even for good man like Cornelius — pious, reverent, influential, liberal, prayerful, obedient, and whatever else — best of people need a Saviour;
   b. He is sufficient — nothing beyond Christ for soul's deepest needs — gives pardon, power, peace, everything;
   c. He is accessible — as to Cornelius, first by Word and then by Spirit;
   d. He is satisfying — not only to be accepted, but to be enjoyed.
2. *All is for Christ*
   a. Our purpose — to win men everywhere;
   b. Our plea — that Christ be accepted as Saviour, Friend, and Lord;
   c. Our power — in proportion as we yield everything to Christ;
   d. Our peace — having surrendered ourselves, we determine to make Him known to everyone else.

Therefore, accept Christ and avoid danger of self-satisfaction, and mistaking of the "good" or the "better" for the "best"!

Study No. 48 — Hearing

ACTS 10:33b

THERE ARE many "model" preachers and sermons in Scripture. Is there anything about "model" hearers? Yes, the Bible is full of instruction and warning for the hearer. Many of Israel's calamities came upon her because she would not hear (cf. Isa. 28:12, 13; Jer. 7:13-15; Zech. 7:13, 14; Mal. 2:2). Some of our Lord's most solemn utterances had to do with hearing — not only "what" (Mark 4:24) to hear, but "how" (Luke 8:18) to hear; and each of the Letters to the Seven Churches of Revelation 2 and 3 ends with the injunction, "He that hath an ear, let him hear." Just as the preacher should make proper preparation beforehand, so his hearers ought to prepare themselves, by prayer to God for keen ears, receptive hearts, and obedient wills.

This was the attitude of Cornelius and his friends as they waited for the coming of Peter (v. 24). In the text before us we shall see —

I. Determination

1. *Based on obedience* — "therefore"
   a. Looking back to God's command (v. 32);
   b. We, too, have Divine injunction about "not forsaking the assembling of ourselves together" (Heb. 10:25).
2. *Shown in punctuality* — "are we . . . here present"
   a. Etiquette, as well as proper preparation, needs attention;
   b. Peter preached all the better because his audience was waiting, not hurrying in at last moment and disturbing him and others;
   c. Keynote of our church service usually struck at beginning — let us be there for it.
3. *Marked by unanimity* — "all"

a. Evidently included every one of group who could possibly be present;
b. Today, do we allow "indisposition" or other excuse to keep us from God's House?

II. Devoutness

God's presence realized — "before God"
1. *In humility* — with entire selflessness (cf. Exod. 3:5, 6, 11);
2. *In sincerity* — with pure motives (cf. Luke 8:18);
3. *In expectancy* — with high hopes (cf. Psa. 62:5).

III. Definiteness

Shown by —
1. *Attention* — "to hear"
   a. Not to see or be seen;
   b. Not to be amused or entertained;
   c. Be sympathetic — not "packed in ice," as some audiences seem, because of unbelief.
2. *Obedience* — "commanded . . . of God"
   a. Not just hearing, nor even preparation of preacher to preach and hearer to hear, but emphasis on duty, preached and heard (cf. v. 6);
   b. Better today if less said about man's delivery and more about God's deliverance.
3. *Faithfulness* — "all things"
   a. Not merely what they wanted to hear, but everything commanded by God;
   b. Overcoming prejudice, which is often strong, of both preacher and hearer, such as —
      (1) Prejudice of race — nationality and religion, as here;
      (2) Prejudice of place — position and wealth;
      (3) Prejudice of face — beauty and appearance;
      (4) Prejudice of pace — ability and knowledge; and, worst of all —
      (5) Prejudice of grace — religious experience and attainment;
   c. Can be removed only by —

(1) Fellowship with God — in whose presence different elements meet on common ground;
(2) Recognition of facts — which are "stubborn things" (cf. Rom. 2:1; 12:10, 16).

Conclusion

The results of such hearing are happy ones:

1. The Saviour is honored;
2. The preacher is encouraged;
3. The Gospel is presented;
4. The guilty, lost, and disheartened are blessed;
5. The Holy Spirit is unhindered;
6. The Church is enlarged;
7. The believer is edified.

"Take heed how *ye* hear!"

Study No. 49 — "Preaching Peace by Jesus Christ"

ACTS 10:36

There are few subjects more prominent in the Word of God than that of peace. It occupies a very important position in the revelation of God's will. We may observe it, for example, in the Apostolic preaching recorded in this Book, and in the salutations and benedictions of St. Paul and the other Apostles. Above all, we note its definite place in their doctrinal teaching. From beginning to end of the Word of God peace is an outstanding theme.

This is due to the fact that peace is concerned with almost every aspect of men's relation to God, and also with practically every part of human life. We read in Scripture of man's need of peace as a sinner; of God's provision of peace for the repentant; of the believer's need of peace in daily experience; of God's inexhaustible supply of peace under all circumstances; and, finally, of the culmination of peace in the Home above. Its prominence is also due to the fact that in it are included and guaranteed all other graces and blessings: spiritual power, spiritual purity, spiritual perception, spiritual progress. These and other elements of the Christian life depend upon peace in the soul. The following are but summaries of the fulness of Scripture teaching on peace which will be found both encouraging and inspiring:

I. The Meaning of Peace

1. Greek word appears to mean a bond, implying union after severance;
2. English word implies a pact, compact, agreement;
3. Hebrew word includes ideas of friendliness, rest, security, completeness.

II. The Need of Peace

1. Peace of conscience in pardon and acceptance (Isa. 48:22; Rom. 3:17);
2. Peace of heart in rest and fellowship (Num. 6:26; 25:12; Psa. 4:8; 29:11).

III. The Provision of Peace

1. Peace with God — barriers removed (Rom. 5:1; John 20:19);
2. Peace of God — burdens relieved (Phil. 4:7; John 20:21); These are also distinguished in John 14:27 — peace as legacy, and peace as gift.

IV. The Source of Peace

1. God of peace (Rom. 15:33; 16:20; 2 Cor. 13:11; Phil. 4:9; 1 Thess. 5:23; Heb. 13:20);
2. Christ (Col. 3:15, A.S.V.; Eph. 2:13, 14).

V. The Media of Peace

1. Christ's Person: as Prince (Isa. 9:6); as Lord (2 Thess. 3:16); as King (Heb. 7:2);
2. Christ's Work (Eph. 2:15; Col. 1:20; Isa. 53:5);
3. Christ's Preaching (Eph. 2:17; Acts 10:36);
4. Christ's Gift (John 14:27).

VI. The Spheres of Peace

1. In Christ (John 16:33);
2. In the Holy Spirit (Rom. 14:17).

VII. The Instrumentalities of Peace

1. The Gospel (Eph. 6:15; Luke 1:79);
2. Faith (Rom. 5:1; 15:13);
3. Spiritually-mindedness (Rom. 8:6).

VIII. The Nature of Peace

1. Great (Psa. 119:165);
2. Deep (Isa. 48:18);
3. Abundant (Psa. 37:11; 72:7; 1 Pet. 1:2; Jude 2);
4. Indescribable (Phil. 4:7);
5. Perfect (Isa. 26:3);
6. Everlasting (Isa. 9:7).

IX. The Power of Peace

1. To fill (Rom. 15:13);
2. To guard (Phil. 4:7);
3. To rule (Col. 3:15 — lit., umpire or arbitrate).

X. The Companions of Peace

1. Grace (Rom. 1:7);
2. Mercy (Gal. 6:16);
3. Righteousness (Rom. 14:17);
4. Joy (Rom. 15:13);
5. Faith (2 Tim. 2:22);
6. Love (2 Cor. 13:11);
7. Life (Rom. 8:6);
8. Holiness (Heb. 12:14);
9. Purity (Jas. 3:17);
10. Gentleness (Jas. 3:17).

XI. The Outcome of Peace

1. In character (Gal. 5:22);
2. In fellowship (Eph. 4:3; 6:23; Mark 9:50; Rom. 12:18; 2 Cor. 13:11; 1 Thess. 5:13);
3. In action (Matt. 5:9; Jas. 3:17);
4. In service (Eph. 6:15).

XII. The possibilities of Peace

1. Through life (Mark 5:34; Luke 7:50);

2. At death (Luke 2:29);
3. In eternity (2 Pet. 3:14).

XIII. The Scope of Peace

1. On earth (Luke 2:14);
2. In heaven (Luke 19:38).

Conclusion

What, then, is the secret of peace? It is fourfold:

1. *Surrender* — to "government" of "Lord of peace" (Isa. 9:7; 2 Thess. 3:16);
2. *Trust* — "perfect peace" and "peace in believing" (Isa. 26:3; Rom. 15:13);
3. *Obedience* — "love" of "law" and "work of righteousness" (Psa. 119:165; Isa. 32:17);
4. *Earnestness* — to "seek" and "follow" peace (1 Pet. 3:11; Heb. 12:14).

From all of these Scriptures we may realize the imperative necessity of experiencing at once, and continually, the things which belong to our peace (cf. Luke 19:42), and following after them (cf. Rom. 14:19).

I go on my way victorious;
I am done with the pain and strife;
I drink of the mighty river
That flows from the wells of life;
And I hear the silent voices
Like the swell of a sleeping sea;
And my heart, O Lord, rejoices—
It has found its rest in Thee!

Study No. 50 — The Church at Antioch

ACTS 11:19-30

WE CANNOT fully realize today the revolutionary change it was to Jewish Christians to see the Gospel extending to the Gentiles. Verse 19 goes back to 8:4 and continues the story of the dispersion which followed the death of Stephen, the third of the four ways in which the extension of the Church was made. The first two had been through Philip to the Ethiopian and through Peter to Cornelius. Perhaps this is the chronological order, although the exact time between is unknown. It is very likely, however, that the witness of Jewish believers to Greeks at Antioch (vs. 20, 21) was due to the incident regarding Cornelius becoming generally known. The fourth line of preparation for the extension of the Gospel to the Gentiles was the conversion of Saul, and this provided the man, the instrument, as the others prepared the way.

Antioch, the capital of Syria, the third city of the Roman Empire (after Rome and Alexandria), with a population of half a million, was to be the center from which "foreign missions" would start. Already it was the scene of the first Gentile Church, and this was such an important Church that it calls for special study:

I. The Birth of the Church (vs. 19-21) — Leading to Christ

1. *Preparation* (v. 19)
   a. Made by scattering of Jerusalem believers by persecution;
   b. But preaching at first limited to Jews, through ignorance.
2. *Progress* (v. 20)
   a. Followed because some believers from Cyrus and Cyrene obeyed spontaneous impulse of opening hearts to Grecians as well;
   b. Message very simple — just Person of "the Lord Jesus" — Divine and human aspects of the Saviour.

3. *Power* (v. 21)
   a. Quickly seen in blessing of God on testimony;
   b. Thus, a few unknown believers, laymen, ordinary Christians, started work in great Syrian city which became center of Gentile Christian world.

II. The Nourishment of the Church (vs. 22-24) — Living for Christ

1. *Sympathy* (v. 22)
   a. News reached mother-church in Jerusalem;
   b. Best available helper sent in proof of interest — Barnabas, "son of exhortation" (4:36, A.S.V.).
2. *Strength* (v. 23)
   a. Barnabas soon realized what had happened and rejoiced in it;
   b. Carried out his role of exhorter, urging all to keep close to the Lord whom they had found.
3. *Success* (v. 24)
   a. His counsel came from his character — "for" he had —
      (1) Goodness;
      (2) Fulness of the Spirit;
      (3) Faith;
   b. Result of presence of so fine a man was —
      (1) Increased blessing;
      (2) Blessed increase.

III. The Growth of the Church (vs. 25, 26) — Laboring for Christ

1. *Assistance* (vs. 25, 26a)
   a. Work too much for Barnabas alone, so set out to get very man for situation, Saul of Tarsus;
   b. Note fine spirit — no self-seeking or jealousy.
2. *Advance* (v. 26b)
   a. Fellowship in assembly for "a whole year";
   b. Instruction in truth for "much people."
3. *Acknowledgment* (v. 26c)
   a. Further progress attracted notice;

b. Testimony obtained new name for believers — "Christians"* (cf. 26:28; 1 Pet. 4:16):
   (1) Word contains Hebrew, Greek, and Latin elements:
      (a) Expresses Jewish thought — root equivalent of "Messiah," "Anointed One";
      (b) Shows Greek language in substantive — *"Christ"*
      (c) Includes Latin language in adjectival ending — *"iani"* (English, *"ians"*);
   (2) This universality reminder of title on Cross (cf. John 19:19, 20);

   N.B. (1) Alexander Smellie says heathen contemporaries "heard its adherents talk continually of one *Christus,* making their boast of Him, and discovering in Him a Magnet to draw their hearts, and a Monarch to establish His control over their lives. So they dubbed them, half in ridicule but with shrewd and true instinct, the *Christiani,* Christ's men and women"; (2) Northcote Deck says: "It seems significant of God's designs for us that we are not called by His personal name of Jesus, which signifies 'He shall save His people from their sins.' He has purposed that, but much more than that. He desires not just pardoned criminals, but privileged children. So we are called after His official name . . . meaning 'anointed.' . . . As the Scripture expresses it, this 'anointing which ye have received abideth' (1 John 2:27). So our general name of Christian implies not only that we have been cleansed from our sins, but that we have been anointed by the Holy Ghost and made nigh for a purpose of walking with God."

   Thy Name we own, Lord Jesus,
   And humbly walk before Thee;
   And while we live to Thee we'd give
   All blessing, worship, glory.

IV. The Vitality of the Church (vs. 27-30) — Loving in Christ

1. *Intercourse* (v. 27)

---

*See also Study No. 55, under XII, p. 223.

a. Between mother-church and daughter-church;
b. Between Jewish church and Gentile church.

2. *Instruction* (v. 28)
   a. By Agabus, prophet from Jerusalem;
   b. Through the Spirit, prophesied widespread famine.
3. *Interest* (vs. 29, 30)
   a. Personal — "every man according to his ability" — not dependent on mood or fad;
   b. Practical — giving determined, done, delivered.

Conclusion

The Church at Antioch was a wonderful church. It was —

1. Born in adversity;
2. Varied in elements;
3. Evangelistic in power;
4. Earnest in work;
5. Mighty in influence;
6. Liberal in giving;
7. Missionary in spirit.

A church well taught is always a church that lives well and works well. Is our church like the one at Antioch?

Study No. 51 — Soul-Winning

ACTS 11:20, 21

In these verses we are introduced to the first lay foreign missionaries. Dispersed on account of persecution, certain men from Cyrus and Cyrene "travelled as far as . . . Antioch," and "spake unto the Grecians, preaching the Lord Jesus."

I. A Spontaneous Impulse Obeyed

1. *Kindliness of heart*
   a. Gospel enlarges sympathies and warms feelings;
   b. Gospel enables believer to think of others, with "heart at leisure from itself, to soothe and sympathize."
2. *Possession of Christ*
   a. Their Master real — consciousness of His presence lighting way and inspiring action;
   b. Their obligation strong — they could not but speak (cf. 4:20; Jer. 20:9).

II. A Largehearted Sympathy Manifested

1. *Barrier broken down*
   a. This meant much then — more than we can realize;
   b. But true Christian feeling not to be hindered — natural prejudice ignored.
2. *Truth grasped*
   a. No distinction between "home" and "foreign" — cf. "made of one blood all nations" (17:26);
   b. Christ delivers from narrowness — widening consciousness so that we are citizens of world, not mere taxpayers of county or residents of town or of countryside.

III. A Notable Message Delivered

These men had clear, full realization of twofold truth:

1. *A Saviour* — "Jesus" (cf. Matt. 1:21) — salvation from sin;

2. *Master* — "the Lord" (cf. John 21:7) — redemption, then rule — life in care of Another.

IV. A Simple Form Used

1. *Natural* — no sermon or dissertation, but just ordinary conversation;
2. *Personal* — not hearsay, but their own experience (cf. Num. 10:29; John 9:25).

V. A Mighty Helper Realized

"The hand of the Lord was with them" (v. 21) —

1. *In guidance* — cf. 1 Kings 18:46; 2 Kings 3:15; Ezek. 1:3;
2. *In power* — cf. Exod. 15:6; Neh. 2:8.

VI. A Glorious Result Achieved

1. *In numbers* — cf. Pentecost — shows what God can do through faithful witness;
2. *In reality* — "turned unto the Lord" as well as "believed" — far better one real convert than fifty who merely assent.

VII. A Universal Obligation Suggested

1. *Because of loyalty to Christ* — saved to serve — cf. 1 Cor. 9:16; 2 Cor. 4:10, 11;
2. *Because witness expected of all believers* — not solely responsibility of priesthood, clerics, etc., but everyone a worker, our goal and our privilege.

Conclusion

Let us see in these verses —

1. *A Rebuke*
   a. What life! What work! What reality! What simplicity!
   b. Are they ours?
2. *A Hint*
   a. The way to live, to work, to speak;
   b. Is it ours?
3. *An Encouragement*
   a. The same God now;
   b. Is He ours?

Only a word for the Master,
Lovingly, quietly said;
Only a word, yet the Master heard,
And some fainting souls were fed.

Only a look of remonstrance,
Sorrowful, tender, and deep;
Only a look, yet a strong man shook
And went forth alone to weep.

Only some act of devotion,
Willingly, joyfully done;
Surely 'twas nought (so the proud world thought),
But yet souls for Christ were won.

Only an hour with the children,
Pleasantly, cheerfully given;
Yet seed was sown, in that hour alone,
Which would bring forth fruit for heaven.

Only—! —but Jesus is looking
Constantly, tenderly down
To earth; and He sees those who strive Him to please,
And has promised their witness to crown.

Study No. 52 — Barnabas (2)*

ACTS 11:22-26

"LET EVERY MAN prove his own work," wrote the Apostle Paul (Gal. 6:4); and he also mentioned "diversities and gifts" (1 Cor.12:4). We shall profit by noting the work and gifts of Barnabas and how they may be ours.

I. Removing Difficulties (v. 22)

1. Was right man for smoothing rough corners;
2. Had confidence of all (cf. 9:27; 15:2, 12, 25);

   N.B. Difficulties arising today, as then, give opportunities to overcome prejudice and abate friction.

II. Helping Believers (v. 23)

1. His exhortations helped Christians to continue; particularly weak ones (cf. 15:37-39);
2. His co-operation about gifts brought relief to brethren in Jerusalem (cf. 11:30);
3. His gladness here and rejoicing (cf. 15:31) cheered fellow-Christians;

   N.B. Today we are to "do good . . . especially unto them who are of the household of faith" (Gal. 6:10).

III. Winning Souls (v. 24)

1. Through others chiefly, for souls won when believers made fit;
2. Barnabas' main work with believers (cf. 9:29), encouraging evangelism;
3. Antioch first missionary church — missions must be prepared for;

   N.B. Christ's work still done largely by individual dealing

---

*For other studies of Barnabas, see pp. 105, 214. 216, 296.

with souls — way opens and Holy Spirit found to be working "at both ends."

IV. Enlisting Workers (vs. 25, 26)

1. Barnabas had already sponsored Saul and saved him for Church (cf. 9:27); now he sets him to work on first special assignment;
2. Yet little knew full worth and power of protege;
   N.B. Our goal today should be every Christian a worker.

Conclusion

1. Barnabas was a man of character — all from within;
2. Christ was the Source of character — all of grace.

Study No. 53 — Barnabas (3)

ACTS 11:24

WE ARE SO APT to associate Pentecost with miracles and marvels that we fail to realize its power for ordinary life. Secular biography often depicts characters so far above normal that they seem impossible to emulate; but not so Scriptural biographies. This is because the same grace which activated the lives of the spiritually great is available for all. Seven men serving tables (cf. 6:2-6) needed the Holy Spirit just as surely as did their apostolic leaders.

Luke, the friend of Paul, wrote this brief but arresting description of Barnabas, the colleague whom the Apostle mentions in 1 Cor. 9:6 after their difference of opinion. Luke's words answer three questions about Barnabas: What he was, why he was what he was, and how he was what he was.

I. The Stream — "He was a good man"

1. *Its meaning*:
   a. Good man means man like God;
   b. Not simply amiable, but more — possessed of active, positive elements of virtue.

---

*For other studies of Barnabas, see pp. 105, 213, 216, 296.

2. *Its characteristics*:
   a. Generosity;
   b. Sympathy;
   c. Clearsightedness;
   d. Self-forgetfulness;
   e. Self-sacrifice;
   N.B. Need today not so much for clever men as for good men.

II. The Source — "He was . . . full of the Holy Ghost"
1. *Stream must have source* — life of Barnabas issued from the Holy Spirit of God:
   a. It was not particularly striking — in fact, would seem ordinary; but —
   b. It was under complete control of the Holy Ghost;
   c. Its strength was due to full surrender after conversion.
2. *Source must have channel* — devotion of Barnabas a link between God and His Church:
   a. It was miraculous;
   b. It was not to be limited to period covered by Book of Acts;
   c. It was not for spiritual work only, but for material — cf. similar description for deacons (6:3, 5);
   N.B. Need today in Church life — every Christian a worker.

III. The Secret — "He was . . full . . of faith"
Why is faith the one condition of receiving the Spirit?
1. *It admits Christ in trust*:
   a. Dependence on Him undertaken;
   b. Independence of Him relinquished.
2. *It allows Christ to remain*:
   a. Surrender to Him sustained;
   b. Hindrances to Him removed.
3. *It attends Christ in obedience*:
   a. Willing to do His will;
   b. Prepared to do His work;

N.B. Need today for those who will take God at His Word.

Conclusion

Can the "biography" of Barnabas be ours?

1. *The condition*
   a. Desire for God's glory;
   b. Renunciation of sin;
   c. Willingness to obey.
2. *The Result*
   a. Believe, not feel, Christ's salvation;
   b. Rely on belief and surrender self to Him;
   c. Find peace, power, joy, at the Cross;
   d. Pass on experience to others.

Study No. 54 — Barnabas (4)*

ACTS 11:25, 26

Every man's life is made up of three elements: what he does, what he is, and how he is what he is and does what he does; or, conduct, character, and causation. In our study of the life of Barnabas we have often considered all of these elements: his conduct, one of goodness; his character, one of faith; and the causation, or motive power, of his whole career, the Holy Spirit of God. The present verse gives us a sidelight on the second of these, his character:

I. Open-mindedness

1. As Jew, and as Levite (cf. 4:36), naturally power for good;
2. Had listened to Saul (cf. 9:26, 27);
3. Is now sent to Antioch (cf. v. 22), perhaps to guard against abuse of Christian liberty or guile of false leaders.

II. Clear-sightedness

1. As to Saul — saw great possibilities (cf. 9:26, 27);

*For other studies of Barnabas, see pp. 105, 213, 214, 296.

2. As to Antioch — saw reality of work (cf. v. 23);
3. As to Saul in relation to Antioch — saw ministry needed, with —
   a. Fresher view;
   b. Clearer insight;
   c. Wider culture;
   d. Firmer hand;
4. As to self — saw own limitations in contrast with other characters and thought Antioch needed someone greater than he.

III. Large-heartedness

1. In the Church at Jerusalem — had shown great generosity (cf. 4:36, 37);
2. In the work at Antioch —
   a. Evidently found it different from what represented or expected;
   b. But, being man of good grace, was "glad" (v. 23);
   c. Felt situation beyond him, and so, with true self-effacement, sought Saul;
   d. Then returned with him and divided leadership in association and in teaching for "a whole year" (v. 26).

IV. True-spiritedness

1. Stages of humility — especially noteworthy since Barnabas probably older man:
   a. Befriending Saul (cf. 9:26, 27) — over him;
   b. Consulting Saul (cf. 11:25, 26) — equal with him;
   c. Following Saul (cf. 13:13, 45, 46, 50; 14:12, etc.) — under him.
2. Notes on humility:
   a. Next to man who achieves great things is man who is incapable of greatness and yet sees and encourages it in another;
   b. He often accomplishes more by sympathy than by actual labor, more by absence of jealousy and recognition of merit than by exercise of personal ambition;

c. Not only ready to acknowledge power of another at distance but, which takes more grace, willing to have him near enough to eclipse his own light and take his place;
d. Absence of anxiety for personal credit — ready for association without selfish ends in view.

Conclusion

Paul wrote later: "To me to live is Christ" (Phil. 1:21). Thus we may sum up Barnabas:
1. *His Conduct* — inspired by Christ;
2. *His Character* — infilled with Christ.
Are we like Barnabas?

Study No. 55 — Names for the People of God

ACTS 11:26

"What's in a name?" The answer to this familiar question, as implied by Shakespeare, suggests that to us a name often means little or nothing. But to the Jew it meant a great deal, for names, as a rule, had a real meaning and purpose. It is this thought that gives so much point and force to the various titles of God's people found in the New Testament. Let us look at those names and titles that are associated with personal life and relationships, placing special emphasis on the one mentioned in this passage, "Christians." Each name has a definite meaning and reminds us of what Christians are intended to be. They were referred to as:

I. Believers (Acts 5:14; 1 Tim. 4:12; also Gr. of Acts 10:45; 16:1)

Belief, faith, is foundation of all other and subsequent relationships with God:

1. *Faith is trust*:
   a. Credence of intellect; confidence of heart; consent of will;

b. Reliance of soul on Word of God; response of soul to God Himself;

c. Initial act by which we become united to Christ; continued attitude whereby we abide in Him.

2. *Faith is trust in a Person*:

a. Faith nothing apart from object;

b. Trust in Person of Christ even more important than belief in facts or truths;

c. Gr. usages suggest following:

(1) We credit God as the Truth;

(2) We rest on Him as our Foundation;

(3) We move towards Him as our Goal;

(4) We abide in Him as our Life;

d. Faith is outgoing of entire personality — intellect, emotion, will — in surrender to Divine Person.

II. **Children** (1 John 3:10, etc.; Rom. 9:26, etc.)

Result of believing — we become children, or sons, of God through faith (cf. Gal. 3:26; John 1:12):

1. *Children* — term used largely by St. John:

a. Possessing new life and new nature (cf. John 1:12; 3:6);

b. Needing Father's care because of feebleness (cf. John 11:52);

c. Growing gradually to maturity (cf. 1 John 2:12-14; 3:1-3).

2. *Sons* — term used largely by St. Paul:

a. Signifying privilege, dignity, responsibility, experience (cf. Eph. 1:5, etc.);

b. Denoting child having reached his majority and, therefore, his spiritual maturity (cf. Rom. 8:14-17; Gal. 4:1-7);

c. Stating, not nature, but standing, not life, but position (cf. Rom. 8:1-16; Gal. 4:1-7).

N.B. Cf. John's concept of New Birth with Paul's concept of Adoption (John 3:3; Rom. 8:15).

III. Disciples (Matt. 10:1; etc.; Acts 6:1, etc.)

Term found frequently during Christ's earthly ministry and in Acts:

1. *Disciples are learners*:
   a. Meaning pupils at school, under instruction, teachable, eager, with intellects awake;
   b. Showing life needs growth, and growth needs truth.
2. *Disciples are more than learners*:
   a. Manlier word than pupils or scholars — these are schoolroom words, emphasizing mere instruction, and representing only part of discipleship;
   b. Better definition is thinker — one under mental, moral, and spiritual stimulus;
   c. Term involves personal influence as well as instruction — imbibing Christ's Spirit as well as learning from Him;
   d. Word not used in Epistles, perhaps because true disciple has not only learned about Christ, he has "learned Christ" (Eph. 4:20);
   e. Note connection, etymological and spiritual, between disciple and discipline — first is developed by second (cf. Job 36:7-11).

IV. Saints (Acts 9:13, etc.)

Very frequent title for Christians, especially in Epistles:

1. *Its Meaning*
   a. Separation — from uncleanness and ordinary life, and to God (cf. Tabernacle, priests, etc., Exod. 25:8; 28:1-3);
   b. Dedication — consecrated to God for His use (cf. Rom. 6:13; 12:1);
   c. Purification — result in character of separation and dedication.
2. *Its Use*

   Care needed here, for usage has narrowed:

   a. In Roman Catholicism — "saint" belongs to exclusive group supposed to be especially holy, and to be venerated, often mistakenly worshipped;

b. In Protestantism — "saint" most august title for Apostle or Evangelist; but —
c. In New Testament — all true members of Christ's Church called "saints," Gr., "holy ones," (cf. John 17:19).

V. Servants (Acts 4:29; Rom. 6:14-23, etc.)

Arising out of our relationship as "children," our position as "sons," and God's possession of us as "saints" comes thought of service, labor; by love of Him we are servants —

1. *Of God*
   a. His possession — cf. slavery, property, "living chattels";
   b. In His service — for work in His vineyard, and to do His will.
2. *For God*
   a. Representing Him to man (2 Cor. 5:20):
      (1) Witnessing to His truth;
      (2) Warring against His enemies;
      (3) Winning men to His Kingdom; and —
      (4) Watching for souls — workmen that need not be ashamed (cf. 2 Tim. 2:15);
   b. Serving brethren in His Spirit (cf. Luke 22:26, 27; Gal. 5:13), and thus glorifying God.

V. Faithful (Acts 16:15; Eph. 1:1, etc.)

Term varies in meaning between "trusting" and "trustworthy";

1. *Reliance on God,* or dependence;
2. *God's reliance on us,* or dependableness;
3. *Reliability for God;* can men depend on us?

As "saint" means dedicated, so "faithful" means devoted — in position and practice.

VII. Brethren (Acts 9:30; Rom. 7:1, etc.)

Very frequent title in N. T. — cf. "brotherhood" (1 Pet. 2:17; 5:9, Gr.):

1. *With common life* — one Father, tie of nature;
2. *With common interests* — if life real, obligations realized and fulfilled;
3. *With common love* — cf. "brotherly love" (1 Pet. 1:22;

3:8) — new bond never before seen (cf. John 13:34, 35) — reciprocal feelings making for genuine unity.

VIII. Friends (John 15:14, 15)

Only one man in O. T. was called "Friend of God" — Abraham (cf. 2 Chron. 20:7; Isa. 41:8; Jas. 2:23):

1. *This designation now applied to all Christians;*
2. *Highest possibility in Christian life* is fellowship with God (1 John 1:3), and only friends hold true fellowship;
3. *Therefore,* note four associated aspects of Christian life: sonship, friendship, worship, fellowship:
   a. Son is more than son — he is friend;
   b. Worshipper does more than worship — he holds fellowship.

IX. Beloved (Col. 3:12, etc.)

Term denotes special personal affection — cf. O.T. use (e.g., Deut. 33:12; Psa. 127:2; Song of Sol. 2:16). In N.T. it has two applications:

1. *Beloved of God* (cf. Rom. 1:7);
2. *Beloved of fellow-Christians* (Rom. 16:8, etc.).

X. Heirs (Rom. 8:17)

Thought of inheritance in N.T. unlike ours; it includes —

1. *Possession as well as prospect;*
2. *Experience as well as expectation;*
3. *Present enjoyment of spiritual blessings and "earnest"* (Eph. 1:14) *of complete possession hereafter.*

XI. "His Own" (John 13:1)

One of most striking of titles (cf. John 10:3, 4, 12; Luke 18:7); it suggests —

1. *Special possession by God;*
2. *Special protection for God;*
3. *Special affection from God.*

But here, in Acts 11:26, we are told that the distinctive title bestowed on the disciples was —

XII. Christians (cf. 26:28; 1 Pet. 4:16)

1. *How was it given?*
   a. Not by enemies — they used terms, "Nazarenes," "Galileans";
   b. But Divinely:
      (1) Word here translated "were called," and found only eight times in N.T., means in every other place voicing of Divine oracle — translated also "warned" and "revealed" (cf. Heb. 12:25; Matt. 2:12, 22);
      (2) Not ordinary word "to call," so significance must be same here as elsewhere, viz., name "Christian" really given, or prompted, by God.
      N.B. Albert Barnes, great Presbyterian, said: "The name was evidently given because they were followers of Christ. That it was given in derision is not probable. It was readily assumed by the Apostles. It is the most honored name that can be conferred on a mortal, a name which rises above every other name. It is a bond to unite in one family all those who love the Lord Jesus."
2. *Why was it given?*
   a. To fulfil prophecy (cf. Isa. 62:2; 65:15);
   b. To emphasize universality, sinking differences in common bond.
3. *Where was it given?*
   a. Antioch in Syria, city of large population, mart of East and West;
   b. Had combination of Roman rule, Greek commerce, and Jewish religion.
4. *What was its meaning?*
   a. Word itself includes —
      (1) Hebrew idea, as equivalent of "Messiah," or "Anointed";
      (2) Greek language, in substantive root, "*Christos,*" "Christ";
      (3) Latin usage, in adjectival ending, "*iani,*" "ians," or "anointed ones";

b. This universality is reminder of inscription on Cross (cf. John 19:20), with threefold language of religion, culture, and authority — Christian name, as well as Christian faith, is universal;

c. Its significance describes our relation to Christ — united with the Anointed (cf. 10:38), and anointed by Him (cf. 2 Cor. 1:21; 1 John 2:27) — union and unction.

5. *What is its relation to other names as above?*

a. It includes them, for they are all in and through Christ:

(1) With Christ the Great Object of our faith, we are Believers;

(2) By faith in Christ we are born again, as Children, Sons;

(3) In following Christ, we become Disciples;

(4) Because Christ is "made unto us sanctification" (1 Cor. 1:30), we are accounted Saints;

(5) With desire to work for Christ as Master, we are designated Servants;

(6) In allegiance to Christ we are included among the Faithful;

(7) In relationship to God through Christ we are all Brethren;

(8) In fellowship with Christ we are among His Friends;

(9) In surrender to Christ we are called His Beloved;

(10) In expectation from Christ we are accounted His Heirs;

(11) In redemption by Christ we are purchased as His Own.

b. It is defined by them — what is it to be a Christian? It is to be all of these;

N.B. Joseph Parker said: "By Christians I understand Christ followers, Christ lovers, Christ worshippers, Christ ones. Were we what we ought to be in integrity, in simplicity, and in equity of soul, there should be no nobler designation known amongst man, and no other should be needed. The one name that we ought to have is Christian."

c. It becomes wider term because it includes all other names given to Christ's followers; it is narrow because it excludes all such for one who has no relationship to Christ.

Conclusion

It is suggestive, and perhaps significant, that the word "Christian" has become the most universal of all names for the followers of Christ, so that, precious as it is, it may easily be lightly or loosely used. Therefore, let me test myself by all the other terms which it includes:

1. Am I a Believer in Christ?
2. Am I a Child, a Son of God?
3. Am I a Disciple, learning of Christ?
4. Am I a Saint, consecrated to God?
5. Am I a Servant, working for Christ?
6. Am I among the Faithful to God?
7. Am I one of the Brethren and filled with love for them?
8. Am I one of God's Friends?
9. Am I one of His Beloved?
10. Am I one of His Heirs?
11. Am I one of His very Own?

If the answers are all in the affirmative, then I am in the company of those who "were called Christians first in Antioch" — I am a Christian! Seeing, then, that all these privileges and prospects are mine, what manner of person ought I to be "in all holy conversation and godliness" (2 Pet. 3:11)?

Study No. 56 — What Is a Christian?*

ACTS 11:26

WHEN A COIN has been so long in use that its impression is almost effaced, it is not easy to recapture its appearance as it came from the mint. Words are like coins — they are worn down by usage, and not only their appearance, but their meaning is altered — in some cases entirely changed, as in the word "prevent."

The word "Christian" often has a different meaning now from the one it had in Apostolic times. In the days when it was difficult and often dangerous to be a Christian, it meant much; nowadays, when it is usually easy to call oneself a Christian, it may mean little or nothing.

The origin of the word is full of interest. Antioch was a city which combined Greek, Roman, and Jewish elements, and the word "Christian," used here for the first time, was more a mark of universality than any of the other names — such as Nazarenes, Galileans, brethren, disciples — by which the followers of Jesus had hitherto been known. Names like these often distinguished between Jews and Gentiles, but in the word "Christian" they were united.

Let us try to find out the true meaning; let us, as it were, recover the markings of the coin. On one face of it may be found the word "Union," for to be a Christian is to be —

I. United to Christ

1. *"Christian" is "Christ's Man"*

   a. Association with Him — points to Person, not system;

---

*Appears in full in *The Christian Life and How to Live It* published by Moody Press, Chicago, and also by The Church Book Room Press, London. Outline used by permission.

b. Union with Him — is twofold:
   (1) Union of Life:
      (a) His life becomes ours — Christ in us (cf. Gal. 2:20);
      (b) It begins — we are "born" (John 1:13), not merely baptized;
      (c) It grows — we feed "on Him in our hearts by faith" (Book of Common Prayer), not merely on Holy Communion;
   (2) Union of Love:
      Our love is fixed on Him in return for His (1 John 4:19):
      (a) We become His — we are in Him;
      (b) We recognize His claim to our loyalty;
      (c) We respond to His call for our devotion.

2. *"Christianity is Christ"**
   a. His Person for worship;
   b. His Sacrifice for trust;
   c. His Life for example;
   d. His Truth for guide;
   e. His Obedience for endeavor;
   f. His Coming for hope;
   g. His Glory for motive;
   Or,
   a. For us — a Sufficient Sacrifice;
   b. In us — a Living Power;
   c. Under us — a Sure Foundation;
   d. Around us — a Wall of Fire;
   e. Over us — a Blessed Master;
   f. Beside us — a Present Friend;
   g. Before us — an Eternal Hope.
   N.B. Am I thus united to Christ? If not, how may I be? Faith in Him is the link.

On the other face of the coin is found the word, "Unction," for to be a Christian is also to be —

---

*See author's volume with this title (Wm. B. Eerdmans Publishing Co., 1955).

II. Anointed by Christ

1. Since "Christ" means "Anointed One," so "Christians" means "anointed ones."
2. Cf. anointing oil in O. T. at consecration of prophets, priests, and kings, symbolizing Holy Spirit;
3. As Jesus was thus anointed (cf. 10:38), so also His followers (cf. 2 Cor. 1: 21, 22; 1 John 2:20, 27), receiving Holy Spirit for —
   a. Purity:
      (1) Cleansing heart from defilement (cf. Matt. 5:8);
      (2) Clearing mind of darkness (cf. Eph. 5:3-9);
   b. Power:
      (1) To walk with God — in fellowship and intercession (cf. Mic. 3:8);
      (2) To work for man — in witness and service (cf. Acts 1:8);
   c. Practice:
      (1) In holiness — salvation and sanctification;
      (2) In helpfulness — service and sacrifice;
      These two not intended to be separated — nowadays they too often are, and so no power.
      N.B. Am I thus anointed by Christ? Nothing less than this is to be a Christian.

Conclusion

1. *What is the N.T. ideal of a Christian?*
   a. Every Christian a convert — no compromisers;
   b. Every convert an active, aggressive agent — no substitutes;
   c. Every agent a fully consecrated, intensely vitalized worker no lukewarm ones;
   d. Every worker endued with power from on High.
2. *How may I attain this ideal?*
   a. Trust Christ as Saviour;
   b. Surrender to Christ as Lord;
   c. Serve Christ as Master;
   d. Speak to and of Christ as Friend.

O, who this day will rejoicing say,
With a grateful heart and free,
"Thou King Divine, my life shall be Thine,
I consecrate all to Thee."

We daily live and we daily give
For some object near the heart,
Some purpose bold, some name we hold
Where the gushing life-springs start;

But oh, 'tis wise, when the heart can rise
And carry its wealth away
Where the angels fall — He deserveth all
That we at His feet can lay.

A life that serves where a love deserves
The life and the love we give
Is a life sublime on the fields of time,
A life it is grand to live.

Then let each one this day rejoicing say,
With a grateful heart and free,
"Thou King Divine, my life shall be Thine,
I consecrate all to Thee."

Study No. 57 — Peter Delivered from Prison (1)

ACTS 12:1-25

THIS LAST important reference to Peter in Acts (except 15:7-11) is in connection with the persecution by Herod. Two serious crises in the life of the young Church had been met already: persecution by the Jewish ecclesiastical authorities (chaps. 3 and 4), and Pharisaic narrowness shown by some Jewish Christians (chaps. 10 and 11). Now comes a conflict with the State, and Peter, as one of the Church's leaders, is again brought into prominence.

In 11:29 to 12:25, we have a picture of Church life amid the untoward circumstances of simultaneous famine and persecution. Physical hunger was relieved by means of timely assistance from the Church at Antioch, delivered by Barnabas and Saul (cf. 11:29, 30), who evidently stayed in Jerusalem through this period (cf. 12:25) of —

I. Danger (vs. 1-4)

It was characterized by —

1. *Wickedness* (vs. 1)
   a. The man — Herod Agrippa I, grandson of Herod the Great (cf. Matt. 2), and father of Paul's Agrippa (cf. 25:13 to 26:32);
   b. The act — persecuting Christians to gain favor with Jews (cf. v. 3); and by striking at leaders intended to deal mortal blow at Church.
2. *Murder* (v. 2)
   a. The victim — James the son of Zebedee, a "son of thunder" (cf. Mark 3:17);
   b. The narrative — very short, only two words in Gr.:
      (1) Cf. long account of Stephen's death (6:8 to 8:2) — this because James' death not concerned with Church's

development, as was Stephen's, so statement not amplified;

(2) Cf. James' death with Peter's release (vs. 7-10);

(3) Cf. it with James' desire expressed to Christ (Mark 10:35-37);

(4) Cf. experiences of two brothers, James and John: one the first Apostle to go, by martyrdom of quick and untimely death, the other the last (John 21:22, 23; Rev. 1:1, 2, 4, 9), by martyrdom of prolonged suffering and loneliness.

3. *Imprisonment* (vs. 3, 4)

a. The prisoner — Peter, recognized leader of Apostles;

b. The reason — further to please Jews;

c. The delay — not to offend feeling of community by desecrating festival by execution — curious blend of formalism and wickedness;

N.B. Religious scruples often nothing but pious regard for times and seasons, e.g., spending Lent preparing for Easter rather than in true penitence; spending Sunday doing accounts for Monday rather than in true worship, rest, or service;

d. The guard — Peter in charge of sixteen soldiers, probably four on duty for each watch — to prevent escape, as on former occasion (cf. 5:18-28) — remarkable testimony to Peter's importance and power behind him.

II. Deliverance (vs. 5-11)

1. *Intercession* (v. 5)

Church doing duty meanwhile in earnest, definite, united, unceasing prayer, in home of John Mark (cf. v. 12).

2. *Calmness* (v. 6)

a. In face of unusual severity — Peter handcuffed to two soldiers — perfect peace on very night of contemplated execution;

b. This was sleep of unquestioning trust in God (cf. Psa. 127:2), as contrasted with two former occasions when he had fallen asleep (see Study No. 60, p. 243):

(1) Through unripeness of experience (Luke 9:32);
(2) Through unfaithfulness of life (Matt. 26:40).

3. *Interposition* (v. 7)
   a. Vividly and fully depicted — angel's presence, light, action, words;
   b. Instant and remarkable result — chains fell off hands;

Then boldly let our faith address
The throne of grace and power;
We shall obtain delivering grace
In every needed hour.

4. *Obedience* (vs. 8, 9)
   a. Prompt, unquestioning — very different from attitude before Pentecost;
   b. At each step his response perfect.
5. *Freedom* (vs. 10, 11)
   a. Angel did for Peter only what Peter could not do for self, then "departed" (v. 10) — instance of true Divine deliverance or revelation; has been called "glory of the commonplace" (cf. Luke 2:15);
   b. Events so crowded, swift, and extraordinary that Peter had not grasped reality of deliverance; but now his freedom not only perfect, but conscious (cf. v. 11 with v. 9, and Psa. 126:1 with Psa. 118:23).

III. **Delight** (vs. 12-17)

1. *Fellowship* (v. 12)
   a. Thought — at once Peter thinks of other Christians;
   b. Action — characteristic of him to go where believers were (cf. 4:23).
2. *Reception* (vs. 13, 14)
   "A damsel came to answer (v. 13, A.R.V.):
   a. Her name — Rhoda, "rose," queen of flowers, pure and sweet;
   b. Her work — to tend door, perhaps as maid in "house of Mary" (v. 12);
   c. Her attitude — one of gladness at hearing Peter's voice, for she must have known him and been interested in him;

d. Her message — Peter there, so prayer answered — simple faith accepts;
e. Her earnestness — confident affirmation (cf. v. 15, A.S.V.)

3. *Incredulity* (v. 15)
   a. Denial — so strong that Rhoda was accused of being mad;
   b. Suggestion — to explain appearance supernaturally.

4. *Astonishment* (v. 16)
   a. Doubt and despair turned to surprise and joy;
   b. Evidently there had been no expectation that answer would come in form of deliverance — James had not been spared, so why should Peter be?
   c. Early Church could pray unselfishly (cf. 4:29), so perhaps here they had asked that Peter might be enabled to witness good confession — "for him" (v. 5), not for his deliverance.

4. *Explanation* (v. 17)
   a. Peter calmed their excitement by gesture and by word;
   b. Recounting remarkable experience, gave glory to "the Lord";
   c. Then commanded those present to report to James (the Lord's brother, cf. 15:13; 21:18; Gal. 2:9, 12; Jas. 1:1), and "brethren," while he departed for "another place."

IV. Death (vs. 18-23)

1. *Of Keepers* (vs. 18, 19)
   a. Their bewilderment (v. 18) very natural under circumstances — Peter had been secured by two soldiers (v.6), two chains (v.6), and two guards (v. 10, A.S.V.);
   b. Herod's anger also to be expected (v. 19), and action in line with custom of times (cf. Matt. 28:11-15).

2. *Of King* (vs. 20-23)
   a. One of Luke's historical references, connecting action of his book with contemporary happenings;
   b. Fate of Herod illustrates statement in Second Commandment — "I the Lord thy God am a jealous God" (Exod. 20:5).

V. Development (vs. 24, 25)

1. *Dissemination* (v. 24)
   a. There follows one of milestones of Church progress: "the word of God grew and multiplied" (cf. 2:14; 4:4, 32; 5:14; 6:7; 8:4, 25; 9:31; 11:24);
   b. In view of death of James, this was another instance of blood of martyrs being blessedly used as seed of Church.
2. *Departure* (v. 25)
   a. Barnabas and Saul had at same time completed their mission in Jerusalem;
   b. Taking John Mark with them, they now returned to Antioch, where great new ministry awaited them.

Conclusion

In this narrative are illustrated the three greatest powers in the universe:

1. *The Power of Satan*
   a. Mighty, causing trouble and suffering;
   b. But limited — not almighty — "thus far and no farther";
   c. Doomed — end and defeat certain;
   Therefore, we must trust, and wait, and watch, and work.
2. *The Power of God*
   a. In human extremity — never too late;
   b. In apparent impossibility — all appearances against deliverance;
   c. In complete victory — as in this case, Peter delivered, Herod destroyed, Church reassured, so now;
   Therefore, we must claim promise of Isa. 54:17: "No weapon that is formed against thee shall prosper."
3. *The Power of Prayer*
   a. Possessing God — because human will linked to His, His resources guaranteed;
   b. Overcoming Satan — because when united to God victory certain;
   c. Blessing man — because bringing —
      (1) As to Peter, quiet conscience, perfect security, patient hope;

(2) As to Church, comfort in trial, testing of character, confirmation of faith.

Therefore, we must use this power of prayer, in order to appropriate the power of God against the power of Satan and be victorious.

Study No. 58 — Peter Delivered from Prison (2)

ACTS 12:1-17

GOOD AND EVIL have always been in conflict. Every part of the Bible illustrates this fact, beginning with the scene in the Garden of Eden, where God said to the serpent: "I will put enmity between thee and the woman, and between thy seed and her seed" (Gen. 3:16). Yet there is a limit, and as to the sea, so to the power of evil, God has said: "Hitherto shalt thou come but no further" (Job 38:11). In this narrative we see how evil man brought the Church of Christ into —

I. Peril (vs. 1-5a)

1. *By murder of James* — first of Twelve to be martyred;
2. *By imprisonment of Peter* — through Herod's —
   a. Malignity — against "certain of the church" (v. 1);
   b. Servility — to please Jews (v. 3);
   c. Hypocrisy — pious regard for Passover (v. 4) while plotting evil against God's children;
   Illus.: Giving up smoking during Lent, then staying up till midnight Easter Even to enjoy first post-Lenten self-indulgence!

"But" (v. 5) pitched battle between Herod and Church, Satan and God, joined through —

II. Prayer (vs. 5b, 12)

1. *United* — "the church" (v. 5); "many" (v. 12);
2. *Unceasing* — "without ceasing" (K.J.V.);
3. *Earnest* — "earnestly" (A.S.V., from Gr. "to stretch out,"

implying intensity by which participants nerve themselves and then, as it were, stretch themselves to full length and strength in order to do their very utmost);

4. *Definite* — "unto God for him" (v. 5) — neither object nor subject in doubt;

   Cf. pattern in 6:4 — "we will give ourselves continually to prayer."

Then came answer, in —

III. Peace (v. 6)

Cf. Circumstances — place, time, conditions — with Peter's two other recorded sleeps (Luke 9:32; Mark 14:37; also see Study No. 60, p. 243); explanation lies in —

1. *Pardoned heart* — possession of God's love (cf. Psa. 27:2);
2. *Pure conscience* — knowledge of God's will (cf. 1 Tim. 3:9);
3. *Perfect trust* — assurance of God's might (cf. Eph. 1:19).

IV. Power (vs. 7-10)

1. *Extremity* — all appearances against deliverance, but God never too late;
2. *Ease* — angel overcame walls, chains, gates, men;
3. *Extent* — complete — all Peter could not do for himself.

V. Perception (vs. 11-17)

1. *Instant* — Peter had seen angel in prison and thought it was vision (cf. v. 9); but quickly realized truth, saying, "Now I know of a surety —" (v. 11), implying former hope and trust;
2. *Gradual* — Church members had heard about Peter at gate and thought it was angel (cf. v. 15); and were "astonished" (v. 16) because they expected less than complete answer to prayer;

   N.B. Psalmist says not only he will direct his prayer to God, but he "will look up" (Psa. 5:3) — i.e., in expectation of answer;

   Illus.: To prayer meeting for rain only one member brought umbrella!

Conclusion

1. *Power of Satan* — real, yet limited and not to be overrated;
2. *Peace of Believer* — deep, perfect, and may be practical reality today;
3. *Prayer of Church* — essential, earnest, and should be believing and prevailing;
4. *Power of God* — great, victorious, and our inner line of defense;
5. *Praise of All* — faithful and faithless — but whose will be the sweeter?

Study No. 59 — James, The Brother of John

ACTS 12:2

Translation into a foreign language is admittedly difficult, and sometimes impossible. Each language has its own genius and its own idiom, and the work of reproduction is often a serious problem. We are told, however, by those who are qualified in linguistics that the Bible is in some respects one of the easiest books to translate, because of the universality both of its appeal and its application.

There is another translation that is often difficult, but it is essential, a work of reproduction that is constantly taking place. This may be described as the translation of truth into life, of thought into experience, of ideals into reality, of knowledge into obedience, of principles into practice: after the teaching, daily life; after the mountain top, the valley; after an atmosphere of fellowship, the sphere of faithfulness, perhaps in the face of indifference and opposition. It may help us as Christians if we look at this work of translating ideals into reality as we find it exemplified in the life of one of our Lord's disciples. In the first recording of his name he is called "James the son of Zebedee," and in this, the last historical mention of him, he is referred to as "James the brother of John."

There were three methods by which our Lord exercised His earthly ministry: the miracles, the teaching, and the training of the Twelve Apostles. Of these, the third was obviously the most important, because the most permanent and far-reaching. The miracles might in time have been forgotten; the teaching, though its influence might have lasted longer, would not have had the effect that it had during the time of the Master's presence, were it not for the Apostles who, as the unique and qualified exponents of His Gospel, founded the Church. This, we know from St. Paul, was "built upon the foundation of the apostles and prophets, Jesus Christ Himself being the chief corner stone" (Eph. 2:20). Thus, everything that we can discover about one of these important men is worthy of our careful attention. Truth is hereby shown to be translated into life, and doctrine transfused into duty. In the case of James there were six stages:

I. Discipleship (John 1:35-42)

1. It is inferred that second of two disciples of the Baptist was John himself and that he, like Andrew, brought "his own brother," James, to Jesus;
2. Discipleship is undertaken through contact:
   a. Coming to Christ (vs. 37, 38);
   b. Abiding with Christ (vs. 39);
   N.B. Not mere knowledge, or reading, or opportunities for Christian fellowship, or privileges in connection with Church; all these count for nothing until and unless there is actual touch with Jesus Christ.

II. Service (Matt. 4:21, 22)

1. All four disciples had gone back to daily work and ordinary life, so this, after few months, was fresh call to special service, or ministry (v. 21);
2. Always second stage in disciple's career — many forms of service, but response to call should be both prompt and complete (v. 22);
   N.B. We are "saved to serve" — if new life does not express itself in service, in home, school, business, church, we shall have limited our experience of Christ.

III. Apostleship (Matt. 10:1, 2)

1. Further step called for by special circumstances — James, one of "his twelve disciples" (v. 1) becomes one of "the twelve apostles" (v. 2);
2. Looking towards future, e.g., founding of Church, meant special preparation of its nucleus;
3. The Seventy (cf. Luke 10:1-24) never heard of again — doubtless because mission temporary, to prepare way for Christ's last journey to Jerusalem; but Twelve intended to be permanent group of "ones sent forth" (cf. Heb. 3:1);
4. In one sense, no one else can be as they were (cf. Acts 1:8, 22, 25), but there is such thing as "apostolic succession" — succession of truth, of life, of ministry; and it is no mere play on words that such is best proved by apostolic success, now as then;

   N.B. We are each called to some special, it may be unique, service — something no other Christian, no other Church member can do for God.

IV. Disposition

1. James and his brother were descriptively surnamed "sons of thunder" (Mark 3:17); he was thus a man of burning zeal;
2. James was one who offered to "command fire to come down from heaven, and consume" foes (Luke 9:54-56); he was thus a man of impulsive indignation;
3. James was one who requested pre-eminence in kingdom and boasted of valor (cf. Matt. 20:20-23; Mark 10:35-40); he was thus a man of ignorant ambition;
4. So James was instance of Christ's use of unpromising material, after He has controlled, purified and guided it — like difference between stone unpolished and polished;

   N.B. According to average Christian experience, disposition, or temperament, often very last element of man affected by grace of God; but grace may and should have powerful influence over character — our temper, tendencies to sloth, selfishness, arrogance, etc. Our Christian walk should certainly not be intermittent, but continuous, enduring (cf. Matt. 24:13).

V. Training

1. Note six-fold work of Christ in James' life, by which he saw —
   a. Power of Christ — by miracle (Mark 5:37);
   b. Glory of Christ — by transfiguration (Matt. 17:1);
   c. Love of Christ — by forebearance (Luke 9:56);
   d. Spirit of Christ — by compassion and correction (Mark 10:35);
   e. Wisdom of Christ — by revelation of future (Mark 13:3ff);
   f. Sufferings of Christ — by witness of agony (Mark 14:33).
2. We may infer influence of Christ exerted on James' life, by inclusion in inner circle, included:
   a. Truth for his mind;
   b. Love for his heart;
   c. Law for his conscience;
   d. Grace for his soul;

      N.B. In a word, Christ stamped His image strongly upon this man, just as He did on more outstanding Peter and John.

VI. Revelation

1. Of the Risen Christ (1 Ior. 15:5; cf. Rev. 1:9-18)
   a. James obviously included among "the twelve," though we have no details about effect of resurrection on him; but he became conscious of the living Lord;
   b. We have same need today — revelation of resurrection for true perspective (cf. Rev. 1:18);

      N.B. Jesus does not re-enact His Passion; to announce at Good Friday service hymn like "Jesus Christ is Risen Today," would sound incongruous — yes, but it is true, for — After Easter, always Easter!
2. Of the Holy Spirit (Acts 1:13, 14; 2:1-4)

a. James in Upper Room with others, in prayer and expectation (cf. 1:13, 14);
b. With them was equipped by the Spirit on Day of Pentecost (cf. 2:1-4);
c. Thus we see everything else in discipleship and training intended to lead up to gift of Holy Spirit, whose presence in life and service is heart of Christian Gospel (cf. Gal. 3:14).

VII. Culmination (Acts 12:2)

1. Martyrdom — "killed . . . with the sword" — "cup" and "baptism" (Mark 10:38, 39) experienced by one brother in one short, swift act; by other brother, in long life of consecrated service.
2. Testimony — "slain with the sword" (Heb. 11:37), "slain for the Word of God" (Rev. 6:9) — was quiet, steady work of Spirit on James' life fruitless? No, everything found flowering in final witness for Christ (cf. Phil. 1:20, 21);
   Illus.: James like "century plant" which grows for many years before it suddenly buds and blossoms most marvellously.

Conclusion

1. *The Call of Divine Grace*
   To —
   a. Salvation;
   b. Sanctification;
   c. Service;
   d. Suffering.
   These experiences true of James and ought to be true of every one of us.
2. *The Course of Divine Grace*
   By —
   a. Testing of temperament;
   b. Training of character;
   c. Transforming of personality.
   These intended to result in us too.

3. *The Crown of Divine Grace*

Is —

a. Faithfulness to Christ in service;

b. Fellowship with Christ in suffering;

c. Fulness of Christ in glory.

These to be the goals of our Christian lives.

Thus we go on, not knowing what will befall us, but knowing Christ. We have only to yield, to trust, to obey, and then His truth will illuminate us, His grace will work in us, His presence will comfort us, His love will inspire us, His coming will incite us, and His glory will crown our days. Whether in life or in death, whether in suffering or in service, to use Dante's fine phrase, "in His will is our peace." This is the supreme requirement, the one thing needful. Paul's way of expressing the same ideal is "to me to live is Christ" (Phil. 1:21) — receiving everything from Him, seeing everything in Him, doing everything for Him; Christ at all times, Christ in all circumstances, Christ at all costs, Christ for all our actualities, and Christ for all our possibilities. We go our way individually, it may be solitarily, but wherever we go, whatever we do, and whenever God may call us Home, His grace will be sufficient for us, since He is able to meet our every need, from this time forth, and even for evermore.

Study No. 60 — Peter's Three Sleeps

ACTS 12:6

Much of Christ's ministry as recorded in the Gospels had to do with the training of the Twelve Apostles. Of these dozen men, three, Peter, James, and John, were admitted to special intimacy and were often dealt with by their Master as though members of a separate, advanced class. Of this small group of three, Peter was the most prominent, not so much for merit as for the faults that too often accompany it; and in Peter's life story we have the record of three times when he was off guard, relaxed, asleep. On each occasion there was something that he did not know.

I. The Sleep of Unripe Experience (Luke 9:32)

1. Peter had recently made his great confession (vs. 20,28), with deep conviction as to Christ's Person and character;
2. In Transfiguration (vs. 27-36) Christ doubtless intended to reveal much more of Himself and His program; but Peter and companions were too sleepy;
3. What they must have missed! Saw some of His glory (v.32), but heard nothing about His "exodus" (v. 31, Gr.); N.B. So no wonder it is written of Peter, after his impulsive speech, made on awakening, "not knowing what he said" (v. 33)!

II. The Sleep of Unfaithful Life (Mark 14:37)

1. Peter was what we might call converted; he had just been warned of weakness (v. 30); and he had made two vigorous protestations of strength (vs. 29, 31);
2. His Master had great need of loyal support — yet he slept;
3. What he missed through unfaithfulness! What joy to Christ had Peter, whom He especially addresses (v. 37),

been able to "watch one hour"! And what strength against his own temptation had he both watched and prayed (cf. v. 38)!

N.B. So no wonder it is written of Peter, as well as of other two favored disciples, "neither wist they what to answer Him" (v. 40)!

III. The Sleep of Unquestioning Trust (Acts 12:6)

This was different kind of slumber:

1. In the presence of danger — perfect calm;
2. In the eyes of God — pardoned heart;
3. In the consciousness of duty done — pure conscience;

N.B. So no wonder it is written of Peter, "he . . . wist not that it was true which was done by the angel; but thought he saw a vision" (v. 9) — i.e., so yielded to will of God was he since Pentecost that he could mistake reality of deliverance and not be disturbed! (Cf. 4:19, 20; Phil. 1:20, 21; 2 Tim. 2:11; 4:6; 1 Pet. 1:6, 7; 3:14; 4:19).

Conclusion

These episodes when Peter lacked knowledge teach us —

1. *God's Constant Purposes*
   a. Of using daily experience for training;
   b. Of showing glory of Christian life in every circumstance.
2. *God's Simple Conditions*
   a. That we open our spiritual eyes to see, instead of closing them in sleep;
   b. That we be faithful to present light even as we look towards that which belongs to perfect day. "Whereupon," let us say with St. Paul (26:19), "I was not disobedient unto the heavenly vision."

Study No. 61 —

The Commencement of Foreign Missions

ACTS 13:1-52

PAUL'S TITLE "Apostle of the Gentiles" (Rom. 11:13) has been well rendered "Missionary to the Nations." Here is a new departure, the first foreign missionary journey, from a new center — not Jerusalem, but Antioch, center of Gentile Christianity. In some respects the journey is a model for all similar service, for the emphasis in this chapter is on the Holy Spirit of God. We note that the Apostles were, in verses 1-3, separated for Him; in verses 4, 5, sent by Him, and, in verses 6-52, strengthened in Him for every step of the way.

I. The Missionary Call (vs. 1-4a)

1. *The Varied Gifts* (v. 1) — in position and capacity:
   a. Teachers at Antioch were all Hellenic or Greek-speaking Jews, unless, as some think, "Simeon that was called Niger" was African;

   b. "Manaen the foster-brother of Herod the tetrarch" (A.S.V.) means friend, comrade, "milk-brother" of Herod Antipas (cf. Luke 13:31, 32);

   c. Barnabas mentioned first, Saul last at this stage (cf. vs. 1, 2 with vs. 13, 43, 46, 50, etc.);
   N.B. A. B. Simpson said: "What a wonderful galaxy of strangely different types of character so blended as to represent humanity and catholicity in its largest circumference! God wants these elements in the Church. . . . He wants us all to be one in the blending of our gifts and temperaments under the fusing power of the blessed Holy Ghost."

2. *The Daily Life* (v. 2a) — of Church leaders one of —
   a. Service — "while they ministered . . . the Holy Spirit said —" (Gr.) — doing duty of moment leads to opportunity for fuller revelation;
   b. Self-denial — "and fasted" — doubtless included much time spent in prayer — attitude that has been called "marching on one's knees."
3. *The Divine Commission* (v. 2b)
   a. How? By separation to Holy Spirit;
   b. Whom? Barnabas and Saul, founders of churches;
   c. Whither? For special work to which they had already been designated — "I have called them" (cf. v. 47; 22:21);
   N.B. Barnabas and Saul doubtless knew this already — waiting only to be separated and sent.
4. *The Human Attestation* (v. 3)
   a. Perception — by being spiritually alive;
   b. Intercession — by fasting and prayer;
   c. Consecration — by laying on of hands;
   d. Commendation — by loving dismissal;
   e. Recognition — by retaining responsibility (cf. 14:26-27).
5. *The Divine Authorization* (v. 4a)
   a. By authority of the Holy Ghost;
   b. With ability given by Him.
6. *Complete Obedience* (v. 4b)
   a. Intelligent — with definite destination, perhaps already planned;
   b. Immediate — with hearty co-operation and no hesitation.

II. The Missionary Work (vs. 4c-13)

1. *Evangelization* (vs. 4c-6)
   a. Scene of first effort Cyprus, home of Barnabas — using natural contacts;
   b. Subjects of first effort Jews (cf. Rom. 1:16) — then "through the isle" (v. 6) to Paphos, where they found Jewish influence on Gentile.

2. *Inquiry* (v. 7)
   a. First inquirer Roman, Sergius Paulus;
   b. His position important — that of proconsul or deputy;
   c. His character "prudent" — "man of understanding" (A.S.V.).

3. *Opposition* (vs. 6, 8)
   a. The man — Elymas, or Bar-jesus, the sorcerer — Jew and false prophet;
   b. The action — "seeking to turn away . . . from the faith" — strong Greek word meaning to turn thoroughly, diversely;
   c. The contrast — Satan's influence real — "When you open heaven, you also open hell."

4. *Judgment* (vs. 9-11)
   a. Keen insight of Paul (who now comes to fore) — here, into Jewish sin — cf. 14:9, into Gentile need;
   b. Solemn rebuke by Paul — "thou son of the devil" (A.S.V.); contrast —
      (1) Paul "filled with the Holy Ghost" (v. 9); and —
      (2) Elymas "full of all subtility and all mischief" (v. 10);
   c. Heavy punishment through Paul — temporary blindness; contrast —
      (1) "Seeking to turn away the deputy from the faith" (v. 8); and —
      (2) "Seeking some to lead him by the hand" (v. 11); N.B. Cf. difference between treatment of Elymas and of Simon Magus (8:9-24); see Study No. 35, p. 144).

5. *Conversion* (v. 12)
   a. Strong impression made on deputy;
   b. His acceptance of new faith immediate and complete.

6. *Disappointment* (v. 13)
   a. Defection of John Mark, "their attendant" (v. 5, A.S.V.), must have been blow to others;

b. Due either to fickleness, narrowness, or fear of unknown Gentile territory (cf. 15:37-40).

7. *Satisfaction* (vs. 2, 4, 9)
   a. Spirit-separated (v. 2);
   b. Spirit-sent (v. 4);
   c. Spirit-saturated (v. 9).
   N.B. Change of Apostle's name from Saul to Paul: perhaps because of conversion (as converts from heathenism today), or because of humility ("*paulos*" Gr. for "little," rather than grander title of Saul, Israel's first king, which means "desired"), or even in relation to Sergius Paulus (lit., Little Sergius) Apostle is said here to be also called "Paulus," "little"; but, best, because chief work from now on was to be among Gentiles and Greek name more appropriate and convenient.

III. The Missionary Message (vs. 14-41)

1. *Scene* — Antioch in Pisidia (v. 14), great trade center of Asia Minor, to be carefully distinguished from Antioch in Syria (v. 1), from which they had started (v. 4).

2. *Subject* — this first missionary sermon addressed to Jews, delivered in synagogue, and appropriate to circumstances:
   a. Reviews Jewish history leading up to David (vs. 16-22);
   b. Shows Jesus was of David's seed (vs. 23-25);
   c. Declares message of salvation based on resurrection (vs. 26-37);
   d. Offers Gospel and warns hearers of consequences of rejection (vs. 38-41).

IV. The Missionary Results (vs. 42-52)

1. *Hearty Acceptance* (vs. 42, 44, 48, 49) by Gentiles, who rejoiced to —
   a. Hear more;
   b. Learn that God's purposes extended to them;
   c. Glorify His Word;
   d. Believe on Christ;
   e. Pass on good news.

2. *Intense Opposition* (vs. 45-47, 50) by Jews who, though solemly warned, countered with —
   a. Envy of Gentiles;
   b. Opposition of Paul's message;
   c. Contradiction of God's truth;
   d. Blasphemy of God's Name;
   e. Persecution of God's messengers.
3. *Great Opportunity* (vs. 46-48, 51, 52)
   a. For Gentiles, to whom Apostles now definitely turned (vs. 46-48, 51);
   b. For Gospel message, which even bitterness of Jews could not seriously injure (v. 49);
   c. For Gospel messengers, resulting in fresh fillings "with joy, and with the Holy Ghost," (v. 52).

Conclusion

1. *The Demands of Missionary Work*
   a. Best talent — two men most useful at home;
   b. Divine call — after years of preparation;
   c. Full consecration — separated, or no use;
   d. Christian sympathy — support of home church;
   e. True living — faith, faithfulness, courage;
   f. Divine power — motivation of the Holy Spirit.
2. *The Difficulties of Missionary Work*
   a. Home ties, hard to break;
   b. Journeying perils, by sea and land;
   c. Satanic influence, to be broken;
   d. Human opposition, to be overcome;
   e. Varying experiences, no two alike;
   f. Fickle friends, as well as fearful foes.
3. *The Delights of Missionary Work*
   a. Divine leadings;
   b. Grand opportunities;
   c. Real interest;
   d. Necessary power;
   e. Divine blessing;
   f. Full compensation.

   N.B. He who sends forth (v. 4) fills full (vs. 9, 52).

Study No. 62 — Two Questions about Missions

ACTS 13:2-4,9-11, 47

IN THIS BOOK of Acts, the inspired record of development in the Divine purpose, early Christianity is seen to be truly "A Tale of Two Cities," Jerusalem and Antioch. The former may be said to represent the Church at home, or Home Missions, and the latter the Church abroad, or Foreign Missions, the extension of the Gospel ministry to the ends of the earth. These verses lead us to ask —

I. What Does God Think of Missions?

1. *He chooses ablest workers for them;*
   a. Cf. Barnabas and Saul as founders and leaders as well as preachers;
   b. Both surely indispensable in home church — but no.
2. *He takes chosen workers from important work:*
   a. Antioch capital of Syria — population half million — great center of Roman, Greek, and Jewish life;
   b. Yet Barnabas and Saul appointed to unknown field;
   c. We often plead "heathen at home"; but is imperfection of church argument for neglecting lost outside?
   d. Rather, let best workers go, giving others opportunities for service in home field to which God will call them.
3. *He qualifies workers for missions:*
   a. He calls (v. 2)
      (1) When? While ministering to Him at home;
      (2) How? By direct choice and separation;
   b. He commissions (vs. 3, 4)
      (1) By the Holy Spirit;
      (2) Through Church fellowship;
   c. He controls (vs. 9-11)
      (1) Granting perception;
      (2) Giving boldness.

But we must also inquire —

II. What Do You Think of Missions?

What part should they play in Christian life?

1. *There should be a sense of compulsion*:
   a. Cf. Gr. of Luke 24:44-48: "must . . . behooved";
   b. Said not only of suffering, death, and resurrection of Christ, but of "repentance and remission of sins" being "preached in His Name among all nations" (v. 47).
2. *There should be a width of vision*:
   a. Best to climb high and gain wide view of landscape;
   b. Missions supply this to Church and individual member — or else danger of routine.
3. *There should be a devotion to others*:
   a. In secular life, some men give themselves to work; others expect work given to them;
   Illus.: Physician who makes medicine his servant for own purposes, or is himself servant of medicine, and of patients;
   b. So work of God should be end and not means.
4. *There should be a largeness of spiritual life*:
   a. Interest in missions brings unselfishness;
   b. Without it as apex, church life imperfectly built.

Conclusion

How shall I participate in missionary work?

1. Read about it;
2. Pray for it;
3. Give to it;
4. Go into it;
5. Help others go into it;
6. Encourage my children to go into it, even pray them into it.

Give of thy sons to bear the message glorious;
Give of thy wealth to speed them on their way;
Pour out thy soul for them in prayer victorious;
And all thou spendest Jesus will repay.
Publish glad tidings, tidings of peace;
Tidings of Jesus, redemption and release.

—Mary A. Thomson

Study No. 63 — The Keynote of Missionary Work

ACTS 13:2, 3, 4, 9

In this account of the beginning of foreign missions are to be found the germs of a number of principles and methods, especially in regard to the function of the Holy Spirit in missionary work. He is the supreme fact and factor in all Christian ministry, and without Him our orthodoxy, our churchmanship, our talents are worthless.

I. The Call (v. 2)

1. *What it was*:
   a. To Divinely appointed work — "the work whereunto I have called them" (cf. 2 Tim. 1:11);
   b. To Divinely possessed workers — "separate now (Gr.) to Me" (cf. 1 Tim. 2:7).
2. *When it came*:
   a. At time when Church in top spiritual condition;
   b. When workers engaged in service ("ministered to the Lord") and in fasting.
3. *How it came*:
   a. In accordance with Divine prophecy (cf. 9:15, 16);
   b. First, by detachment — from Antioch ministry; then, by attachment — to foreign missionary endeavor.

II. The Commission (vs. 3, 4)

1. *By the Church*:
   a. Sanction — "fasted . . . prayed . . . laid hands" (v. 3);
   b. Sympathy — close connection, if not control (cf. 14:28, Gr.);
   N.B. Not like certain workers nowadays independent of Church, with no responsibility, or continuity, or authority.

2. *By the Holy Spirit*:

   a. Authority not only human, but Divine — "sent forth by the Holy Ghost" (v. 4);

   b. Armed with His power (cf. vs. 9-11), and His joy (cf. v. 52).

III. The Equipment (v. 9)

"Filled with the Holy Ghost" for —

1. *Insight*:

   a. Cf. "set his eyes on him" with "stedfastly beholding him, and perceiving" (14:9) — enabled both to detect him and to recognize need;

   b. Intimate knowledge necessary for Jewish work (chap. 13) and for Gentile work (chap. 14) alike.

2. *Instruction*:

   To fulfill Christ's promise: "The Spirit of truth . . . will guide you into all truth" (John 16:13). Note the means:

   a. "The Word of God" (vs. 5:7, 44, 46);

   b. "The Word of this salvation" (v. 26);

   c. "The Word of His grace" (14:3; see also 20:32);

   d. "The Word of the Lord" (v. 49).

3. *Influence*:

   a. Utterance

      (1) Cleansing (cf. Isa. 6:6, 7);

      (2) Liberty (cf. 2:4; Col. 4:3);

      (3) Courage (cf. Eph. 6:19);

      (4) Joy (cf. 1 Thess. 1:6);

   b. Power

      Expressed by two Gr. words in N.T. (cf. both in Luke 4:36):

      (1) *Dunamis* — strength (cf. our word dynamite);

      (2) *Exousia* — authority (lit., from, deriving from, property);

      Christian missionary results come from this twofold force;

c. Holiness
   How obtained and maintained? By —
   (1) Prayer (cf. 1 Pet. 2:5);
   (2) Word of God (cf. Eph. 4:21-24);
   (3) Trust (cf. Rom. 12:1);
   (4) Obedience (cf. Rom. 6:19-22).

Conclusion

"I believe in the Holy Ghost," we say in the Apostles' Creed:

1. *For the past* — "having been filled (Gr.) with the Holy Ghost" (cf. 4:8);
2. *For the present* — "full of the Holy Ghost" (cf. 6:3, 5);
3. *For the future* — "kept on being filled (Gr.) . . . with the Holy Ghost" (cf. 13:52).

Yes, He calls, He commissions, He equips — all three; and these are never separated. If He calls, He commissions; and if He commissions, He equips. Has He called, commissioned, equipped you?

Study No. 64 — A Model of Christian Preaching

ACTS 13:16-43

WHAT SHOULD Christian preaching be like? What should it always include? Here, in the first of St. Paul's recorded addresses, which was also the first foreign missionary sermon ever delivered, we have a model to follow.

I. The Basis of Christian Preaching (vs. 16-23)

This was here, and always should be, Holy Scripture — "the ministry of the Word" (6:4):

1. *Knowledge of its Contents* — e.g., here:
   a. History of Israel in Egypt and Canaan;
   b. Facts about Samuel, Saul, and David.
2. *Recognition of its Author*:
   a. God's Person — permeating it, and supplying unity and cohesion;

b. God's Workings — leading up to Christ's coming.

II. The Theme of Christian Preaching (vs. 23-37)

This was here, and always should be, the Person and Work of our Lord — not only what, but who (cf. Col. 1:27);

1. *His Person*:
   - a. As Saviour (cf. 17:13; 1 Cor. 2:2);
   - b. As Lord (cf. 2:36; 2 Cor. 4:5);

     N.B. All doctrines and duties mentioned while preaching must be linked to Him, for truth lies in Him and is therefore living; so throughout Acts (cf. 5:42; 8:5, 35; 9:20, etc.).

2. *His Work*:

   Based on His Person, it includes:
   - a. His Life (vs. 23-26) — "John," adducing strong contemporary witness;
   - b. His Death (vs. 27-29) — "they," identifying wilfully ignorant agents of sin;
   - c. His Resurrection (vs. 30-37):
     - (1) The significance — "God," indicating vindication of Christ's work (v. 30);
     - (2) The evidence — "we" producing eyewitnesses (vs. 31, 32);
     - (3) The fulfilment — "written," marshalling Scripture prophecy (vs. 33-37);

       N.B. Announcement of these "glad tidings" (v. 32) should never be omitted, for offer is "to you" (v.26), "unto us" (v. 33).

III. The Application of Christian Preaching (vs. 38-41)

Based on offer of Christ's Person and Work to man, it should include:

1. *Blessings of faith* (vs. 38, 39)
   - a. Forgiveness — sin pardoned (v. 38) — never before defined, only typified by sending away scapegoat (cf. Lev. 16:10);

b. Righteousness — sinner justified (v. 39) — completely, as neither law of Moses nor works of man could ever do; N.B. This Paul's first teaching of great doctrine of justification by faith: cf. Rom. 5:1, where it is joined to peace; Gal. 5:6, where faith, works, and love are joined, or, root, fruit, spirit.

2. *Warnings of unbelief* (vs. 40, 41)
   a. "Beware!" (v. 40) — of dire consequences foretold by prophets;
   b. "Behold!" (v. 41) — "work" of God, which He will "work" in spite of despising and disbelieving man (cf. Hab. 1:5; also Isa. 43:13);
   N.B. Condition of receipt of blessing and avoidance of judgment always faith, belief, trust. We need faith even to eat in this life; much more, to get to heaven in the next!

IV. The Consequences of Christian Preaching (vs. 42, 43)

These should be as outlined here:

1. Some hearers, like Jews, depart, because message is so strong as to be unacceptable to them;
2. Others, like Gentiles, remain, beseeching more teaching because their hearts have been touched by Gospel; and —
3. Preacher, like Apostles, persuades individuals that they "continue in the grace of God," i.e., stay where they are, within sound of Gospel, retaining what they have learned.

Conclusion

People are still saying to the Christian preacher: "Sir, we would see Jesus."

Oh, that all preaching might indeed exemplify —

1. A Divine Theme;
2. A Redemptive Character;
3. An Individual Appeal;
4. A Definite Offer;
5. A Solemn Alternative;
6. A Simple Secret.

Said Ian Maclaren: "Every sentence should suggest Christ, and every sermon . . . should leave the hearers at the feet of Christ. The chief effort of every sermon should be to unveil Christ, and the chief art of all preaching is to exalt Christ."

Study No. 65 —

"The Word of This Salvation" (A Fragment)

ACTS 13:26

SALVATION IS —

1. *Personal*
   "To you is the word" — as telegram to addressee, as diagnosis to patient;
2. *Powerful*
   Christ saves from penalty, power, and presence of sin — able to deal with man's past, present, and future;
3. *Peaceful*
   After war with sin comes peace with God;
4. *Precious*
   Results may be tested by various circumstances, e.g., youth, old age, sorrow, poverty, and found to wear well.
5. *Perfect*
   No want unsatisfied: pardon, life, peace, liberty, healing, cleansing, refreshment, comfort, strength;
6. *Present*
   "Is sent" — now! God's grace, "unmerited favor," brings instant hope, but also great responsibility, since time is short.

Conclusion

How shall this "word" be treated?

1. There may be refusal;
2. There may be delay in reception;

3. There may be pretence; or —
4. There may be instant and sincere acceptance of "so great salvation" (Heb. 2:3) and, with this —
5. There should be complete surrender to "the Author of eternal salvation" (Heb. 5:9).

Study No. 66 —

Paul's Witness to the Resurrection (1)*

ACTS 13:30

LET US IMAGINE a minister of the Gospel calling on an old Christian of no intellectual attainments or education, to put before him the usual arguments for the Resurrection of Christ: the evidence of the Gospels, the evidence of the Church, etc. To this reasoned discourse the old man might well reply: "I cannot understand your arguments, sir, but I know Christ is alive; I know it by what He has done for me."

Someone else could bear a similar testimony to complete change in and new direction for his life — St. Paul, the great Apostle to the Gentiles. Here he makes a simple, definite statement: "But God raised Him from the dead." Let us turn to Paul for his personal witness to the Resurrection. We see him, first, as —

I. The Persecutor

Paul was man of —

1. *Powerful intellect*:
   a. Had training of thinker;
   b. Home was Jerusalem, center of Judaism;
   c. Was member of Sanhedrin.
2. *Strong feeling*:

* For another treatment of general subject see Study No. 107, p. 426, and for more complete treatment of this one, see author's *Christianity Is Christ*, chap. 11 (Wm. B. Eerdmans Publishing Co., 1955).

a. Influenced by intellect; when man's intellect feeble, feelings feeble, and, as in Paul's case, strength of mind makes for strength of feeling;
b. His feelings gave him force and purpose, emphasizing words, resolutions, actions.

3. *Intense conscientiousness*:
   a. Training as Jew made his conscience sensitive to light he had;
   b. Learned to hate Christ and Christianity as foes of Judaism, in Jerusalem and even to Damascus.

4. *Determined will*:
   a. Combination like foregoing — strength of intellect, feeling and conscience — bound to influence will;
   b. Note strong wording: "punished . . . compelled . . . exceedingly mad . . . persecuted" (26:11); "breathing out threatenings and slaughter" (9:1); "made havoc . . . dragging (Gr.) men and women . . . to prison" (8:3).

But, suddenly, Paul is seen as —

II. The Believer

1. *He is convicted of error* — in spite of his past and his worldly interests.
2. *He undergoes complete change of life and purpose* — preaching instead of persecuting.
3. *His conversion still insoluble problem to world* — as F. C. Baur admitted, no psychological or dialectical analysis sufficient to explain mystery of act by which God revealed His Son to Paul.

And, finally, we see him as —

III. The Apostle

1. *New life begun* — conversion but commencement of Christian experience — after 25 years in entirely different direction, and with seemingly everything to lose and nothing to gain.
2. *New life tested* — as Paul himself recounts (cf. 2 Cor. 4:8-18; 11:23-33).

3. *New life permanent* — amid praying, laboring, suffering for his converts, he experienced perfect satisfaction (cf. 2 Cor. 1:5-7).
4. *New life vigorous* — he was strong personality, yet self-confessed echo of Christ (cf. Gal. 3:20).

Conclusion

1. *If Paul's testimony is true, his conversion was real.* He bears three marks of good witness:
   a. Intelligence;
   b. Candor;
   c. Disinterestedness.
2. *If Paul's conversion was real, Christ arose from the dead;*
   a. Conversion made entire change in life — old gone, new had come;
   b. Conversion brought consciousness of forgiveness, clarified vision, joy of salvation;
   c. Conversion gave new direction to life — present and future changed as well as past, pointing to new powers, principles, prospects.

   Is all this possible from one who is dead? No, —
3. *Paul's experience claims Resurrection of Christ as fact;* it produced in him not only personal change, but —
   a. That system of thought he calls "my Gospel" (Rom. 2:16) — set forth in Christianity of Epistles, and still subject of study and object of respect;
   b. That influence on the world which is so well known and so valued today.
4. *We can verify all this for ourselves in same way as St. Paul;*
   a. By surrender to Christ;
   b. By service for Christ;

   And then we "may know Him, and the power of His resurrection" (Phil. 3:10).

Study No. 67 — The Sequel to a Sermon

ACTS 13:42-52

In verses 16-41 of this chapter we have the record of the first foreign missionary sermon; now we see the results of it. The account of them is of great value, a source of both guidance and inspiration to us today.

I. Great Encouragement (vs. 42-44)

1. *Real Interest* (v. 42)
   a. Impression made on congregation;
   b. Desire for more next time on part of Gentiles.
2. *Remarkable Earnestness* (v. 43)
   a. Persistence — "followed";
   b. Continuance — "continue in the grace of God," i.e., conversion evident.
3. *Increasing Readiness* (v. 44)
   a. General — "almost the whole city";
   b. Specific — "the next sabbath day came . . . to hear the Word of God."

II. Bitter Opposition (vs. 45-47)

1. *Intense Hostility* (v. 45)
   a. Cause — "envy";
   b. Character — "contradicting and blaspheming";
   N.B. Attitude of wilful blasphemy and deliberate rejection of known truth is essential nature of "unpardonable sin" (cf. Mark 3:29, 30).
2. *Increased Power* (v. 46)
   a. Boldness — "waxed bold";
   b. Plainness — "we turn to the Gentiles";
   N.B. It often takes opposition to bring out firmness of resolve in doing of God's will.

3. *Impressive Testimony* (v. 47)
   a. To purpose of the Lord — "I have set thee for a light of the Gentiles";
   b. To reason for His action — "for salvation unto the ends of the earth" (cf. 9:15; Isa. 42:6);
   N.B. Missionary to Manchuria told of seeing displayed ambitious slogan of Standard Oil depot there: "Get the Light into Every Dark Corner of the World"! Multitudes of towns and villages lighted with kerosene oil of West, but we have been slower to bring them light of Gospel.

III. **Wider Opportunity** (vs. 48, 49)

1. *Acceptance* (vs. 48, 49)
   a. "Word of the Lord" glorified by Gentiles (v. 48);
   b. "Word of the Lord" extended among Gentiles (v. 49);
   N.B. Cf. v. 48 with v. 46 for two aspects of doctrine of foreordination to eternal life, Divine and human. Bible emphasizes both but never attempts to reconcile them, because when kept closely associated and duly emphazised, no practical difficulty.
2. *Persecution* (vs. 50, 51)
   a. "Raised" (v. 50) — even among "devout," "honorable," "chief" people;
   b. Repudiated (v. 51) — in manner commanded by Master (cf. Matt. 10:14, 15; Luke 10:10-12);
   N.B. Sad that thus early in foreign missions history His servants obliged to carry out this direction.
3. *Blessedness* (v. 52)
   a. Its nature — "filled with joy";
   b. Its secret — "filled . . . with the Holy Ghost" — He remained with disciples though teachers gone.

Conclusion

1. *Variety of Results*
   a. Receptiveness and success (vs. 42-44, 48, 49);
   b. Opposition and persecution (vs. 45, 50);
   c. Interruption and incompleteness (v. 51).

2. *Causes of Variety*
   a. Openmindedness (vs. 42-44); prejudice (v. 45);
   b. Belief (v. 48); repudiation (v. 46);
   c. Contentment (v. 52); contention (v. 50).
3. *Contrasts of Action*
   a. In acceptance, exhortation (v. 43);
   b. In opposition, boldness (v. 46);
   c. In rejection, warning (v. 46);
   d. In persecution, withdrawal to continue elsewhere, not to give up.

Therefore, now as then, Christian workers, home or foreign, must —

1. Trust on!
2. Speak on!
3. Work on!

"Be ye steadfast, unmoveable, always abounding in the work of the Lord, forasmuch as ye know that your labor is not in vain in the Lord" (1 Cor. 15:58).

Study No. 68 — Eternal Life (A Fragment)

ACTS 13:48

CHRISTIAN HISTORY and present-day experience demonstrate the miracle wrought in the lives of "twice-born men." It is indeed the miracle of eternal life.

I. Christ Brings Believers out of Death into Life

1. Eternal life is not mere endless existence; its chief characteristic is —
   a. Not its quantity, but its quality;
   b. Not its duration, but its character.
2. Eternal life is entirely different from natural life, "dead in trespasses and sins" (Eph. 2:1).

II. Christ Brings Believers into a Life that is His own Life

1. Eternal life is the life of Christ — "he that hath the Son

hath life; and he that hath not the Son of God hath not life" (1 John 5:12).

2. Eternal life is a new life — "all things are become new" (2 Cor. 5:17).
3. Eternal life has changed bondage to freedom — "Christ hath made us free" (Gal. 5:1).

III. Christ Brings Believers into a Life of Supernatural Power

1. Eternal life is a "walk" in which "the righteousness of the law might be fulfilled in us" (Rom. 8:4).
2. Eternal life is for "the servants of Christ, doing the will of God from the heart" (Eph. 6:6).

Conclusion

Only Christ can accomplish this in the life of a redeemed sinner. Have you "passed from death unto life" (1 John 3:14)?

Study No. 69 — "Joy and . . . the Holy Ghost"*

ACTS 13:52

If one should ask what one thing characterized the Christians of the New Testament, the answer would be, their joy. Is this true of Christians today? Is joy one of the marks distinguishing them from the people of the world?

It may be argued that life is different now; but is it any less bright or easy? Is it not rather, in many ways, more so? The abolition of slavery from so much of the world is only one example of the amelioration of conditions in the old order which were not conducive to joy. The very presence of Christianity and its undeniable influence on life is, of course, the most striking instance of this. The fact is that joy is like the peace of God — the world can neither give it nor take it away; and it comes to the heart of the believer as one of the most precious parts of "the fruit of the Spirit" (Gal. 5:22).

---

* Adapted from *Sermon Outlines,* p. 107 (Wm. B. Eerdmans Publishing Co.)

I. **Joy — What It means**

1. *Joy is condition,* state of soul due to being right with God.
2. *Joy is not happiness:*
   a. Happiness is dependent on happy circumstances, on what happens; joy is independent of these;
   b. Happiness is affected by what one has; joy by what one is;
   c. Happiness comes from experience of good as distinct from evil; joy from experience of God apart from good or evil;
   d. Happiness comes through things outside which stir feelings within; joy leaps within, from God in the heart and soul;
   Illus.: Happiness like changing surface of ocean; joy like ocean bed, untouched by change of wind or atmosphere.
3. *Joy has three elements:*
   a. Retrospection on revelation — faith, because of past;
   b. Aspiration after realization — love, in present;
   c. Preparation in anticipation — hope, for future.

II. **Joy — For Whom It is**

For "the disciples" —

1. *Those who belong to Christ* — not the world;
2. *All those who belong to Christ* — not favored few only, but all "called to be saints" (Rom. 1:7).

III. **Joy — What It Does**

1. *It fortifies* — mind with truth and will with grace (cf. Neh. 8:10);
2. *It satisfies* — soul with fellowship and heart with love (cf. Psa. 16:11);
   N.B. Ethiopian eunuch (8:26-40) "went on his way rejoicing" even though but a new convert with scanty knowledge, bereft of teacher, absolutely alone; so also here, new converts in Pisidian Antioch (cf. v. 48), whose evangelists had departed (cf. vs. 50, 51).

IV. Joy — How It Comes

1. *With "the Holy Ghost"* — incoming, indwelling, upon conversion;
2. *By being "filled with the Holy Ghost"* (v. 9) — God's Holy Spirit entering the yielded life, empty of self and of world, and bringing the "joy of the Lord" (Neh. 8:10), the "joy of salvation" (Psa. 51:12).

Conclusion

Some of us have fallen away from the New Testament ideal of the joyous Christian life, and we need to return to it. How are we to do this?

1. Admit the Holy Spirit to the heart;
2. Permit Him to reveal Christ to the soul;
3. Commit to Him the life; and then —
4. Transmit the resultant joy to others.

Study No. 70 — "The Smile that Won't Come Off"

ACTS 13:52

IN LONDON, years ago, some large pictures of cheerful faces appeared in the advertising of a certain food product, and with them the caption, "The Smile That Won't Come Off." The faces belonged to those in various occupations who were supposed to have enjoyed eating the particular food so much that it caused a perpetual smile. The words of the advertisement set one to wondering whether it was possible for man to have that which is indicated by a perpetual smile, namely, inward satisfaction expressing itself in the features of the face; and then one was reminded of certain words from an Old Book which are said to have been written in order that "joy may be full" (1 John 1:4). Quite unconsciously, but very really, the advertisement was bearing witness to one of God's purposes for human life, viz., that it should be full of joy, of peace, and of deep satisfaction, and that it should show this happy condition in face and manner on every possible occasion.

What is a smile? It is surely the expression of a combination of certain physical, mental, and emotional elements in human life, and perhaps may be described as the outward and visible sign of an inward and emotional content and enjoyment.

I. There are some smiles that will "come off."

1. Smile of drunkard, little better than idiotic leer, will assuredly "come off," for no "drunkards . . . shall inherit the kingdom of God" (1 Cor. 6:10);
2. Smile of impure and sensual man will undoubtedly "come off," for "there shall in no wise enter into" the city of God "anything that defileth" (Rev. 21:27);
3. Smile of dishonest man and gambler will also "come off," for "the kingdom of God is . . . righteousness" (Rom. 14:17);
4. Smile of proud, self-satisfied man, with supreme contempt for others, will also "come off," since gateway to heaven is low, and only humble-minded and true-hearted can stoop to enter (cf. Matt. 19:23, 24).

Indeed, we may be sure that every smile that results from gratification obtained through sin will assuredly "come off," because sin does not satisfy eternal needs of life: "Whosoever drinketh of this water shall thirst again" (John 4:13).

II. There are some smiles that last for a very long time.

1. Smile of total abstainer takes long time to "come off," for his head is clearer, his body healthier, his eyes brighter, his step lighter, his pocket heavier, his soul safer, by avoidance of alcohol;
2. Smile of pure and right-living man will also stay on longer than that of man who abuses his body or mind;
3. Smile of honest man also lasts long time, for when he pays his way, supports his family, never gets into debt, and is able to look whole world in face, he has perfect right to smile of contentment and satisfaction, as he does duty to God and man in this respect;

Yet it must be said with all possible plainness that total abstinence, purity, or honesty, by themselves or even practised together, are utterly insufficient to produce a smile that will never "come off." Life of man much wider than any or all of these, and goes much deeper than anything connected with everyday affairs. The fact is —

III. There is only one "smile that won't come off."

It is the one on the face of a Christian, a true follower of the Lord Jesus, for Christianity alone touches springs of life and sounds depths of being. This is because Christian has fourfold joy in his heart, filling his soul, and showing itself in his life:

1. *The joy of salvation*
   a. Like Philippian jailor (cf. 16:34), man who accepts Christ is able to rejoice in God when he believes;
   b. All through history of early Christians, as disciples in our text, their experience was always accompanied by joy —
      (1) Of complete forgiveness, covering guilt of sin;
      (2) Of instantaneous pardon, blotting out condemnation of sin;
      (3) Of perfect righteousness, promising deliverance from sin.
2. *The joy of sanctification*
   a. Our Christian life commences with new birth by presence of Holy Spirit in our hearts (see text again), and His work is —
      (1) To make us holy;
      (2) To consecrate our lives to God; and —
      (3) To enable us to witness for Him;
   b. His presence and work bring joy, for He produces purity —
      (1) Of thought;
      (2) Of motive;
      (3) Of desire;
      (4) Of action.

3. *The joy of service*
   a. Only man healthy and strong in body knows joy of physical work, and Christian whose soul is healthy and true to God will delight in privilege and opportunity of service:
      (1) Witnessing for his Master;
      (2) Working in His behalf;
      (3) Waging warfare against His enemies;
   b. This service always brings joy:
      (1) Of soul-winning;
      (2) Of speaking a good word;
      (3) Of doing a kind action;
      (4) Of living for God, always and everywhere.
4. *The joy of satisfaction*
   a. Christian life is, above and beyond all, life of daily fellowship with God in Christ (cf. 1 John 1:3), and this becomes ours through communion of Holy Ghost as, day by day —
      (1) Soul learns more of glory of Master;
      (2) Spirit reveals more of Christ and bestows more grace;
   b. Consequence is soul exults in Christ and testifies to truth of words "satisfied with favour, full with the blessing of the Lord" (Deut. 33:23);
   c. This produces constant and ever-increasing satisfaction within, and result is buoyancy of spirit, spontaneity of heart, and vigor of life.

Thus, Christian experience deepens and widens as days go on, and finally there is promise of God that "everlasting joy" shall be upon our heads (cf. Isa. 35:10).

Conclusion

This is indeed the source of "the smile that won't come off," and it may be ours if we will —

1. Give ourselves into the Father's keeping;
2. Accept by faith Christ's great salvation;

3. Welcome into our souls the Holy Spirit; and —
4. Trust God to lead and use us day by day.

Then shall we know what it is to be Christian in reality and in truth, and the testimony of our lives will be that "the Lord hath done great things for us, whereof we are glad" (Psa. 126:3).

Study No. 71 — "Through Peril, Toil, and Pain"

ACTS 14:1-28

BECAUSE of the persecution of Pisidian Antioch, Paul and Barnabas fled to Iconium, about eighty miles away (cf. 13:50, 51) and, finding similar opposition there, went on after some time to Lystra (v. 6) and Derbe (vs. 6, 20). After staying there they retraced their steps until they came back at last to Antioch in Syria (vs. 21-28). The details of this part of the First Missionary Journey are so full that the greatest possible care will be necessary to avoid losing sight of the main narrative and teaching.

I. The Progress (vs. 1-7)

1. Work at Iconium marked, as at Antioch, by —
   a. Success (v. 1);
   b. Opposition (v. 2);
2. But Paul and Barnabas not prevented from —
   a. Remaining long time; and —
   b. Witnessing to God by word and deed (v. 3).
3. Finally, persecution became acute and they fled to Lystra (vs. 4-7).

II. The Power (vs. 8-10)

At Lystra —

1. Man born crippled heard Paul speak (vs. 8, 9);
2. Apostle looked keenly at him, perceived his faith, and gave command to stand (vs. 9, 10);
3. Obedience of faith brought immediate blessing of healing (v. 10).

III. The Popularity (vs. 11-13)

Outcome of miracle:

1. Crowds attributed it to apostles themselves;
2. Said two gods had come down in likeness of men:
   a. Jupiter (Latin name for Zeus, chief deity and national god of Greeks) — Barnabas; perhaps because he was physically taller and more impressive in appearance;
   b. Mercury (or Hermes, deity of eloquent speech) — Paul; for obvious reason of leadership along this line (cf. 1 Cor. 2:1);
3. Priest of Jupiter, who had temple there, tried to sacrifice oxen.

   N.B. Confirmation of record from archeology — discovery at Lystra about 1909 of two ancient inscriptions referring to both gods.

IV. The Plea (vs. 14-18)

1. *The Audience*
   a. Apostles could not for an instant accept worship;
   b. Instead, pleaded with people not to worship them since they, too, were but men.
2. *The Appeal*
   a. Used occasion to urge turning from such "vanities" to living, loving God of creation;
   b. Significant that with these heathen people, living in and around what we might call country town, Paul seems to have started by proclaiming elementary truths of natural religion, instead of taking up at once distinctive Christian message of redemption — leading from known to unknown.
3. *The Application*
   a. But God of nature (v. 15), and of history (v. 16) is also God of providence (v. 17), and of grace (cf. 21-23, where Lystra is again mentioned);
   b. Also, it is evident "these sayings" were hasty method by which apostles "restrained" the people from doing proposed sacrifice (v. 18);

c. Then came interruption of Jewish persecutors from Antioch and Iconium.

V. The Persecution (v. 19)

These Jews —

1. Persuaded people of Lystra to turn against Paul;
2. Stoned him, permitted by fickle crowd;
3. Dragged him out of city; and —
4. Left him for dead.

VI. The Program (vs. 20-22)

1. But Apostle not yet finished, for God raised him from what was thought to be death (cf. 7:58, 59; 2 Cor. 11:25), and he was able next day to depart for Derbe, thirty miles away. N.B. Some hold this apparent death at Lystra corresponds to Paul's statement about himself as "caught up to the third heaven" (2 Cor. 12:2) and hearing "unspeakable words" (v. 4). If so, what blessed spiritual compensation, just after physical attack! In any case, Apostle occupied unique relation to God in connection with knowledge of heavenly things.
2. Notwithstanding everything, Paul and Barnabas persisted, continuing their ministry by —
   a. Preaching — "preached the Gospel to that city" (v. 21), i.e., Derbe;
   b. Teaching — "taught many" (v. 21); "confirming . . . and exhorting" (v. 22);
   c. Organizing — "ordained . . . elders in every church" (v. 23).

   N.B. Cf. "much tribulation" (v. 22; John 16:33) with "easy" yoke and "light" burden of (Matt. 11:30): two different aspects of Christian experience. Our Lord's yoke and burden refer to those things He Himself places upon us, while tribulation is that which comes from world — not His active, primary will for us, but allowed by Him as natural outcome of our profession, overruled for our good and good of His cause.

3. Note Apostles returned to very three cities where they had been so persecuted — did not avoid them but must have been in each long enough on return trip to allow for founding of local church (cf. v. 23).

VII. The Provision (v. 23)

1. Thus, in addition to confirming, exhorting, and warning (v. 22), Apostles took steps to ordain leaders in each church, in order to —
   a. Perpetuate its existence, and —
   b. Guarantee its progress.
2. Individualism in church matters not encouraged in N.T. — instead, cooperation, order, succession, responsibility, example, unity.

VIII. The Praise (vs. 24-28)

1. After long return journey, preaching Word en route, Apostles finally arrived at Antioch in Syria, whence they had started (vs. 24-26).
2. Important and fitting that they should gather together church which had recommended them to God in starting out (vs. 26, 27; 13:3);
3. Told wonderful story of way God had opened doors among Gentiles (v. 27).
   N.B. This is record of first missionary meeting in Christian Church, with report from field.

Conclusion

St. Paul's First Missionary Journey is of special importance because it shows how Apostle did his work and how he behaved in presence of difficulties.

1. Preaching was suited to audience, whether informed Jews (chap. 13), or more immature Gentile heathen (chap. 14).
2. Personal attitude was one of —
   a. Sympathy at sight of need;
   b. Courage in face of danger;
   c. Persistence in midst of opposition;
   d. Tact when confronted with delicate situations.

3. Primary concern was evangelism, proclamation of Gospel to those not yet Christian.
4. Provision was made for continuance and development of Church by appointing responsible successors.

Thus, whether in presence of faith or of fickleness, or even of frustration, Paul displayed firmness and faithfulness. Have we heard the messenger of the Gospel, heeded the message, and honored the Master?

Study No. 72 — God's Witness to Mankind

ACTS 14:17

"ROGATION DAYS" in the calendar of the Church of England were originated for the purpose of praying for the harvest; they are also held later in the year as occasions of thanksgiving for abundant crops and safety in gathering them. In either case, they are full of teaching for all willing to learn, since Nature around us should always remind us of God.

The context of this verse is striking. The people of Lystra, having just witnessed a miracle performed by the Apostle Paul, called him and his companion Barnabas "gods . . . in the likeness of men" (v. 11), and proposed a sacrifice to them. Perhaps it was the sight of the "oxen and garlands" brought by the priest of Jupiter for the purpose of sacrifice that prompted Paul to make his stirring appeal to the people on the grounds of Nature and its witness to the one true God.

I. God's Witness — Its Method

1. Simple — "rain from heaven"
   a. Ordinary, not at all marvelous;
   b. Nature is manifestation of God, its First Cause.
2. Constant — "fruitful seasons"
   a. Through centuries the same, with no suspensions;
   b. Nature shows forth power, love, faithfulness of God.

II. God's Witness — Its Meaning

1. Life-giving — "filling our hearts with food"
   a. For strength;
   b. For work.
2. Joy-giving — "filling our hearts with . . . gladness"
   a. For health;
   b. For contentment.

III. God's Witness — Its Message

We may well continue in imagination Paul's interrupted speech which, we are persuaded, would have assuredly led his hearers into higher realms of thought and aspiration; and thus we may consider some other witnesses to God which he must have mentioned on his return to Lystra (cf. vs. 21-23):

1. World history;
2. The Bible;
3. The Lord Jesus;
4. The Holy Spirit;
5. The changed lives of believers because of two elements of spiritual life suggested in this verse:
   a. Christ our Food;
   b. Christ our Joy.

Conclusion

Today's tendency is to forget that Nature is God's witness:

1. The witness is true — God is faithful;
2. The witness is to be believed — God is love.

Will you not trust Him?

Study No. 73 — Two Problems of Missionary Work

ACTS 14:21-28

THE EARLIER PART of the chapter gives an account of missionary resourcefulness in the face of alternating persecutions and honors. It also indicates both spiritual insight into an individual case and faithful testimony before a crowd. But these closing verses give the reader a glimpse into two of the important problems which beset missionary work in those early days and with which church history is often repeated in the mission fields of today.

I. The Problem of the Native Churches (vs. 21-23)

Gospel had been preached and disciples made (v. 21, A.S.V.; cf. Matt. 28:19, A.S.V.); but conversion not everything. Strong local churches and devoted pastoral work necessary to efficient evangelization and growth (cf. Eph. 4:11, 12).

1. *Organization was essential* (vs. 22, 23a)
   a. Souls were confirmed, or established;
   b. Disciples were exhorted to continue (cf. 13:43);
   c. Believers were told with great plainness what to expect in Christian life;
   d. Elders were ordained to lead. Yet —
2. *Organism was to be in direct relation to Christ* (v. 23b)
   a. Apostles set example of prayer and fasting;
   b. They commended each church to the Lord; and so —
3. *Organism and organization were to be inseparable*:
   a. Organism only would mean disorder;
   b. Organization only would invite disaster.
   N.B. Thus, most important problem in native churches was correlation of two, and for this all possible grace and wisdom were needed. We have same problem today;

to solve it we must use every means available and then trust Holy Spirit's power to complete task.

II. The Problem of the Church at Home (vs. 24-28)

After journey back to home base (vs. 24, 25), Apostles arrived at Antioch, and there held first missionary meeting in history:

1. *The Place*

   Antioch:

   a. Third city of the world — important, wealthy, sinful;

   b. Because from thence they had gone out, "recommended" (v. 26; "committed," A.S.V., "handed over," Gr.) to grace of God.

2. *The Deputation*

   Paul and Barnabas, who had been —

   a. "Sent forth by the Holy Ghost" (13:4);

   b. "Filled with the Holy Ghost" (13:9); and whose —

   c. "Work" was now "fulfilled" (v. 26).

   N.B. "Long" stay in Antioch not all "deputation work," but doubtless opportunity for exerting personal influence in everyday living (cf. v. 28).

3. *The Audience*

   Antioch Church (v. 27), who had —

   a. "Laid their hands on them"; and —

   b. "Sent them away" (13:3);

   N.B. Whole congregation apparently concerned with foreign missions.

4. *The Addresses*

   Simple narrations of fact, not sermons, nor even evangelistic appeals:

   a. "All that God had done with them"; and —

   b. "How He had opened the door of faith unto the Gentiles" (v. 27);

   N.B. God given all glory for both doing and opening.

5. *The Teaching*

   Missionary work thus shown to be —

   a. Duty of church;

b. Subject for prayer;
c. Asset to history;
d. Cause of God.
N.B. Thus, most important problem in home church was and still is how to inspire and maintain steadfast prayer, sympathetic interest, and sacrificial giving in relation to missions.

Conclusion

What is the true attitude in every church and between churches and missions?

1. *Prayerful commendation;*
2. *Spiritual sympathy;*
3. *Cordial co-operation.*

This is a work of the Holy Spirit of God; let us listen for His voice, obey His commands, and trust His wisdom and protection.

Study No. 74 — "Handed Over"

ACTS 14:26; 15:26; I Peter 2:21, 23

The dictionary defines a plumb line as one which, by means of a weight suspended from it, may be used to "determine verticality." Scripture is full of plumb lines, in the form of words and ideas that, when applied to human behavior, test the "verticality," the sincerity or the zeal, of the Christian or of the Church. One of these is a word which appears more than one hundred times in the Greek Testament, often with the significance of "commit," "yield," or "deliver up." In the American Revised Version of the first and third of our references, this Greek word is translated "committed" whereas in the second one it is translated "hazarded." In each of the three a very fair approximation of the meaning would be our modern phrase, "handed over," in the sense of surrender. As we consider them in the light of this thought, let us test our own "verticality" in the spiritual life, especially in relation to the missionary cause.

I. **Missionary Church** (Acts 14:26)

Christian group at Antioch is here characterized by —

1. *Service*:
   "Work" to be "fulfilled";
2. *Strength*:
   "The grace of God" to be trusted;
3. *Surrender*:
   "From whence they had been committed" (A.S.V.), in prayer and in fasting (cf. 13:3), i.e., "handed over" to God for His "work."

Are these things true of our churches?

II. **Missionary Workers** (Acts 15:26)

Paul and Barnabas are here said to have shared in —

1. *Sacrifice*:
   "Have hazarded" — they had "handed over" everything to the Lord;
2. *Surrender*:
   "Their lives" — all that they were, and all that they had — talents, confidence, courage, readiness, possessions; because they had as —
3. *Stimulus*:
   "The Name of our Lord Jesus Christ" — great motive for all Christian work.

Are these things true of our missionaries?

III. **Missionary Example** (1 Pet. 2:21, 23)

Here, it is the Master who is described:

1. *Suffering*:
   "Christ also suffered" (v. 21);
2. *Surrender*:
   Even He "kept on committing (handing over) Himself" (v. 23, Gr.);
3. *Security*:

"To Him that judgeth righteously," v. 23, i.e., to God His Father, and ours in him — the One who does all things well.

Are these things also true of us all as His faithful followers?

Conclusion

This surrender must be definite, unreserved, irrevocable. We must "deposit" ourselves with God and abide there (cf. 2 Tim. 1:12). It is the attitude expressed by the frequent O. T. phrase, "Here am I" (cf. Isa. 6:8, etc.). It means —

1. The placing of the whole life at God's disposal; and —
2. The response of the whole personality, mind, body and soul, to His love and grace in Christ.

It is only by faith that we thus "hand over" ourselves to Him. Have we done this?

Study No. 75 — Grace* (A Word Study)

ACTS 14:26

"Grace" is one of the greatest words in the Bible because it so truly expresses God's character and attitude in relation to man. It comes from two or three roots in Hebrew and Greek. The Hebrew substantive means "favor" and the corresponding adjective means "favorable," "gracious." In the Greek, we find derivatives meaning "gift," to "forgive," to "bestow graciously," to "rejoice," to "give thanks," etc. In English, derived from Latin, we have "gratis," "gratitude," "gracious," "graceful," "gratuity," etc. The subject is large, with many aspects; and the Scripture passages are numerous and well worthy of close study.

I. The Meaning of Grace

Root means to "give pleasure," and branches out in two directions, one in relation to giver, other in relation to recipient —

* See also "Grace," chapter V in author's *Grace and Power* (Wm. B. Eerdmans Publishing Co., 1949).

or, graciousness and gratitude, leading in turn to graciousness towards others. When applied only to God, the Supreme Giver, idea has two distinct yet connected aspects:

1. *The Divine Attitude*
   - a. Grace means God's favor and good will towards mankind in natural state — cf. Virgin Mary described as "favored" or "graced" (Luke 1:28);
   - b. This favor manifested without regard to merit; indeed, grace and merit are complete opposites; and thus grace is —
     - (1) Spontaneous — not prompted from outside;
     - (2) Free — no conditions required;
     - (3) Generous — no stint shown;
     - (4) Abiding — no cessation experienced;
   - c. It is opposed to "wrath," which means judicial displeasure against sin;
   - d. But it must be distinguished from mercy even though mercy is one of its methods of expression; mercy is related to misery and to (negatively) non-deserving, while grace is related to redemption and to (positively) undeserving.
2. *The Divine Action*
   - a. Grace means help to man as helpless and needy:
     - (1) Not only benevolence but also benefaction;
     - (2) Not simply feeling but also force;
     - (3) Not solely good will but also good work;
   - b. It is Divine favor expressed in and proved by Divine gift — attitude manifested by action;
   - c. Thus, from "grace" comes "gift," invariably implying gift of or from grace (cf. Rom. 5:15; 12:6; 1 Cor. 4:7).

These two ideas are thus connected and united as Cause and Effect, telling of God's Heart and God's Hand.

II. The Source of Grace

1. *God*
   - a. As here and elsewhere in Acts (cf. 15:40; 18:27; 20:24), "the grace of God" is prominent (cf. also Rom. 5:15; Heb. 2:9);

b. Also to be noted is "the God of all grace" (1 Pet. 5:10; cf. 1 Cor. 2:12).

2. *Christ*
"The grace of our Lord Jesus Christ" (15:11; 2 Cor. 8:9; 13:13; Gal. 1:6; cf. Rom. 5:15; John 1:14, 17).

3. *The Holy Spirit*
"The Spirit of Grace" (Heb. 10:29).

III. The Manifestation of Grace

1. *From the Divine Side*
   a. Commenced in God's purpose (2 Tim. 1:9);
   b. Embodied in God's revelation (Tit. 2:11; cf. Gal. 3:18);
   c. Declared in God's Gospel (20:24);
   d. Bestowed in God's gift (Rom. 5:15; 12:3, 6; 15:15; Gal. 2:9; Eph. 4:7);
   e. Intended for God's glory (Eph. 1:6).
2. *To the Human Side*
   a. Realized in man's life (1 Pet. 3:7);
   b. Witnessed in man's conduct (11:23).

IV. The Work of Grace

1. *The Means*
   a. Election (Rom. 11:5);
   b. Calling (Gal. 1:15);
   c. Justification (Rom. 3:24; Col. 2:13; 3:13; Tit. 3:7);
   d. Salvation (Eph. 2:5, 8; Tit. 2:11);
   e. Faith (18:27);
   f. Instruction (Tit. 2:11, 12);
   g. Equipment (14:26; 1 Cor. 15:10; 2 Tim. 2:1);
   h. Rule (Rom. 5:21; 6:14; Heb. 4:16);
   i. Hope (2 Thess. 2:16);
   j. Establishment (Heb. 13:9).
2. *The Measure*
   a. Sufficiency (2 Cor. 9:8; 12:9);
   b. Greatness (4:33);
   c. Fulness (John 1:14);
   d. Abundance (2 Cor. 4:15; 9:8, 14; Rom. 5:17, 20; 1 Tim. 1:14);

e. Wealth (Eph. 1:7; 2:7);
f. Increase (Jas. 4:6; 2 Pet. 1:2).

V. The Glory of Grace

1. *The Character*
   a. Divine (Luke 2:40);
   b. True (1 Pet. 5:12);
   c. Free (Rom. 3:24);
   d. Individual (Eph. 4:7; 1 Pet. 4:10).
2. *The Companions*
   a. Truth (John 1:14, 17);
   b. Apostleship (Rom. 1:5);
   c. Peace (Rom. 1:7; 1 Tim. 1:2);
   d. Righteousness (Rom. 5:21);
   e. Mercy (1 Tim. 1:2).

VI. The Aspects of Grace

1. *As a Source*
   a. "Out of" (Gal. 5:4);
   b. "From" (1 Cor. 1:3).
2. *As a Standard*
   "According to" (Rom. 4:4, 16; 12:6; 2 Tim. 1:9);
3. *As a Means*
   a. "Through" (Rom. 12:3; 15:15);
   b. "By" (Rom. 3:24);
   c. "To" (14:26).
4. *As a Principle*
   "Under" (Rom. 6:14; 11:6).
5. *As a Sphere*
   "In" (Rom. 5:15, Gr.; 2 Thess. 2:16, Gr.).
6. *As a Power*
   "Upon" (4:33; Luke 2:40).
7. *As a Companion*
   "With" (1 Cor. 15:10; Rom. 16:20, 24).

VII. The Conditions of Grace

1. *Positive*
   a. From God (Rom. 5:15);

b. Through the Word (14:3; 20:32);
c. By faith (Eph. 2:8);
d. In humility (Jas. 4:6; 1 Pet. 5:5).

2. *Negative*
a. Not of self (Eph. 2:5, 8);
b. Not by works (Rom. 11:6; Eph. 2:8, 9);
c. Not of debt (Rom. 4:4);
d. Not by law (Rom. 6:14).

VIII. The Response to Grace

1. *The Use*
a. Finding (Heb. 4:16);
b. Receiving (2 Cor. 6:1);
c. Knowing (2 Cor. 8:9; Col. 1:6);
d. Having (Heb. 12:28);
e. Standing (Rom. 5:2; 1 Pet. 5:12);
f. Growing (2 Pet. 3:18);
g. Dispensing (1 Pet. 4:10; Eph. 4:29);
h. Sharing (Phil. 1:7);
i. Continuing (13:43);
j. Inheriting (1 Pet. 3:7);
k. Expecting (1 Pet. 1:13).

2. *The Misuse*
a. Receiving in vain (2 Cor. 6:1);
b. Failing (Heb. 12:15);
c. Falling (Gal. 5:4);
d. Changing (Jude 4);
e. Presuming (Rom. 6:1);
f. Insulting (Heb. 10:29).

IX. The Expression of Grace

1. *Towards God*
a. Singing (Col. 3:16);
b. Praise (Eph. 1:6).

2. *Towards Man*
a. Speech (Col. 4:6; Eph. 4:29);
b. Liberality (2 Cor. 8:19);
c. Witness (20:24; Eph. 3:8).

Conclusion

Hort defines grace as "free bounty." As such it brings great joy and is the source of power in daily living:

1. *Etymologically* — grace is a term referring to the beautiful which gives delight;
2. *Theologically* — grace means God's favor as seen in the gift of His Son;
3. *Practically* — grace implies God's presence and redemptive power in human life.

Blending all these aspects, we may realize grace as God's spontaneous gift which causes pleasure and produces blessing in the lives of all who have accepted it.

Grace first contrived a way
To save rebellious man;
And all the steps that grace display,
Which drew the wondrous plan.

Grace all the work shall crown
Through everlasting days;
It lays in heaven the topmost stone,
And well deserves the praise.

Oh, let Thy grace inspire
My soul with strength Divine!
May all my powers to Thee aspire,
And all my days be Thine!

—PHILIP DODDRIDGE

Study No. 76 — The Council at Jerusalem

ACTS 15:1-35

THIS CHAPTER records what has been well called "the Magna Carta of the Christian Church," and also its first conference or congress. Another great problem of early Christianity was to be settled by the laying down of a principle, that of salvation by faith and not by works or by the keeping of the Mosaic law. It was a battle for Gentile Christian liberty, the first skirmish of which is recorded in 6:1-6, the second in 11:1-18, and which was now to be renewed and fought to a finish. In chapter 11, the Gentiles had been shown to be entitled to eternal life. But what were to be the conditions? Let us trace the account here:

I. The Difficulty (v. 1)

1. *The Problem*
   a. Not whether Gentiles could be saved — that had already been settled, as in case of Cornelius (cf. 11:17);
   b. It was, On what grounds were Gentiles to be saved?
2. *The Protagonists*
   a. Paul and Barnabas — declared "God had . . . opened the door of faith unto the Gentiles" (14:27);
   b. "Certain men from Judaea," evidently of narrow Jewish "sect of the Pharisees" (v. 5) — said to Gentiles of Antioch that unless they were circumcised according to Mosaic law they could not be saved; i.e., non-Jews to be admitted to Christian Church must first submit to all Jewish ordinances (cf. v. 5).

II. The Dissension (v. 2a)

1. *The Argument* — question caused great difference of opinion at Antioch — "no small . . . disputation."

2. *The Issue* — very grave, involving universality of Christianity, work of St. Paul and, indeed, Gospel itself.

III. The Deputation (vs. 2b-4)

1. *The Appointment* — so much at stake it was found necessary to send Paul and Barnabas with others to Jerusalem to take counsel (v. 2b).
2. *The Journey* — told story en route of "conversion of Gentiles," and "caused great joy" in all churches (v. 3).
3. *The Arrival* — received by Jerusalem church, including "apostles and elders," and again reported what "God had done with them" (v. 4).

IV. The Discussion (vs. 5-21)

1. *The Contention* (v. 5)

   Narrow party soon expressed opposition, reiterating declaration concerning Gentiles and Mosaic law quoted in v. 1;

   N.B. Campbell Morgan once said of tendency of Jerusalem Church to compromise with Judaism: "There is a toleration in religion which is treachery. There are hours when the Church must say 'No,' to those who ask communion with her in the doing of her work upon the basis of compromise . . . If the Church . . . today were aloof from the maxims of the age, . . . bearing her witness alone to the all-sufficiency of Christ, and the perfection of His salvation, . . . it would be to her that men would look in the hour of their heartbreak and material need. The reason why men do not look to the Church today is that she has destroyed her own influence by compromise."
2. *The Conclave* (vs. 6-21)

   Result was serious consideration, proceeding along three main lines:

   a. The address of Peter (vs. 7-11)

      After some disputing, Apostle arose and gave simple, fine narration of facts in his own experience, showing —

      (1) What God's action had been in giving Holy Spirit to Gentiles (vs. 7, 8), and drawing conclusion that —

      (2) Proposal to circumcise Gentiles was at once unneces-

sary and impossible in light of God's dealings with Cornelius and friends (v. 9); and, therefore, that —

(3) Salvation was exactly the same for all peoples "through the grace of the Lord Jesus Christ" (vs. 10, 11);

N.B. How patiently Peter had bided his time before interposing! Cf. "much disputing" (v. 7); no longer, as in old days, determined to be first, he was indeed growing in grace.

b. The testimony of Barnabas and Paul (v. 12)

(1) Their message equally impressive as they declared "what miracles and wonders God had wrought by them";

(2) Here is another convincing appeal to facts;

c. The judgment of James (vs. 13-21)

Now came from president of council —

(1) Assent to Peter's argument — how God for first time (Gr.) had "visited the Gentiles" (v. 14, A.S.V.) i.e., those in house of Cornelius;

(2) Appeal to Scripture — which had indicated way of salvation, but had also prescribed circumcision and other regulations pointing to superior privileges of Jews over those of other peoples — looks forward to restitution of Israel, and backward to beginning of world (vs. 15-18);

(3) Agreement between Scripture and Peter's argument — as James showed how to save liberty of Gentiles, convictions of Jews, and authority of Scriptures — i.e., not essential for Gentiles to become Jews in order to become Christians, so long as they were true to God in other respects (vs. 19-21).

Thus, on Scripture and on experience, case rested, and discussion was closed.

V. The Decision (vs. 22-29)

Result of conference was —

1. *Pharisees silenced and other Jews soothed;*

2. *Gentiles of Antioch reassured by letter that —*
   a. Narrow brethren had not been authorized by mother Church at Jerusalem, but that Paul and Barnabas, Judas and Silas were now being sent (vs. 22-27);
   b. Gentile Christians should assume no heavier burden than certain moral safeguards which "seemed good" to observe, according to leading of Holy Spirit (vs. 28, 29).

Thus, compromise made for sake of unity was not of principle but of conduct.

VI. The Development (vs. 30-35)

1. *Return of Apostles with letter* caused great joy in church of Antioch "because of the exhortation" (vs. 30, 31, Gr.).
2. *Confirmation by Judas and Silas* safeguarded and set forward principle of church liberty and mutual love (vs. 32-34).
3. *Continuation by Paul and Barnabas* of teaching and preaching of Word was doubtless occasion of great blessing in all aspects of church life (v. 35).

Conclusion

1. *Difficulties in a church constitute real test of vital Christianity of its members.* How are such difficulties dealt with?
   a. They should be faced frankly;
   b. They should be discussed fully;
   c. They should be decided amicably;
   d. Decisions on them should be accepted heartily.
2. *The distinguishing characteristics of this first Church council were —*
   a. Its frank discussion (v. 7);
   b. Its simple creed (v. 11);
   c. Its teachable spirit (vs. 12, 13);
   d. Its rule of faith (vs. 15-18);
   e. Its liberal decision (vs. 19-21);
   f. Its perfect agreement (v. 22);
   g. Its Divine Head (v. 28).

   When problems are dealt with in a spirit of prayer, trust, love, and obedience, they soon find their solution in the power of the Spirit of God.

3. *The decision at Jerusalem was a victory for —*
   a. Freedom over bondage;
   b. Breadth over narrowness;
   c. Universality over nationality;
   d. Christianity over sectarianism.

   This was the great theme of the entire Epistle to the Galatians, and the liberty gained by means of Paul's testimony, written and spoken, affected the whole of Christianity at that time and has left its mark upon it until this day. Are we standing fast "in the liberty wherewith Christ hath made us free" (Gal. 5:1)?

Study No. 77 — Faith

ACTS 15:9

THERE ARE few things in the New Testament more obvious than the emphasis laid on faith. Here in this verse our hearts are said to be purified by faith. We are justified by faith (Rom. 5:1), we live by faith (Gal. 2:20), we stand by faith (2 Cor. 1:24), and we walk by faith (2 Cor. 5:7). Christ dwells in our hearts by faith (Eph. 3:17), and by faith we are victorious over the world (1 John 5:14). Perhaps the very familiarity of it tends to make us overlook its meaning, necessity, and importance. We fail to do justice to its depth of meaning and fulness of power in connection with every aspect of the Christian life.

But amid all the stress laid on faith in the New Testament, one thing is missing, and that is a prayer *for* faith. The prayer *of* faith is often found, but never the prayer *for* it. We shall see the reason for this in due course. The nearest approach to it is the prayer "Lord, increase our faith" (Luke 17:5); and yet even here the reply of Christ virtually is, Use the faith you possess and you will have more. This shows that faith is an act and an attitude towards God. Let us see what it does and what is its warrant:

I. The Attitude of Faith

1. *Faith Reckons*

   There is perhaps no aspect of faith that needs such careful, constant attention as this:

   a. "Reckon" (Rom. 6:11) is metaphor from accounting, with two "columns" of spiritual "figures": on one side, Death and Sin; on the other, Resurrection and Deliverance;

   b. Christian is to make careful calculation in order to reckon himself dead to one side and alive to other;

   c. This reckoning is one of faith, not of feeling; whether he feels it or not, facts of Christ's redemption are for him, and his faith reckons them such and lives accordingly;

   d. Thus, results of redemption are put to his account, imputed, reckoned to belong to him for pardon, life, holiness.

2. *Faith Responds*

   On basis of reckoning comes second element:

   a. "Yield" (Rom. 6:13) —

      (1) Self to God, as one alive from dead; and —

      (2) Members as instruments of righteousness in His hand;

   b. This surrender means —

      (1) Life at God's disposal; and —

      (2) Soul responding to His love and grace in Christ; and —

   c. It is by faith that this committal is made.

3. *Faith Receives*

   Outgoing of faith in reckoning and responding met by corresponding in-taking:

   a. "Receive" (Gal. 3:14) — one of great words of N.T. (cf. John 1:6; 2 Cor. 6:1, etc.);

   b. Christian not only to ask, but to accept; not only to pray, but to give thanks for answer;

   c. It is faith that accepts, appropriates, applies — one of prime essentials of true Christian life.

4. *Faith Rests*

   Greatest word of Christ for spiritual experience is —

a. "Abide" (John 15:4); it means nothing more nor less than remaining where we are:
   (1) In Christ for pardon? Abide there.
   (2) In Christ for power? Abide there.
   (3) In Christ for life? Abide there.

b. Our union with Him so real and close that He does not say He is root and we branches, but "I am the *Vine,* ye are the branches" (John 15:5), for vine includes branches as well as root.

c. It is faith that enables us to accept this position and to abide in it:
   (1) We continue in His Word (John 8:31) by believing it;
   (2) We continue in His love (John 15:9) by believing it.

Faith thus includes the whole of our attitude to God: it submits to Him in everything; it admits Him to everything; it commits to Him everything; it permits Him to do everything; and it transmits for Him everything. Our inner life must learn, and experience, and express the secrets of faith. But how can this be attained? Because there is —

II. The Warrant of Faith

1. *Faith must have a foundation*:
   a. If this be sure we need not concern ourselves with reality or quality of our faith;
   b. As healthy man is not always occupied with thought of health, so man of God with true foundation for faith is not continually concerned with fact or depth of faith.
2. *This foundation is the Word of God* (Rom. 10:17):
   a. Herein lies explanation of absence of prayer for faith from N. T. — would be unnecessary and futile;
   b. Faith does not come down from heaven in answer to prayer; it springs up in soul in response to Divine Word;
   c. Faith is believing, trusting, crediting, confiding — and

must have something to believe and credit, Someone in whom to trust and confide;

d. Faith will rise and will grow even as we enter more fully into mind, will, and character of God as revealed in Scripture: if we study it but seldom, our faith will be poor because we know not God; if our meditation in it be constant, our faith will be strong because they "who know their God shall be strong" (Dan. 11:32).

Conclusion

1. *Faith is man's response to God's revelation*
   a. This will be in accordance with his knowledge of contents of revelation;
   b. This in turn will lead to knowledge of God Himself which is secret of faith and also of power in Christian life.
2. *Faith is supreme factor in study of God's revelation*
   a. World needs spiritual men;
   b. Secret of spirituality is fellowship with God;
   c. Secret of fellowship is time spent with God through His Word.

From the act will come the habit, and from the habit the character; and we shall enter more fully into His character and the revelation of Himself in Christ. Our faith in Him will indeed be the means of purifying our hearts, "even as He is pure" (1 John 3:3). Is this faith ours?

Study No. 78 — Silas

ACTS 15:22, 32-34, 40

IN THE STUDY of human character, we must consider not only the salient features of a man's mind and disposition, but also the circumstances of every kind that limit and direct his action. Of all these circumstances, his relation to other men is one of the most important, for his companions almost constitute parts of his character. Is not a man known by the company he keeps? Yes, because they, his companions, act on him, and he on them.

This was true of St. Paul, who had so many companions and friends. Human friendships played a great part in his life and exerted a strong influence on it. His first Christian friend, and in some respects the most important, was Barnabas, his second Silas, or Silvanus, who is mentioned for the first time here.

I. His History

1. As one of "chief men among the brethren" of Jerusalem church, was sent to Antioch with Paul and Barnabas to bear letter from council addressed to Gentile Christians (vs. 22, 23).
2. Was commanded to repeat "the same things by mouth" (v. 27).
3. Was called prophet, one who exhorted and confirmed his brethren (v. 32).
4. Chose to remain at Antioch, leaving church at Jerusalem, doubtless to be with Paul (v. 34).
5. Was chosen by Paul as companion on Second Missionary Journey (15:40 to 18:22), visiting Asia Minor, Philippi, Thessalonica, Berea, Corinth.

6. Was mentioned by Paul in three Epistles: to Corinth, as having preached there (2 Cor. 1:19); to Thessalonica, as joining in salutations (1 Thess. 1:1; 2 Thess. 1:1).
7. Was entrusted with Peter's First Epistle to Jews scattered abroad (1 Pet. 5:12).

II. His Character

1. Experienced — intellectually as well as spiritually — called prophet (cf. 1 Cor. 14:3).
2. Authoritative — described as "chief among the brethren" in Jerusalem — would be great help to Paul in re-visiting Derbe and Lystra and delivering "decrees" from Jerusalem, especially if confidence in Paul shaken by absence of Barnabas.
3. Large-hearted — from Jerusalem to Paul — from Paul to Peter.
4. Constant — accompanied Paul from place to place, and called "faithful brother" by Peter (1 Pet. 5:12).

Conclusion

1. Silas helped Paul — with companionship, faithfulness.
2. Paul helped Silas — with inspiration, teaching.

This profitable friendship was of and through God's Holy Spirit, and for His glory. How about our friendships?

Study No. 79 — Barnabas (5)*

ACTS 15:36-41; GAL. 2:13

In the modern watch there is always a balance-wheel, a delicate part that provides compensation — for heat and for cold, in upright or recumbent positions — so that the action of the watch may remain constant under all circumstances. Such a perfect balance as this is missing from human nature on account of sin. In every life some bias may be detected; no one is ever wholly right, impartial, balanced. We see this truth illustrated all through the Bible, for Scripture never glorifies man, only God.

There was a lack of balance in Barnabas, a strain of weakness even in so fine a character as his. Let us consider what these two passages, taking the latter first, reveal as to —

I. The Facts

1. *The Passive Side* (Gal. 2:13)
   - a. The Dispute:
     - (1) We may regard dispute at Antioch mentioned in this passage (vs. 11-21) as having happened prior to council at Jerusalem (cf. Acts 15:6-29);
     - (2) Not likely or even possible for Peter to be so weak after strong attitude recorded in Acts 15:7-11, but firmness at Jerusalem could naturally follow mistake at Antioch;
   - b. The Dissimulation:
     - (1) Same is probably true of Barnabas, who shared Paul's stand at Jerusalem, but in Antioch "was carried away" by dissimulation of Peter and other Jewish Christians;

* For other Studies on Barnabas, see, pp. 90, 105, 213-218, 296.

(2) This was serious crisis for Paul, who stood alone on matter of principle, not only of liberty but of charity; whereas Barnabas, the charitable, yielded, probably because of inherent weakness.

2. *The Active Side* (Acts 15:36-41)

a. The Dissension (vs. 36-39a)

(1) In planning Second Missionary Journey, Barnabas, with natural feelings towards young relative, wished to take him again — "blood is thicker than water";

(2) Paul, just as naturally, remembered Mark's desertion (cf. 13:13) and would not agree — wanted work of confirming churches (cf. v. 41) to be lasting and ministry consistent; also, it may be, Mark may have objected to free offer of salvation to Gentiles (see also Study No. 80, under II, 2 & 3, pp. 300, 301);

(3) Outcome was sharp contention and severance — two Apostles never worked together again;

(4) Yet with no animosity — Barnabas mentioned in Paul's Epistles (1 Cor. 9:6; Gal. 2:1, 9, 13; Col. 4:10); and Mark, having developed spiritually, is commended (Col. 4:10; 2 Tim. 4:11; Philem. 24);

b. The Division (vs. 39b-41)

(1) God overruled difference of opinion and thus two parties of missionaries set out instead of one, and Cyprus was re-visited;

N.B. R. V. Bingham reminds us that trouble doubtless led to calling forth of Silas and finding of Timothy, revealing to Mark his weakness and bringing about change in him; and thinks it unlikely that because Barnabas missed God's first plan for his life he was discarded from service.

(2) But Church seems to have sided with Paul (cf. v. 40 with 39b), and Barnabas drops out of sight, as far as record in Acts is concerned.

II. The Truths

1. *The power of circumstances and associations is a test of character*:
   a. Connection of Barnabas with Mark not to be compared with friendship and fellowship of Paul which were never fully resumed;
   b. Partiality to kin and warm-hearted generosity need caution where there are positions to fill, especially in church affairs — nepotism, or appointment of relatives when feelings influence judgment, can be discredit to Christianity.

2. *Past grace is no guarantee of future faithfulness*:
   a. Tendencies lurking within do not appear all at once, but only come to light as there are objects to attract them, unless counteracting power is brought to bear;
   b. It has been said: "No one is safe till he gets to heaven" — i.e., safe from sins, shortcomings, imperfections of character, the fruits of sinful human nature.

3. *A man's strongest point is often his weakest*:
   a. Note some strong points of Biblical characters:
      (1) Abraham — faith;
      (2) Moses — meekness;
      (3) Elijah — bravery;
      (4) John — love;
      (5) Barnabas — kindness;
      With all of these may be cited related weaknesses;
   b. Many pride themselves on strong point which is really weak point — e.g., speaking one's mind;
   c. Defects of qualities show tendency of finest characters to run off into error:
      (1) Barnabas had ready facility for giving and receiving confidence, and for securing co-operation;
      (2) Such good qualities carry with them danger of easy yielding and desire to please at expense of principle;
      (3) We, too, may carry acquiescence and gentleness to point of unfaithfulness.

Conclusion

The story of Barnabas is the story of a noble life: its initial step, its genuine spirit, its splendid service, its hidden secret, and — its solitary speck. How may such a character defect as his be checked? By abiding in Christ:

1. *This will strengthen us for His work;*
2. *We shall become channels for the grace of God;* and —
3. *Our characters and our lives will be all-round and full-orbed,* "perfect and complete in all the will of God" (Col. 4:12).

Study No. 80 — "John, Whose Surname Was Mark"

ACTS 15:37

THE AUTHOR of the second Gospel is first mentioned by name in Acts 12:12, though some think he was the "young man" mentioned in Mark 14:51. But since this chapter contains the account of the turning-point of Mark's career, it is fitting to study his whole Christian experience at this point.

I. His Background

1. *Name*
   a. "Mark" — or "Marcus" (Col. 4:10) — was Latin surname; "John," Jewish given name, meaning "grace of God";
   b. Both found here and in 12:12; "John" alone in 13:5, 13; and "Mark" alone in 15:39 and thenceforward.
2. *Connections*
   a. His mother was Jewish, Mary of Jerusalem, whose house was center for Christian assemblage, where Peter naturally went upon his release from prison (cf. 12:12);
   b. Nothing known of father, but Barnabas was his cousin (not uncle; see Gr. of Col. 4:10); so Apostles took him to Antioch (cf. 12:25);

c. May have been led to Christ by Peter (cf. "Marcus my son," 1 Pet. 5:13, though this may have been mere indication of intimate association in ministry) — names always linked by early Christian writers.

II. His Early Ministry

1. *Service*

a. Mark's association with Barnabas was natural, and he became "attendant" (13:15, marg.) of his cousin and of Paul on First Missionary Journey;

b. Greek word signifies "under-rower" on ship — hidden and humble in function, but very necessary and useful; perhaps Mark assisted in making arrangements;

c. Experience thus gained with such able, consecrated men as Paul and Barnabas must have been both interesting and valuable.

2. *Failure*

a. Mark left Paul and Barnabas at Perga, in midst of expedition, and returned home to Jerusalem (cf. 13:13);

b. Why? We can only surmise:

(1) Beyond Perga, work would grow in difficulty — but perhaps hardly likely this alone led Mark to shrink from experiences in interior of Asia Minor (cf. 2 Cor. 11:23-27);

(2) Charles E. Wilson asks: "Was it thought of his mother, a widow? Maybe St. Paul — the intrepid — was led to go farther than St. Mark expected when he started. Note only St. Paul and St. Barnabas were 'called.' Was St. Mark in advance of God's purpose for him?"

(3) Dr. Farmer, in International Standard Bible Encyclopedia, thinks Mark objected to offer of salvation to Gentiles on condition of faith alone; says there are hints that Mark's family, like Paul's, were Hebrews of the Hebrews; and suggests significance

of his being given in 13:5-13 his Hebrew name alone lies in what happened at Paphos — Roman deputy becoming believer.

3. *Repudiation*

a. For second missionary journey (15:36), Barnabas naturally wished young cousin to be included again for practical reasons (v. 37);

b. Paul's strong remonstrance on principle (v. 38) is further indication that question of free salvation for Gentiles may have been cause of trouble, since that subject stirred his feelings more deeply than any other (cf. Gal. 2:4, 5, 14-21, etc.);

c. On it, either before or after this time, even Barnabas himself betrayed weakness (cf. Gal. 2:13 and see Study No. 79, under I, 1, p. 296);

d. Perhaps it is fair to say that both men were right in regard to Mark, from different points of view: Paul in refusing to take along one so prejudiced or unreliable on tour certain to be full of difficulties; and Barnabas in wanting to give his young kinsman another chance;

e. But both were manifestly wrong in indulging in "contention" so "sharp" that they "parted asunder one from the other" (15:39), especially since they were so apparently suited to serve God together.

f. It would seem that Church sided with Paul (cf. v. 40 with 39b);

N.B. When Christians have conscientious differences they should "agree to differ" without doing violence to character or testimony; but where "line of cleavage" has to be drawn is between Christian and non-Christian, true churchman and apostate (cf. Heb. 6:4-9) — here there is to be no compromise, for line is usually one's attitude to the Bible.

III. His Later Experience

1. *Sympathy*
   a. Shown to Mark by Barnabas, "son of consolation" (4:36) — another striking instance of tenderness and large-heartedness of his nature;
   b. Doubtless expected John Mark after all to "make good" — so took young man back with him to Cyprus, his own home (cf. 4:36).
2. *Training*
   a. Though nothing heard of Mark for about eleven years, sequel proves cousin's kindness great blessing to him;
   b. But Paul's refusal must also have been factor in discipline;
   c. As ever, both tenderness and severity, in right relation and proportion, are needed for highest development of youth (cf. Rom. 2:1-11; 11:22).
3. *Contribution*
   a. As minister of Christ:
      (1) Fact that Mark was at Rome with Paul (cf. Philem. 24) shows breach healed by then;
      (2) One of faithful few among Jewish Christians, he is described by Paul as "fellow-worker" and "comfort" (Col. 4:10, 11);
      (3) Called "profitable . . . for the ministry" (2 Tim. 4:11; cf. Philem. 11);
      (4) Peter's reference to him (1 Pet. 5:13) may date from time after Paul's death, which would prove Mark still faithfully laboring — in Babylon, from which Peter was writing;
      (5) Tradition says Mark preached in Egypt and North Africa, founding great Church of Alexandria; and one of world's finest basilicas — St. Mark's, Venice — named for him;
      N.B. Quarrel between Paul and Barnabas apparently made up, for Paul later speaks kindly of his old friend (cf. 1 Cor. 9:6).

b. As writer of Second Gospel:
   (1) Writing represents teaching and influence of Peter — idea mentioned by tradition and confirmed by Gospel itself;
   (2) Scope of Gospel corresponds to outline of Peter's address in house of Cornelius (cf. 10:37-43); and keynote said to be Mark 10:45;
   (3) Whole book in harmony with Peter's character — active, impulsive, forthright, rather than argumentative, logical, doctrinal;
   (4) Intended for Gentiles rather than for Jews, and especially for Romans because of their dominant admiration of force — with Mark emphasizing activity and power of Christ rather than words, and constantly using expression "straightway" (cf. "swiftly" of Julius Caesar's commentaries on his Gallic Wars) and certain words of Latin origin, such as "legion," "centurion," etc.;
   (5) But most important is clear reference in Mark to great idea of Isaiah known as "the Servant of Jehovah" (cf. Isa. 52:13 to 53:12); singularly appropriate for author, who was servant to Barnabas, Paul and, probably, Peter, to have depicted our Lord as the Divine Servant.

Conclusion

We may summarize the life and character of John Mark by the following elements:

1. *Faith* — clearly indicated by his discipleship;
2. *Fear* — if this was cause of his return home;
3. *Fickleness* — in not continuing in God's work;
4. *Faithlessness* — in lack of loyalty to God's will;
5. *Forcefulness* — something worth while in him, as seen by recovery;
6. *Faithfulness* — shown during years between Paul's refusal of him and approval;

7. *Fellowship* — especially with two such outstanding men as Peter and Paul.

Here is both warning and encouragement for us today: let personality and effort "be strong in the Lord" (Eph. 6:10).

—That all my powers with all their might
In Thy sole glory may unite.

—CHARLES WESLEY

Study No. 81 —

Paul Starts on His Second Missionary Journey

ACTS 15:40 to 16:8

THIS SECOND MISSIONARY JOURNEY of Paul's may well be taken as a model by travelling evangelists and Christian workers.

I. Seeking Helpers (15:40 to 16:3a)

1. *Paul's Need*
   a. Could have been independent, yet made best choice in taking helpers (cf. Christ's example — 12 disciples — 70 sent out two by two);
   b. Silas chosen first (15:40), and then Timothy (16:1-3a).
2. *Paul's Action*
   a. Chose Silas as one of "chief men among the brethren" and therefore presumably mature, to take place of Barnabas;
   b. Chose Timothy, who was young, to take place of Mark — Paul always lover of young, but they must be true:
      (1) Timothy interested in spiritual things from early days, through mother and grandmother (cf. 2 Tim. 1:5; 3:14, 15);

(2) Apparently led to Christ by or through Paul on first visit to Lystra (cf. 14:18-23; 2 Tim. 1:2, 18; 2 Tim. 2:1; Phil. 2:22).

II. Strengthening Converts (15:41; 16:4, 5)

1. *Confirming* (15:41) — cf. past (14:22; 15:32);
2. *Delivering* (16:4) — letter from Jerusalem (cf. 15:30, 31);
3. *Increasing* (16:5) — always result of strengthening believers;

N.B. Work among Christians essential to character of church and of converts (cf. Eph. 4:16).

III. Winning Outsiders (v. 3b)

1. *Paul's Precaution*

Favoring circumcision in case of Timothy and not in that of Titus (cf. Gal. 2:3-5) may seem inconsistent, especially in view of recent declaration in Jerusalem (cf. 15:24), copies of which he was even now delivering (v. 4); but —

a. Timothy, half-Jew, was circumcised for sake of Jews whom Paul wished to reach for Christ, using synagogues as bases — or storm of protest would have gathered around him, impeding further progress;
b. Titus, Gentile, was not circumcised because those who insisted on rite for non-Jews were Christians who should have known better than to try to burden Gospel of grace with yoke of Law (cf. 15:10, 28).

2. *Paul's Pronouncement*

Note his own words to people of that very region (Gal. 5:6; 6:15) — rite of circumcision so unimportant as to rule out controversy.

IV. Following Spirit (vs. 6-8)

1. *Knowing His will* — by words, events, impressions;
2. *Obeying His will* — by sanctified understanding and imagination;

N.B. R. V. Bingham says: "When you get guidance through dreams, weigh well the proper conclusion with surrounding providences, scriptural injunctions, and sanctified judgment under the Divine Spirit. Paul had them all concurring in the course he took."

Conclusion

1. *The Need of the Church*
   a. The true faith;
   b. To be continually established, or strengthened, in that faith.
2. *The Provision for the Church*
   a. The right teaching;
   b. The chosen teachers.
3. *The Result in the Church*
   a. Great increase (Gr. of v. 5);
   b. Daily increase.
4. *The Challenge to the Church*
   a. To ascertain the leading of the Holy Spirit;
   b. To carry His Gospel to the regions beyond.

Where do we stand?

Study No. 82 — Three Conversions

ACTS 16:1, 3, 15, 23-34

One of the glories of Christianity is its power of perpetual adaptation to human needs; another is its great variety of method in meeting the needs and dealing with the needy. Christianity takes men as they are and works on their natures and through their circumstances. The purpose of the working is the same in each case, but the methods are very different. In this chapter are recorded three conversions to Christianity — all by means of the same messenger, but by such different ways to the one goal.

I. The Youth — Timothy (v.1)

1. *Introduction* (cf. 2 Tim. 3:14, 15)
   a. Family circle — boy, mother, grandmother, seen in relation to Scriptures;
   b. Ideal home centers around Bible reading and study;
   N.B. Father probably Greek proselyte and may well have died before this.
2. *Influence of Paul* (cf. 14:8-23)
   a. Original visit to Lystra seven years before, so Timothy then quite young boy;
   b. Product of home training, godly example, and knowledge of Scriptures fruitful ground for evangelist or pastor;
   c. Care of Christ's "lambs" (John 21:15) one of most important phases of Christian work.
3. *Characteristics of conversion* ("believed," v. 1)
   a. Probably through miracle of healing and subsequent persecution of Paul during former visit;
   b. No violent change noted — just experience leading to belief, his door into Kingdom;
   c. This ought always to be so with children of Christian household — each "disciple" (v. 1) from cradle, never knowing date, only reality, of regeneration* — unconscious of Divine influence at first, but God made very real through hearing and reading of Scriptures and through lives and examples of relatives; thus, only need is for acceptance;
   *Illus.***: Child too young to know absent father, yet recognizes him instantly on return through fine portrait faithfully shown by mother; likewise, child may early draw parallel between Heavenly Father and earthly one (cf. Psa. 103:13; Matt. 7:11).

II. The Woman — Lydia (vs. 13-15)

1. *Introduction* (vs. 13, 14a)
   a. Business woman, in Philippi from Thyatira — already

---

*See also author's *Outline Studies in the Gospel of Luke,* pp. 273, 274.
** From author's own family life.

Jewish adherent, although European by residence;

b. Doubtless knew Scriptures — was accustomed to frequent place of prayer.

2. *Influence of Paul* (v. 14b)
   a. Gave careful attention to new teaching from him;
   b. Found it fitted in with what she knew already.

3. *Characteristics of conversion* (vs. 14, 15)
   a. Passed quietly into Kingdom but, because adult, would always know time as well as fact;
   b. Heart (v. 14) and home (v. 15) both opened in humility;
   c. So now, grace often comes simply and fits in exactly, bringing consciousness of newness of life (Rom. 6:4) and of spirit (Rom. 7:6).

III. The Man — The Jailor (vs.23-24)

1. *Introduction* (vs. 23, 24)
   a. Probably rough, hard individual chosen for such a position;
   b. Evidently opposed to Paul and Silas, or else frankly sadistic, for he used gratuitous cruelty in placing their feet in stocks.

2. *Influence of Paul* (vs. 25-32)
   a. Jailor's first reaction — to earthquake — was terrified, attempt on own life;
   b. His second reaction — to Paul's words of reassurance — was precipitate, trembling prostration before Apostles, release from stocks, and anguished inquiry as to salvation;
   c. Apostles' reply one of classics of Gospel regarding both faith and salvation:
      (1) "Believe on the Lord" — faith (in the Name, cf. Rom. 10:13);
      (2) "Believe on . . . Jesus" — repentance (from sin, cf. Matt. 1:21);
      (3) "Believe on . . . Christ" — acceptance (of God's Anointed One, cf. Luke 2:26):

N.B. Alexander Maclaren said: "If He is 'Lord,' that implies His sovereignty and . . . His Divinity. If He is 'Jesus,' that implies His Incarnation. If He is the 'Christ,' that implies that He is the fulfilment of all the ancient dispensation of priest and sacrifice."

(4) "— And thou shalt be saved, and thy house" — salvation (complete, immediate, and providing for another Christian family; cf. 1 Cor. 1:16; 2 Tim. 4:19).

3. *Characteristics of conversion* (vs. 33, 34)

a. Paul's assurance (v. 28) led jailor out of one fear only to bring on another and deeper fear (v. 29), but this soon relieved by message of Gospel (vs. 30, 31);

b. Change in this man's life complete — he could never forget either day or hour, or deny reality of his conversion;

c. Change in his life also rapid — answer to those who say they do not believe in sudden conversions:

(1) Cure of soothsayer was rapid (cf. v. 18); and —

(2) Capture of Apostles was immediate (cf. vs. 19-22); and —

(3) Fright of jailor was instantaneous (vs. 27-29); so —

(4) Faith was instantly called forth (vs. 33, 34);
N.B. R. V. Bingham said: "Some people ridicule sudden conversions, but they do not know God. It does not take God any more time to save a soul than it did for Him to breathe into man's nostrils the breath of life in the beginning. Paul presents no long process of reform to this man; he simply 'spake unto him the word of the Lord' and uplifted an almighty Saviour as the object of faith."

Conclusion

1. *Conversion is a unique characteristic of Christianity.*
   a. Before Christianity, the old world, as Thomas Carlyle remarked, knew nothing of conversion;
   b. Nor does world of today — conversion absent from all other religious systems, even to bafflement of students of comparative religion, according to William James;
   c. But Christianity not only makes good people better, as might be claimed for other faiths, but it makes bad people good.

2. *Conversion takes varied forms.*
   In this chapter —
   a. The youth was brought up naturally into Christ;
   b. The woman was led step by step towards the truth;
   c. The man was granted a quick and mighty change from old to new;
   N.B. Of Bishop Paget it was written: "He came to a man's conscience as he would come into a sick-room, treading softly. He took infinite care never to be abrupt or overbearing. It was of the very essence of his honor as a gentleman, his religion as a Christian." But of William Booth it is said: "His voice was like the sea-wind; when it blew abroad, men's souls in the salt wilderness astray came multitudinous rolling in to God."

3. *Conversion is in effect always the same.*
   In this chapter —
   a. All heard the Word;
   b. All felt a sense of need;
   c. All accepted Christ as Saviour and Lord;
   d. All proved conversion in life:
      (1) Timothy, by following Paul and Silas;
      (2) Lydia, by welcoming them into her house; and —
      (3) The jailor, by doing his best to compensate them, washing their wounds and giving them food and shelter.

Conversion, therefore, finds its importance not in the method, but in the fact. Thus, the question is not, How were you saved? but, Have you been saved? And the answer must therefore be categorical, Yes, or No!

With a lowly, contrite spirit, kneeling at the Saviour's feet,
Thou canst know this very moment pardon — precious, pure, and sweet;
Let the angels bear the tidings upwards to the courts of heaven!
Let them sing with holy rapture, o'er another soul forgiven!

Fanny J. Crosby

Study No. 83 — Timothy

ACTS 16:1-3

After the defection of John Mark it seems as though St. Paul again felt the need of young life around him as he travelled and preached. Timothy, therefore, was chosen to become his minister or assistant, and we know more of him than of any other companion of the Apostle. In his life and work we see —

I. The Career of a Minister

1. *Early Influences* (2 Tim. 1:1-6; 3:14, 15)

   a. Probably native of Lystra in Asia Minor, visited twice by Paul and Barnabas in first missionary journey (14:8-23);

   b. Mother was Jewess, though father Gentile — Timothy heir of two generations of piety, showing power of Christian motherhood, for mother, Eunice, and grandmother, Lois, had taught him Scriptures from babyhood;

c. He or they possibly witnessed miracle of healing and subsequent persecution of Paul — impressed that one so manifestly of God should suffer and almost die for faith.

2. *Definite Conversion* (1 Tim. 1:2, 18; 2 Tim. 2:1)

a. Since Paul calls Timothy his "own son (or, true child) in the faith," and his "dearly beloved son," it seems clear boy was led to Christ by Apostle during his first missionary journey;

b. Was instance of child-conversion, which should never be despised but, on contrary, should be emphasized today — not only possible, but normal, especially in Christian home;

Illus.: Only one converted in Scottish country church one year was "Little Robbie," and old minister was sadly discouraged; but child later became Robert Moffat, great pioneer missionary.

3. *Special Work* (16:1-3)

a. At time of Paul's second visit to Lystra, Timothy had grown from boy into young man, referred to as "a certain disciple" (v. 1);

b. Significantly described as having good reputation among Christians of locality (v. 2; cf. v. 3; 1 Tim. 3:7) — important in view of work before him;

c. From then on, Timothy was Paul's companion and fellow-worker (cf. 17:14, 15; 18:5; 19:22; 20:4; Rom. 16:21; 1 Cor. 4:17; 16:10, 11; 2 Cor. 1:19; 1 Thess. 3:2, 6; all of 1 and 2 Timothy; Heb. 13:23);

d. We may but surmise whether Timothy was indeed able to "come before winter" at end of Apostle's life (cf. 2 Tim. 4:21).

4. *Fine Spirit* (Phil. 2:19-23)

a. Timothy was only man who could be sent with confidence that he would unselfishly consider best interests of Philippian Christians;

b. Faithful not only in relation to church, but to Paul himself — two were like father and son;
c. All through, Timothy was Paul's most trusted and loved companion, sympathizer, helper, messenger.

II. The Character of a Minister

1. *Qualifications of Timothy for the Christian Ministry*
   a. His good foundation and Christian background:
      (1) Principle of his home was faith (v. 1; 2 Tim. 1:5);
      (2) Method of training was through Scriptures (2 Tim. 3:14, 15);
   b. His possession of Christian life — discipleship (v. 1);
   c. His good reputation in local church (v. 2);
   d. His being under fine influence of Paul, which gave him —
      (1) Strength — balancing feminine softness of home influence, and possibly timidity of temperament and delicate constitution (cf. 1 Tim. 6:12; 2 Tim. 2:3, etc);
      (2) Wisdom — teaching him truth more and more fully (cf. 1 Tim. 1:4; 3:15; 6:20; 2 Tim. 2:15, etc.);
      (3) Self-reliance — justifying Apostle's trust in him — no "leading-strings" for such an able young man (cf. 1 Tim. 1:3; 4:6-16; 2 Tim. 1:6, 7, etc.);
   e. His knowledge and full use of Word of God (cf. 2 Tim. 3:14-17;
   f. His splendid spirit of unselfishness (Phil. 2:19-23).

2. *The Christian Ministry Today*

   One of great Puritans said, "God had only one Son and He made Him a minister" (cf. Mark 10:45).
   a. N.T. clear and constant in its references to Christian ministry (cf. 1 Tim. 1:12; 4:6-16, etc.);
   b. History shows some of greatest men have been ministers, e.g.: Augustine, Luther, Calvin, Wesley, Spurgeon;
   c. Experience proves ministry affords —
      (1) Finest possible opportunity of doing good, for winning men and women to Christ is highest service;

(2) Greatest joy and satisfaction in life;
Illus.: Ian Maclaren, famous novelist, whose real name was Dr. Charles Watson, Liverpool preacher, never forsook pulpit, and even refused certain generous offer from publisher, saying: "I should be tempted sometimes to think of my literary work when I ought to be thinking of my work for God and Christ among my people."

Conclusion

Timothy is the only one in the N.T. to whom is given the old prophetic title "Man of God" (1 Tim. 6:11). What does it indicate?

1. *Godliness* — being deeply concerned with God, by means of —
   a. Reading His Word — God speaking to man; and —
   b. Prayer — man speaking to God.
2. *Manliness* — having —
   a. Truth in the mind;
   b. Love in the heart; and —
   c. Righteousness in the life.
3. *Manliness is due to Godliness* — cause and effect:
   a. Grace of God in Christ first makes man godly;
   b. Then it proceeds to make him manly.

Thus Paul and Timothy were one in Christ and one for Christ.

Study No. 84 — On to Europe (1)

ACTS 16:6-18

WHAT IS THE GREATEST event in history? Moses bringing Israel out of Egypt? The founding of Rome? No; according to the great scholar Fairbairn, it was Paul at Troas, first gazing and then going across the Aegean to Europe. For four thousand years Asia had been the cradle of the human race, but now it was to give place in importance to Europe, which was to become the center of Christianity. Alexander of Macedon who, four hundred years before, had dreamed of one empire and one language, had "builded better than he knew," for the diffusion of the Greek tongue had made the spread of the Gospel possible. Thus Paul's Second Missionary Journey was fraught with infinite possibilities.

As this chapter opens we see Paul concerned still with Jewish Christianity in Asia (vs. 1-7); then come days of transition (vs. 8-12); and then the beginning of missionary work on another continent (vs. 13-18). Each development was distinct and each was guided by God.

I. The Divine Check (vs. 6, 7)

1. *Man's Impulses*

   Paul's plan was —

   a. To re-visit churches of First Journey (cf. 15:36, 41; 16:4, 5);

   b. To preach in great centers from Antioch to Ephesus, capital of Asia Minor.

2. *God's Restraints*

   a. Paul "forbidden" (v. 6) to go north — "suffered . . . not" (v. 7) to go north-east;

b. We do not know how God made known His will, but there was some definite and possibly extraordinary indication, perhaps by vision or by voice;
c. Paul may have felt it strange and puzzling, even wrong;
d. But he obeyed and awaited revelation of God's way (cf. Psa. 37:23) to do God's will and accomplish His work;

N.B. Cf. v. 7 with 1 Thess. 2:18, "Satan hindered us." Paul understood how to distinguish between guidance of Holy Spirit and hindrance of Satan, though we do not know circumstances that led him to do so in these particular cases. In the one, the Spirit did not allow him to labor in Bithynia because He had other purposes; in the other, some human opposition was probably Satan's instrument against Apostle. Spirit-taught believer will be guided similarly, for spiritual perception is mark of growing, mature Christian (cf. Phil. 1:9; Heb. 5:14).

II. The Distinct Call (vs. 8, 9)

Arrived at Troas, great seaport (Troy), Paul soon learned reason for hindrances;

1. *The Need*
   a. "A man" — indicating humanity;
   b. "Of Macedonia" — suggesting helplessness of Greek intellect and futility of Roman power;
   c. "Come . . . and help us" — because of —
      (1) Intellectual destitution;
      (2) Social distress;
      (3) Moral degradation;
      (4) Spiritual desire.
2. *The Testimony*
   a. To power of Gospel — it could "help";
   b. To need of messenger — including himself in word "us";
   N.B. What about continuing need of Asia — "heathen at home"? But is imperfection here reason for complete ignorance there? Cf. Christ's plan in 1:8.

III. The Decided Conviction (v. 10)

Realization of God's will brought —

1. *Complete Unanimity*

   Four men involved in plan:

   a. Original party — Paul, Silas, Timothy;

   b. New fellow-worker — Luke, physician and author of Acts:

      (1) Note first instance of word "we" indicating his inclusion (cf. 16:11-17; 20:6-15; 21:1-18; 27:1 to 28:16);

      (2) Writers have suggested "man of Macedonia" was Luke himself, since he was Greek.

2. *Incontestable Proof*

   In their discussion they "put two and two together" (Gr. word translated "concluding" in A.S.V., "assuredly gathering" in K.J.V., means "to put together, to examine, to prove").

IV. The Definite Consecration (vs. 11-13)

1. *The Action*

   a. Immediate endeavor (v. 10) resulted in prompt obedience to known truth — always secret of blessing;

   b. To know was to act.

2. *The Arrival*

   a. Philippi "chief city" of region but Roman "colony" — military, not commercial center, so evidently Jewish residents few;

   b. But Paul sought out best opportunity and used it.

V. The Direct Consequences (vs. 14-18)

1. *The Acceptance*

   Two women were first European converts. Where was "man of Macedonia"?

   a. Lydia (vs. 14, 15) — led simply to Christ and soon showed results in her life;

   b. Soothsaying girl (vs. 16-18) — first opposed, but was finally delivered by power of Christ.

2. *The Opposition* (vs. 16, 17)

a. Christianity never long without it;
b. Perversion of human life and practice of gross falsehood due to Satanic power;
c. Worst of all, they involved clear testimony to God and salvation — awful patronage of good by evil.

3. *The Triumph* (v. 18)
a. By power of Divine Name, Paul gained immediate, complete victory over evil spirit;
b. Christ will not tolerate evil, but wars against it in every form;
N.B. J. N. Darby said: "The spirit of Python can flatter the servants of God in order to gain them; it can speak of God, of the most high God, even of the way of salvation, but not of Christ, Lord and Saviour . . . When the world unites itself to Christians their testimony is lost, and the fault is always that of the Christians. They accept the world because they have already lost true spirituality, the love of Christ rejected by the world."

Conclusion

1. *Man's Need of Help*
He needs —
a. Knowledge of God;
b. Pardon of sins;
c. Power for life;
d. Hope for the future.

2. *God's Help for Man*
The Holy Spirit as "Paraclete" — one called alongside to help — sheds light on the Gospel as —
a. Good news brought — information;
b. Good news wrought — impartation;
c. Good news believed — imputation.

Jesus, I will trust Thee, trust Thee with my soul;
Guilty, lost, and helpless, Thou canst make me whole.
There is none in heaven or on earth like Thee;
Thou hast died for sinners, therefore, Lord, for me.
—M. J. Walker

Study No. 85 — On to Europe (2)

ACTS 16:9-15

THE FIRST WORK of the Christian Church, and therefore of every member of it, is the duty of winning men and women to Christ, the truest kind of "Church extension," of which we hear so much today. Winning others is appropriately and abundantly illustrated by the earliest work of Paul in Europe, on his Second Missionary Journey.

I. The Divine Call (vs. 9, 10)

1. *A Cry* (v. 9)
   a. Exact circumstances of vision unknown — "man of Macedonia" may have been Luke himself (cf. "we" in next verse);
   b. But character typical — "man" — human being, helpless, weary of self;
   c. His greatest need inability to help self — confidence shown in Gospel to supply it.

2. *A Conviction* (v. 10)
   a. Recognition of need led to conviction on part of Paul and companions as to will of God;
   b. Call of God often heard through human voice;
   c. This especially so when hindrance in other directions experienced (cf. vs. 6, 7).

II. The Human Response (vs. 11-13)

1. *Promptness* (vs. 11, 12)
   a. With destination Europe and duty to preach Gospel, party left Troas and journeyed via most direct route;
   b. Not tarrying anywhere, they went at once to most important city of Macedonia, Philippi.

2. *Aggressiveness*: (vs. 13)
   a. On first opportunity, sabbath, sought out Jews in place of prayer — apparently found only women;
   b. If "man of Macedonia" specific person, where was he? Apostles must have wondered as to means used to summon them;
   c. Perhaps explanation lies in Philippi being "Roman colony" (cf. v. 12, A.S.V.), military rather than commercial, so Jewish men few and probably no synagogue (cf. v. 13, with v. 40; 17:1).
3. *Simplicity* (v. 13)
   Both message and method quiet and simple — four men and group of women meeting to speak and hear Word — best way of winning others to Christ.

III. The Consequent Blessing (vs. 14,15)

Three stages in spiritual experience of Lydia, first European convert:

1. *Conviction of need* (v. 14)
   a. Attention to Gospel;
   b. Admittance of Gospel.
2. *Conversion to Christ* (v. 15)
   a. Acceptance of Him;
   b. Acknowledgement of Him.
3. *Constraint of messengers* (vs. 15, 40)
   a. Acceptance through faith;
   b. Affection through faithfulness.

Conclusion

1. *God's Call to Work*
   a. Human need — fields white to harvest (v. 9; cf. John 4:35);
   b. Personal readiness — abiding in presence of God, patiently waiting till darkness clears (vs. 6, 7);
   c. Prompt action — immediate endeavor (v. 10);
   d. Complete conviction — "assuredly gathering" (v. 10);
   e. Spiritual power — "the Holy Ghost" (v. 6); "the Spirit" (v. 7); "the Lord" (v. 10).

2. *God's Care in Work*

   a. Guiding — preventing as well as enabling — mere open door not everything, it must be "effectual" (1 Cor. 16:9), for way is God's as well as work;

   b. Preserving — "straight course" across sea or land — circumstances made favorable;

   c. Using — teaching and personal work like picking fruit by hand;

   d. Blessing — opening of hearts by the Lord sure sign — message makes friends for messengers.

Thus, the work of winning others to Christ is in every sense worth while. Are we doing it?

Study No. 86 — On to Europe (3)

ACTS 16:13-15

In 1620 a ship left Plymouth, England, with men of strong hearts and intense love of liberty as passengers. In that ship were the seeds of civilization to be developed under new circumstances, the seeds of life as we find it in the United States today. But this departure, though fraught with destiny, is not to be compared with the one in A.D. 52, when four men went down to the quay at Troas. One was Paul, the leader, strong, determined, fearless; another was Silas, an earnest preacher; a third was Luke, the cultured professional man, physician and writer; and the fourth was but a youth as yet untried, Timothy by name. In that ship were the seeds of life for Europe; up to then, Asia had led the world. The story of taking the Gospel to the Greek world is so simply told that we may fail to realize that in that voyage was the making of Europe and with it of America.

I. Convocation (v. 13)

What a strange one!

1. *The time* — "on the sabbath" — usual day for worship, but this type of meeting was different;
2. *The place* — "by a river side" — it was in open air, probably no synagogue in Philippi;
3. *The manner* — "sat down, and spake" — free, simple, informal, with nothing set or elaborate about service, just prayer and an opportunity of testimony for Christ.

What an insignificant way of opening up a continent!

II. Congregation (v. 13)

It was made up of women. Where were the men? Perhaps there was to be another time for them (cf. v. 40), or Jewish men were few in this Roman colony because there was little commerce, or they had been banished. Yet it is hereby shown that —

1. *The Gospel is universally adapted.*
   a. If it were primarily a cult, its force and power would depend on its appeal to trained minds of, say, philosophers;
   b. But because it is a recital of facts — "good news" — love of God to sinners, salvation through Christ, etc. — it appeals first to hearts of people who may be quite ordinary, who may include women or children as well as men; and after that to their heads.
2. *The Gospel is universally uplifting.*
   a. Woman in West is man's companion — not, as in East, his slave;
   b. Difference in status due to Gospel — not to political revolt, but to silent revolution through oneness in Christ.
3. *The Gospel is universally influential.*
   a. It touches all of life, including place and power of woman;
   b. Her influence on race now greater than man's: if she acts worthily, she is regal; if unworthily, reprehensible;
   c. It is often said that women keep up Church; if so, still more do they keep up society and its standards — e.g.,

greatest English reigns were those of Elizabeth and Victoria;

d. In short, woman's influence on race since Paul's arrival in Europe indicates unmistakeably what Gospel can do.

III. **Conversion** (vs. 14, 15)

Lydia, one of these women in Philippi, first convert made in Europe:

1. *Her Calling* — business, implying enterprise, independence, ability;
2. *Her Character,* — thoughtful, a proselyte to Judaism but evidently not spiritually satisfied — generous, ready to show hospitality and kindness;
3. *Her Conversion* — definite, true, blessed, by Divine grace through hearing of Gospel.

Conclusion

1. *The Message*
   a. Man or woman may be worthy, industrious, religious;
   b. Yet change of heart necessary — one thing needful (cf. Luke 10:42).
2. *The Method*
   a. Personal, human, informal — yet Divinely guided;
   b. Only one talk — Christian faith often quiet growth, like stream at source.
3. *The Might*
   a. Resulted in open heart (v. 14) and open home (vs. 15, 40):

A Christian home, wide swings the door,
Enter thou in, a happy guest;
God's love thy purpose, thy reward,
And in His fellowship thy rest.

A Christian home, so Lydia came
The Lord's Apostle welcoming in;
Worthy was she His own to name
For He had washed her from her sin.

b. Change affected not only Lydia, but "her household" which shared in rite of baptism (v. 15);
c. Yes, change was complete, because effected by One who "searcheth the reins and hearts" (Rev. 2:23) and has said, "Behold, I stand at the door, and knock" (Rev. 3:20):

O Lord, with shame and sorrow
We open now the door;
Dear Saviour, enter, enter,
And leave us never more!
—W. Walsham How

Study No. 87 — The Opened Heart

ACTS 16:14

Lydia is the first Christian in Europe of whom there is a definite record. Whatever superiority Europe and America have over Asia and Africa dates from this conversion of a woman. The explanation of all that Christianity has done lies in these words: "Whose heart the Lord opened."

Lydia represents both trade and religion. She had some enlightenment, both intellectual and spiritual, and she quickly responded to more light.

I. The Heart

1. *What it is*

   Center of our moral life, including —

   a. Intellect — thinking;
   b. Emotions — feeling;
   c. Will — determining.

2. *What it means*

   Essence of our whole being, our personality, as emphasized in Scripture:

   a. It contains "the issues of life" (Prov. 4:23);

b. From it "proceed evil thoughts" (Mark 7:21);
c. With it "man believeth unto righteousness" (Rom. 10:10); and —
d. God offers man "a new heart" (Ezek. 36:26).

II. The Heart Closed

1. *How it is closed*
Shutting out Christ, so that —
a. Intellect against truth — deliberate;
b. Emotions against love — defiant;
c. Will against grace — disobedient.
2. *Why it is closed*
Because of sin:
a. Sin in nature — root;
b. Sins in practice, especially such as prejudice, avarice, worldliness — fruit.

III. The Heart Opened

1. *The Source*
"The Lord," and only He — by means of His Holy Spirit, through truth of Gospel.
2. *The Methods*
a. Sometimes by earthquake (cf. v. 26), but more often by more light, soul is made —
(1) Sensible of Divine mercy;
(2) Dissatisfied with world;
(3) Fearful of consequences of neglect;
b. Here, method was quiet — nothing startling, just growing conviction of existence of something deeper.
3. *The Proofs*
a. Conviction, confession, conversion, consecration;
b. Opened heart includes opening of ear, mind, will, tongue, hands, home.
N.B. A. B. Simpson said: "It was not Paul that converted Lydia, but the Lord opened Lydia's heart . . . It is the sun that makes the photograph, not the artist. And so the work of the Acts of the Apostles, the work of the Church of God to the end of time, the work of

every minister and every missionary, the conversion and sanctification of every soul is God's and God's alone."

Conclusion

1. *The Need*

   A worshipper, earnest and sincere, whose heart desired more light.

2. *The Condition*

   Willingness, door of heart never forced (cf. Rev. 3:20).

3. *The Hope*

   No heart too tightly closed.

   Down in the human heart, crushed by the tempter
   Feelings lie buried that grace can restore.
   —Fanny J. Crosby

Study No. 88 — Opposition in Europe (1)

ACTS 16:16-24

CHRISTIANITY is never long in encountering opposition. This had been true in Jerusalem, in Cyprus, and in Asia Minor, and it was true now, in Europe. Christianity had run counter to the religious interests of the Jews, but here it was found contrary to the personal interests of the Greeks and to the national interests of the Romans. Here is the first instance of heathen opposition to Christianity in Europe.

I. The Power of Human Sin (vs. 16, 17)

1. *Perversion of human life*
   a. Slavery — womanhood in subjection to man made in God's image;
   b. Avarice — womanhood used to man's profit — contrast with Lydia, independent "seller," woman of business.
2. *Practice of gross falsehood*
   a. Soothsaying — craft, deceit, fortune-telling;

b. Diabolism — more than trickery — Gr., "a spirit, a Python" — in mythology, dragon guarding Delphi and slain by Apollo; its powers supposed to have been passed on to him and through him to others — often associated with ventriloquism, clairvoyance, frenzy, and demon-worship. Cf. India and Ceylon today.

3. *Profession of true religion*
   a. Testimony — true and clear, in spite of evil source;
   b. Patronage — yet awful, not to be allowed; cf. fallen angels, probably finest imitators of holiness.

II. The Power of Divine Grace (v. 18)

1. *Bold attack*
   a. Such testimony not permitted — has "neither part nor lot in this matter" (cf. 8:21);
   b. Church not to be patronized by devil, nor to be built by his money;
   c. Truth not to be taken on irreverent lips.
2. *Complete victory*
   a. Deliverance from devil;
   b. Intolerance of sin, injustice, and oppression.
3. *Glorious result*
   a. When? Immediately — "he came out the same hour";
   b. How? Divinely — "in the name of Jesus Christ" — this alone gives power over devil;

   N.B. Alexander Smellie wrote: "Each of us has his master, just as surely as the Python-possessed damsel of long ago. At first it is Satan who leads us bound and does with us whatever he wills. But Christ can spoil the strong man, and take from him his goods."

III. The Power of Sinful Opposition (vs. 19-24)

1. *Thwarted* — not concerned with morals, only with gain (v. 19);
2. *Hypocritical* — lying accusations (vs. 20, 21);
3. *Real* — stripes and imprisonment (vs. 22, 23);
4. *Vindictive* — inner prison and stocks (v. 24).

Conclusion

1. *We have similar problems today.*
   a. National — cf. opium, drink, gambling, vice, etc. — all protected by vested interests, so opposition to Christian message certain;
   b. Individual — here is crux of matter — sin of man's heart should be dealt with first, before sins of society.
2. *We have the same solution today.*
   Christ and His Gospel!

He breaks the power of cancelled sin,
He sets the prisoner free;
His blood can make the foulest clean,
His blood availed for me.
—Charles Wesley

Study No. 89 — Opposition in Europe (2)

ACTS 16:19-40

Heathen opposition to the Gospel of Christ had to do with personal interests rather than with the religious considerations that had motivated the Jewish enmity to it. Here is the account of Paul's experience of opposition in the European city of Philippi:

I. Suffering Persecution (vs. 19-24)

1. *Hatred* (v. 19)
   a. Cause — then as now:
      (1) Gains gone — miracle (cf. vs. 16:18) had aroused great rage because of financial loss; cf. this demon-possessed girl with demoniac of Gospels (Matt. 8:28-34; Mark 5:1-20; Luke 8:26-39);
      (2) Today, revivals always hinder evil men's work;
   b. Character — then as now:

(1) Resentment — always felt if Christians come out strongly against sin;

(2) Today, sinners apt to tell Christian worker to attend to sick and heathen, but not to bother them.

2. *Injustice* (vs. 19-21)

a. Apprehension — then as now:

(1) Not really concern for welfare of city, only for own selfish ends;

(2) Today, civic pride often not important if gains gone or threatened;

b. Accusation — then as now:

(1) Jews vs. Romans — Apostles, working from one motive, credited with another;

(2) Today also, Christian workers often wilfully misunderstood.

3. *Cruelty* (vs. 22-24)

a. Insolence — then as now:

(1) "These men, being Jews . . ." (cf. v. 20) — hostility towards Jews not exclusively modern — always have suffered for nationality and for religion — so here, met with concerted violence;

(2) "And teach customs . . ." (cf. v. 21) — what Jewish customs harmful? Neither accusers nor mob could have said if asked — so today;

b. Infliction — then as now — in certain parts of world if not our own:

(1) Indignity — "rent off their clothes";

(2) Injury — "beat them . . . laid many stripes upon them";

(3) Imprisonment — "cast them into prison";

(4) Insult — "the jailor . . . having received such a charge, . . . made their feet fast in the stocks."

II. Proclaiming Salvation (vs. 25-32)

1. *Rejoicing* (v. 25)

a. Anomaly:

(1) In spite of persecution and pain, these Christian prisoners prayed and praised;
N.B. (a) Tertullian wrote: "Legs did not feel because souls were in heaven!"
(b) Spurgeon said: "Paul and Silas sing in the stocks because their minds are at ease, while Herod frets on his throne because conscience makes him a coward. Happiness lies not in the outward, but in the inward. A crust of bread from one heart brings a song, from another a thousand acres of ripening grain can produce no thanksgiving."

(2) What a time — midnight! What a place — prison! Strange time and place for church service;

b. Audience:

(1) Prisoners "were listening" (A.S.V) — what a rare opportunity!

(2) Never before had such things occurred — little had these criminals expected so remarkable a band of fellow-prisoners.

2. *Reaffirmation* (v. 26)
"Great earthquake" resulted in supernaturally —

a. Shaken foundations;

b. Opened doors;

c. Loosened bands;

Guarding His own, the Lord was in this earthquake (cf. 1 Kings 19:11), using it to work His sovereign will.

3. *Reassurance* (vs. 27, 28)
Effect of earthquake —

a. On jailor was abject fear, and attempted suicide;

b. On Paul was sympathy with plight of jailor, and command of situation.

4. *Redemption* (vs. 29-31)

a. Sinner led out of one fear only to experience another — first, for his skin, second, for his soul;

b. Salvation shown to be belief on, not merely about, "the Lord Jesus Christ" (v. 31).

III. Gathering Fruit (vs. 32-34)

1. *Word preached* (vs. 32)
   a. To head of house;
   b. To household.
2. *Kindness shown* (vs. 33, 34)
   a. Healing;
   b. Hospitality.
3. *Confession made* (v. 33)
   a. By baptism;
   b. Promptly and fully.
4. *Joy experienced* (v. 34)
   a. Because of "having believed God" (marg.);
   b. Full of peace and power of grace.

IV. Maintaining Rights (vs. 35-40)

1. *Change in attitude* (vs. 35-39)
   a. On Paul's part (vs. 35-37):
      (1) Had suffered indignity, wrong, and cruelty, but God's purposes had been fulfilled;
      (2) Now it was necessary to show rights of position — would not go out as criminals — true and proper pride and independence for sake of church in Lydia's house (cf. v. 40);
   b. On magistrates' part (vs. 38, 39):
      (1) Knew it to be wholly illegal to treat Roman citizens thus;
      (2) Proved it by fear and improvement in procedure.
2. *Comfort in fellowship* (v. 40)
   a. Invitation again accepted (cf. v. 15) — out of prison, into Christian home;
   b. Mutual edification enjoyed — before departure, gathered with "saints in Jesus Christ which are at Philippi" (Phil. 1:1).

Conclusion

The first Christian witness in Europe was, in spite of stiff opposition, strong, manly, true, courageous. It came from vital contact with Christ and the grace of God through faith in His Name — the dynamic of Christianity:

1. *The Worker*

   Paul here exemplified —

   a. Faith in God — did not question vision in spite of hardship that followed it;
   b. Firmness of spirit — not a murmur under persecution, nor was he daunted by circumstances;
   c. Faithfulness to duty — singing and witnessing in midst of suffering, radiating Divine influence in darkness;
   d. Feeling for fearful — willing to reassure even persecutor;
   e. Fearlessness of attitude — seen not only in endurance of pain, but in subsequent protest to magistrates when time was ripe.

2. *The Convert*

   Jailor had contact with Christ through faith — not in a creed, which is but a guidepost, but in a Person, who is the Goal — not in truths about Christ, but in Christ Himself who is the Truth. Here are the steps he took:

   a. Need felt;
   b. Desire expressed;
   c. Willingness shown;
   d. Truth accepted;
   e. Surrender made;
   f. Joy experienced;
   g. Reality proved.

   Thus, in the Europe of the First Century, amid heathen opposition, the presence of God was realized; the peace of God was enjoyed; the power of God was experienced. How is it in the Europe and the America of the Twentieth Century?

   May we, His children, truthfully say with the poet:

Content with beholding His face,
My all to His pleasure resigned,
No changes of season or place
Would make any change in my mind.

While blest with a sense of His love,
A palace a toy would appear;
And prisons would palaces prove
If Jesus would dwell with me there.

Study No. 90 —

The Conversion of the Philippian Jailer

ACTS 16:25-36

ONE OF THE outstanding characteristics of Christianity is its variety of methods in dealing with men. It takes them as they are and works along the line of their individual temperaments and circumstances. The object is the same — salvation for the soul; but the means vary, taking different ways to one goal. This is shown very clearly in the present chapter, as we compare with the conversion of Lydia and Paul's dealings with the young woman possessed of a demon the transformation wrought in the life of the jailer.

I. Testimony for God (vs. 25, 28, 31)

1. *Words of Solace* — prayer and praise offered by Paul and Silas on their own account, but heard by prisoners, fellows in discomfort (v. 25);
2. *Words of Sympathy* — addressed to jailer in reassurance after earthquake (v. 28);
3. *Words of Salvation* — addressed to jailer in invitation (v. 31);

   N.B. What is our testimony, especially in face of difficulty?

II. Conviction of Sin (v. 29)

1. *Jailer "trembling for fear"* (A.S.V.) — knew something very wrong, life not right;
2. *His post in danger?* Yes, but more — his soul (cf. 14, 17);
3. *Probably remembered* unnecessarily cruel treatment of Paul and Silas (cf. v. 24).

III. Anxiety of Soul (v. 30)

Jailer's question, eternally echoed by sinners, was —

1. *Submissive* — What must —"
2. *Personal* — "I —"
3. *Practical* — "do —"
4. *Definite* — "to be saved?"
   a. "Saved" always in strong contrast to "lost" — cf. similar contrast of lost sheep, silver, son, with "found" (Luke 15:6, 9, 24)*;
   b. Still psychologically true to life — to be saved great need of soul;
   N.B. Alexander MacLaren: "What does salvation mean? It means the opposite of being lost, and unless you and I have laid hold of Jesus Christ we are lost . . . It means the opposite of being in danger, being safe; and unless you and I have laid hold of Jesus Christ we are in danger."
   N.B. Have we ever asked this all-important question? Do we know how to answer it?

IV. Salvation from Sin (vs. 31-36)

1. *Immediate change* — note steps:
   a. Heard (vs. 31, 32);
   b. Accepted (v. 33);
   c. Confessed (vs. 33, 34).
2. *Entire change* — note proofs:
   a. Helped (v. 33);
   b. Was baptized (v. 33);
   c. Welcomed (v. 34);
   d. Rejoiced (v. 34);

---

* See author's *Outline Studies in Luke,* pp. 236 ff.

e. Showed courtesy (v. 36);
N.B. Have we ever doubted "sudden conversions"? But here is one: influences may well be many and far back, and yet action sudden. Cf. flower from bud; and one swift blow often cleaner cut than sawing or filing.

Conclusion

1. *"What must I do to be saved?"* (v. 30)
   a. The need — salvation, safety;
   Danger caused by sin — its guilt, its power, its presence;
   b. The provision — the Lord Jesus Christ;
   Redeemer from all three — in past, in present, and in future;
   c. The means — belief, faith, committal to a Person;
   Shown by hearing, accepting, obeying.

2. *What must I do to be lost?*
   No elaboration of answer to this question, for it consists of just one word: Nothing!
   Are *you* saved, or are you lost? "Believe on the Lord Jesus Christ, and thou shalt be saved!"

Study No. 91 — The Gospel in Thessalonica

ACTS 17:1-9

THE ACTS OF THE APOSTLES covers a period of thirty years and is centered about thirteen cities of the ancient world: Jerusalem, the two Antiochs, Lystra, Derbe, Iconium, Philippi, Thessalonica, Berea, Athens, Corinth, Ephesus, and Rome. Of these, Thessalonica is interesting because, as the modern Salonika, prominent in the history of the Great War of 1914-18, the city is one of the few on the list that survive today. Named in honor of a Macedonian victory over the Thessalonians, it was and still is an important center because of three rivers which there flow into the sea.

In verses 1 and 2, we read that there was a Jewish synagogue in Thessalonica and that Paul attended it on three sabbath days, "as his manner was." By so doing he was obeying God's holy commandment, enjoying religious fellowship, and furthering his own spiritual welfare. It is even possible that the word rendered here "sabbath days" may mean "weeks," as it translated elsewhere (cf. Mark 16: 2,9; Luke 18:12; 1 Cor. 16:2), implying daily discussions in the synagogue.

It will be profitable for us to compare the Christian approach then and now —its message, its methods, its materials; and we may refer also to Paul's Letters to the Thessalonians.

I. The Gospel Preached (vs. 1-3)

1. *Its Divine Authority* (vs. 2, 3a)
   a. Based on "the Scriptures" available then, viz., O.T.;
   b. Proved by means of reasoning with hearers — our word "dialectic" comes from this Gr. word — suggests constant discussion, which included:
   (1) "Opening," or explaining, revealing, letting in light (cf. 16:14);

(2) "Alleging," or affirming, setting forth, laying before audience.

2. *Its Direct Argument* (v. 3b)
   a. That Messiah must die as atonement for sin — doctrine very objectionable to Jews, preventing them from accepting Christianity (cf. 1 Cor. 1:18, 23);
   N.B. Even Apostles had received this concept with difficulty (cf. Matt. 16:21, 22; Luke 24:25, 26);
   b. That Messiah must rise again as proof of victory (cf. 2:23-36; 13:29-37).

3. *Its Distinct Appeal* (v. 3c)
   a. Jesus is this Saviour who died and rose again;
   b. His Messiahship is evidenced by His personal history:
      (1) His supernatural origin;
      (2) His superlative power;
      (3) His startling omniscience;
      (4) His simple majesty of speech;
      (5) His sublime departure from this world;
      (6) His supreme achievement of redemption;
      N.B. The same Gospel today: A Divine Person died and rose again, according to the Scriptures (cf. 1 Cor. 15:3, 4).

4. *Its Definite Assurance* (vs. 2c, 3c; also 1 Thess. 1:5)
   a. By the Word — "out of the Scriptures" — "our gospel came . . . in word";
   b. By the Preacher — "whom I preach" — "in power" — of thought and of feeling;
   c. By the Spirit — "in the Holy Ghost."

II. The Gospel Received (v. 4)

1. *Its Wide Influence*
   a. Regardless of religion or nationality — "devout Greeks" (cf. Eph. 2:11-22) — Gentile adherents of Jewish faith, not yet admitted by circumcision (cf. 13:43);
   b. Regardless of position or sex — "chief women" (cf. Gal. 3:28) — ladies of high birth and strong influence in city, probably Macedonians;

N.B. Some regard this verse as description of extension of work beyond the three weeks in synagogue (cf. 1 and 2 Thess.).

2. *Its Immediate Power*
   a. Because "received " not as mere "word of men," but as "Word of God, which effectually worketh" (1 Thess. 2:13);
   b. Because "received" not only as doctrine, but as rule of conduct — "how . . . to walk and to please God" (1 Thess. 4:1).

3. *Its Permanent Result*
   a. Faith — "believed" (v. 4), or "were persuaded" (A.S.V.) — reception of Gospel immediate and real;
   b. Fellowship — "consorted with Paul and Silas" (v. 4), or "took sides, cast in lot" (Gr.) — reproduction of Gospel brought Christian cooperation;
   c. Fortitude — "certain brethren" dragged (A.S.V.) "unto the rulers of the city" (v. 6) — reality of Gospel in lives gave endurance under persecution.

III. The Gospel Opposed (vs. 5-9)

1. *Its Perennial Persecutors* (v. 5a)
   a. Once again, "Jews which believed not" showed their jealousy and enmity against evangelization of Gentiles (cf. 13:45, 50; 14:5, 19; 1 Thess. 2:14-16);
   b. Loungers in marketplace ("certain vile fellows of the rabble," A.S.V.) influenced to stir up strife against missionaries — Thessalonians seem to have been notorious for laziness (cf. 2 Thess. 3:10-13), so easily used by Jews.

2. *Its Determined Persecution* (vs. 5b-9)
   a. First attack on house of Jason where missionaries were staying, though not in at time; Jason name of Christian at Corinth (cf. Rom. 16:21), thought by many to be same person — may have been either Jewish or Gentile convert, but Jason is Greek form of Hebrew Joshua;

b. Not finding Paul and companions, Jews determined to wreak vengeance on Jason by bringing him and other believers before magistrates and charging them with associating with men who had "turned the world upside down, " i.e., were seditious;
Illus.: Asked about a certain evangelist who was doing a fine work, man replied: "Have you not read about certain men in Acts who turned the world upside down? Well, I believe this man is a relative of those!"

c. In view of Emperor's decrees against treason (v. 7), this charge was crafty, and Paul's teaching about Christ's Lordship might easily have given color to accusation in eyes of mob, who did not distinguish between spiritual and earthly kingship; cf. accusation against Christ Himself (Luke 23:1-5; John 18:28-40);

d. Only after authorities required "security" of Jason and "the rest" (A.S.V.), legal term meaning what is now called bail, were they released.

Conclusion

Note Paul's summing up of Thessalonian Christianity in 1 Thess. 1:3-10. He recalls particularly their —

1. *"Work of Faith"* (v. 3)
— "how ye turned to God from idols" (v. 9);
2. *"Labour of Love"* (v. 3)
— "to serve the living and true God" (v. 9);
3. *"Patience of Hope"* (v. 3)
— "to wait for His Son from heaven" (v. 10).

Have *you* faced the claims of Christ?
Are *you* "persuaded' (Acts 17:4, marg.)?
Are *you* therefore willing to count the cost of discipleship?

Study No. 92 — The Gospel at Berea

ACTS 17:10-15

When the Thessalonian Christians, to avoid further trouble, sent Paul and Silas away by night, they chose as destination Berea, a city about fifty miles to the southwest. It is now called Veria, and in it are more than seventy "hidden churches" dating back to the Turkish persecution of Greek Christians. There is also a small park with a modern speaker's stand which bears the name of "St. Paul's Pulpit," all of which would seem to bear out the statements in these verses.

I. The Gospel Considered (vs. 10, 11)

1. *The Receptive Audience*
   a. Again Paul entered synagogue and reception this time was excellent;
   b. Berean Jews "more noble than those in Thessalonica" (v. 11) — word means literally noble by birth, but doubtless refers here to liberal character and large-hearted disposition that should accompany privilege;
   c. They also showed "readiness of mind" — cf. "readiness to will" (2 Cor. 8:11) — made ready, surely, by Holy Spirit's influence.

2. *The Reverent Attitude*
   a. Bereans also willing to give Paul's message consideration in light of daily study of Scripture (cf. Deut. 6:6-9; John 5:39);
   b. This Jewish reception of Gospel unique in Paul's experience, and probably due to isolated geographical position of city in mountains of Greece, and consequent eagerness to learn about something new.

II. The Gospel Accepted (v. 12)

1. *The Natural Outcome*
   a. "Therefore many of them believed" — reverence for and reliance on Word of God always means reception of Gospel and reproduction by its means (cf. Psa. 19:7-14; John 5:46);
   b. Again women of Macedonia are prominent (cf. v. 4; 13:50), but in Berea men, too, were not lacking in response.
2. *The Compressed Account*
   a. Probably intended to include much more than appears on surface (cf. 13:44-49);
   b. Significant that name "Berean" often used to this day for Bible study bands, etc.

III. The Gospel Hindered (vs. 13-15)

1. *The Bad Example*
   a. Peaceful mission did not last long, for Jews of Macedonia repeated action of those of Galatia (cf. 14:19) and, coming from Thessalonica to Berea, were determined to oppose Paul and his companions (cf. 1 Thess. 2:15, 16);
   b. Their one idea was to make trouble and take advantage of ignorance and prejudice.
2. *The Immediate Results*
   a. Berean brethren, probably including Sopater (cf. 20:4; Rom. 16:21), took Paul to sea-coast and thence to Athens;
   b. Silas and Timothy remained behind to establish new converts in both Berea and Thessalonica (cf. 1 Thess. 3:1, 2);
   c. Macedonian situation doubtless easier and safer with prime mover gone against whom Jewish hostility was chiefly directed;
   d. Bereans returning carried Paul's orders to rejoin him — which took place at Corinth (cf. v. 16 with 18:5), showing unexpected interruption of Paul's stay at Athens (cf. vs. 32, 33);

e. Nothing known of Berean church after this, unless implied by 20:4, 2 Cor. 8:1, and 1 Thess. 4:10 — Paul's short time there for instruction would be source of anxiety to him which reunion with associates would relieve.

Conclusion

The Berean attitude to the Gospel was characterized by —

1. *Receptivity*
   — reverent attention;
2. *Research*
   — reasoning activity;
3. *Revelation*
   — resulting acceptance.

Here my choicest treasure's hid;
Here my best comfort lies;
Here my desires are satisfied,
And here my hopes arise.
Then let me love my Bible more,
And take a fresh delight
By day to read those wonders o'er,
And meditate by night.

Study No. 93 — Paul at Athens

ACTS 17:16-34

PAUL AT ATHENS offers one of the finest illustrations of the Gospel in relation to mankind, of Christianity faced with the wisdom of the world, and of Christ revealed with reference to human thought. Paul's great working principle is expressed in his First Epistle to Corinth (9:22): "I am made all things to all men, that I might by all means save some." Thus, in preaching, he adapted himself to his audiences, whether Jews or Gentiles, cultured or ignorant. At Athens Christianity met the best thought of the day, and since Paul claimed that the Gospel was for all he seized this opportunity to include men of culture, education, and philosophy. Sir William Ramsay calls it in some ways the most "picturesque and interesting incident in his whole career."

Athens was different from any other place that Paul had visited, since it was, indeed, unique. It was the most celebrated city in Greece, the home of literature and art, famous in politics and thought. Although under the Romans at this time, Athens was still the intellectual center and university city of the world, so that its importance can hardly be exaggerated. Paul at Tarsus had come under the influence of Greek culture, and must have realized the outstanding importance of Athens, for he was able to appreciate its learning and admire its glories. Most important of all, he was able, as a true servant of Christ, to realize its spiritual needs.

It is sometimes thought that Paul made a mistake at Athens in the philosophical manner of his address, an error which showed itself in comparative failure. But this does not seem to be warranted by anything found in the story, or even in the first Epistle to the Corinthians, as is so often claimed. Paul's words as given in the English versions of 1 Cor. 2:2 are not the correct interpretation of the original. A careful study of the Greek will show that he does not here limit his preaching to the proclamation of the Cross. Indeed, he tells us in verse 6 that among mature Christians he preaches Divine wisdom. Verse 2 is part of his solemn warning to the Corinthians in their exaltation of human wisdom (see 1:10 to 4:21 as one whole section of Paul's letter). What he means is that he had made up his mind about one subject, i.e., Christ crucified, and that at all costs he was going to deliver that message, whatever else he should be led to discuss when he arrived in Corinth. There may have been circumstances in that city very different to those obtaining in Athens, which necessitated a prominent, not to say a predominant, preaching of Christ crucified. Certainly the prevailing sins of the two places were not the same. This text, according to the Greek, does not at all imply that the Cross was the only thing made known by Paul. The true meaning will be shown if we render the text, not "I determined — not to know," but rather "I did not determine — to know," the negative modifying the word "determined," not the word "know."

In Athens Paul is adapting himself to his audience and, in view of what we know of that city, it is not surprising that there are so few results. Fortunately, the spiritual quality of a sermon does not depend on the numbers of people moved by it. We have already seen how Paul addressed Jews (13:16-41), and uncultured Gentiles (14:15-17); here we have a striking instance of still another method of apostolic preaching. We see Paul facing the highest intellects of his day and speaking with a wonderful combination of faithfulness and tact. Theologically speaking, he gave an illustration of a trained Semite who believed in the Divine transcendence dealing with trained Aryans who believed in the Divine immanence. He started from their belief in immanence (v. 23), and led them to see that the immanent, indwelling God was also the transcendent, supreme Being, above men and nature alike (vs. 24-27). Then Paul reverted to immanence (v. 28), and lastly showed the overwhelming transcendence of God (vs. 29-31). How versatile was the Apostle to the Gentiles in proclaiming His Master's Gospel!

I. God's Worship Neglected (v. 16)

1. *What Paul saw* — "the city wholly given to idolatry"
   While waiting for his friends to join him (see v. 15), could not but notice remarkable number of temples, shrines, altars, idols.
2. *What Paul Felt* — "his spirit was stirred in him"
   Instead of being impressed by beauty of sculpture and architecture, he looked at them from religious standpoint and was roused to strong indignation at terrible idolatry and insult to God (cf. Rom. 1:22, 23).

II. God's Message Delivered (vs. 17, 18)

1. *To the Jews* (v. 17)
   Thus stirred, Paul began his work as usual in local synagogue.
2. *To the devout Greeks* (v. 17)
   Some Athenians evidently not satisfied with idolatry and were seeking one true God.
3. *To men of all sorts* (vs. 17, 18)
   a. Daily "in the market" (cf. 16:19), open space in center of city where people congregated — spot in Athens crowded with works of art and used by teachers for lectures to their students;
   b. Here were "philosophers" of two opposing schools:
      (1) Epicureans — followers of Epicurus, born about 400 years before — taught pleasure as main purpose of life and regarded gods as living in calm happiness far removed from all earthly things;
      N.B. "But," says Alexander Smellie, "Paul 'preached unto them Jesus.' Jesus, who brings God near to bless us! Jesus, through whom God says to laboring and heavy-laden men, 'I will give you rest'! Jesus in whom God died because He cannot let us die!"
      (2) Stoics — followers of Zeno, born about 300 years before — taught practice of virtue for own sake, fatalism, and discipline of endurance;
      N.B. "And," says Dr. Smellie again, "Paul 'preached unto them Jesus,' . . . Jesus, who sets us the loftiest

standard of duty in His example, and furnishes us with the strongest motive for duty in His love, and imparts to us the indispensable impulse of duty in His indwelling life."

c. Both philosophies had natural tendency to dispense with God, whether in pleasure or in pride — one materialistic, and other pantheistic;

d. Paul's theme, "Jesus and the resurrection," made all these men curious, calling him "babbler," term of Athenian slang, as one writer suggests — implying one who picks up scraps of knowledge and retails them, one utterly outside ordinary university culture, adventurer hunting for living and pretending to wisdom he does not possess;

e. But Paul was soon seen to be earnest, capable speaker.

III. God's Servant Examined (vs. 19-21)

1. *The Outcome*

a. Paul led to Areopagus, or "Hill of Mars," named from trial of god Mars supposed to have taken place there;

b. Word also used of council accustomed to meet there (cf. v. 34), so Paul may have been taken before this body to give account of teaching.

2. *The Statement*

a. Athenians, and strangers attracted by fame of city, probably made it fashion at least to pretend to be concerned with intellectual problems and especially with novelties in thought;

b. Contemporary writers spoke of idle inquisitiveness, though man's true object is not speculation, but service, not curiosity, but consecration.

IV. God's Person Unknown (vs. 22, 23)

With exquisite tact, Paul began address, adapting himself to audience like old Greek orators, and saying, in effect, that in Athens God was —

1. *Feared*

   People were "very religious" (A.R.V.) — "too divinity-fearing" (Gr.), or carrying religion rather far, superstitious in the sense of excessive dread of supernatural;

2. *Worshipped*

   But along with other "objects of . . . worship" (A.S.V.) — not given sole place which is His due;

3. *Unrealized*

   "Ignorantly" (v. 23) is, rather, "unconsciously" — altar to "Unknown God" probably both expression of sincere longing and striking confession of ignorance and fear; thus God was worshipped with mistaken piety.

V. God's Truth Declared (vs. 24-28)

Paul started where Greeks left off and, as they did not know O.T., made no reference to it, but instead, to true God along two main lines:

1. *In Nature*

   a. The Person of God:

      (1) Creator — "God that made the world and all things therein" (v. 24);

      (2) Ruler — "seeing He is Lord of heaven and earth, dwelleth not in temples made with hands" (v. 24);

      (3) Life-giver — "He giveth to all life, and breath, and all things" (v. 25);

   b. The Worship of God:

      (1) Spiritual — "neither is worshipped with men's hands, as though He needeth anything" (v. 25; cf. Psa. 50:7-15) — i.e., He is Spirit (cf. John 4:24, Gr.);

      (2) Intelligent — thus, Paul implies, altar of ignorant worship (cf. v. 23), built by human effort, was not only totally unnecessary, but against witness of Nature.

2. *In Man*

   a. The Work of God:

(1) Universality — "hath made of one blood all nations of men" (v. 26) — therefore, one God for whole world;

(2) Providence — "hath determined . . . times . . . and . . . bounds" (v. 26; cf. Deut. 32:8);

b. The Purpose of God:

(1) Man seeking and finding Him — "that they should seek the Lord, . . . and find Him" (v. 27);

(2) Man realizing his sphere in Him — "in Him we live, and move, and have our being" (v. 28);
N.B. Note quotation from Greek poets (Aratus and Cleanthes, both Stoics, in which man is called God's "offspring," or "race" (Gr.), as in creation — not His children or sons, as in redemption.

VI. God's Gospel Proclaimed (vs. 29-31)

From God in Nature and in Man, Paul proceeded to his special subject of God in Christ:

1. *In Relation to Past* (vs. 29, 30a)

a. Human ignorance — in spite of having been made "in the image of God" (Gen. 1:27), man had made images for His worship and had ignored His true nature;

b. Divine mercy — God had overlooked for a time this ignorance (cf. 14:16) and "sins that are past" (Rom. 3:25), awaiting opportunity of revelation in Christ.

2. *In Relation to Present* (v. 30b)

a. Universal repentance now called for;

b. All reasons for ignorance removed in Christ.

3. *In Relation to Future* (v. 31)

a. Day set for righteous judgment of all mankind;

b. Proof of it given in resurrection of Judge from dead;
N.B. A. B. Simpson said that "the message . . . deserves to be written in letters of gold . . . The whole address could be repeated in five or six minutes, and yet it outweighs whole volumes of philosophy, theology and diluted homiletics."

VII. God's Offer Received (vs. 32-34)

Mention of resurrection caused interruption, and it seemed impossible for Paul to go further. This enables us to see threefold result of his address:

1. *Ridicule* (v. 32a)

   a. From Epicureans, because they did not believe in life after death;

   b. From Stoics, because, though believing in future existence of soul, they were not ready to adopt doctrine of resurrection of body.

2. *Procrastination* (v. 32b)

   Either —

   a. Courteous dismissal by inquisitive, who left at point of moral pressure; or —

   b. Adjournment for further inquiry by those who may have been keenly desirous of hearing more.

   But in both cases, we are told, "Paul departed from among them" (v. 33). When conscience touched, natural man refuses to listen further. However, in case of few, there was —

3. *Acceptance* (v. 34)

   a. Some "clave" — strong Greek word used for contrast, signifying unnatural or, as here, supernatural union;

   b. Some "believed" — including two conspicuous people, Dionysius, important judge, and Damaris, woman who may have been foreign and not very reputable, since Greek women of respectability seem never to have appeared in public gatherings; thus, these names may have been early instance of many such contrasts among believers;

   N.B. Paul never returned to Athens nor addressed another word to her people, so far as is known. Perhaps, though he could bear opposition, he was led to disregard indifference.

Conclusion

1. *The Messenger of God*

   Paul at his best as orator and preacher:

   a. His introduction was conciliatory (v. 22);
   b. His proposition was clear (v.23);
   c. His exposition was concise (vs. 24-28);
   d. His application was cogent (vs. 29-31).

2. *The Message about God*

   a. How did Paul characterize Him? As —
      (1) Divine Creator (v. 24);
      (2) Universal Lord (v. 24);
      (3) Bountiful Giver (v. 25);
      (4) Almighty Ruler (v. 26);
      (5) Unseen Spirit (vs. 27, 28a);
      (6) Tender Father (vs. 28b-30);
      (7) Righteous Judge (v. 31).
   b. How did Paul speak about Him? With —
      (1) Tact — approached considerately, awakening interest without arousing prejudice (v. 22);
      (2) Fairness — recognized hearers' position, finding common starting-point (v. 23);
      (3) Truth — stated positively as well as negatively, reminding of God's essentially spiritual being (vs. 24, 25);
      (4) Attractiveness — assured of God's Fatherhood, emphasizing uplifting power of Gospel (vs. 26, 27);
      (5) Appeal — spoke to inner consciousness of man, devoting secular wisdom to sacred use (vs. 28, 29);
      (6) Faithfulness — told them ignorance not only error, but sin, declaring God's full revelation (vs. 30, 31);
      (7) Trust — showed no discouragement when efforts not notably successful, leaving results to Him (vs. 32-34; 18:1).

For today's messenger from God, Christ must be in the mind for knowledge, in the heart for trust, in the will for surrender, and in the life for obedience.

Study No. 94 — Paul's Message to Athens

ACTS 17:30, 31

IT IS WELL KNOWN that a single drop of iodine is strong enough to impregnate a large quantity of water; that a small quantity of yeast will leaven a large lump of dough; and that a colored glass held in front of the eye will tinge everything seen with the same color. It is equally true that one idea, one desire, or one motive in a man's mind can color and influence the whole of his life. The desire to get on in business will often so take possession of a man that everything will be considered solely in reference to it. The desire of a student to amass knowledge will frequently cause him to ask concerning everything he meets whether it will add to his store of information. The desire of a young man to rise to high position will probably so possess his mind and heart as to cause him to bend everything in life to his aim. The same is true in spiritual matters, as we find from this incident of St. Paul at Athens. There was one all-embracing idea in his mind, one all-absorbing feeling in his heart, one all-powerful motive in his will, and that was GOD! Everything in his whole life was colored, influenced, and controlled by God. To him God was everything, and by him everything was considered in relation to God.

The Apostle was waiting at Athens for his friends Silas and Timothy to rejoin him, but his waiting was more energetic than most men's toil, for he at once was stirred to testify concerning his God. Paul was in a city, perhaps the most renowned in the then known world, where the human form, art, architecture, poetry, wisdom had been manifested at their highest point of excellence; a city where a man of Paul's culture could have spent days and weeks with a burning interest, examining the numerous statues, some by Phidias, generally acknowledged to be the greatest sculptor of all time. Such a visitor might have explored the various places of note and appreciated to the full their historic associations. But no, none of these things moved Paul, except in one way, in relation to God. The statues of Jupiter and Mercury, the Acropolis, the Parthenon — all these and much more went for nothing in the presence of the idolatry on all sides, showing so clearly that the Athenians were without the true God and, therefore, without hope in the world. One thing especially had caught Paul's eye, an altar with a strange inscription — "To the Unknown God." In this he saw at once a proof of the need for God and of the inability of the natural man to find Him.

Such universal idolatry impelled the Apostle to speak out, reasoning with Jew and Gentile, in synagogue and market-place. When his preaching of Christ had aroused curiosity, Paul was led by certain philosophers in his audience to Mars Hill, where there was doubtless a better opportunity for discussion, perhaps in the meeting-place of the city council, or Areopagus. There he presented God to these people, saying in effect, "You Athenians have given me a text. I start where you leave off. The God you acknowledge and worship without knowing, I declare to you!" Then he proceeded to state the true conception of God as Creator, Life-Giver, and Preserver, affirming that in Him all men live, and move, and have their being. Thus did Paul attempt to bring home to the people of Athens the knowledge of the true God. If we dwell for a little on the two verses which follow at this point in his discourse, we shall find that there were four things about God that Paul emphasized before his learned audience.

I. The Forbearance of God — "the times of ignorance therefore God overlooked" (v. 30, A.S.V.).

1. *The Nature of This Ignorance*

   a. Ignorance of God Himself:

      (1) Pagan worship regarded deity as practically confined to temple, as prince holding court in such and such a city;

      (2) It also had different gods for different places, and consisted of homage paid to statues whose very beauty,

in many cases, tended to fix thought more on themselves than on deity they represented;

b. Ignorance of Man's Relation to God:
   (1) Pagans thought of God as afar off, unconcerned with world and having no relationship to it;
   (2) To them He had no conscious connection with them and so they lived day after day as though He did not really exist.

2. *The Cause of This Ignorance*
   a. Sin:
      (1) God had made man upright and in full communion with Himself, but sin entered, separating them;
      (2) Gradually, though very really, knowledge of God and man's relationship to Him faded, resulting in pagan worship of Greece and other nations (cf. Rom. 1:19-25);
   b. Self-will:
      (1) This is always included in sin and is opposite of submission to God;
      (2) Result is dense ignorance and blank despair suggested by inscription on Athenian altar already mentioned.

3. *The Overlooking of This Ignorance*
   a. How did God overlook it?
      (1) By not granting further knowledge of Himself; centuries passed and darkness grew dense and more terrible;
      (2) By not punishing pagan nations — Assyria, Babylon, Persia, Media, Greece, Rome, all allowed to continue in own ways to this point (except in so far as they had contact with Israel);
   b. Why did God overlook it?
      Sin was surely not disregarded as of no moment; far from it — sin is sin at all times, and God would not be God if He were ever indifferent to it:
      (1) Ignoring of sin was temporary, in order to prove

human need of God and inability to find Him (cf. 1 Cor. 1:21);

(2) Still more, because of Divine plan of salvation to send Someone who should come and dispel ignorance and banish darkness — "when the fulness of time was come, God sent forth His Son" (Gal. 4:4);

(3) Cf. man's ignorance of God in John 1:18 with his new relationship to God in John 3:5 — Gospel is revelation of Christ as One able to destroy work of Devil shown in man's ignorance and sin.

II. The Commandment of God — "but now commandeth all men everywhere to repent" (v. 30)

No longer forbearance on part of God:

1. *Why?*
   a. Time of testing over — altar proved "world by wisdom knew not God" (1 Cor. 1:21);
   b. Work of salvation completed — object of Christ's coming was threefold (see I John 5:20, 21);
      (1) To reveal God to man — "that we may know Him that is true";
      (2) To show man's relation to God — "we are in Him that is true";
      (3) To deal with sin as cause of former ignorance — "keep yourselves from idols."
2. *What instead of forbearance?*

   Repentance — crux of message of Paul to Athens:
   a. What it is:
      (1) New reflection as to past (Gr., "after-thought"), and new resolution as to future;
      (2) Change of mind about God and man's relation to Him, issuing in change of life; and —
      (3) Starting to live in light, instead of in darkness;
   b. What it is not:

      Not atonement, for that has been wrought;
   c. What it does:

(1) Gives mind new perception of sin as fact;
(2) Gives heart new repulsion against sin as guilt before God;
(3) Gives will new choice of God's law and truth and holiness;

d. How it must be experienced:
(1) It must be done at once — "now" — God gave man up for long time to own devices, but new day has dawned; world many thousands of years old, but we today still date letters from "now" of redemption;
(2) It must be done by all — "all men" — not by one or two; as none exempt from ignorance of sin, so none excused from change which repentance brings;
(3) It must be done in all places — "everywhere" — no place on earth where sin has not reached; and so there must be no place where light of Gospel shall not penetrate and God's message of repentance be proclaimed.

III. The Appointment of God — "because He hath appointed a day, in the which He will judge the world in righteousness by that Man whom He hath ordained" (v.31)

1. *The Future Judgment*

a. Inevitable — "He will judge"
(1) Fact of judgment must have sounded novel to Athenian ears, although old fable had told of Minos and Rhadamanthus in Hades;
(2) But human philosophy had succeeded mythology, obscuring even vague idea of future punishment; so Paul resolutely preached judgment to come;
(3) Such preaching much needed today — knowledge of coming judgment best human guarantee of morality;
(4) Even believer needs thought of "judgment seat of Christ" (Rom. 14:10; 2 Cor. 5:10), to steady him and solemnize life:
(a) Christ "bare our sins" (1 Pet. 2:24), and "there is therefore now no condemnation" (Rom. 8:1),

but sins of believers are principally associated with unfaithfulness of life and service;

(b) We can hide much from fellow-man, and many things are not what they seem; but day is coming when every motive, desire, and action will be laid bare before Christ;

(c) This judgment will not involve eternal destiny, but distinctions of reward;

(5) But, according to other passages, Christ is coming not merely to judge world, but also, and first, to take His people to be with Him; only subsequently will He return to earth for judgment;

(6) Emphasis on judgment, however, is abundantly warranted by many Scripture references.

b. Universal — "the world"

(1) Not one exception because of merit — "we must all appear" (2 Cor. 5:10);

(2) Not one missing because of status — "the dead, small and great, stand before God" (Rev. 20:12);

(3) All will be there to give account and to receive according to deeds done in body (cf. again Rom. 14:10 and 2 Cor. 5:10).

c. Righteous — "in righteousness"

(1) Every allowance will be made for defect of ability through defect of opportunity;

(2) But at the same time full answer will be demanded for every disregard of privilege, every abuse of opportunity;

(3) Those who never heard Gospel and are still in ignorance of sin through no fault of their own will be judged according to privileges, few or many;

(4) But those to whom has come God's command to repent will be judged differently;

(5) In all cases, however, "shall not the Judge of all the earth do right?" (Gen. 18:25)

N.B. Four distinct judgments are mentioned in N.T.: (1) of sin on Cross (cf. John 12:31); (2) of believers in regard to faithfulness since conversion (cf. 2 Cor. 5:10); (3) of living nations before millennium (cf. Matt. 25:31-46); and (4) of unconverted at Great White Throne (cf. Rev. 20:11-15).

But perhaps greater novelty in St. Paul's message to the Athenians was what he said about —

2. *The Judge*

A "Man" — why?

a. Because, being one with us, He will know our frame (cf. Psa. 103:14), and therefore have that sympathy that is so necessary to true, righteous judgment;
b. Because, since Man who died is Man who lives and who will judge, we shall be shown to be without excuse in meeting as Judge Him whom as Saviour we have either accepted or rejected;
c. Because God has ordained Him and thus set His seal on Him, honoring Him because of His life and work (cf. John 5:22, 23, 27).

This, then, is message of Gospel — judgment inevitable, universal, and righteous, by Man ordained of God, with close connection between it and previous call to repentance. This call of God will have to be accounted for in day when Christ shall judge secrets of all hearts, according to Paul's Gospel (cf. Rom. 2:16). To make quite sure of this, and in order that there be no mistake, we now have God's proof of future judgment:

IV. The Assurance of God — "whereof He hath given assurance unto all men, in that He hath raised Him from the dead" (v. 31)

Judgment does not rest simply on word, but on fact:

1. *The Resurrection of Christ*

a. This "assurance" is given by God — why?

(1) Resurrection proves many things, among them God's thought of Christ and purpose for Christ which included appointment of Him as Judge of all men;

(2) Fact that God raised Him from dead is God's testimony to world that there will be future judgment of sin by Him;

(3) No fact in whole range of history more certain or more capable of proof than Resurrection of Jesus Christ, and it carries with it certainty of judgment to come;

b. This "assurance" given to all — how?

(1) By fact that Holy Spirit is now in world, stirring, convicting, converting, and sanctifying men's hearts;

(2) If Christ had not risen and ascended, Holy Spirit would not have descended (cf. John 16:7); but now He is here.

From the Resurrection of Christ is implied —

2. *The Resurrection of All*

a. This "assurance" shows reality of future life — death is not full stop, or period, to sentence of life, but only a colon or comma, and narrative is continued and completed in world to come;

b. This "assurance" includes "resurrection of the dead" (v. 32), i.e., of all men — word in original is "out of," i.e., as pledge or proof that all will be raised; Man has been raised, man will be raised (cf. John 5:19-29).

Conclusion

1. *What, then, was Paul's message at Athens?*
   a. The Longsuffering of God concerning past ignorance;
   b. The Law of God concerning present duty; and —
   c. The Judgment of God concerning future life.
2. *What was the result of Paul's sermon?*
   a. As far as immediate results were concerned, preaching was comparative failure, and St. Paul departed without having founded church, and probably discouraged and lonely;
   b. Some Athenians mocked, others procrastinated, and only a few believed:

(1) Those who mocked did so at any such idea as resurrection of the dead, especially of body, which was to them totally absurd;

(2) Some put off — would they live to hear him again? Would he preach to them a second time? No, he did not; they consulted first their own convenience, and so they never heard him again. When, if ever, they desired to do so, he had gone.

3. *What was the cause of such a barren result?*

Simply this — majority left him at point of moral pressure:

a. As long as he tickled fancy or intrigued mind with novel ideas about God, they were interested, but when he came close home to conscience and claimed change of life and submission to Christ they left him; speculations about God, yes; change and amendment of life, and acceptance of Christ, no;

b. How is it with us now? You probably would not mock and jeer truth of God, but possibly you may let opportunity to accept it pass and defer decision to more convenient season; you may have heard Gospel so often as to be practically indifferent to it. Let us therefore face truth now and yield to God in —

(1) Conviction of intellect;
(2) Confidence of heart;
(3) Control of will; and —
(4) Conversion of life.

4. *After all, then, was St. Paul's preaching at Athens really a failure?*

a. No, indeed! He founded no church there, but one grew up later and from it came some of our most noble martyrs; Christian school at Athens became noted and even the very Parthenon became dedicated — however mistakenly — to worship of mother of this Galilean of whom Paul spoke, instead of that of pagan goddess. Thus Paul's sermon at Athens was beginning of end of pagan worship;

b. Scoffers did not dream that one day this discourse would be more read and discussed than all those of their famous scholars put together — had no idea that Paul had pronounced sentence of death over all this ancient polytheism and idolatry; simple and brief as discourse was, it was great page in history of religion and Christian Church;

c. Even Demosthenes fulminating against Philip of Macedon was nothing in comparison with this fiery little Jew with weak presence and contemptible speech (cf. 2 Cor. 10:10), because Paul stood, as it were, foursquare in strength of almighty God;

d. Moreover, statues of Jupiter and Minerva, and philosophies of Plato, Socrates, and Aristotle were as nothing beside power of true God, of Athens, Greece, Europe, and world; and ever-to-be-admired fictions of Homer were vain compared with true story of that Galilean who died on a cross;

e. There in Athens was the Christian "folly" (1 Cor. 1:21, 25, 27; 3:18), face to face with wisdom and glory of world, and it has so far conquered and will continue to conquer (cf. 1 Cor. 15:25; Heb. 2:8, 9);

f. Victories of past are pledge of victories of future; present Saviour will become future Victor; and throne of grace now will become throne of power and judgment then (cf. Matt. 25:46; Phil. 2:10; Rev. 11:15).

Thus, there comes the message of God to everyone: "See that ye refuse not Him that speaketh" (Heb. 12:25); "To you is the word of this salvation sent" (13:26); "Now is the day of salvation" (2 Cor. 6:2).

Study No. 95 — Paul at Corinth, And After

ACTS 18:1-28

THE CONTRAST between Paul's experiences in Athens (17:16-34) and those in Corinth is very striking. The two cities are only forty miles apart, and yet, while Paul's work in Athens was not marked by any striking success, in Corinth he did some of the best and most widely influential work of his life. The length of time spent there shows the importance of the city, which was the capital of the Roman province of Achaia, or Greece. To go from Athens, the intellectual center, to Corinth, the political and commercial center, was something like going from, say, Oxford or Cambridge to London, or from Boston to Washington or New York. Corinth on its isthmus was an ancient and famous city, with two harbors uniting two seas, the Aegean and the Adriatic, and it lay on the direct route from Rome to the East. It had a large, mixed population, was famous for the Isthmian Games, and was also notorious for its wickedness, its very name being a by-word for terrible sin.

Such an important place was the right one for the Apostle Paul, who must have been a lover of great cities, for he evidently felt at home when in the center of things. Furthermore, his active, business-like temperament would probably feel more attracted to the Corinthians than to the word-splitters of Athens. There were five stages in his Corinth experience:

I. Discipleship — Paul and His Life (vs. 1-4)

1. *Wayfaring* (v.1)
   a. When Paul came to Corinth he was feeling weak and fearful (cf. 1 Cor. 2:3), yet on he pressed, assured that God who knows where He wants His servants had brought him thus far;

b. Must often have reviewed whole journey — prevented from preaching in several places, until at Troas he felt God guiding him to Europe; but even in Macedonia no great sense of need shown, and work continually opposed — cf. Philippi, Thessalonica, Berea, Athens;

c. Yet clearly all things hastening him on; and here was Corinth, great center where he was to make long stay and not only preach, but have occasion and opportunity for writing at least two important Epistles (1 and 2 Thess.).

2. *Waiting* (vs. 2, 3)

a. While waiting for Timothy and Silas (cf. v. 5), Paul found Jewish couple with whom he formed friendship that proved one of greatest comforts of his life — Aquila, of Pontus, with wife Priscilla, lately arrived from Italy, Jews having been expelled from Rome by edict of Emperor;
N.B. Roman writer Suetonius says cause of edict was frequent rioting among Jews "at the instigation of Chrestus" — meaning probably friction due to preaching of Jesus as the "Christ" or Messiah, for we know that Jews from Rome had been present at Pentecost (cf. 2:10; Rom. 1:8);

b. Not known definitely whether already Christians, or whether Aquila and Priscilla converted through this contact with Paul, but doubtless never regretted their coming nor taking in their great lodger (cf. v. 26; Rom. 16:3; 1 Cor. 16:19; 2 Tim. 4:19);

c. Of same trade, tent-makers, and this brought them together:

(1) Custom of Jewish parents, whatever social status, to teach son manual trade;

(2) Apostle frequently supported himself by his own work, so as not to be burden on others (cf. 20:34; 1 Cor. 4:12; 1 Thess. 2:9; 2 Thess. 3:8);

(3) Thus at first Paul seems to have spent weekdays working at his trade, because of economic pressure;

N.B. Tarsus, his birthplace, had famous industry of making tents from goats' hair called *cilicium* (after province Cilicia), such as are still in use today.

3. *Witnessing* (v. 4)
   a. Paul had found work and home, so now was free to preach in synagogue every sabbath;
   b. His message may be deduced from 1 Cor. 1 and 2, with twofold appeal:
      (1) "Reasoned" — to mind and conscience — expounding Scriptures, and placing truth carefully before audience in proclaiming Christ as fulfilment of prophecy;
      (2) "Persuaded" — to heart and will — "wooing note," as J. H. Jowett calls it, pointing men to Christ and urging them to accept Gospel message;
   c. Greeks attending synagogue would be God-fearing people interested in Judaism;
      N.B. Thus we have interesting picture of Paul's ordinary life as friend, fellow-worker, and lodger of Aquila and Priscilla, using spare time to bear witness to his Master.

II. Apostleship — Paul and His Work (vs. 5-8)

1. *Faithfulness* (vs. 5-6)
   a. Arrival of companions from Macedonia cheered him with good report from Thessalonica (cf. 1 Thess. 3:5-8), and with gifts from Philippi (cf. 2 Cor. 11:9; Phil. 4:15) which freed him, apparently, for full-time ministry of apostle again;
   b. Description of Paul as "pressed in the spirit" (v. 5, K.J.V.), or "constrained by the Word" (A.S.V.), suggests that under stimulus of love for Christ and real craving to impart knowledge of Gospel (cf. 1 Cor. 9:16; 2 Cor. 5:14), Paul began fresh campaign of testimony to his Master as Messiah;
   c. But inevitable opposition arose — deliberate and organized this time, for wording of v. 6 suggests Jews definitely

ranged themselves against Gospel while they "blasphemed" (cf. 13:45), i.e., spoke evil of Christ;

d. Then Paul showed devotion to faith in equally definite action and speech:
   (1) Shaking of raiment symbolic of disclaiming all responsibility (cf. same Gr. word for shaking dust from feet in 13:51; Matt. 10:14; Mark 6:11);
   (2) Expression about blood being upon head also familiar to Jews, as implying full responsibility transferred to themselves with its attendant danger (cf. Josh. 2:19; 2 Sam. 1:16; Matt. 27:25);
   N.B. Cf. this passage and 13:45 with Matt. 12:31 — "the blasphemy against the Holy Ghost" which "shall not be forgiven unto men" — as illustrative of same sinful tendency, deliberate rejection of known truth, continuation in which is essential nature of "unpardonable sin."

e. Paul's conscience clear, having done all in his power (cf. 20:26), so determined now to turn to general body of Gentiles, marking solemn close of first stage of work in Corinth — similar separation already elsewhere and occurs again in Ephesus (cf. 19:9).

2. *Fearlessness* (vs. 7, 8)
   a. Even so, with courage made strong by love, Paul only went next door, in spite of risk from synagogue, taking for center house of Justus:
      (1) Believer not mentioned elsewhere by name in N.T., but was evidently Gentile attracted to synagogue by desire for purer faith;
      (2) Influenced by Paul's preaching, was ready to open house to him in order to give opportunity for welcoming Jews or proselytes wanting to hear more;
   b. One thus led to Christ none other than ruler of synagogue, Crispus — mentioned again as having been baptized by Paul (cf. 1 Cor. 1:14); his conversion must have angered Jews more than ever, as "many of the Corinthians" (v. 8) followed his example.

III. Fellowship — Paul and His God (vs. 9-11)

1. *Human Extremity*
   a. Comparatively few converts at Athens, after stress and strain in Macedonia, together with disheartening conflicts of early part of stay in Corinth, when in physical and spiritual weakness — and now excitement of dawning success — would have profound psychological effect on Paul;
   b. As is often case, there was probably reaction of feeling, one of risks of accomplishment; they may have included touch of fear and temptation to silence;

But Christianity can master human moods, and at this critical Juncture in Paul's ministry there was —

2. *Divine Manifestation* (vs. 9, 10)
   Just when Paul needed it, the Lord appeared to him (cf. 23:11; 27:23), another instance of grace being shaped to human need, providing —
   a. Encouragement (v. 9)
      (1) "Stop fearing" (Gr.) — Paul told not to begin to despond or to dread further trouble; he was to continue to speak out boldly;
      (2) God's ambassador must not faint through discouragement or feel himself led to move elsewhere — ability in speech great endowment for Christian work;
   b. Assurance (v. 10a)
      (1) Paul told of God's presence and protection — "I Myself (emphatic in Gr.) am with thee";
      (2) Nothing was to prevent his continued testimony (cf. 1 Cor. 9:16), for Divine plan not to be set aside or hindered by man;
   c. Reassurance (v. 10b)
      (1) Paul told of "much people in this city" to be gathered out by preaching of Gospel — jewels, as it were, in cesspool of Corinth (cf. 1 Kings 19:18; John 10:16; 11:52; 2 Tim. 2:19);

(2) In every congregation many are only waiting to be garnered as Christian worker endeavors to reap as well as sow (cf. Christ's emphasis on "harvest," Luke 10:2; John 4:35);

N.B. C. H. Spurgeon wrote: "This should be a great encouragement . . . since God has among the vilest of the vile . . . an elect people who must be saved. When you take the Word to them, you do so because God has ordained you to be the messenger of life to their souls, and they must receive it, for so the decree of predestination runs . . . They are Christ's property . . . God is not unfaithful, to forget the price His Son has paid . . . Tens of thousands of redeemed ones are not regenerated yet, but regenerated they must be; and this is our comfort, when we go forth to them with the quickening Word of God . . . 'Neither pray I for these alone,' saith the great Intercessor; 'but for them also which shall believe on Me though their word.' "

d. Security

Here, then, are two commands and two corresponding reasons for them which are introduced by same causal preposition, "for" or "because":

(1) "Be not afraid" (v. 9) . . . for I am with thee" (v. 10);

(2) "Speak, and hold not thy peace" (v. 9) . . . "for I have much people in this city" (v. 10):

N.B. For other examples of similar usage, see Luke 2:7; 21:28; Phil. 2:26.

3. *Human Recognition* (v. 11)

a. Obedience — result of such clear directions was that Paul settled down for another period of work, remaining in Corinth at least eighteen months (cf. v. 18);

b. Opportunity — result of following will of God was period of —

(1) Preaching, with spread of Gospel throughout whole of Achaia (2 Cor. 1:1), including Cenchrea, a port of Corinth (cf. Rom. 16:1); and —

(2) Writing, with two Thessalonian Epistles dating from this period.

IV. Hardship — Paul and His Enemies (vs. 12-17)

Another interruption came by means of new effort on part of Jews, who were not disposed to leave Paul alone:

1. *The Assault* (v. 12)
   a. Roman authority in Ephesus at that time was Gallio, elder brother of Seneca, famous philosopher who was favorite and tutor of Emperor Nero;
   b. Jews evidently sought to take advantage of arrival of new "proconsul" (A.S.V.), though contemporary evidence shows Gallio to have had amiable disposition;
   c. Made unanimous "insurrection against Paul" and with violence brought him into court.

2. *The Accusation* (v. 13)
   a. Charge against Paul was that he persuaded men to worship God contrary to law of Roman Empire;
   b. This may mean —
      (1) Accusation similar to that at Philippi (cf. 16:21); or —
      (2) Accusation made that Paul had opposed Jewish law which had received legal sanction;
      N.B. Two classes of religion at that time in Empire, known respectively as "legal religion" and "illegal religion."

3. *The Attitude* (vs. 14-16)
   a. Gallio evidently saw true state of case, accusation being absurd and hollow, and felt no need to summon defense, as though for crime;
   b. Told accusers, therefore, it was matter of mere discussion and he could not be concerned with question of words and names; so dismissed case and cleared court;

c. Attitude may appear to have been one of contempt, but Ramsay regards decision of Gallio as "charter of Christian freedom."

4. *The Aftermath* (v. 17)

a. Gentile crowd used opportunity to vent spleen on Jews;

b. Laid hold of ruler of synagogue, Sosthenes, who had probably succeeded Crispus and perhaps was leader of Jewish party against Paul; if he is person mentioned in Paul's Letter (cf. 1 Cor. 1:1), must have been converted after this event, perhaps because of it;

N.B. A. C. Gaebelein believed he is same, "for the grace of God delights to take up such characters and show in them what grace can do";

c. Gallio seems to have taken no notice of action against Sosthenes, perhaps thinking Jews deserved such treatment;

d. Some writers think that words "Gallio cared for none of these things" mean he was entirely indifferent to matters of religion;

N.B. Alexander Smellie, however, felt Gallio "is too frequently crowned with a condemnation he does not deserve," and said he may teach us "much that is profitable and wise," i.e., refusing to meddle, leaving trifling wrongs to compose themselves, placing duty above disputes, righteousness above policy, law of God above expediency or popularity.

V. Companionship — Paul and His Friends (vs. 18-28)

1. *Paul Departing* (v. 18)

a. Not known whether "many days" (v. 18, A.S.V.) within or in addition to eighteen months (cf. v. 11), but at length Paul left Corinth for Asia and Syria, taking with him Aquila and Priscilla — Silas and Timothy not mentioned as accompanying him;

b. Paul evidently thought it necessary to take vow of Nazarite (cf. Num. 6:1-21), perhaps for purpose of —

(1) Winning Jews at Ephesus; and/or —

(2) Making good impression in Jerusalem;

c. In any case, although ready to vindicate freedom of Gentiles, Paul himself often conformed to customs of his own people (cf. 20:6; 21:18-26; 1 Cor. 9:20);
N.B. Cenchrea was eastern port of Corinth whence Paul would sail.

2. *Paul at Ephesus* (vs. 19-21)
   a. Arrived in two or three days at Ephesus, capital of Roman province of Asia (cf. 2:9) and, after Corinth, next great city on route from Rome to East; ship called there on way to Caesarea;
   b. This first visit short, but even so Paul found it impossible to avoid bearing testimony, especially because Jews numerous, important, and evidently tolerant;
   c. Left Ephesus under protest, but Priscilla and Aquila remained, perhaps on business but also to witness (cf. v. 26), and were there when he returned (cf. 1 Cor. 16:19).

3. *Paul Travelling* (vs. 22, 23)
   a. At length reached Caesarea and, wanting to keep feast at Jerusalem (cf. v. 21), and probably to fulfil his voluntary vow (cf. v. 18), hurried to Jerusalem — "went up and saluted the church" before going "down to Antioch" (v. 22), his starting-place (cf. 15:35-41);
   b. This was Paul's fourth visit to Jerusalem (cf. 9:26; 11:30; 15:2; 21:17), and we have no particulars of it;
   c. After "some time" in Antioch, Paul commenced his third missionary journey by visiting "all the country of Galatia and Phrygia in order, strengthening all the disciples" (v. 23).

4. *Apollos at Ephesus* (vs. 24-28)
   Another Christian companion is here introduced:
   a. His antecedents (v. 24a)
      (1) Jewish by nationality;
      (2) Born in Alexandria;
   b. His equipment (vs. 24b, 25a)
      (1) Eloquence in speech;
      (2) Might in Scriptures;

(3) Instruction in way of the Lord;
(4) Fervency in spirit;

c. His diligence (v. 25b)
   (1) In speaking of things of the Lord;
   (2) In teaching — even though only baptism he knew was that of John the Baptist (cf. John 1:33; 19:1-7):

d. His zeal (v. 26)
   (1) Boldness in Jewish synagogue;
   (2) Teachableness in Christian home;

e. His influence (vs. 27, 28)
   (1) Being recommended by brethren in Ephesus to those in Achaia (v. 27a);
   (2) Helping believers in Christian life (v. 27b);
   (3) Convincing unbelievers of Christ's Messiahship, publicly, and by means of Scripture (v. 28).

Conclusion

This chapter provides an epitome of practical Christianity:

1. Home life (vs. 3, 26);
2. Daily toil (v. 3);
3. Sabbath worship (vs. 4, 19, 26, 28);
4. Gospel testimony (vs. 5,11, 19, 27, 28);
5. Great faithfulness (vs. 6, 25, 26);
6. Loving compassion (vs. 7, 21, 25);
7. Spiritual communion (vs. 9, 10);
8. Inevitable suffering (v. 12).

"In all these things, we are more than conquerors through Him that loved us" (Rom. 8:37).

Study No. 96 — Paul at Ephesus

ACTS 19:1-41

ON A PREVIOUS JOURNEY, Paul had been forbidden by the Holy Spirit to preach the Gospel in Asia, the region of which Ephesus was the chief city (cf. 16:6). This was for some Divine reason at that particular juncture, but now the proper time had come. After revisiting the Galatian churches, Paul was permitted to enter this Roman province which covered the entire western part of the region known today as Asia Minor. Here he did what was, in some respects, the greatest work of his career. He describes it as "a great door and effectual," though there were "many adversaries" (1 Cor. 16:8, 9), and he remained in the Asian metropolis for about three years (vs. 10, 22; 20:1, 31).

Ephesus was one of the three most ancient and famous cities in the East, Antioch and Alexandria being the others. It was a center of commerce, with a direct road to Rome, so that it was also a naturally fine center for Paul's work. But it had a great pagan temple (see v. 27) of marvellous architectural beauty, with 127 columns. This was one of the Seven Wonders of the World and devoted to the worship of the goddess Diana. There was also a great theater (see v. 29) said to have held 24,000 people. Ephesus was included in the "seven churches which are in Asia" (Rev. 1:4; 2:1-7). In the account of Paul's stay there, we may see —

I. Christian Experience Enlarged (vs. 1-7)

Route to Ephesus seems to have been taken by Paul on foot over high ground ("upper country," v. 1, A.S.V.) covering distance of something like 200 miles.

1. *The Holy Spirit Declared* (vs. 1-4)

Beginning of work in Ephesus associated with about dozen disciples of John the Baptist — last mention of him in N.T.;

these men, about 25 years after his death, and far from Jerusalem, striking testimony to his influence:

a. Ignorance (vs. 1, 2)

(1) When Paul asked question about their receiving Holy Spirit at conversion ("when ye believed," v. 2, A.S.V.), we are to understand he found they had never heard of Pentecost, i.e., of promise of Baptist (cf. John 1:33) being fully fulfilled; "we did not . . . hear whether the Holy Spirit was given" rather than "whether there be any Holy Ghost," as translated by K.J.V.;

(2) Thus, their knowledge was narrow and partial;

b. Interest (v. 3)

(1) Evidently these men began to realize they were living only in spiritual dawn and it was necessary to be introduced into spiritual noonday, as indicated by gift of Holy Spirit and everything involved in Pentecost (cf. John 7:39);

(2) Their sincerity was real, for they had been living up to light they possessed;

N.B. It is usually thought reason for episode being mentioned here is these disciples were like Apollos (cf. 18:25), who also needed to enter into fulness of Christian blessing (cf. 18:26), and who may indeed have been one of them (cf. 18:24 with 19:1);

c. Instruction (v. 4)

Seeing their willingness to listen, Paul made clear distinction between two baptisms, i.e., "of repentance" and "in the Name of the Lord Jesus."

2. *The Holy Spirit Conferred* (vs. 5-7)

a. Action (v. 5)

Paul's baptism of men resulted in their receiving not only Holy Spirit Himself, but His Divine gifts also — "tongues," and prophecy, or teaching;

b. Assurance (vs. 6, 7)

Thus they proved themselves by what they did, and showed they had received not simply indwelling, but anointing; N.B. We must always distinguish between ordinary grace and miraculous gifts of Spirit; latter peculiarly needed then, but God uses former also to His glory, now as then.

II. Christian Message Given (vs. 8-20)

1. *The Word of God Resisted* (vs. 8, 9)

a. Opportunity (v. 8)

At first, Jews seem to have been less hostile than in other places, and Paul, as was custom, used synagogue and spoke there "boldly for the space of three months, disputing and persuading";

b. Opposition (v. 9a)

But it was not long before they protested, and result probably more severe because of hardness and disobedience against "the Way" (cf. 1 Cor. 15:32);

N.B. Special notice should be taken of description of Christianity as "the Way," meaning that which provides direction for life (v. 9; cf. v. 23, also 9:2; 22:4; 24:14, 22; and 18:25; John 14:6). C. G. Trumbull wrote: "Jesus does not merely show us the way; He *is* the Way . . . The Way is not a method, but a Man . . . not a path, and not a persuasion, but a Person . . . not a direction, but Deity . . . not a course, but Christ . . . not a line, but a Life";

c. Outcome (v. 9b)

This necessitated definite separation of disciples from synagogue, and Paul apparently hired lecture hall of pagan teacher, one Tyrannus, demonstrating flexibility of method and readiness to make new plans;
N.B. It was at this time that news came from Corinth which led to writing of First Corinthians.

2. *The Word of God Attested* (vs. 10-20)
   a. Perseverance (v. 10a)
   Meanwhile, Gospel spread everywhere for "space of two years" — sometimes difficult to maintain witness for so long, especially in face of opposition;
   b. Proclamation (v. 10b)
   "All . . . in Asia heard the Word of the Lord Jesus" — and yet it would seem that Paul never left Ephesus, but rather made it center of influence by means of companions who evangelized neighboring places in one of most populous of Roman provinces:
      (1) Thus, though Colosse so near Ephesus, Paul seems never to have visited it (cf. Col. 1:4, 7, 9; 2:1);
      (2) It was almost certainly at this time that Seven Churches in Asia (cf. Rev. 1-3) were founded;
   c. Power (vs. 11, 12)
   Not only by speech, but also by action Paul bore witness for God, who wrought "special miracles" of healing through him;
   d. Pretence (vs. 13-17)
      (1) Another striking testimony to Gospel was incident connected with "seven sons of one Sceva" (vs. 13, 14), who tried to imitate casting out of evil spirits in Name of Jesus;
      (2) Result was immediate disaster to these men which had marvellous influence on Jews and Greeks alike — "fear fell on them all, and the Name of the Lord Jesus was magnified" (v. 17);
   e. Penitence (vs. 18, 19)
      (1) Perhaps greatest testimony was confession on part of magicians, for they brought books and publicly burned them;
      (2) Value was something like $10,000, so destruction severe and sufficient test of sincerity;
      Illus.: Modern counterpart — gay young Oxford student named Fremantle, convicted of sin, made

bonfire of books and photographs in college yard, confessed sins, gave up secular profession, spent one more year at Oxford, then went to foreign field to labor for Christ;

f. Predominance (v. 20)

No wonder, then, that "mightily grew the Word of God and prevailed" — both verbs in imperfect tense in Gr. — Word "kept on" being heard and received:

(1) "Grew" — wide diffusion by means of preaching;

(2) "Prevailed" — great influence through acceptance.

III. Christian Influence Opposed (vs. 21-41)

1. *Culmination* (vs. 21, 22)

a. With v. 20, fifth division of Book closes; cf. summaries at end of each: 6:7; 9:31; 12:24; 16:5;

b. This division covers missionary effort of St. Paul at its height, from Philippi to Ephesus;

c. Some think v. 21 key to remainder of life in his great desire and determination to see Rome;

d. But it was necessary first to go again to Jerusalem, with collection (cf. 2 Cor. 8 and 9), visiting "Macedonia and Achaia" (v. 21) en route;

e. Here commences sixth and closing section of Acts (19:21 to 28:31), to which all else has been leading up; further details not needed — only necessary to tell why Paul left Ephesus and how he came to reach Rome at length;

f. It was now possible for Paul to leave Ephesus, for work was practically at an end; but he stayed there some time longer, sending before him into Macedonia Timothy and Erastus (cf. Rom. 16:23; 2 Tim 4:20).

2. *Complaint* (v. 23)

a. Commotion: Then arose entirely new form of opposition, unlike anything preceding — "no small stir," or rioting, "concerning the Way" (A.S.V.), or because of preaching of Christ and His Gospel;

b. Comparison: This disturbance very fully reported, compared with scant notice given to other important events — perhaps because —
   (1) It showed vast extent of work done by Apostle in two years; and —
   (2) It revealed underlying spirit against Christianity; N.B. Theodore Parker called this section, "Old Complaints and New Reproaches."

3. *Cleverness* (vs. 24-28)
   a. Craft (vs. 24, 25)
      City owed much of prominence to popularity of worship of goddess Diana, and trade in silver shrines — small images of goddess or of temple, specimens of which still exist — had become seriously diminished; striking testimony to Paul's influence (cf. v. 26);
   b. Craftiness (vs. 26-28)
      (1) Christianity as a "way," a life, inevitably rouses opposition, and silversmith Demetrius is typical of "those that oppose themselves" (2 Tim. 2:25) in cunning and selfishness — under guise of defense of idols, tried to stir up people, though sheer greed was at base of action — "by this craft we have our wealth" (v. 25);
      (2) Thus, commerce and religion used by self-seeking and superstition, two of Gospel's most virulent foes; N.B. Note how greed leads to demand for monopoly in popular religion (cf. vs. 27, 28).

4. *Calmness* (vs. 29-34)
   a. Cruelty (v. 29)
      Mob immediately seized two of Paul's companions, Gaius of Derbe (cf. 20:4), and Aristarchus of Thessalonica (cf. 20:4; 27:2; Col. 4:10; Philem. 24);
   b. Courage (v. 30a)
      Note calm attitude of Apostle — with absolute trust in God and His cause, and with manly piety, he was ready to go in among enraged crowd in theater (vs. 29, 30);

e. Caution (vs. 30b, 31)

(1) But twofold pressure brought to bear prevented risk of his life, — that of disciples (v. 30), and of "certain of the chief of Asia, which were his friends" (v. 31);

(2) These "Asiarchs" (A.S.V.) were provincial magnates whose duties were partly religious and partly political, and fact of their friendship speaks volumes for Paul's influence;

d. Confusion (vs. 32, 33)

(1) Meanwhile, assembly in utter confusion, majority not even knowing reason for coming together (v. 32);

(2) Endeavor on part of a Jew, Alexander (otherwise unknown, unless mentioned in 1 Tim. 1:20 and/or 2 Tim. 4:14) to explain matters prolonged uproar and prevented hearing, because of strong Gentile opposition to all things Jewish (vs. 33, 34);

e. Clamor (v. 34)

Two hours of shouting followed — few things more irrational and less open to conviction than excited mob.

5. *Coolness* (vs. 35-41)

a. Counsel (vs. 35-40)

(1) Now city official, town clerk, or secretary to city assembly, takes sagacious action, coming to fore and advising quiet (vs. 35, 36);

(2) Ephesus was free city, Romans allowing it its own government subject to imperial supervision, but dependent on proper behavior; so town clerk, afraid uproar would lead to abolition of privilege, —

(a) Cites dignity of city as center of Diana's worship;

(b) Tells crowd men seized not guilty of sacrilege; and —

(c) Pleads with Demetrius and friends to deal with matter before courts (vs. 37-40);

N.B. "Deputies," or "proconsuls" (v. 38, A.S.V.), were, of course, Roman governors;

b. Character (v.41)

Clerk's action sufficient to quell disturbance and shows what can be done by man of strong personality, even in face of turbulent crowd;

N.B. Great detail of account appears to indicate Luke's desire to emphasize impossibility of case made out against Christianity, except by illegal means.

Conclusion

There is nothing in this chapter more striking than the contrast between those who sacrificed everything for God (vs. 17-20) and those who sacrificed everything for gain (vs. 23-38). "Vested interests" exert an immense power when attacked by the Gospel. In Lystra there had been the opposition of ignorant paganism (14:8-19); in Athens it was the opposition of cultured heathenism (17:32); in Corinth it was the opposition of philosophical scepticism (18:5-17); while in Ephesus it was the fear of earthly loss through change of religion. It is significant that covetousness was often associated either with heathenism or with debased Judaism, as in the case of Simon Magus (chap. 8), of Elymas (chap. 13), and of the masters of the slave girl (chap. 16).

1. *Opposition in Ephesus*

   Uproar was only one instance of way in which Gospel was opposed — devil had one of his greatest strongholds in that wonderful city, so it is not surprising that he did his utmost to thwart St. Paul in numerous ways:

   a. Hardness (v. 9) — on part of Jewish unbelievers, blaspheming "that Way" (cf. 18:6);
   b. Hypocrisy (v. 13) — on part of exorcists, using religion as cloak for evil-doing;
   c. Hatred (v. 28) — on part of silversmiths, inciting mob to violence.

2. *Opposition in Ephesus Overcome*

   a. It is particularly important to notice how these difficulties were dealt with:

      (1) Hardness was countered by separation (v. 9);

(2) Hypocrisy was countered by exposure (vs. 15, 16);

(3) Hatred was controlled by reason (vs. 35-41);

b. Meanwhile, without compromising his message, or modifying his tone, Paul was proclaiming Person and work of Christ and power of Holy Spirit (vs. 6:10, 13); no wonder we read of Name of the Lord Jesus being magnified (v. 17), and the Word of the Lord growing mightily and prevailing (v. 20), for there were —

(1) A full Gospel appreciated;

(2) A supreme Christ accepted;

(3) A living Spirit acknowledged.

But Sceva and his sons, and Demetrius and his followers still live, and it is only too possible under the guise of religion to exert the most utter deception and selfishness. The secret of all true Christian living is summed up in Paul's words to the Galatians: "Not I, but Christ" (Gal. 2:20). When Christ fills the soul, there is "the expulsive power of a new affection," and we realize what the Apostle meant when he told Timothy, "Godliness with contentment is great gain."

Study No. 97 — Paul's Ministry at Ephesus (1)

ACTS 19:1-20

EPHESUS was undoubtedly among the most important spheres of the Apostle's ministry. His stay there was a great testimony to his Master, for we read that "the Name of the Lord Jesus was magnified" (v. 17). Let us consider how this was done and the resulting victory for the cause of Christianity:

I. Preparation (vs. 1-7)

1. *Partial Ignorance* (vs. 1, 2)

   On returning to Ephesus on his third journey (cf. 18:19-21), Paul found disciples, but they had never heard of Pentecost.
2. *Past Influence* (v. 3)

   These were disciples of John the Baptist, who had been dead many years, yet was still remembered here in far-off Ephesus.
3. *Precious Instruction* (vs. 4, 5)

   Paul lost no time in giving them necessary information implied in John's teaching, showing them their low spiritual level, and leading them into full blessing of Christianity.
4. *Powerful Initiation* (vs. 6, 7)

   Holy Spirit as given at Pentecost being outside their experience thus far, here were another twelve disciples who were now "endued with power from on high" (Luke 24:49), and this was at once proved by miraculous results (cf. 1:4);

   N.B. There are those today who may be said to be living as though Pentecost had never taken place. Historically, they are on this side of it; spiritually they are on the other.* Yet there can be no true evangelism without God's Holy Ghost power.

---

* For fuller treatment of this subject, see Study No. 2, p. 28.

II. Preaching (v. 8)

1. *Where?* — "the synagogue," where Paul had witnessed before (cf. 18:19), i.e., "to the Jew first" (Rom. 1:16).
2. *What?* — "the things concerning the kingdom of God," entered only by New Birth (cf. John 3:3-5).
3. *How?* — with —
   a. Physical boldness — "spake boldly";
   b. Intellectual power — "disputing," or "reasoning" (A.S.V.);
   c. Spiritual earnestness — "persuading";
   N.B. When these are combined there is effectual preaching. Note especially order and union of second and third — only through intelligent understanding can there be true spiritual acceptance.

III. Perversity (v. 9)

1. *Its Character*:
   a. Hardening of heart — "divers were hardened";
   b. Lack of faith — "believed not";
   c. Wickedness of speech — "spake evil."
2. *Its Consequence*:
   a. Departure of Paul — "he departed from them";
   b. Separation of disciples — "separated the disciples";
   c. Intensification of witness — "disputing daily in the school" — i.e., instead of weekly in synagogue;

   N.B. (1) Extent of depravity of these Jews indicated not merely in rejection (negative) of Gospel, but also in opposition (positive) to it (cf. 2 Cor. 2:15, 16);
   (2) Description here of Christianity as "the Way" (A.S.V.) implies "way of salvation" (16:17), and "way of holiness" (Isa. 35:8), and also reminds us of Christ Himself as "the Way" (John 14:6).

IV. Persistence (v. 10)

1. *The Duration*
   Work continued daily for no less than two years.
2. *The Influence*

"Word of the Lord Jesus" reached all countryside around, "Asia" meaning Roman province covering part of what is now called Asia Minor, and including districts of Seven Churches (cf. Rev. 2 and 3), probably founded then; N.B. Today, Ephesus is ruin and no Christian church has been there for centuries, because warnings of Rev. 2:1-7 went unheeded.

V. Power (vs. 11, 12)

1. *Manifestation* (v. 11)

"Special miracles" doubtless much needed in circumstances.

2. *Blessing* (v. 12)

Healing of diseases and exorcism of evil spirits were indeed "special" results which gave strong testimony to power of Christ at this critical juncture;

N.B. Cf. corresponding results in Peter's experience (5:15, 16) at another crisis in Church history.

VI. Pretense (vs. 13-16)

1. *The Remarkable Action* (vs. 13, 14)

a. Its Character — Satanic imitation of God's work;

b. Its significance — "sincerest form of flattery";

N.B. Alexander Smellie says: "Where you have the reality, you will have the caricature and counterfeit. The falsetto of miracle is magic; and Ephesus had magicians who tried to imitate Christ's Apostle . . . They had no formula or talisman except a stolen one . . . They traded at second-hand with another person's Saviour and Lord."

2. *The Surprising Effect* (vs. 15, 16)

a. The question — another proof of reality of demon possession and Satanic knowledge (cf. 16:16-18; Mark 1:23, 24; Jas. 2:19);

b. The action — unique testimony to Christianity, for demons recognized imposture.

VII. Proof (vs. 17-19)

1. *Three Marks of Reality*
   a. Conviction (v. 17) — "fear fell on them all";
   b. Confession (v. 18) — "many that believed came, and confessed";
   c. Consecration (v. 19) — "brought their books together, and burned them before all men."
2. *Three Marks of Relapse*
   How sad to read in Rev. 2:4 that Ephesian church had left its "first love" — and with it, of course, lost its power, because it had (v. 5) —
   a. No sense of sin — "remember";
   b. No penitence of soul — "repent"; and —
   c. No witness for God — "remove."

VIII. Progress (v. 20)

Effect on "the word of God," or Gospel message, was twofold:

1. *Growth* — "increased" (cf. 6:7);
2. *Influence* — "multiplied" (cf. 12-24);
   N.B. Note also v. 17 — "the Name of the Lord Jesus was magnified" (cf. Isa. 9:6) — another striking example of relation of Incarnate Word to Written Word.

Conclusion

Paul always went where life was at its height, its swiftest tempo, i.e., to cities — depending on his converts to evangelize surrounding places, as Colosse had been reached from Ephesus (cf. Col. 2:1). We may sum up his Ephesian sojourn thus:

1. The church founded, and two disciples left there (18:19-21);
2. His return (19:1);
3. His work among partial disciples (vs. 2-7);
4. His work among unconverted Jews (vs. 8, 9);
5. His work among receptive Gentiles and Jews (vs. 9, 10);
6. His work meeting with great blessing (vs. 11, 12);
7. His work meeting with Satanic opposition (vs. 13-16; cf. 1 Cor. 15:32);
8. His work meeting with renewed blessing (vs. 17-20);

9. His work meeting with renewed opposition (vs. 21-41; cf. 2 Cor 1:8);
10. His departure (20:1);
11. His farewell appeal (20:17-38).

These events and the Epistle to the Ephesians show how important and far-reaching was the work in that great city which was such a challenge to the Apostle. Says Dr. Smellie: "For two years Paul had been in Ephesus, . . . and all Asia heard the Word. It is an arousal for which we ought to pray . . . The evil spirits of our age, like those of the first century . . . are afraid of one man alone — the man who owes everything to Jesus Christ, and in whom Jesus Christ lives and walks day after day."

Study No. 98 — Paul's Ministry at Ephesus (2)

ACTS 19:1-20

It is interesting to study accounts of battles from the standpoint of tactics and methods of generalship. On a visit to the battlefield of Waterloo, for example, one is enabled the better to grasp its significance in history if he is instructed in the strategies employed by the two great contending generals, Napoleon and the Duke of Wellington. So it is in the realm of spiritual warfare as carried on by leaders greatly used of God. St. Paul, as we follow his career in the Acts of the Apostles, is the finest example of the use of Christian strategy. We may say that he left behind him a chain of great fortresses — the churches established in the cities he used as preaching centers — all the way from Antioch to Rome. From these, other soldiers of the Cross emerged to join forces against paganism and subsequent forms of evil.

Of these centers Ephesus was one of the most important, for here Paul did a very remarkable work for three years (cf. 20:31). In 19:20, which sums up this whole passage, we read of two results of that work upon "the word of God," the Gospel message:

I. Wide Diffusion (vs. 1-12)

"So mightily grew the Word of God" — and this growth came by Preaching:

1. *Instruction of Partial Disciples* (vs. 1-7)
   a. These needed fuller light and power;
   b. They then became channels of blessing.
2. *Discussion with Unregenerate Jews* (vs. 8, 9)
   a. First, in synagogue for three months, "disputing and persuading the things concerning the kingdom of God" (v. 8);
   b. Then, separated, "disputing daily in the school of one Tyrannus" (v. 9).
3. *Inclusion of Open-minded Gentiles* (v. 10)
   a. Rejection by majority of Jews turned Paul towards non-Jews, as so invariably elsewhere;
   b. Continuation for two years, so that "all they which dwelt in Asia heard the word of the Lord Jesus."
4. *Manifestation of Special Miracles* (vs. 11, 12)
   a. Confirming word of mouth by "virtue" of body (cf. Luke 8:46);
   b. But influence called "special" (v. 11) — needed for particular time and circumstances.

II. Great Influence (vs. 13-19)

"So mightily . . . the Word of God . . . prevailed" — and this prevalence, or prevailing, came by Hearing, as Gospel message made fourfold effect:

1. *On Enemies, Confusion* (vs. 13-16) — intensified by testimony of evil spirit;
2. *On Populace, Conversion* (v. 17) — fear was vehicle of conviction, especially to superstitious;
3. *On Believers, Confession* (v. 18) — magnifying of Christ's Name in accessions (v. 17) brought conviction also to Christians;

4. *On Magicians, Consecration* (v. 19) — reality of Christian profession amply proven.

Conclusion

Several times in Acts we are told of the progress of the Word of the Lord in the hands of its defenders. It "increased" (6:7); it "grew and multiplied" (12:14); it was "glorified" and "published," or, as we would say today, "publicized" (13:48, 49); and, here "grew and prevailed," first by preaching, or diffusion, and then by hearing, or influence. What are the secrets of this twofold process, subjective and objective?

1. *The Secret of True Preaching*

   This may be summed up by use of the words of 1 Thess. 1:5:

   a. What it is not — "not in word only":

      (1) Not mere eloquence (cf. 1 Cor. 2:1; 13:1), though Paul later asked Ephesians to pray that "utterance" might be given him (cf. Eph. 6:19);

      (2) Not even knowledge only (cf. 1 Cor. 1:17b; 2:1, 4, 5; 13:2), though Paul did not despise it (cf. 22:3; Col. 3:10);

      N.B. Cf. 1 Cor. 1:5, where both "utterance" and "knowledge" are included in riches of grace;

   b. What it is —

      (1) Powerful — "in power";

      (2) Spirit-filled — "in the holy Ghost";

      (3) Confident — "in much assurance";

      N.B. It must also be accompanied by consistent living — "ye know what manner of men we were."

2. *The Secret of Fruitful Hearing*

   This might be called "heeding" and is illustrated in lives of Thessalonians as we read in 2 Thess. 3:1;

   a. Word of God must have "free course," or "run" (A.S.V.) — nothing allowed to stand in its way;

   b. Word of God must be "glorified" — given all credit as message of eternal life in Christ (cf. Gal. 6:14).

Such preaching and such hearing are just as possible today. We have exactly the same need for them — but also the same God, the same Christ, the same Gospel; and so, whether in pulpit or in pew, let us "take heed to speak that which the Lord hath put in" our "mouth" (Num. 23:12); and let us "take heed therefore how" we "hear" (Luke 8:18).

Study No. 99 — Paul as Pastor

ACTS 20:1-38

THE FIGURE of the shepherd in the Bible is very familiar with regard to things spiritual. Our Lord is called the Good Shepherd who died (John 10:11; Psa. 22), the Great Shepherd who lives (Heb. 13:20; Psa. 23), and the Chief Shepherd who is coming again (1 Pet. 5:4; Psa. 24). Ministers of Christ are also appropriately described as shepherds and their people as sheep (e.g., Ezek. 34:1-24). In the present chapter we have a beautiful picture of Paul as the spiritual shepherd, or pastor, of God's sheep.

The Apostle had a special reason for going to Jerusalem. He hoped, by means of a collection taken in Macedonia and Achaia on behalf of the poor of that city, to unite more closely the two great sections of the Church, Jewish and Gentile (cf. Rom. 15:25-27). Evidently he did not expect to see again his friends in Asia and Macedonia, and so the record of the journey is full of poignancy and also of valuable detail.

I. **Ephesus to Troas** (vs. 1-6)

1. *The Plan* (v. 1)
   a. After uproar at Ephesus (19:23-41), Paul left for Macedonia, according to intention (19:21); en route, he landed at Troas to wait for Titus, who had been sent to Corinth, probably with First Epistle;
   b. But because of anxiety (cf. 2 Cor. 2:12, 13) and perhaps illness (cf. 2 Cor. 1:8-10), Paul cut stay short and went

on to Macedonia alone, where Titus rejoined him, probably at Philippi (2 Cor. 7:5-7).

2. *Progress* (vs. 2, 3a)
   a. Then followed tour occupying several months, including Thessalonica and Berea, and giving churches "much exhortation" (v. 2); apparently journey extended as far as Illyricum, province on Adriatic Sea, north of Macedonia (cf. Rom. 15:19);
   b. Next came journey into Greece, or Achaia, as intended (cf. 19:21); Paul may not have revisited Athens, but certainly stayed at Corinth for a third time (cf. 2 Cor. 12:14; 13:1; 1 Cor. 16:5-7; Rom. 16:23), remaining three months (v. 3), writing and sending off his Epistle to the Romans.

3. *The Plot* (v. 3)
   a. It was then his purpose to sail direct for Jerusalem in time for Passover, but Jewish plot was discovered and led to alteration of plans;
   b. It is usually thought Jews planned to get rid of him during voyage of pilgrim ship, perhaps by pushing him overboard from crowded deck; cf. other plots on Paul's life (9:24; 18:12; 21:27-32; 23:12-22; 25:3);
   c. Consequently, he decided to return through Macedonia, much longer route, thus abandoning idea of observing Passover at Jerusalem; instead, planned to reach there by Pentecost, fifty days later (cf. v. 16).

4. *The Party* (vs. 4-6)
   a. Several of Paul's friends accompanied him into Asia, doubtless as delegates from Gentile churches carrying contributions for Jerusalem (cf. 1 Cor. 16:3, 4), and preceding him waited at Troas;
   b. At Philippi Luke seems to have joined party (vs. 5, 6) — second "we" section, to 21:25.

II. Paul at Troas (vs. 7-12)

Story of Sunday at Troas noteworthy for —

1. *Christian gathering on Lord's Day,* first day of week (cf. 1 Cor. 16:2);
2. *Celebration of Lord's Supper in evening* — so evening communion not only permissible, but practical and helpful reenactment of original institution (cf. Mark 14:17; 1 Cor. 11:23); also in accordance with rule of primitive Church for nearly 150 years;
3. *Sermon by Paul* — about which we know nothing except its length;
4. *Death of Eutychus,* through fall while asleep — even Paul's sermons could not keep everyone awake!
5. *Miracle by Apostle* (cf. 1 Kings 17:19-24; 2 Kings 4:32-37).

III. Troas to Miletus (vs. 13-17)

1. *By Land* (v. 13)
   Apostle's companions set sail for Assos, while he went on foot, probably to gain opportunity for quiet fellowship with God, in view of what lay ahead;

2. *By Water* (vs. 14, 15)
   From Assos all journeyed together by sea to Miletus, then important seaport (though now some ten miles inland), about 25 miles south of Ephesus.

IV. Paul at Miletus (vs. 16-38)

To prevent further delay, Paul summoned elders of church at Ephesus, rather than go there again (vs. 16, 17). To them he delivered solemn and beautiful address. With one exception (cf. v. 3), this chapter has to do exclusively with Paul's associations with believers. His discourse to Ephesian elders (vs. 18-35) is only example we possess of an address to Christians, all other speeches in Acts being of different nature because addressed to non-Christian audiences. It included:

1. *A Look Backward* (vs. 18-21)
   Paul first calls attention to his life in their midst "from the first day" (v. 18) and for "the space of three years" (v. 31):

a. The character of his ministry (v. 19) — seen as "serving the Lord" in threefold way, by —
   (1) Humility, or "lowliness" (A.S.V.);
   (2) Tears — recorded on three different occasions and connected with —
      (a) Unconverted, as here;
      (b) Inconsistent Christians (2 Cor. 2:4); and —
      (c) Unworthy ministers (Phil. 3:18);
   (3) Trials (A.S.V.) — due to Jewish plots of which we have no details (cf. 19:13);

b. The methods of his ministry (v. 20) — shown to have been —
   (1) Well-rounded — "kept back nothing that was profitable";
   (2) Public — "have taught you publicly" (cf. 16:37); and —
   (3) Private — "from house to house" (cf. 2:46; 1 Cor. 16:19; 1 Thess. 2:11);
      (a) Ministerial work undoubtedly pastoral as well as homiletical — visitation and consultation both essential, as in case of physician and patient, and closely related to preaching;
      (b) Intercourse with people will enrich and make ministry real, practical, sympathetic, alive:
      (c) Minister's every-day life will either deepen or remove impression of sermon;
      Illus.: Scottish pastor once said to be on weekdays invisible and on Sundays incomprehensible! Another way of expressing unfortunate contrast is, "He preaches cream, but he lives skim milk!"

c. The message of his ministry (v. 21) — declared to have included —
   (1) "Repentance" — turning from sin to God; and —
   (2) "Faith" — trusting Christ for salvation.
   These two doctrines fundamental requirements of Gospel — letting go of sin and laying hold of Christ (cf. 1 Thess. 1:9, 10);

N.B. This personal review of the Apostle's life and ministry necessary as vindication after serious attacks against him (cf. Gal. 1:10; 1 Thess. 2:3-5; 2 Cor. 10:7-18; 12:15-18).

2. *A Look Forward* (vs. 22-24)

Then Paul turns to future and tells his audience:

a. He was on his way to Jerusalem "bound in the spirit," which means either constrained by the Holy Spirit, perhaps through prophets like Agabus (21:10, 11), or, as Scofield believes, impelled by his own spirit, motivated by hope that Gentile Christian gifts to poor saints in Jerusalem (cf. Rom. 15:25-28) would open hearts of law-bound Jewish believers to "gospel of the grace of God" (v. 24);

b. He desired to "finish" or "fill full" his ministry; cf. with word used in Col. 4:17 and 2 Tim. 4:5;

c. He did not know "the things" that should befall him (v. 22), but "none of these things" moved him (v. 24):

I know not what will befall me; God hangs a mist o'er my eyes;
And thus, each step of my onward path, He makes new scenes arise,
And every joy He sends to me comes like a glad surprise.

For perhaps the dreaded future is less bitter than I think;
The Lord may sweeten the waters before I stoop to drink;
Or, if Marah must be Marah, He will stand beside the brink.

O restful, blissful ignorance! 'Tis blessed not to know;
It keeps me still in those mighty arms which will not let me go,
And lulls my weariness to rest on the bosom which loves me so.

So I go on not knowing — I would not if I might;
I would rather walk in the dark with God than go alone
in the light;
I would rather walk with Him by faith than walk alone
by sight.

3. *A Look Inward* (vs. 25-31)

Then came necessity for some pastoral counsel and warnings based on what Paul did know, viz., that these Ephesian Christians would not see him again:

a. He bore solemn testimony to the past (vs. 25-27), namely, that he had worked conscientiously for their salvation, and had declared entire plan and purpose of God:
   (1) Cf. Epistle to Ephesians in its wealth of doctrine and fulness of exposition;
   (2) Few things in N. T. more impressive than Gospel as truth and disciples as witnesses;
   (3) Call same today to proclaim by lip and life whole counsel of God, to withhold nothing, to reveal all His will, "whether they will hear, or whether they will forbear" (Ezek. 2:11);

b. He called for special care in the present (v. 28), on part of elders in regard both to themselves and to their people:
   (1) To selves, on account of flock — "take heed therefore unto yourselves" — no man set over such a charge can possibly be indifferent to greatness and solemnity of position;
   (2) To flock, by care of selves — "and to all the flock" — they had been appointed by Holy Spirit as "overseers," or shepherds, and "ensamples" (1 Pet. 5:3): people of God, as sheep, are Christ's blood-bought possession "purchased with His own blood";
   (3) To doctrine, for sake of both selves and flock — "feed the church of God" (cf. 1 Tim. 4:16) — if leaders right with God and their doctrine true to His Word, flock will assuredly be secure, and ministry increasing blessing to people, joy to selves, and glory to God;

N.B. (1) Interesting that same men called "elders" (Gr., *presbuterous*) in v. 17 here in v. 28 described as "bishops" (A.S.V.), or "overseers" (Gr., *episkopous*). Throughout N.T., two terms represent two aspects of same office, one referring to seniority and other to supervision. Later on, offices were distinguished, and are to this day;

(2) Some authorities prefer "the Church of the Lord" (v. 28) because of objection to phrase "God . . . purchased with His own blood." But since our Saviour was God as well as Man, expression, however strange, is theologically correct; and "Church of God" is frequently found in N.T., while other phrase is not. Purchase of Church with Christ's own blood significant testimony to redemptive work (cf. Eph. 1:7; 1 Pet. 1:18, 19);

e. He warned of serious dangers in the future (vs. 29-31):

(1) These dangers were —

(a) From without — "grievous wolves" (v. 29) — false teachers would enter Church and cause great trouble (cf. Matt. 7:15; Rev. 2:2);

(b) From within — "of your own selves" (v. 30) — even professing Christians would lead others astray (cf. Ezek. 34:1-10; 2 Tim. 4:3, 4);

(2) It was for this reason these Ephesian elders were to be on alert — "therefore watch" — and to recall what Apostle himself had done during his time with them — "and remember" his —

(a) Lengthy visitation — "by the space of three years";

(b) Continuous exertion — "I ceased not . . . night and day";

(c) Tender fidelity — "to warn . . . with tears";

(d) Personal work — "every one."

4. *A Look Upward* (v. 32)

Then, as he left them, he commended them "to God and to the Word of His grace," emphasizing gracious revelation that constitutes secret of Christian progress (cf. Heb. 1:1, 2), and three important elements of Christian life through this precious possession, namely, the Word of God:

a. Edification — "to build you up"
By the Word —
(1) We are begotten (1 Pet. 1:23);
(2) We are quickened (Psa. 119:50);
(3) We grow (1 Pet. 2:2);

b. Inheritance — "to give you an inheritance"
By the Word —
(1) We are fed (Jer. 15:16);
(2) We are led (Psa. 25:5);
(3) We are satisfied (Psa. 119:193);

c. Sanctification — "among all them which are sanctified"
By the Word —
(1) We are protected (Psa. 119:11);
(2) We are cleansed (John 15:3);
(3) We are sanctified (John 17:17).

Thus, from first to last, we find reality, illumination, and satisfaction in fellowship with Christ through God's Word. St. Paul then provides —

5. *Another Look Backward* (vs. 33-35)

a. He pointed again to his own life and showed it to be absolutely free of self-interest and greed (v. 33);
N.B. Someone has said: "There is no evil into which men have not been led by the love of money," and cites Ananias and Sapphira (5:2); Simon Magus (8:18); Felix (24:26); Judas (Matt. 26:15); Gehazi (2 Kings 5:22); Haman (Esth. 3:9); false priests and prophets Mic. 3:11); Roman soldiers (Matt. 28:12, 13). Cf. also 1 Tim. 6:10; Heb. 13:5;

b. Paul showed his hands, as he spoke (v. 34), hardened by toil in tentmaking (cf. 18:3), thereby proving in his life reality of own teaching (v. 35a);

N.B. Yet he did not necessarily intend all ministers to imitate him in regard to toil (cf. 1 Cor. 9:14; 1 Tim. 5:17, 18);

c. He referred to saying of our Lord (v. 35b), only one recorded in N.T. outside Gospels (cf. Luke 14:12) — Paul's own life perfect example of this dictum (cf. Rom. 12:13; 1 Thess. 5:14):
N.B. Dr. Smellie calls it "one of the *Logia* of the Lord," and says: "There must be many such, which the Gospels do not record on any of their pages. 'It is more blessed to give than to receive.' More blessed it is, because it is more Godlike . . . it is more fruitful . . . It is the consequence and consummation of receiving. So let me remember and obey the words of the Lord Jesus. And let me thank St. Paul that he has preserved for me a flower of the Master's speech which is not enshrined in the Evangel itself."

V. Paul Leaving Miletus (vs. 36-38)

1. *Prayer* (v. 36)

a. Having commended friends to God (v. 32), Apostle "prayed with them all";

b. We know some of his petitions, intercessions, and thanksgivings from his Epistles (cf., e.g., Eph. 1:15-19), and there are few more precious subjects for meditation and imitation;

c. Most of them concerned with others rather than with himself, as doubtless here, especially with needs of their spiritual life (cf. Eph. 3:14-19, etc.).

2. *Parting* (vs. 37, 38)

a. Touching description of scene shows how deeply Ephesian elders loved man who had led them to Christ, and what they felt in losing beloved leader;

b. After all blessings he had brought them, they knew they probably would never see him again (cf. 21:5, 6, 13).

Conclusion

It is noteworthy that there are in this passage three phrases indicative of what the Apostle Paul had been preaching and teaching:

1. *"The grace of God"* (v. 24)
   a. This seems to represent, in particular, the elementary, fundamental truths of the Gospel in relation to our Lord as Saviour;
   b. When we commence the Christian life, we are but "children" (1 John 2:12).
2. *"The kingdom of God"* (v. 25)
   a. This perhaps indicates fuller and deeper truth as taught to those who had been Christians for some time, and refers to the rule and sovereignty of God, present and future;
   b. As we grow in grace and become "young men" (I John 2:13), we are strong in relation to the "kingdom" and the truth concerning it.
3. *"The whole counsel of God"* (v. 27)
   a. This undoubtedly refers to the deepest and fullest of spiritual truths, suited to those who had been mature Christians for a long time;
   b. As we proceed further and become spiritual "fathers" (1 John 2:14), Christians of ripe experience, we have appreciation and understanding of Scriptural teaching as a whole.

Thus did the Apostle feed his flock of the first century and us, his followers of today, with "food convenient" (Prov. 30:8). May we who are preachers and teachers and personal workers emulate him!

I thank Thee, Lord, for using me for Thee to work and speak;
However trembling is the hand, the voice however weak.
O honor, higher, truer far than earthly fame could bring,
Thus to be used, in service blest, for such a glorious King!
—Horatius Bonar

Study No. 100 — The Church of God (2)*

ACTS 20:28

THE DOCTRINE of the Church, the essential truth concerning the Church of Christ, is to be found in the Word of God, and nowhere else. Taking our stand on the Bible, we must refuse to go outside its pages for anything which concerns the *esse* of the Church, its essential being. Further, we must decline to read the New Testament through the glasses of Church History in order to learn essential truth. Scripture alone, and not Scripture interpreted and exemplified by even the sub-Apostolic Church, is our rule of faith. The primitive Church is to be sought for in the New Testament alone, and sought there, not because of its antiquity or even its purity, but because of its immediate connection with Christ and His Apostles, and because it was founded by our Lord and guided by His uniquely inspired apostles. We therefore place the New Testament high and alone as our authority; we take its evidence alone, and not conjointly with that of the Fathers; we emphasize Scripture only, because it is unique and supreme as the source of all necessary primitive and positive truth concerning the Church.

Consider these three main points of New Testament teaching:

I. The Founding of the Church

Our Lord clearly established a Society which in the Apostolic writings is called a Church (Gr., *ekklesia,* those called out); and we note its —

1. *Essence*

   Word in N.T. has threefold application:

   a. It is used of local Church, in particular city or in particular house (e.g., Rom. 16:1-5);

   b. It is used of Church universal regarded as aggregate of local Churches of that time (e.g., 1 Cor. 10:32; 12:28);

* For another treatment of this general subject, see Study No. 22, p. 101.

c. It is used of the Church universal regarded as ideal, as apart from time, and as realizing God's purposes of redemption (e.g., here, and in Eph. 1:22):
   (1) Scripture never limits Church to or identifies it with officials or offices, but applies word to whole body of believers;
   Illus.: No N.T. Christian should speak of "entering the Church" when he means only entering ministry;
   (2) Scripture always distinguishes between Church as visible and local, and as spiritual and ideal, though truly real — i.e., that which constitutes true being of Church is invisible and spiritual.

To become members of this Society, we must find its —

2. *Entrance*

Process, according to Acts 2, is as follows:

a. Christ preached (vs. 14-40);
b. Christ accepted by faith (v. 41);
c. Christ confessed in baptism (v. 41); and —
d. Christ adding penitent believers to Church (vs. 41, 47);

N.B. True order: God in Christ, individual, Church — not Christ, Church, individual; though members of Church are often media in relation to knowledge and acceptance of Gospel. Justification of individual primary in N.T.; it was also reason for and basis of Reformation — faith in Christ first, then fellowship with His Church.

II. The Functions of the Church

Reasons for existence of Church are that it may be for Gospel of Christ a means of —

1. *Expression*

Christ's work made provision for association among those in Him, exemplified in Acts 2:42:

a. Instruction — "continued stedfastly in the apostles' doctrine";
b. Fellowship — "and fellowship";
c. Sacrament — "and in breaking of bread";
d. Worship — "and in prayers."

Everything thus points to community bound by spiritual ties, expressing common life in simple yet adequate forms; N.B. No faintest trace in N.T. of either mediaeval or modern conception of Church as mother, as though it had entity apart from members who compose it. Correlation of God as Father and Church as mother only possible to degenerate thought and unscriptural language of men and organizations far removed from simplicity that is in Christ. Even if need to personify at all, Church is not mother but at most nurse (cf. 1 Thess. 2:7).

2. *Extension*

Through members of Church, knowledge of Christ is to be continually extended; after life in Christ and love to Christ comes labor for Christ, and so we find N.T. Churches "abounding in the work of the Lord" (I Cor. 15:58), which included —

a. Preaching the Word;
b. Administering the Sacraments;
c. Building up believers.

With "diversities of gifts" (1 Cor. 12:4), there was something for each member to do: and though in practical experience later Churches have not maintained standard of N.T., yet it is still ideal — "all at it and always at it";

N.B. All this is possible because Holy Spirit is immanent in Church by means of individual Christians in whom He dwells. This truth of His immanence must always be carefully balanced and rigidly guarded by truth of His Divine transcendence and sovereignty, and His primary, direct, and continuous contact with individual believers.

III. The Form of the Church

This is brought before us primarily under characteristics of —

1. *Unity*

a. This is based on possession of spiritual life;
b. It is manifested in sevenfold way, according to Eph. 4:3-6:
   (1) One body;
   (2) One Spirit;
   (3) One hope;

(4) One Lord;
(5) One faith;
(6) One baptism;
(7) One God and Father of all;

c. It is illustrated by records of earliest Church in Acts 2 to 4;
d. It was of life rather than of organization; of spirituality, not of officialism;
e. It was ethical, not hierarchical;

2. *Polity*

a. This was simple and developed gradually as needed:
(1) At first, Apostles only officials; then came deacons — Jerusalem;
(2) Prophets and teachers — Syria;
(3) Elders — Asia Minor;
(4) Bishops and deacons — Philippi;
(5) Bishops or presbyters, and other officials — Ephesus;

b. Thus there was adaptability, with no one form binding upon all;
N.B. List of offices in 1 Cor. 12:28 differs from that in Eph. 4:11, indicating consideration given to particular and varying needs;

c. There are indications of threefold function of ministry in N.T., viz., bishops or presbyters, elders, and deacons, but nothing so clear as to be absolutely or permanently binding;

d. We may therefore use argument from silence; that if any one form had been vital to existence of Church it would have been as clearly stated as every essential point concerning God, Christ, Salvation, Immortality, etc.;

e. There is true succession, not of officials or offices, but of truth and life; Apostles as such had no successors, for their authority was incapable of transmission; and mere outward transmission of particular ministry no necessary guarantee of authenticity;
N.B. Cf. Caiaphas, accepted as in true succession from Aaron, but condemned by very Scriptures he guarded (cf. Matt. 26:62-66);

f. There is no substitute for Christ but Holy Spirit, the "other Comforter" (John 14:16), and historical continuity is best preserved and guaranteed by unity of Spirit in doctrine of Apostles; it was to Church as whole that promise of perpetuity was given, for it contains within itself, by continued gift of Christ's grace, all things necessary for preservation, purity, power, progress, permanence;

g. There are no spiritual mercies outside covenant of God in Christ; but covenant is wholly independent of this or that Church polity;

N.B. Fairbairn says: "Nor does the existence of particular churches with differing polities break the unity of the Church visible, while their faith and love constitute the unity of the Church invisible";

h. As long as Church keeps to Apostolic Word, and lives Apostolic life, it will remain, whatever its outward polity, Apostolic Church.

Conclusion

Of all the foregoing these three things are the practical sum:

1. *The Church's Membership*
   a. Church as visible is congregation of faithful men among whom —
      (1) Word of God is preached;
      (2) Sacraments are duly administered; and —
      (3) Discipline is exercised;
   b. Church as spiritual is community of those who are Christians, the "society of the saved";
   c. Into this Church men come by union with Christ through His death on the Cross;
   d. In this Church they abide through presence of Holy Spirit, each member exercising gift or gifts bestowed by Him.
2. *The Church's Ministry*
   a. Only ministry *is* a ministry, not a hierarchy;
   b. Only priesthood is that of each believer;
   c. Only sacrifice is that of ourselves.

3. *The Church's Message*

Only true doctrinal perspective may be summed up in words "Christianity is Christ":*

a. What are called "High" views of Church visible have usually brought low views of Church spiritual and of Christ, Head of Church; where Church tends to precede, Christ tends to recede; where Church is stressed as depository of grace, Christ is neglected as Source of grace;

b. But if Church takes its rightful place, Christ is exalted —

(1) In Godhead of His Person;
(2) In completeness of His Sacrifice;
(3) In power of His Resurrection;
(4) In perfection of His Righteousness;
(5) In uniqueness of His Priesthood;

And the Holy Ghost is manifested —

(1) As direct Revealer of Christ to soul;
(2) As immediate and not mediated Source of grace to all believers;
(3) As Divine Illuminator of Word to each disciple.

Then we shall obtain, maintain, and retain in its true position the primitive and positive truth of the Church as that body of which Christ is the Head; in which the Spirit dwells as the present, continuous and permanent life; to which all the promises of God are made; outside which no one can ever be saved; from which no believer can ever be excommunicated; and against which the gates of Hades shall never prevail. Amen, Hallelujah!

---

* For author's enlargement of statement, see his volume of this title (Wm. B. Eerdmans Publishing Co., 1955).

Study No. 101 — Expository Preaching

ACTS 20:32

EXPOSITORY PREACHING is based on the Bible and indicates that it is from the Bible that we elicit our teaching. It is essentially for instruction and information, so that the expository preacher will always be in particular a teacher.

This does not for a moment rule out what is called evangelistic preaching. We believe that all preaching should be evangelistic; but evangelistic preaching is not always associated with the exposition of Scripture, though it may be greatly enriched and strengthened when the evangelist is also a teacher. However, expository preachers are teachers of believers rather than evangelists and their preaching is mainly didactic. They are usually men in the regular ministry who, located in one particular place, are intent on giving their people Scripture teaching and thus "feed the Church of God" (v. 28).

I. Four Types of Expository Preaching

There may be more, but these will cover a good deal of ground:

1. *The Exposition of a Text or Passage*
   a. All textual preaching should be expository, or, as has often been said, text taken out of context may become pretext; and —
   b. Expository preaching should be textual, i.e., based on actual words of Scripture, however wide its scope;
   N.B. Alexander McLaren was ideal in this respect — at once expository and textual preacher.

2. *The Exposition of a Topic*
   a. This may be preaching on some Bible word, or phrase, or subject;

b. It should be expository, presenting subject matter logically and in detail, as found all through Scripture.

3. *The Exposition of a Biography*
   a. Over half of Bible is history, and history is largely concerned with records of individual lives; e.g., taking six men out of Genesis would leave little;
   b. Biographies yield thoughts, messages, and applications where least expected, and give one of finest opportunities of expository preaching; e.g., impossible to consider Abraham's life without learning about faith.

4. *The Exposition of a Book*
   a. Bible in volume form is one book, but name comes from Greek *biblia,* books, so it is also "Divine Library," as Campbell Morgan calls it;
   b. Since God has given this Book in such divisions, study of one particular book is of immense value; based upon Bible, it is explanatory of whole, and ideally suited to instruction of those who belong to God, its Divine Author.

II. Four Reasons Why Expository Preaching is Important

1. *It is of Value to Ourselves*
   a. "Water never rises above its level" — what we are will determine our preaching, and what we do will never rise above what we are;
   b. Expository preaching will increase what we need to emphasize, knowledge of Bible:
      (1) We shall never be able to preach acceptably unless we know subject thoroughly;
      (2) In mastering it, we should always have large margin of information that comes from study; as Lord Bacon used to say, "Reading makes a full man" — and we need to be "full" in order to be true expositors of the Word in all its fulness in limited time allotted; N.B. Alexander McLaren said everything he was he owed to studying chapter of Bible each day.

2. *It Gives Knowledge to Our Hearers*
   a. There is call almost every day for passing on of this

knowledge to congregations or individuals, and here expository preaching is invaluable;

b. This is said to be day of education and enlightenment, but it is also day of very grave ignorance of God's Word, and best way of counteracting this condition is expository preaching.

3. *It Helps in the Building Up of Believers*
   a. According to our text, "the Word of His grace . . . is able to build you up," and does so much more fully than anything else; that is meaning of word "edification" (cf. 1 Cor. 14:3; Eph. 4:12, etc.; note also Psa. 37:31; 119:11);
   b. Note strong emphasis in Paul's Epistles on Christian walk rather than on missionary work; this is because if walk is right there will be work done, and no need of appeal:
      (1) Highest ideal of Christian life is urged; justification, sanctification, consecration, separation, and holy association for every believer;
      (2) To attain this ideal there is nothing to be compared to knowledge of and love for Bible;
      (3) Backsliding can usually be traced to neglect of prayer and Bible study; and in churches where there is expository preaching members will be not only built up but kept up.
4. *It Points to Christ, the Living Word*
   a. People may forget about preacher but will feel they have had message from God; let him pray before going into pulpit:

      When telling Thy salvation free,
      Let all-absorbing thoughts of Thee
      My mind and soul engross;
      When all the hearts are bowed and stirred
      Beneath the influence of Thy Word,
      Hide me behind Thy Cross.

   b. If preacher has this ideal he will see value of expository preaching, because it will not be himself speaking but his Lord (1 Cor. 15:10; Gal. 2:20);
      Illus.: Scholarly preacher who gave his people "dry"

sermons found one Sunday morning note on pulpit that read, "Sir, we would see Jesus." Wise enough to take hint, he preached unto them Jesus, in fulness of God's Word. After some weeks, he found another note: "Then were the disciples glad when they saw the Lord";

c. If we preach Word as we should, we shall always preach Jesus also — not so much *what* but *whom;*
Illus.: Speaking of three preachers, gentleman once said, "If I go and listen to *him,* he preaches 'Her' — the Church; if I go and listen to *him,* he preaches 'It' — doctrine; but whenever I hear *him* he preaches 'Him' — Christ." "He," "She," "It" — in Christ the Church takes her rightful place and doctrine is seen to be vital truth concerning both.

Conclusion

In Colossians 1 are to be found three aspects of the ministry which are appropriate to sum up the true preacher:

1. *He is a Minister of Christ* — "a faithful minister of Christ" (v. 7) — he must exalt Christ in all his preaching;
2. *He is a Minister of the Gospel* — "the gospel . . . whereof I Paul am made a minister" (v. 23) — first Christ, then the Gospel;
3. *He is a Minister of the Church* — "the church, whereof I am made a minister" (vs. 24, 25) — that is the Scriptural order — Christ, the Gospel, the Church.

Thus the expository preacher will have every opportunity of proclaiming the whole counsel of God. He will preach the living Christ first and foremost, and in so doing will preach the Gospel of Christ, and will build up the Church of Christ.

Study No. 102 — Widening Witness

ACTS 21:1-40

A PHRASE of Shakespeare is often quoted: "There is a soul of goodness in things evil"; and we are accustomed to refer to "bringing good out of evil." While the intention of these phrases is doubtless correct, they are literally wrong, because evil is always evil and there is no "soul of goodness" in it; and therefore it is impossible to "bring good out" of it. But what is usually meant is that God can and does overrule evil for good. There is a Divine permission of evil and then an overruling of it for the carrying out of great purposes. It was thus in the lives of men like Joseph, David, Nebuchadnezzar; so also was it in the imprisonment of John Bunyan and in the opposition to Christianity on the part of men like Voltaire and Strauss. In this chapter we shall see how wrong-doing was made to issue in blessing and witness in the experience of the Apostle Paul.

While Paul was among the Gentiles, what about the Church in Jerusalem? Christianity was tolerated there only as a sect of Judaism, not as an organization including Gentiles. And yet, according to Romans 4, written from Corinth only a few weeks previous to the events recorded in this chapter, there was no real difference between Jews and Gentiles originally; any difference at present was due to God's dealings; and Paul was convinced that God had sent him especially to the Gentiles. In this connection it is interesting also to study Romans 9 to 11.

Why was Paul so determined to go up to Jerusalem? Was it to prove the obstinacy of the Jews? Not only was his message rejected during the ensuing two-year period covered by chapters 21-27, but not a single conversion to Christianity is recorded. Did the opposition to Paul's methods come from Christian Jews? We do not know, but at any rate it was not from the Jerusalem Church as such this time.

This passage is part of the last and longest section of Acts, which is descriptive of Paul's progress towards Rome (19:21 to 28:31). The detail at this point is remarkable and seems to indicate that in the view of the writer great events were taking place. That, says Ramsay, is because this part of Luke's book concerns a crisis in the fate of both Paul and the Church.

I. Journeying to Jerusalem (vs. 1-17)

1. *En Route* (vs. 1-3)
   a. Parting from Ephesian elders at Miletus must have been great wrench (cf. 20:36 to 21:1a);
   b. But it was necessary for Paul and his party to leave them and sail south, skirting coast of Asia Minor, touching at islands of Cos and Rhodes, and landing at Patara in Lycia;
   c. Here they found ship which took them past Cyprus and landed them at Tyre, in Syria.
2. *At Tyre* (vs. 4-6)
   a. Remained there one week and enjoyed fellowship with Christians, who tried to dissuade Paul from going to Jerusalem;
   b. But again came time to depart, and once more we note beautiful spirit — love had discovered love and expressed it; picture of men with wives and children, all kneeling in prayer on seashore, reveals wonderful possibilities of Christian affection within space of single week — what a man was Paul to have drawn out so much love!
3. *At Caesarea* (vs. 7-14)
   a. Then came one-day call at Ptolemais and arrival at Caesarea, where Paul was guest of Philip the evangelist (cf. 6:5; 8:5-40) and seized another welcome opportunity for fellowship — again, Luke characteristically notes part played by Christian womanhood;
   b. Stay there was longer and during it prophet Agabus (cf. 11:27, 28) gave symbolic warning to Paul against

going to Jerusalem; and this was strengthened by general agreement;

c. But Paul's determination was reiterated so courageously that his friends finally concurred in his conviction of God's will for him.

4. *Arrival* (vs. 15-17)

a. Certain Christians of Caesarea accompanying them, they again took up their "baggage" (v. 15, A.S.V., i.e., that which was to be "carried"), and completed journey to Jerusalem;

b. With them also was Mnason, evidently one of earliest converts, perhaps dating from Pentecost or before, who was to provide lodging for Paul and party;

c. On arrival they were given warm welcome by Jerusalem Christians, probably first privately and unofficially.

II. In Jerusalem Again (vs. 18-40)

1. *The Meeting* (vs. 18-20a)

a. Next day came public gathering, with James, brother of our Lord, as presiding officer and chief authority (cf. 12:17; 15:13-21), and with other leaders present;

b. Paul told in detail what God had done among Gentiles through him, and result was repeated praise to God.

2. *The Proposal* (vs. 20b-25)

a. Yet it was thought important to take immediate action to show Jews Paul's true position in regard to Judaism; perhaps, while Church as body was hearty in reception of him, leaders were somewhat timid about his effect on narrow-minded believers;

b. "Many thousands of Jews" (v. 20, Gr., "myriads," or tens of thousands) seems to refer to Jewish believers then gathered in city for feast, including not only Jerusalem Christians, but others from elsewhere, showing great progress of Gospel among Jews;

c. These were all zealous observers of law, though accepting Jesus as Messiah — impossible position which could not last very long;

d. But in order to conciliate them, it was suggested that Paul should become responsible for four poor Jewish Christians who had taken upon themselves Nazarite vow (cf. 18:18; Num. 6:1-21); this would be proof of his readiness as Jew to observe law though, so far as Gentiles were concerned, James and elders stood by what had already been decided (cf. 15:19-29).

3. *The Action* (v. 26)
   a. Paul responded to suggestion in order to avoid friction and to conciliate Jewish Christians;
   b. We may wonder how Paul could harmonize action here with attitude expressed in Gal. 2:3-9; it has been suggested that —
      (1) He was doing only what he himself had urged in 1 Cor. 9:19-23 (cf. 18:18; Rom. 14);
      (2) He had great hopes at this time of uniting Jewish and Gentile believers (cf. Rom. 15:25-28);
      N.B. Four parties should here be distinguished: Pharisees, Sadducees, Jewish Christians, Gentile Christians;
   c. In any case, Paul never allowed apparent inconsistencies of outward action to interfere with constant loyalty to inner principles;
   d. True Christian attitude may be summed up in words — "Not compromise at the expense of truth, but comprehensiveness for the sake of truth."

4. *The Outcome* (vs. 27-36)
   a. Paul's object just about to be attained (v. 27) when sudden interruption took place: Jews from Asia, specially hostile to him because of events at and near Ephesus (cf. 19:8-41; 20:19), had come to Jerusalem for Pentecost, and naturally had them freshly in mind;
   b. Prejudice and bigotry easily inflamed, so populace soon stirred up by means of false charges:
      (1) Having seen Paul in company of an Ephesian, Trophimus (cf. 20:4; 2 Tim. 4:20), they supposed Paul had brought him, a Gentile, into inner portion

of temple, contrary to law, instead of leaving him in court of Gentiles;

(2) Perhaps this barrier was "middle wall of partition" (Eph. 2:14);

(3) Seeing Paul busy with ceremonies in inner court where only Jews were permitted, enemies from Asia assumed Trophimus to have been there too;

c. Paul then seized and dragged "out of the temple," i.e., from inner to outer court — Jews not willing to defile temple even though quite ready to take human life elsewhere, so far will religious intolerance go;

d. But news of disturbance reached Roman commander, Claudius Lysias by name (cf. 23:26), for cloisters in court of Gentiles communicated with fortress of Antonia, occupied by Roman garrison;

e. From this eminence, "chief captain" and soldiers ran down just in time to prevent Paul from being beaten to death; and, having ordered Paul to be chained, Lysias made inquiry as to prisoner's identity and charges made against him;

f. Such was uproar that Lysias then ordered Paul to be taken into castle; and, realizing Paul was escaping, crowd surged upon soldiers who had literally to lift and carry him out of reach; cf. uproar at Ephesus (19:32,33).

5. *The Appeal* (vs. 37-40)

a. When Paul asked to be allowed to speak to chief captain, he was met by surprised question, for Lysias astonished to hear Greek language of culture from prisoner;

b. Thought Paul Egyptian fanatic who had recently posed as prophet and collected large number of men called "Assassins" (A.S.V.) because each carried dagger under his garments, for purpose of overpowering Romans and seizing Jerusalem; military measures had been taken against movement and Egyptian leader had run away;

c. Captain's conclusion rather natural one, but Paul's reply clearly showed mistake:

(1) He was Jew by race and, as such, had perfect right to enter inner court of temple; and —

(2) So far from being alien Egyptian, he was citizen of Tarsus, "no mean city" (v. 39) and site of important university;

N.B. Much depends on these two elements in life — whence man comes, as to race and family, and where born and grows up, as to surroundings; or, heredity and environment;

9. Result was immediate permission to address people, and so in "a great silence" Paul was heard "in the Hebrew tongue" (v. 40; cf. 22:2).

Conclusion

There is no word so frequent in the Acts of the Apostles to express true Christianity as the word "witness" (cf. 1:8; 2:32; 10:39, etc.). This chapter is a revelation of Paul as a witness (cf. 22:15; 26:16), able and anxious to pass on to others what he had learned and received:

1. *How Did Paul Witness?*
   a. By his effect on others, eliciting their thought, love, sympathy, sorrow, and prayers, because of their debt to him in Christ;
   b. By his personal character, displaying tenderness, strength, conscientiousness, courage, trust, largeheartedness;
   c. By his risking all for Christ, with danger foretold, felt, and faced;
   d. By his boldness of speech, both to fellow-Christians and to unbelieving Jews and Gentiles.
2. *Why Could Paul Witness?*
   a. Because he was continually in touch with God the Father;
   b. Because Christ was real and precious to him —all and in all;
   c. Because the Holy Spirit filled his soul with Divine grace and guidance.

When we come thus into union and communion with God, Father, Son, and Holy Spirit, our thoughts, feelings, desires, manner, character, conduct, and speech all will witness to Him "Whose we are and Whom we serve."

Study No. 103 — Full Surrender

ACTS 21:13

ONE OF LIFE'S greatest problems is to know when to give way and when not to give way. On the one hand, a man may consider himself conscientious when, instead, he is pursuing a mistaken course through sheer obstinacy. On the other hand, weakness is wrong and even dangerous.

There is an illustration of this problem in the experience of St. Paul at Caesarea where we find, apparently, the Holy Spirit leading on two conflicting lines. While still in Ephesus, Paul had been quite clear as to the necessity of going again to Jerusalem (cf. 19:21), and this conviction was strengthened by the time he reached Miletus (cf. 20:16, 22). While it would seem that the "spirit" mentioned in these passages is Paul's own and not the Holy Spirit, yet it is hardly likely that in a Christian of the great Apostle's calibre such a strong purpose would be in opposition to the will of God. On the other hand, the disciples at Tyre and the prophet Agabus at Caesarea were obviously inspired by the Holy Spirit to warn Paul of what he would encounter if he persisted in his course of action. But then his friends added to this message an argument against his going to Jerusalem (v. 12), and this he could not accept.

A. B. Simpson has expressed it thus: "We see the Apostle's leading by the Spirit apparently contradicted by another leading of the Spirit, and yet in the end we find his first leading was sustained, the second appearing to be only a test that brought out the more fully his fidelity to God."

In all of this we may see some of the elements of Paul's personality:

I. His Sorrow — "What mean ye to weep and to break mine heart?"

1. *Human affection occupied large place in Paul's life*:
   a. At Tyre, for instance, had stayed only one week, yet had won disciples' hearts, including those of wives and children (cf. v. 5); and —
   b. All along way, hospitality had been generously offered and gratefully received (cf. 20:6; 21:4, 8, 16).

But —

2. *Human affection sometimes interposed unduly*:
   a. Disciples of Caesarea caused themselves sorrow — "What mean ye to weep —?" and also caused their beloved leader sorrow — "What mean ye . . . to break my heart?"
   b. This distress for Paul was intensified when his own comrades joined in persuasive entreaty — "both we, and they of that place, besought him —" (v. 12).

II. His Spirit — "I am ready not to be bound only, but also to die"

1. *Paul was ready to suffer.*
   a. This was great test of reality (cf. Phil. 3:10; Heb. 11:25);
   b. Suffering often follows surrender (cf. 5:41; 9:16).
2. *Paul was ready to die.*
   a. This was greatest test of love (cf. 2 Tim. 4:6, 8);
   b. Readiness to die follows readiness to live (cf. Rom. 1:15); N.B. Note other types of readiness urged in N.T.: to do good works (1 Tim. 6:18; Tit. 3:1); to bear Christian testimony (1 Pet. 3:15); to meet our Lord at His coming (Matt. 24:44; 25:10); and all summed up in readiness of mind (Acts 17:11), and readiness of will (2 Cor. 8:11).

III. His Secret — "for the name of the Lord Jesus"

1. *"The Name"*
   a. Meant full revelation of Christ to His Apostle;

b. Provided basis for later declaration, "To me to live is Christ" (Phil. 1:21):

"To me to live is Christ" — and yet the days
Are days of toiling men;
We rise at morn, and tread the beaten ways,
And lay us down again.

How is it that this base, unsightly life
Can yet be "Christ" alone —
Our common need, and weariness, and strife,
While common days wear on?

Then saw I how before a Master wise
A shapeless stone was set;
He said, "Therein a form of beauty lies,
Though none behold it yet.

When all beside it shall be hewn away,
That glorious shape shall stand
In beauty of the eternal day
Of a fair, unsullied land."

2. *"For the Name"*

Signifies in Greek "on behalf of the Name," so that to suffer or to die was to Paul —

a. A reward — privilege leading to joy and glory; and —
b. A responsibility — duty providing present power and future possibilities.

Conclusion

These three elements in Paul's life may be summed up in —

1. *Three Characteristics*:
   a. His tender heart;
   b. His clear conscience;
   c. His strong yet surrendered will; and in —
2. *One Power*

"The Lord Jesus"

I am the Lord's! O joy beyond expression,
O sweet response to voice of love Divine!
Faith's joyous "Yes" to the assuring whisper,
"Fear not; I have redeemed thee; thou art Mine";
This the transforming word which faith receiveth,
The message which the child-like soul believeth.

I am the Lord's! Yet teach me all it meaneth,
All it involves of love and loyalty,
Of holy service, absolute surrender,
And unreserved obedience unto Thee.
They nearest draw to joy's sublime perfection
Who seek it in the depths of full subjection.

Study No. 104 — "An Old Disciple"

ACTS 21:16

IN THESE FEW WORDS is one of the shortest of Biblical biographies, that of Mnason who, according to the Greek adjective used of him, was an "early" disciple, his conversion dating back possibly to Pentecost, or even to Christ's earthly life. Another conjecture is that Mnason was a product of either Paul's ministry on the island of Cyrus, the initial stop on the First Missionary Journey (cf. 13:4-13), or of the home missions work of Barnabas (cf. 4:36; 15:39). In any case, Mnason was at least middle-aged at this time and probably older — what we would call elderly, if not really aged. Living now in Jerusalem, he had apparently been visiting the Christians of Caesarea. We may certainly think of Mnason as a mature Christian and a man of property, and consider his —

I. Faithfulness

We know that in Mnason's life there had been —

1. *Conversion*
   a. Mnason had become disciple of Christ many years before;
   b. It is easy to begin almost anything, especially in youth; cf. Paul's words to Galatians (5:7), "Ye did run well."
2. *Continuance*
   a. But Mnason had also continued in discipleship; cf. Paul himself (e.g., Phil. 3:10-14), and Daniel (6:10-13);
   b. Perils of middle life very real — physical, mental, social, so also spiritual; cf. Psalmist's phrase, "destruction that wasteth at noonday" (91:6).

II. Receptiveness

Word "disciple" means learner; Mnason was one —

1. *With the Heart*
   a. Gesture of welcoming Paul to his home showed freshness of sympathy;
   b. This is rare in older people, who are apt to resent new ways as "newfangled," and to prefer old friends and habits.
2. *With the Head*
   a. Mnason was one who, while holding fast old, saw good reasons to welcome new;
   b. Secret is found in John 8:31: "If ye continue in My Word, then are ye My disciples indeed" — subjecting every movement to standard of Scripture.

III. Usefulness

This was twofold:

1. *Fruitfulness*
   Abiding in Christ all this time, Mnason was living testimony to world and to Church of grace of God bringing —
   a. Christ's power not only to save, but to sanctify (cf. Psa. 92:12-14); and —
   b. Christ's power not only to keep, but to satisfy (cf. Isa. 46:4).
2. *Fellowship*
   Association with such an one as Mnason had great value for Paul, for it included —
   a. Hospitality provided for his stay in Jerusalem;
   b. Countenance lent his great cause; and —
   c. Experience utilized in behalf of his ministry.
   N.B. Alexander McLaren said of Mnason: "Men have spent their lives to win a line in the world's chronicles which are written on sand, and have broken their hearts because they failed; and this passing act of one obscure Christian, in sheltering a little company of travel-stained wayfarers, has made his name a possession forever."

Conclusion

The gracious influence of "one Mnason of Cyprus, an old disciple," reminds us that —

1. *Christian Discipleship is the same today* — for Christ says:
   a. "Come unto Me" (Matt. 11:28) — for conversion;
   b. "Learn of Me" (Matt. 11:29) — for consecration.
2. *Continuance in Discipleship is the same today* — for Christ says:
   a. "Abide in Me" (John 15:4) — for communion;
   b. "Follow Me" (Matt. 4:19) — for conduct.

So, to paraphrase a familiar hymn —

Coming, learning, abiding, following —
Is He sure to bless?
Angels, martyrs, prophets, virgins
Answer, Yes!

Study No. 105 — A Great Christian

ACTS 21:27-40

PAUL'S JOURNEY to Jerusalem was made with the intense desire and great hope of winning the Jewish churches to an acceptance of the Gentile churches, and of uniting them all in Christ. His reception by the Jerusalem church, both private (v.17), and formal (vs. 18-20), was cordial, raising his hopes for the success of his mission. But immediately the issue of law and grace was introduced. Paul was vigorously against keeping the law as the means of salvation, yet as a Jew he naturally continued to practise it; so, with love towards others and the best of intentions, he carried out the plan of the elders (vs.20-26). What followed brought out in sharp contrast Jewish bigotry, Roman power, and Christian consecration.

I. The Jews (vs. 27-31)

They illustrate how man's basest passions can be utilized for profession of religion:

1. *They were prejudiced.*
   Influenced by religious bigotry, they made wrong suppositions.
2. *They were hateful.*
   Filled with cunning, they used false representation of half-truths in order to influence crowd.
3. *They were murderous.*
   In spite of anxiety not to defile Temple, they were willing to take human life near it.

II. The Apostle (vs. 32-40)

1. *He was large-hearted.*
   His co-operation with elders in respect of law in order that he might conciliate and win adversaries proved him —
   a. Not enslaved, but free;
   b. Not hypocritical, but true;
   c. Not backsliding, but obedient.
2. *He was trustful.*
   a. Even in face of misrepresentation, and of apparent yielding of truth to bigotry, his faith did not fail;
   b. He knew God would overrule, causing both Jew and Roman to carry out His purpose.
3. *He was calm.*
   a. Composed in face of attempted murder, he made no rejoinder to mob;
   b. Then, when Romans had rescued him, he used occasion to advantage of Gospel, seizing long-desired opportunity for public testimony to his countrymen in their own language.
   c. He did not "lose his head" because his heart was fixed on God (cf. Psa.112:7).

Conclusion

True Christianity is the same in our day as in Paul's:

1. *Aggressive* — it encounters difficulties;
2. *Large-hearted* — it is liable to misconceptions;

3. *Opposed* — it is part of God's plan;
4. *Consecrated* — it is sure of God's protection, power, and peace.

Study No. 106 — Paul's Defense Before His People

ACTS 22:1-30

This chapter follows closely on the last one and continues the story of St. Paul's experiences in Jerusalem. Permitted to speak to the crowd, he tells the story of his life. Comparison with chapter 9 (see Studies 39-42) shows how the Apostle adapted himself to the occasion and revealed tact, presence of mind, and an earnest desire to impress his hearers and win them for Christ. A man's best defense is often his own experience and not mere argument. In order to appreciate Paul's position, we must first ponder each stage of his appeal, and then note the effect of it on his audience, and the consequences to himself.

I. **The Solemn Plea** (vs. 1-21)
   1. *Conciliation* (vs. 1, 2)
      a. Paul knew patriotic pride of all conservative Jews in national language of that day, Aramaic (cf. 1:19; 21:40), mixture of Hebrew and Syriac;
      b. His use of it was wise, for it predisposed crowd to listen.
   2. *Education* (v. 3)
      a. Paul indicates his early experience to have been exactly like their own, and implies his disposition and training were such as would not lead to change in life without adequate cause;
      b. He declares himself to be a true Jew (cf. 21:39) —
         (1) By birth (cf. 9:11);
         (2) By training (cf. 5:34); and —
         (3) By conviction (cf. 7:58; 8:1; 26:4, 5);
      c. He discusses Jewish law, mentioning —

(1) His own strict adherence to it (cf. 21:20-26; 24:14-18; Gal. 1:14; Phil. 3:5, 6); and, with rare courtesy —
(2) His accusers' zeal for it (cf. 21:20; Rom. 10:1, 2), even though he had come to regard attitude as mistaken.

3. *Persecution* (vs. 4, 5)
   a. Paul adduces, as further proof that he had been one with them in his opposition to Christianity, its ruthless ferocity, for —
      (1) It involved women as well as men;
      (2) It extended even to death; and —
      (3) It included Damascus, city far from Jerusalem;
   b. He gives as witnesses to this the high priest (probably Caiaphas, though when Paul was speaking it was Ananias, cf. 23:2), and "all the estate of the elders" (v. 5) — another instance of fine courtesy and tact ;
   N.B. Here, again, we read of Gospel as "the Way" (cf. 9:2; 19:23), course of life expressive of progress.
4. *Conversion* (vs. 6-16)
   a. In recounting his vision (vs. 6-11), Paul emphasizes supernatural element, as though to say —
      (1) God's action alone explained so great a change in his life; and —
      (2) Time of day (noon) made heavenly light all the more striking and authentic;
   b. In proceeding to vision's outcome (vs. 12-16), Paul's —
      (1) Description of Ananias (v. 12) shows how orthodox he was, unlikely to do or allow anything opposed to Judaism;
      (2) Designation of God (v. 14) indicates true continuity with past; and —
      (3) Delineation of Divine purpose (vs. 14, 15) proves that Paul had been "chosen" (cf. Deut. 7:6; John 15:16; 1 Cor. 1:26-28) to —
         (a) "Know His will";
         (b) "See that Just One";

(c) "Hear the voice of His mouth"; and —

(d) "Be His witness unto all men";

N.B. It has been well said that, since invitation to "come and see" empty tomb is followed by command to "go and tell" (Matt. 28:6, 7), this is God's order for everyone who has had real vision of risen Christ;

(4) Direction to "be baptized" (v. 16) follows logically, and verse must be taken in entirety to avoid misunderstanding, for it emphasizes and balances both Divine and human sides:

(a) There is no doubt that on God's part he who surrenders to Christ is forgiven, and order of this is indicated by tense of Greek words, "having called on the name of the Lord";

(b) On other side, baptism always means introduction into new sphere in which opportunity of remission of sins is afforded; refers to position, not to spiritual condition; and complements (a); cf. same truth on both its sides in 2:38;

(c) Paul is clear, both in his own experience and in that of all other Christians, that no mere mechanical rite can bestow forgiveness, but also that baptism is sign and expression of that attitude of repentance and faith which is sole condition of salvation.

5. *Commission* (vs. 17-21)

Next stage of Paul's experience described in very significant terms, for he had specific reason for including it. This episode is not narrated in chap. 9, but it supplements 9:26-29 (cf. Gal. 1:18, 19):

a. Revelation (vs. 17, 18)

(1) It took place in temple, showing that, although a Christian, he still honored spot on which people were then standing listening to him;

(2) It was in trance (cf. 10:10) that God spoke to him, and sign and sound mentioned to show God was

indeed speaker; and —

(3) It was Divine appeal for haste, indicating danger God knew attached to Paul's presence in Jerusalem (cf. 9:29), and so his visit lasted only fifteen days (cf. Gal. 1:18);

N.B. It was not that Paul had been wrong in going to Jerusalem, which was natural and right in view of past, but that radical changes in his life had caused revulsion of feeling in respect to him;

b. Rejoinder (vs. 19, 20)

(1) Paul's reply to God showed —

(a) He supposed his testimony would carry special weight with those who knew him well; and —

(b) He thought he had special advantages for work in Jerusalem;

(2) But facts proved to be against Paul, for —

(a) His former friends became intensely angered at what they regarded as desertion and change of front, and —

(b) Not even participation in martyrdom of Stephen, which had so impressed Paul (cf. v. 20), would influence them in his favor;

N.B. Word "consenting" used here and in 8:1 suggests thought of pleasurable agreement, indicating Paul's former callous attitude towards martyr's suffering and death (cf. 26:10);

c. Reiteration (v. 21)

God did not reply to Paul's arguments, but —

(1) Commanded him again to leave Jerusalem; and —

(2) Commissioned him to go and preach to Gentiles;

N.B. Apostle wanted audience to realize his work among foreigners was not of his own choice, but was undertaken only after expressed reluctance and under Divine orders.

II. The Stubborn Prejudice (vs. 22, 23)

1. *Opposition Aroused*

a. It is significant that up to that moment all went well, and

Jews listened carefully to what Paul said about Christ;

b. But hated name "Gentiles" proved too much for them, and revived animosity instantly.

2. *Opposition Expressed*

a. They shouted at Paul, saying he ought not to have been kept alive by Romans (cf. 21:33-36; Heb. 11:23);

b. They threw off garments in uncontrollable excitement (cf. 16:22; Luke 19:35);

c. They cast dust into air, mark of intense anger (cf. 2 Sam. 16:13).

III. The Strong Protection (vs. 24-30)

1. *The Plan* (v. 24)

a. Roman authority, compelled to intervene again, and puzzled by new outburst, determined to discover true reason by method of torture;

b. In this examination by cruel scourging, victim was stripped, tied with thongs to pillar or stretched on frame, and lashed with leather straps tipped with lead till he gave information or made confession.

2. *The Protest* (vs. 25-28)

a. But Paul would not be treated thus, and spoke to centurion (cf. 10:1; 27:1), subordinate officer in charge of operation, questioning legality of it;

b. This was because Roman law forbade scourging of any Roman citizen (cf. 16:23, 37, 38);

c. In claiming position Paul showed advantage of citizenship, for first centurion and then captain quickly recognized offense of scourging Roman as liable to severe penalty;

d. But chief captain found it difficult to believe that one whom he regarded as mere Jewish sedition-monger could really be Roman citizen, and so referred proudly to his own citizenship by purchase;

e. Paul, however, could and did claim it by birth (v. 28), though we do not know circumstances leading to his family's obtaining privilege; but it was great thing for Jewish boy to inherit;

N.B. Strictly speaking, it was possible to have Roman citizenship in only three ways:
(1) By birth from citizen parents;
(2) By reward for services;
(3) By freedom after slavery;
But during reign of Emperor Claudius, citizenship was sold, and perhaps it was this that accounted for captain's name of "Claudius Lysias" (23:26).

3. *The Privilege* (vs. 29, 30)
   a. Paul's claim being sufficient to prevent scourging, he was at once released from thongs, and then, because of chief captain's fear of results, set free from chain which doubtless bound him to soldier (cf. 21:33; 12:6; 28:16, 20);
   b. Then, because chief captain still anxious to understand accusation, he summoned "chief priests and their council to appear," and brought Paul unbound before them;
   c. From that time on, friendliness and fairness of Roman authorities is noteworthy, showing it was better for Paul's cause to claim his Roman citizenship rather than to assert his Jewish birth (cf. v. 3).

Conclusion

The Apostle's address to this Jewish crowd is characterized by —
1. *A spirit of conciliation;*
2. *A narration of facts;* and —
3. *A definite object;*

— and yet he met with immediate failure, so far as the Jews were concerned. But the subsequent events show how God overruled and caused both Jews and Romans to carry out His great purpose.

Can we, like Paul, trust in God even when our best efforts for Him seem to fail?

Study No. 107 — Paul's Witness to the Resurrection (2)*

ACTS 22:8

DRIVEN outside a city's walls by a riotous crowd picking up stones as they hurried along, a man with "the face of an angel" calls upon the Lord Jesus to receive his spirit, and then, as the fatal blow descends, he falls asleep in death. One witness of the scene, at least, stands unmoved as he guards the garments of those who have stoned this first martyr for the new faith, and he leaves the spot as hardened as ever in spite of the sight of suffering and death.

Less than thirty years later, in the same city, not far from where he had stood before, stands the man who later became an active persecutor; but now he is not a mere witness in a mob scene, but the chief actor; now he is not free, but chained; now he is the one persecuted, and the time is coming when he, too, will die as a martyr.

What has made the difference between Saul the Persecutor and Paul the Apostle? The vision he had of the Risen Lord Jesus Christ, of whom he speaks so positively in our text. We are thereby reminded that the spiritual experience of Paul is one of the greatest proofs we have of the Resurrction (cf. 26:8, 22, 23). It may be divided into three stages or steps:

I. Enmity Shown — The Man

What a man Paul had been, with —

1. *Powerful Intellect*

   a. He was great thinker, after long, thorough training — Roman at Tarsus, and Hebrew in Jerusalem, under

* For another treatment of general subject, see Study No. 66, p. 258.

Gamaliel, doctor of law with fine reputation (cf. v. 3: 5:34);

b. He was of such mental capacity that intellect ruled emotions by means of compelling convictions.

2. *Strong Impulses*
   a. Feelings that in some men are weak, icy, uninspired, in Paul were like fire;
   b. Through everything they gave warmth to his words, force to his purposes, and resolution to his actions.
3. *Intense Conscientiousness*
   a. Jewish training developed scrupulous regard for law, religion, and demands of conscience;
   b. When man's convictions and feelings are ruled by conscience, he ought to be at his highest and best; but it is also possible, like Paul at this time, merely to "think that he doeth God service" (John 16:2).
4. *Determined Will*
   a. When man of conviction, emotion, and conscientiousness also has strong will, he is a real man, and one to be reckoned with;
   b. This was sort of foe Gospel had to encounter as, with sanction of High Priest, Paul —
      (1) Breathed out "threatenings and slaughter" (9:1);
      (2) "Made havoc of the Church, entering into every house, and haling men and women committed them to prison" (8:3); and —
      (3) "Compelled them to blaspheme" (26:11).
      N.B. Man of such intense individuality would have made his mark anywhere. Cf. twelve disciples who were also strong individualists but who had first known Jesus "in the days of His flesh" (Heb. 5:7), as Paul had not; he first met "Christ risen from the dead" (1 Cor. 15:20; cf. vs. 4, 8).

II. Enmity Overcome — The Convert

In Paul's account of his own conversion, we observe —

1. *Sudden Check*

a. As he set out with party for Damascus, he had apparently no time alone and no compunctions;
b. But as he neared city, with its towers gleaming in noon sunlight, greater light shone upon him, and he fell dazzled to the ground;
c. Light was Divine — "from heaven" (v. 6) — and so was voice (v. 7), for he answered, "Who art Thou, *Lord?*" (v. 8).

2. *Surprising Revelation*
a. Name used — "Jesus of Nazareth" — only time spoken from heaven — not "Lord," or "God," or even "Christ," but hated name, only one Paul had until now accorded Him;
b. Accusation made — "whom thou persecutest" — but what had Paul done to Jesus Himself? Cf. Prov. 14:31; Zech. 2:8; Matt. 18:5; 25:40, 45.

3. *Submissive Response*
a. Saw truth of matter at once, "trembling and astonished" (9:6) — this Man alive!
b. Surrendered to Him at once, placing himself at the "Lord's" disposal — yet no direct revelation then — further test of obedience first (v. 10);
N.B. Nature of manifestation notable — no compulsion — supernatural in form, but open to rejection; resurrection accepted by Paul because convinced of its reality.

III. Enmity Transformed — The Worker

Story of Paul's life demonstrates —

1. *Prompt Action*
a. Attitude not only overcome, but reversed — he who had persecuted now prays (cf. 9:11) and preaches (cf. 9:27);
b. Great change made him endeavor to undo former harm done to cause of Christ (cf. 26:22, 23) — as F. W. H. Meyers has expressed it:

Saints, did I say? with your remembered faces,
Dear men and women, whom I sought and slew!
Ah, when we mingle in the heavenly places
How will I weep to Stephen and to you!

2. *Permanent Allegiance*
   a. Relationship with Christ lasted, with no wavering, no tiring, no regrets;
   b. Thirty years spent in many labors, many countries, in service of Christ till death.
3. *Prolonged Suffering*
   a. Jews were frenzied in enmity to Paul; Gentiles ridiculed him; converts disappointed him; helpers left him (cf. 2 Cor. 16:33; 2 Tim. 3:11);
   b. Yet he continued, declaring, "None of these things move me" (20:24).
4. *Perfect Satisfaction*
   a. Paul's was no forced work, but his life was full, well-rounded;
   b. Hear his exultant voice: "That I may know Him" (Phil. 3:10); "I press toward the mark" (Phil. 3:14);
   c. Then, facing towards home: "I am now ready . . . I have fought . . . I have finished . . . I have kept" (2 Tim. 4:6, 7);

   N.B. During all these years, Paul's personality strong, yet only echo of Risen Christ: his desire was to know Him, his passion to preach Him, and his glory to be His slave. Paul's life motto may truly be said to have been — "Not I, but Christ" (Gal. 2:20).

Conclusion

As we think of all this, we see what a splendid witness Paul was to the Resurrection of Christ:

1. *If his testimony was true, his conversion was real.*

   His witness was marked by —
   a. Intelligence;
   b. Candor;
   c. Disinterestedness;

   — and, therefore, may be presumed reliable and truthful.
2. *If his conversion was real, Christ rose from the dead.*
   a. This is because Paul attributed all to his meeting with the living Christ (cf. 22:6; 26:23; 1 Cor. 9:1; 15:8);
   b. This is the supreme argument for the Gospel, for it is here

that Christianity demonstrates what it does for human life (cf. 4:13, 14).

3. *If Christ rose from the dead, proof of it is —*
   a. Invincible in all — personal experience of Risen Christ has validity because of effect on men's souls; not only have we written record but if all Bible were taken away, we would still have human witness to Resurrection:

   Whoso has felt the Spirit of the Highest
   Cannot confound nor doubt Him nor deny;
   Yea with one voice, O world, tho' thou deniest
   Stand thou on that side, for on this am I."
   —F. W. H. Meyers

   b. Verifiiable by all — circumstances alone different, fact same — contact made between Christ and human soul.

The Risen Christ stands before us now, the Answer to all our desires, all our needs, all our problems, Surrender and see!

This hath He done and shall we not adore Him?
This shall He do and can we still despair?
Come let us quickly fling ourselves before Him,
Cast at His feet the burthen of our care.

Flash from our eyes the glow of our thanksgiving,
Glad and regretful, confident and calm,
Then thro' all life and what is after living
Thrill to the tireless music of a psalm.

Yea, thro' life, death, thro' sorrow and thro' sinning
He shall suffice me, for He hath sufficed;
Christ is the end, for Christ was the beginning,
Christ the beginning, for the end is Christ.

Study No. 108 — The Imitation of Paul

ACTS 22:14, 15

MANY are well acquainted with the book of devotions by Thomas à Kempis called "The Imitation of Christ," but by no means so familiar is Caroline Fry's volume, "Christ Our Example." This, however, is even more valuable because far more Scriptural. Both titles suggest an inspiring ideal; yet may we not have a feeling that they also pose a difficulty, if not an impossibility? This is because we realize that Christ is God as well as Man, and therefore impossible for us to follow fully.

When, however, we consider St. Paul we are on firmer ground. Paul was a man, and what grace did for him it can do for other men. He tells us in I Timothy 1:16 that his life is to be "a pattern to them which should hereafter believe," and in two other passages in his Epistles he speaks of himself as an "ensample" (cf. Phil. 3:17; II Thess. 3:9). Let us therefore follow Paul as, in recounting to the multitude his conversion, he quotes the inspired words of Ananias, the Damascus believer who was sent to reveal God's will for his life.

I. God's Purpose — "that thou shouldest know His will" (v. 14)

1. *An Important Lesson*
   a. God had great purpose in calling Saul; like David, Apostle became ideal for that great plan — "a man after my own heart, which shall fulfill all my will" (13:22);
   b. God's will was to be object of life and realization of everything good:
      (1) God's will is our salvation — "it is not the will of your Father . . . that one . . . should perish" (Matt. 18:14);
      (2) God's will is our sanctification — "this is the will

of God, even your sanctification" (I Thess.4:3);

(3) God's will is our glorification — "I will that they ...may behold My glory" (John 17:24);

N.B. So God has a purpose for each of us:

Teach me, my God and King,
In all things Thee to see,
And what I do in anything,
To do it as for Thee.

2. *A Startling Surprise*
   a. Saul was ignorant of all this — he, Pharisee, scholar, member of Sanhedrin, needed rebuke as well as reassurance;
   b. Name used of God, "the God of our fathers," familiar to Saul (cf. 5:30; 7:32; Exod. 3:13, 15), but he later admitted he had been following "traditions of my fathers" (Gal. 1:14);
   c. Now found it was necessary to lay aside all prejudice — "except ye become converted, and become as little children" (Matt. 18:3);
   N.B. So many fail here — cf. Naaman's "Behold, I thought . . ." (2 Kings 5:11).

II. God's Plan — "that thou shouldest . . . see that Just One, and shouldest hear the voice of His mouth" (v. 14)
God's purpose was to be realized by Saul's

1. *Personal Contact with Jesus* — "see that Just One"
   a. In answer to Saul's startled question, "Who art Thou, Lord?" (v. 8), Christ said, not "I am the Son of God," for Saul could have denied persecuting Him, but "I am Jesus of Nazareth," familiar, hated name;
   b. So now He is called "the Righteous One" (A.S.V.); cf. John 16:10, "of righteousness, because I go to My Father" — Jews had rejected Him but God had exalted Him (cf. 5:30, 31);
   c. Saul had needed proof of this, but now he realized Jesus was indeed with the Father;
   N.B. Today, sight of "the Righteous One" is secret of

Christian life: it saves; it sanctifies; it qualifies; it satisfies;

Illus.: When morning-glory closes at night, not most skillful surgeon with most delicate instrument can open flower without destroying it; but returning sun next day opens it easily, naturally, and safely.

2. *Personal Revelation from Jesus* — "hear the voice of His mouth"
   a. What a blow to Saul's pride, to hear God's voice from source so opposed and hated, the Nazarene!
   b. He was greatest of God's many channels of revelation, and Saul was finding more things in heaven and earth than he had dreamt of;
   N.B. Now, we have God's Word — containing truth, law, wisdom, salvation — everything needful; but do we often give Him opportunity to speak to us through it?

III. God's Project — "for thou shalt be His witness" (v. 15)
All was leading up to this work of witnessing:

1. *The Nature of the Work*
   a. It was not like that of judge — Saul had, as it were, tried that and disaster had resulted for his spiritual life;
   b. It was not like that of echo — vague, empty, lifeless;
   c. It was not like that of book — valuable, but books are not as powerful as "living epistles" (cf. 2 Cor. 3:2, 3);
   d. It was to be that of witness:
      (1) Of life to truth of Gospel;
      (2) Of experience to power of Gospel;
      N.B. No word in N.T. so frequent to express Christian service (cf. 1:8; 4:33; 23:11; 26:22; Luke 24:48; John 1:7; 1 Pet. 5:1; 1 John 1:2; Rev. 20:4).
2. *The Scope of the Work*
   a. "Unto all men" — wherever Saul was to go and whenever he had opportunity to speak;
   b. "Unto all men" — "whosoever" (John 3:16) — everyone to be regarded in light of recipient of testimony for Christ;

N.B. Dynamic of Christianity is life witnessing for God.

3. *The Power of the Work*
   a. To Paul himself — he is telling this years after, but facts of past are still —
      (1) So real that he can rest firmly upon them; and —
      (2) So valuable that he finds them inexhaustible;
   b. To others — an unanswerable argument:
      (1) Paul in Jerusalem might be expected to use eloquence to carry his audience; but —
      (2) No, simply gave personal testimony, the best Christian evidence;
      N.B. There is no greater foe to true Christianity than mere profession — e.g., standing up for Word of God and yet denying it by life; and yet converse is also true — living an exemplary life and yet failing to speak up for belief at any and every opportunity.

Conclusion

1. *God is the Same Today in the Salvation of the Sinner.*
   a. He has called him not merely to be saved, but to be saved to serve;
   b. If content with salvation only, individual may still be unsaved, and should —
      (1) Listen — "hear the voice of His mouth";
      (2) Look — "see the Righteous One";
      (3) Learn — "know His will."
2. *God is the Same Today in the Life of the believer.*
   a. Not merely for happiness, but for helpfulness;
   b. Personal contact with Christ will cause us to —
      (1) Love Him (cf. Eph. 6:24);
      (2) Live for Him (cf. Rom. 14:8);
      (3) Labor with Him (cf. 1 Cor. 15:10).

Do we remind people of Him? What sort of God are we showing to those who will not read the Bible? Can they see God in us? Are we true witnesses?

Lord, touch me now that I may live
For evermore in Thee;
And through the life that Thou wilt give
May ever fruitful be.

Lord, touch me now and make me clean,
So clean, so pure, so white,
As though I had not ever been
A sinner in Thy sight.

Lord, touch my heart that it may be
No longer like a stone;
That it may be henceforth for Thee
A temple and a throne.

Lord, touch my ears that I may hear
The music of Thy voice;
That I may hear the words of cheer
That make my heart rejoice.

Lord, touch my eyes that I may see
The radiance of Thy face;
And touch my tongue that I may be
A herald of Thy grace.

—Edmund Pillifant

Study No. 109 — Paul and His Enemies

ACTS 23:1-35

IT IS NOT always easy to see that "*all* things work together for good to them that love God" (Rom 8:28). We are ready to believe, of course, that *some* things work thus, but that this is true of everything, without exception, is much harder to accept, and still harder to understand. And yet so it is, and unless we believe in the providence of God, the power He has to foresee and provide and overrule, we shall find the Christian life so difficult as to be impossible.

A marked feature of the Book of Acts is the strong hostility shown towards St. Paul, almost from the first mention of him. It increases in force in these later chapters, as he who had been so violently opposed to Christianity now is himself the subject of intense animosity. But goodness invariably arouses wickedness, and the world's hostility was directed toward not only the Apostle, but also the Master whom he loved and the Gospel that he preached. It might well have been hard to see how this hostility, expressed by imprisonment and plot as recorded in this chapter, worked for Paul's good; and yet he himself was perfectly certain about it (cf. Phil. 1:12).

The events follow closely on those of the preceding chapter, and again there is remarkable fulness of detail. Paul was for the time being safe under Roman protection, but his position was not without risk. Rome stood for peace, and even a Roman citizen must not disturb it; so the authorities had to make sure that Paul was not working against the Empire. The trial before the Jewish Sanhedrin (cf. 4:5-23; Matt. 27:1; Mark 15:1; Luke 22:66) was thus intended as a test, and Paul was brought down from the fortress of Antonia and set before them (cf. 22:30).

In this chapter (v. 15) is the last mention of the Sanhedrin in the Book of Acts.

I. The Council (vs. 1-10)

1. *The Altercation* (vs. 1-5)
   a. Paul's attitude here is striking — stood before enemies with true earnestness and with no fear or shame;
   b. Paul's address was familiar one of "men and brethren" (cf. 1:16; 7:2; 13:26; 15:7, 13; 22:1), indicating friendliness and equality;
   c. Paul's assertion was courageous expression of noble heart, stating that as member of Jewish nation he had lived in presence of God with good conscience — Gr., "lived as a citizen with God" (cf. Phil. 1:27); in effect, charges were baseless;
   d. High priest's action was totally unwarranted and illegal — intended to signify blasphemy on part of prisoner (cf. John 18:22, 23); this was Ananias, avaricious and violent, soon to be summoned to Rome for just such acts but, through influence, acquitted;
   e. Paul's answer was bold declaration that God would deal with Ananias, hypocrite of fair appearance but of inward wickedness (cf. Matt. 23:27); this prophecy was fulfilled only a few years later, when he was first deposed and then assassinated;
   f. Bystanders' admonition against sacrilege elicited plea of ignorance on part of Paul as to identity of antagonist — perhaps because of defective vision or of long absence from Jerusalem; but some have thought that, feeling keenly injustice, Apostle broke forth in indignation, and that Scripture faithfully records failure in self-control. Others urge it was case of anger without sin (cf. Eph. 4:26), against deplorable conduct of one who ought to have been impartial;
   g. Paul's acknowledgment of error was prompt and so was his expression of loyalty to God's Word (cf. Exod. 22:28; Deut. 17:8-13);

N.B. Most natural view, however, whether Paul was at fault or not, is that he did not recognize high priest, or he would not have said he did not; and therefore his explanation shows his courtesy and generosity.

2. *The Appeal* (vs. 6-10)
   a. Something in procedure of council led Paul to realize there were two parties represented, Pharisees and Sadducees;
   b. Grasping situation, he used it with great effect, cutting across formalities with straightforward declaration that —
      (1) He was Pharisee;
      (2) He believed in resurrection; and —
      (3) This belief was real issue at stake (cf. 26:6-8);
   c. Apostle has been criticized for action, but surely without warrant:
      (1) Motive was high and words were true:
      (2) He was still Jew with right to declare himself;
      (3) He always maintained Judaism led to Christ as fulfillment of law, and he consequently sided with party of religion as against that of rationalism;
      (4) He, as Pharisee as well as Christian, was being opposed by Sadducees who were in power, and who did not believe in supernatural or in future life as Pharisees did (cf. v. 8); and —
      (5) His adherence to Gospel was actually due to appearance of resurrected Christ (cf. 1 Cor. 15:8);
      N.B. (1) Dr. Bartlett in *Century Bible*: "Paul with his keen eye for the logic of a subject was right in his cry; and he was justified in trying to make the Pharisees realize that they had no right to view his case in the same light as the Saddusaic party of the High Priest."
      (2) Neander, as quoted by Hackett, considers St. Paul justified in producing division in assembly, applying well-known dictum, "Divide and conquer" in good sense;
   d. Paul used division, not to further own ends, but for glory

of God, in attempt to witness for Master and win hearers to cause of Gospel;

e. But he was before tribunal intent upon deplorable injustice, so even this method of preventing illegal condemnation had little effect in personal advantage;

f. Protection afforded Paul by Pharisees did not avert danger (cf. vs. 12ff), for outcome was clamor and break-up of council (cf. v. 9), with Roman governor again obliged to protect prisoner by removal to castle (cf. v. 10);
N.B. Emphasis on resurrection in Acts is significant: cf. 1:22; 2:24-32; 3:15; 4:2, 33; 17:18, 32; 24:15, 21.

II. The Cheer (v. 11)

1. *The Appropriateness*
   a. After two days of great strain — physical, mental, emotional, spiritual — vision came as beautiful provision;
   b. Such supernatural intervention was notable feature of early Church (cf. 1:10, 11; 5:19, 20; 7:55, 56; 9:3-8; 10:3, 9-16; 12:7, 8; 16:9, 10; 18:9, 10; 22:17-21; 27:23-25).
2. *The Assurance*
   a. Vision implies Divine approval of Paul's course of action, for there was no rebuke but simply word of encouragement during "the night following" day of grave crisis;
   b. Use of present imperative, "Be of good cheer," suggests he had begun to despond, for adding to strain of recent events were —
      (1) Consciousness of Israel's unbelief (cf. Rom. 9:1-3) and failure of his effort to conciliate Jews;
      (2) Question of his reaching Rome now that he was prisoner;
      (3) Possibility that he had been wrong in persisting in journey to Jerusalem (cf. 19:13; 20:16; 21:13);
   c. But, whatever the past, now came experience of his Lord's presence, acknowledgment of his testimony at Jerusalem, and assurance of fulfilment of his long-cherished hope about Rome;

d. Thus, in unexpected, unimaginable ways, the Master was leading His servant on and, thus reassured, Paul could take fresh courage.

III. The Conspiracy (vs. 12-35)

1. *Formulated* (vs. 12-15)

   Next day new situation arose, as Jews showed fresh animosity against Paul by hatching plot to kill him. It was —

   a. Determined (v. 12) — extent to which opponents were prepared to go clearly shown by solemn oath which placed them under Divine ban of destruction in case they failed;
   b. Strong (v. 13) — conspirators numbered more than forty, enough to surround victim and, if necessary, overpower opposition of guards;
   c. Malign (v. 14) — willingness to tell chief priests and elders their plans shows how far evil is prepared to go in opposition to good;
   d. Clever (v. 15) — they knew even religious leaders would not check them in this murderous project; on the contrary, leaders were asked to expedite it, for opportunity to kill Paul would come as result of request for fresh examination of him.

But conspiracy was —

2. *Found out* (vs. 16-22)

   Defeat of plot combination, so often experienced, of supernatural grace and natural means:

   a. God was overruling in fulfilment of His promise (v. 11), causing both Jews and Romans to carry out His Divine purpose concerning Paul (cf. 9:15);
   b. God was working through unexpected but perfectly simple circumstances:
      (1) Paul's nephew, only relative of his specifically mentioned, may have come up to feast or, like uncle years before, as student (cf. 22:3);
      (2) He may have been one with Paul spiritually, since Romans 16 suggests some of kinsmen were Christians (cf. vs. 7, 11, 21);

(3) But in some way he heard of plot and succeeded in letting his uncle know;

(4) Information was soon passed on through centurion to chief captain, whose attitude to Paul's nephew (v. 19) seems to indicate desire to show kindness to fellow-citizen and make amends for error (cf. 22: 25-30).

And so, conspiracy was —

3. *Foiled* (vs. 23-25)

Information at once led to necessary precautions being taken to protect Paul, including —

a. Removal from Jerusalem and referring of his case to Felix the governor, at Caesarea;
b. Detail of large band of soldiers — 470 in all — regarded as necessary in case of concerted attempt to take Paul;
c. Choice of nighttime hour — 9 P.M. — added precaution to forestall attack;
d. Writing of letter testifying to Paul's innocence in Roman official view — even though it slightly misrepresented facts so as to hide writer's own error and place action in best possible light.

Thus, once more, Paul escaped out of hands of enemies and, although prisoner, was safe, and certain of Roman justice.

Conclusion

Maclaren calls this story "man's mining and God's counter-mining." In it we see —

1. A fresh illustration of old saying that "man is immortal till his work is done";
2. A strong suggestion that life is often altogether different from what is expected;
3. A blessed guarantee that a Christian never really loses, since God only changes the course of his career to bring about greater and nobler ends.

His purposes will ripen fast,
Unfolding every hour;
The bud may have a bitter taste,
But sweet will be the flower.

Blind unbelief is sure to err,
And scan His work in vain;
God is His own interpreter,
And He will make it plain.
—William Cowper

Study No. 110 — Paul and His Lord

ACTS 23:11

NO ONE can read St. Paul's life and Epistles without realizing that he was a man of great projects and plans, of large thoughts of the Gospel and how it was to be made known. It is the wideness of his grasp and the clearness of his view that mark him out as the first Christian statesman. One of his principles was the occupation of great centers, as though in a chain, all the way from Antioch to Rome. But the Apostle was also a man of real simplicity and humanity, with a craving for companionship and a susceptibility to joy and to sorrow. His was a nature of great intensity combined with keen sensibilities.

Hence, though Paul often undertook the important work of giving encouragement to others, he also realized the need of cheer for himself; and never more so than at the critical time recounted in this chapter. His heart was doubtless greatly excited, especially when he considered the apparent thwarting of cherished plans. Let us therefore ponder the verse in which we read of the Divine vision and promise vouchsafed to Paul, and see how God appeared at this juncture as his "very present help in trouble."

I. The Presence of the Lord

1. *It was opportune* — "the night following" — Christ comes in our darkest hour;
2. *It was inspiring* — "the Lord stood by him" — bringing comfort, cheer, and strength, and revealing honor to be conferred on His true servant.

II. The Word of the Lord

1. *It conveyed encouragement* — "be of good cheer" — which, after reaction from that trying day, must have been most welcome. Cf. Christ's message to John the Baptist (Matt. 11:4-6).
2. *It expressed appreciation* — "thou hast testified" — Paul's work had been noticed and approved (cf. Heb. 6:10).

III. The Work of the Lord

1. *It had been witnessing* — "thou hast testified of me" — manifestation of Christian life in action.
2. *It was to be more witnessing* — "so must thou bear witness" — after Jerusalem would come Rome, for reward of labor is still more labor (cf. Luke 19:17), and faithfulness in service leads to wider opportunities. So pressure was not to be relieved, but worker was to be supported and strengthened.

IV. The Purpose of the Lord

1. *It should be realized* — "must" — all events overruled in God's Providence.
2. *It could be realized* — if fear gave way to "cheer" — Paul would indeed be immortal till his work was done, through God's Power.

Conclusion

Thus we see that difficulties —

1. Are no necessary proof of unfaithfulness;
2. Are all known to Christ;
3. Are an incentive to fresh effort; and —
4. Are intended to lead to fuller trust in God (cf. Isa. 50:7).

Do we know all this by personal experience of our Master and Lord?

Study No. 111 — Paul Before Felix

ACTS 24:1-27

It is recorded that Alexander the Great, while visiting a poor philosopher named Diogenes, was asked who, if he were not Alexander, he would like to be. He replied: "If I were not Alexander, I would be Diogenes!" This may seem a strange answer, but perhaps amid all his glory the Grecian conqueror realized that the thoughts of a man like Diogenes would have a more enduring influence than his own achievements. His words are surely a testimony to the supremacy of intellect over rank, of thought over earthly glory. To be a thinker is sometimes greater than to occupy a throne, and today we value Shakespeare, Bacon, and Milton far more highly than the monarchs in whose reigns they lived. The same is true of the chief figures in this chapter, Paul and Felix. The avaricious Roman governor would have been entirely forgotten except for this story, while his prisoner has become one of the greatest influences in the history of the world.

Antonius Felix was a Greek by birth, a younger brother of Pallas, favorite of the Emperor Claudius. His position was due to his brother's influence, and his appointment as procurator of Judaea was made in A.D. 53. Tacitus speaks of Felix as "wielding the power of a king with the mind of a slave." We read of Paul before Felix and yet, in reality, it was Felix before Paul. The Apostle was the central, dominant figure, clad in the dignity of truth and surrounded by the greatness of righteousness. The fulness of the narrative at this point must indicate emphasis on the importance of the period in Paul's life, his slow though inevitable progress toward the imperial city (cf. 1:8).

I. The Prosecution (vs. 1-9)

1. *The Accusers* (v. 1)

a. The high priest, Ananias (cf. 23:2-5);
b. The elders (cf. 23:14);
c. The prosecutor — Tertullus, Roman lawyer:
   (1) Doubtless employed by Jews because of knowledge of Roman law and eloquence in Latin;
   (2) Word "orator" denotes skilled speaker — shown here by flattery of Felix, praising him on grounds Tertullus must have known were untrue and not endorsed by clients (cf. vs. 2, 3);
   (3) Felix had indeed suppressed brigands, dispersed pretender and followers (cf. 21:38), and quelled riots; but he had also caused much discontent and the assassination of a high priest.

2. *The Accusation* (vs. 2-6a)
   Tertullus made three charges against Paul:
   a. Sedition — against state (v. 5a)
      (1) Complete untruth of this obvious;
      (2) Ulterior motive of Jews equally clear;
   b. Sectarianism — against Jewish community (v. 5b)
      (1) Half-truth of this admitted later (v. 14), but unfair to charge Paul with being public nuisance and danger to society because leader of "sect" dubbed "Nazarenes";
      (2) Town of Nazareth used in Acts in connection with name of Jesus (cf. 2:22; 3:6; 4:10; 6:14; 22:8), and often contemptuously (e.g., 6:14), for place had obtained bad name (cf. John 1:46), though we do not know why;
      (3) Here, term "Nazarene" (cf. Matt. 2:23, referring probably to Isa. 11:1; Mark 1:24, etc.) applied first to Christ's followers, and as time went on word became more and more used by Jews to describe despised "heretics" (cf. v. 14);
   c. Sacrilege — against God (v. 6a)
      (1) Charge of sedition (untruth) and severance into new sect (half-truth) made to develop into sin of treating sacred place with irreverence;

(2) Surmise regarding Gentile (21:29) changed into definite accusation of attempted defilement of temple.

3. *The Testimony* (vs. 6b-9)

a. History (vs. 6b-8a)

Tertullus told —

(1) How Jews had laid hold of Paul to be judged according to own law, and —

(2) How Roman representative, Lysias, had forcibly taken him from them, and had commanded accusers to appear before Felix instead;

b. Suggestion (vs. 8b, 9),

(1) Taking v. 8b with v. 22, it would seem Tertullus wanted full information to be obtained from Lysias;

(2) None of these statements, though endorsed by Jews (v. 9), was supported by evidence.

II. The Defence (vs. 10-21)

With fine spirit Paul commenced answer (v. 10) by referring courteously and with truth to Felix as governor who, through unusual length of tenure, was experienced in Jewish affairs; then took up in turn each of three charges:

1. *Against Sedition* (vs. 11-13)

a. Only twelve days had elapsed since arrival in Jerusalem, so that in this short time truth could easily be ascertained, and idea of insurrection obviously incredible;

N.B. Five of these days had elapsed since Paul had left Jerusalem (cf. v. 1);

b. He had gone to worship, not to stir up trouble;

c. Thus, charge emphatically denied because truth of accusation could be so fearlessly challenged.

2. *Against Sectarianism* (vs. 14-16)

a. Paul repudiated any religious offense, while boldly confessing himself a Christian;

b. Described Christianity as "the Way" (cf. 9:2; 19:9, 23; 22:4), course of life involving progress;

c. Term "sect" (v. 5) means party separated from Judaism and believing "heresy" (v. 14), but Paul claimed still to be worshiping God of Jewish ancestors, accepting Scriptures, and looking forward with nation in general to resurrection (cf. Dan. 12:2);

d. In all this there was nothing "sectarian" or divisive; and in such faith and hope Paul did utmost to live conscientious life in sight of God and men, so could not be dangerous to religion or state.

3. *Against Sacrilege* (vs. 17-21)

a. Paul tells how he had come to Jerusalem after long absence, for purpose of bringing alms and offerings (cf. 11:29, 30; 1 Cor. 16:1; 2 Cor. 8:4; 9:1; Rom. 15:25-27);

b. Purification mentioned referred to action connected with Nazarite vow (21:26, 27); and Jews of Asia had caused trouble and misinterpretation of facts and yet had not courage to face Paul;

c. Jews present could not prove misconduct — only thing against him was that he had by utterance about resurrection caused division and uproar in council (vs. 20, 21; cf. 23:6, 7);

N.B. Note how Paul Seizes opportunities to witness for Christ and His truth.

III. The Climax (vs. 22-27)

From this point on in court drama, two chief participants hold stage; but, in spite of outward circumstances, Paul, the prisoner, is dominant figure, and Felix, the judge, falls into background through indecision of attitude:

1. *The Judge*

a. Postponement (v. 22)

(1) Interest vs. indifference — Felix had been too long in country to be deceived by such charges — new faith widely enough accepted that its profession was no crime — so he deferred decision, adjourned case, but did not acquit accused;

(2) Innocence vs. influence — Felix knew Paul to be guiltless, and yet, characteristically, wanted to please Jews;

(3) Integrity vs. inconvenience — Felix made absence of Lysias as chief witness excuse for deferring difficult decision;

b. Provision (v. 23)

(1) Imprisonment to continue — "commanded a centurion to keep Paul" — and yet Felix gave him privileges;

(2) Independence to be granted — "let him have liberty" and —

(3) Indulgence to be allowed — "forbid none of his acquaintance to minister or come unto him";

c. Procrastination (vs. 24-27)

(1) Interest renewed (v. 24) — "after certain days," Felix sent for Paul to tell of "faith in Christ"; as Jewess, wife Drusilla would also have some knowledge of it;

(2) Iniquity admitted (v. 25) — "Felix trembled" — had tempted Drusilla, daughter of Herod Agrippa I (12: 1), from her first husband, so guilty conscience aroused by Apostle's plain speaking about "righteousness, temperance, and judgment to come"; but it was alarm of fear rather than of genuine conviction of sin, for Felix again delayed decision until "convenient season" which, as we know, never came, for he does not seem to have given himself another opportunity to hear Gospel;

(3) Inducement attempted (vs. 26, 27) — "hoped also that money should have been given him of Paul" (v. 26), and yet "willing to shew the Jews a pleasure" (v. 27) — so first "sent for him the oftener" (v. 26) but finally "left Paul bound" (v. 27);

N.B. Perhaps allusions to collection (v. 17) and visits of friends (v. 23) led Felix to think Paul had resources with which to purchase release; but Paul practised righteousness as well as preaching it; so, as Bengel says, "unhappy Felix" (false to his name, which is Latin for "happy") "let go the treasure of the Gospel";

(4) Indifference resumed (v. 27) — "after two years," Felix summoned to Rome (to answer cruelty charges), and his successor appointed — thus disappearing forever, doubtless more hardened than before, and leaving Paul in prison.

2. *The Prisoner*

Paul's outstanding character is seen not only in his public defense (vs. 10-21), but also in the less detailed private talk to Felix and Drusilla (vs. 24, 25). In this can be seen the same faithfulness, frankness, and fearlessness that characterizes his longer statement. Its content was fourfold:

a. Paul preached "righteousness" — need of all men to be right with God — doubtless included proof of man's failure through sin, and God's offer of righteousness in Christ (cf. Rom. 3:19-26);
b. Paul preached "temperance" — self-control, which would come home with great force to both hearers in view of their shameful story (cf. Gal. 5:19-24);
c. Paul preached "judgment to come" — dread penalty of sin persisted in; but also —
d. Paul preached "the faith in Christ" (v. 24) — Divinely provided remedy for sin and provision for both righteousness and self-control.

Thus, the Apostle would show how righteousness could be received, self-control be made possible, and judgment be rendered in both justice and mercy.

Conclusion

Here called to face accusations, the Apostle shows no fear of the false charge of wrong-doing — only the fear of wrong-doing itself. His defense before Felix reveals —

1. *The Character of St. Paul*
   a. His courtesy (v. 10);
   b. His cheerfulness (v. 10);
   c. His candor (vs. 11-13);

   d. His conviction (v. 14);
   e. His confidence (v. 15);
   f. His conscientiousness (v. 16);
   g. His courage (vs. 17-21, 25).

2. *The Circumstances of St. Paul*
   a. His subtle temptation — activity curtailed;
   b. His sad trial — converts and churches robbed of guidance;
   c. His severe test — pressure on character;
   d. His splendid testimony — witness before rulers, both in Jerusalem and in Caesarea;
   e. His simple trust — faith resting on God only.

   The tedious two-year imprisonment gave Paul not only his first real rest in twenty years, but also an opportunity to think more deeply and obtain a clearer view of Christ and his Gospel. Thus his character was tested by circumstances, and he was permitted to develop a profounder faith and a mellower experience. Do we thus utilize the adverse circumstances that sometimes follow our strongest witness for Christ?

Study No. 112 — Christian Manliness

ACTS 24:14-16

"SO WORSHIP I THE GOD OF MY FATHERS," declared St. Paul, never more manly or courageous than in his eloquent defense before Felix; and he went on to speak of having "hope toward God," and "a conscience void of offense toward God, and" he added, "toward men." Manliness and Godliness — are the two compatible today? It is sometimes thought not, but that Christianity fosters only the development of what are sometimes considered the less rugged virtues, the more refined graces. These verses would seem to contradict such a suggestion, for they contain —

I. The Essence of Christian Manliness

Word "worship" indicates service, homage; but worshipper is surely never more of a man than when he harks back to his "fathers," claiming their God as his. Paul develops thought of worship in three ways:

1. *By Believing* (v. 14) — "believing all things which are written in the law and in the prophets" — the Scriptures; no true worship of God except by one who believes His Word.
2. *By Hoping* (v. 15) — "have hope toward God, . . . that there shall be a resurrection of the dead" — the God who is "not the God of the dead, but of the living" (Matt. 22:32).
3. *By Obeying* (v. 16) — "I exercise myself, to have always a conscience void of offense" — never trifling with sin, but sensitive to claims of God and good of fellow-man.

II. The Expression of Christian Manliness

In this faith, hope, and obedience, Paul was doing his utmost to live a genuine Christian life, and his statement about it was —

1. *Clear* — "confess" — like his Master, he "witnessed a good confession" (1 Tim. 6:13);
2. *Personal* — "I" — cf. "confession" of Christ — "I," "my" (John 18:36, 37);
3. *Bold* — "unto thee" — cf. positions of Felix and Paul, Pilate and Christ.

Conclusion

1. *The Source of Christian Manliness is God;*
2. *Its Standard is the Bible;*
3. *Its Substance is character;*
4. *Its Strength is witness;*
5. *Its Secret is faith.*

Let us, like Abraham of old, say a forthright Amen to God: "He believed in the Lord, and He counted it to him for righteousness" (Gen. 15:6).

Study No. 113 — Three Great Principles of Paul's Life

ACTS 24:14-16

The study of literature that affords a self-revelation of the author is of special interest to most readers. In particular, the unconscious revelation of his character is apt to be profitable to others. St. Paul scarcely ever wrote or spoke without revealing himself; his great, intense personality had to overflow his words, as here. Falsely charged with three crimes — sedition, heresy, and sacrilege — he shows the truth about the accusations, and in so doing he reveals the three great principles that summed up his life. These are for us also:

I. **Faith** (v. 14)

1. *Its Object* — Deity — "God"
2. *Its Attitude* — dependence — "believing"
3. *Its Warrant* — Scripture — "the law and . . . the

prophets":

a. Nature of Paul's view of O.T. — it was credible;

b. Extent of Paul's view of O.T. — it was "all" true;

N.B. Cf. his treatment in Rom. 10:8 — faith ever nourished by Scripture because only through His Word can we know God and receive His Son.

II. Hope (v. 15)

1. *Its Object* — again, Deity — God"
2. *Its Attitude* — expectancy — "toward"
3. *Its Substance* — resurrection — "of the dead, both of the just and unjust":

a. "Of the just" — consummation of God's purpose in Christ;

b. "Of the . . . unjust" — vindication of God's righteousness against sin.

III. Conscientiousness (v. 16)

1. *Its Object* — again, Deity, but also fellow men — "toward God, and toward men";
2. *Its Secret* — referring back to faith and hope — "herein";

N.B. Only as heart is right with God can conscience be truly sensitive.

3. *Its Expression* — habitual, systematic — "I exercise myself"

a. "To have always a conscience void of offence" — Gr., to be free from stumbling:

(1) "Toward God" — keeping himself upright;

(2) "Toward men" — not causing anyone else to be tripped up (cf. 1 Cor. 10:32; Phil. 1:10);

b. Paul, living in Divine presence, moment by moment, was consciously right towards God and those around him.

Conclusion

We have seen the recurrence of the Name of God in this passage; but, as a parallel, there is also the use of the personal pronoun, "I":

1. *"I confess"* (v. 14) — the Apostle's courage;
2. *"I worship"* (v. 14) — the Apostle's reverence;

3. "*(I) have hope*" (v. 15) — the Apostle's expectation;
4. "*I exercise*" (v. 16) — the Apostle's example.

Thus did Paul "serve . . . with pure conscience" (2 Tim. 1:3), and so may we, in trust and obedience.

Study No. 114 — Paul, A Man of Conscience

ACTS 24:16

Paul was a man of conscience. How may we define conscience? It is the "knowing" part of us, that which "knows" what is right and what is wrong. The English word comes from *con,* "with," and *science,* "knowledge," and refers to that faculty which "knows with" God's law within us, agreeing with it, assenting to it. Let us look first at conscience in general and then at Paul's conscience in particular:

I. Conscience

1. *The Voices of Conscience*
   These are three:
   a. Warning against evil (Rom. 2:15);
   b. Approval of well-doing (2 Cor. 1:12);
   c. Condemnation of wrong-doing (John 8:9).
2. *The Needs of Conscience*
   These are two:
   a. Illumination from God's Word, lest it be not properly instructed and informed; for by itself conscience may be —
      (1) Evil (Heb. 10:22);
      (2) Defiled (Tit. 1:15);
      (3) Seared (1 Tim. 4:2);
      (4) Weak (1 Cor. 8:7).
   b. Purification by Christ's blood, in order to be made —
      (1) Pure (1 Tim. 3:9; Heb. 9:14);
      (2) Good (1 Pet. 3:16);
      (3) Void of offence (v. 16).

II. Paul's Conscience

1. *It was good* (cf. 23:1; Heb. 13:18);
2. *It was pure* (cf. 2 Tim. 1:3);
3. *It was void of offence* (v. 16; cf. 1 Cor. 10:32, 33; Phil. 1:10) — neither stumbling, nor causing another to stumble (Gr.) — splendid thing to be able to say, and true because —
   a. Paul's life was "before God" — in Divine presence, conscience tested, trained, and taught;
   b. Paul's walk was "before man" — aim was to do full duty to fellows;
   c. Paul's attitude was continual — "always" — not intermittent, but permanent — Christianity to be real must be habitual;
   d. Paul's effort was earnest — "exercise" — like athlete, he took pains, knowing such a life was possible only through devoted endeavor;
   e. Paul's foundation was Christ and His Gospel — "herein" — faith and hope of verses 14 and 15 part of his very being.

Conclusion

1. *This was the Apostle*: great because good, and good because of God's grace (cf. 1 Cor. 15:10);
2. *This can be any Christian*: when life is full of grace (cf. 2 Cor 1:12), it will always be full of goodness (cf. 11:24).

Well will it be for us if we follow Paul as he followed Christ (cf. 1 Cor. 11:1).

Study No. 115 —

Life and Death: A Prisoner's Theme

ACTS 24:25-27

IN THE GREAT REALM of human character, a king is one who sways the destinies of men, and not necessarily one who occupies a throne, however mighty. No pagan monarch can compare with Socrates. The Roman governor Pilate is forgotten, except for that sentence in the Apostles' Creed which stamps him forever as the judge under whom was committed the foulest miscarriage of justice in history. But the Man who, from the human standpoint, was the victim on that awful day, Christ Jesus, shines forth in all the transcendence of His Divine character.

A parallel case is found here, with two other figures strikingly contrasted — another Roman governor, Felix, and another prisoner, Paul. The former has perished in oblivion, save for the stigma of the record, while the latter is, next to Jesus Christ, the greatest influence in the world. This is because Paul was a man of character, and character is power. All life, in every part, is lived according to rule, law, principle — good or bad, high or low. The story of Paul and Felix enables us to discern the real meaning of life lived according to great principles — what true life is and what it is not; and when physical life may become spiritual death.

I. The Principles of Life Laid Down by Paul (v. 25)

"He reasoned" — uttered not mere denunciation, but stern statements based on solid ground of fact and grouped under three headings:

1. *Righteousness — Duty to Fellow-man*

This was first great theme of Paul's discourse and must

have surprised Felix who, with so-called wife Drusilla, had sent for him out of curiosity — heard more than they bargained for from one who, though dependent on governor for liberty, did not hesitate to speak with superb moral courage of justice, of right, to one whose whole life had been one of unrighteousness — rapacity, corruption, murder.

a. The meaning of righteousness:
   (1) It means "right-ness" of outward conduct; but this can be shown only if, also —
   (2) It means "right-ness" of inward principle; for as source so stream;
      (a) But man's inward principles are all unsound and defiled through sin;
      (b) Thus sin is cause of all unrighteousness; cf. picture of man in Gen. 6:5 — "every imagination of the thoughts of his heart was only evil continually" — still as true today as ever.

b. The power of righteousness:
   (1) Greater even than mercy — which is great healer of mankind, administered for ages, but world well-nigh as dark as ever; mightier agent needed in old and young, between man and man, capital and labor, peer and peasant, in society, politics, religion; while mercy lessens existing evil, righteousness prevents its existence; while mercy feeds and clothes poor, righteousness would prevent extremities of need;
   (2) Greater even than charity — which binds up wounds of mankind, but righteousness would prevent their infliction; covers multitude of sins, but righteousness would prevent their commission; rescues from degradation, but righteousness would prevent such a fall.

c. The need of righteousness:
   (1) Not only in lives of vicious, but also in lives of respectable:
      (a) He who has sense of true living and would carry it out must let justice reign in heart, pay

homage to it almost amounting to a passion, must be ready to be, do, suffer for and, if need be, die for it;

(b) He who is thus upright in character is worth more than one who, tender-hearted and charitable, is not careful of obligation to moral conduct; but —

(c) He who blends two, in whom mercy and truth meet together, is finest character of all;

(2) Not only in world in general, but also in life of individual:

(a) In order that righteousness be emphasized universally, beginning must be made singly; and —

(b) In order that righteousness reign supreme on earth, it must first rule individual, owning whole nature of man — mind, heart, will, conscience. Cf. Jerusalem repaired, "every one over against his own house" (Neh. 3:28, 39).

d. The source of righteousness:

(1) Did Paul tell how it could be obtained? Surely he did, for Felix had summoned him to speak "concerning the faith in Christ" (v. 24), that is, Christ's Gospel, of which faith is leading feature and which has cleansing power (cf. Heb. 10:22);

(2) What is this cleansing of inward principle that brings righteousness of outward life? It is not like lopping off diseased branches from corrupt tree, nor applying plaster to cure diseased body, when correct treatment would be attempt to discover and extirpate infection from whole;

(3) What should be thought, then, of one who, discovering unrighteousness in his life, should apply plaster of good works to cure it? Rather, he should seek microbes of indwelling sin and apply Gospel of Christ's atoning blood and Holy Spirit.

Thus, and thus only, can we find, as did Paul, pardon, life, righteousness. Paul's second principle was —

2. *Temperance — Duty to Self*

This also must have surprised Felix and Drusilla:

a. The meaning of temperance:

(1) Word has not merely modern significance — idea of moderation in use of drink, or abstinence from it, partial though important aspect of usage;

(2) Paul referred to self-control of whole man, restraint of every passion, inclination, or desire that might injure life.

b. The power of temperance:

(1) Paul himself exemplified fearlessness and strength of temperate man — nothing finer than moral courage — "feared man so little because he feared God so much";

(2) Was on delicate ground, for modern writer has said Felix "had been in the vilest of positions, in the vilest of all ages, in the vilest of all cities" — had also been courtier in worst of courts and soldier among worst in troops;

(3) Above all, woman listening whom Felix had enticed from husband and home.

c. The need of temperance:

(1) Same principle needed for life of today regarding all forms of desire, mental and physical;

(2) If nature — mind, heart, body — not kept rigidly under control, but gets upper hand, it will lead to destruction:

Illus.: (a) Man's nature compared to high-spirited horse ridden by experienced owner — rider would neither starve animal till all spirit had left it, nor pamper it by letting it have its head; rather would he keep it under firm control, that it might recognize its master, feel his power, and so do his will;

(b) If plant allowed to throw off side shoots, it will never grow far upwards, but if these are clipped it will grow straight and tall; and let our nature run sideways into evil and there can never be uprightness; but keep it checked, after we have been brought into right relationship with Christ, and it will grow pure, high, strong.

d. The source of temperance:
  (1) How may we keep our natures under control? Repeated failure brings discouragement and sense of powerlessness, because Satan has chained us in bondage of sin and is "strong man armed" who keeps "palace" (Luke 11:21);
  (2) Here, again, it is "the faith in Christ" (v. 24), the Gospel, that tells of deliverance; as we trust in Him who is so much stronger than Satan as to be able to enter his house and spoil his goods (cf. Matt. 12:29), we shall be enabled by God's grace to keep our bodies under, and to grow in holiness and in purity, more and more.

The third of these great principles of life is —

3. *Judgment to come — Duty to God*
  a. The meaning of judgment:
    (1) This is clear indication we shall be judged hereafter according to our life here and now;
    (2) On this account we are to frame our lives in light of judgment day.
  b. The power of judgment:
    (1) This is foundation principle of life, that man must take God into consideration and live under influence of world to come;
    (2) Great test will be when secrets of all hearts shall be revealed.
  c. The need of judgment:
    (1) This is essential culmination of life — some people may pass muster with others, or may remain enigmas — e.g., interested in religion, respectable, show some taste for Divine things;
    (2) Yet there may be shrewd suspicions of something wrong at foundation, and Great Day will reveal true character, if not revealed before;

Illus.: Engineers, to clear New York harbor of dangerous rock in channel known as Hell Gate, for years tunneled it and honeycombed it with dynamite. To all appearances it was still same, but when test came and fuse set off rock was at once shivered to atoms; so those regarded as outwardly upright are often being sapped by sin; but day of testing will show they are moral and spiritual wrecks;

(3) Slowly and surely each one of us is writing his character in imperishable letters in now invisible ink of daily habits and sins;

(4) But day is coming when fire of God's perfect holiness will make it all visible and show each one to himself and others as he really is.

d. The instrument of judgment:

(1) This is grave warning that Paul had uttered at Athens, namely, that God had "appointed a day in the which He will judge the world in righteousness by that Man" (17:31), Jesus Christ;

(2) But we can fearlessly face that ordeal before judgment seat of Christ by taking Him now as our Saviour instead of meeting Him as our Judge at the Great White Throne;

(3) Trusting in Him, following Him, abiding in Him, we may have confidence, even boldness, "at that day" (2 Tim. 4:8).

Such are the principles of life laid down by Paul, and the only way to make them vital in daily life is by heeding what he called "the faith in Christ," through whom —

1. We obtain righteousness and live accordingly;
2. We exercise self-control and manifest it; and —
3. We fearlessly face judgment and therefore look forward confidently to the future.

II. The Example of Life Set by Felix (vs. 25-27)

There are few more striking situations on record than this, in which are contrasted a haughty governor and a despised prisoner. Fearlessly and forcefully had this prisoner "reasoned of righteousness, temperance, and judgment to come," and not in vain. What was the effect of such a serious discourse?

1. *Conviction* — "Felix trembled" (v. 25)
   This is first true work of Gospel:
   a. The power of Divine truth:
      Paul's words to Felix like arrows striking home, seeking out petty excuses hitherto used as sop to conscience, and laying bare absurd sophistries that had supported irrational attitudes to past, present, and future:
      (1) As Paul reasoned of righteousness, Felix glanced back over past stained with rapacity and cruelty;
      (2) As Paul reasoned of temperance, Felix saw beside him one reminder of his wrong desires and passions;
      (3) As Paul reasoned of judgment to come, Felix acknowledged existence of great Being to whom he would be accountable.
   b. The standard of Divine truth
      Gospel, not man himself, is true standard of life and righteousness:
      (1) Man likes to frame own principles of life and set own standard, often excusing actions under pretty names — slips, failings, weaknesses, indiscretions, etc.; but when God's principles and standards are brought to bear on them they stand out in all their hideousness as sins;
      (2) Man's own conscience alone is not wholly reliable guide, since he may bribe, deceive, throttle it; so —
      (3) Man needs standard outside of and different from own, in order to show him himself in true colors;
      Illus.: Merchant is not allowed to use own standard for weights and measures, but must have them tested periodically by government standard.
   c. The application of Divine truth
      (1) Man may admit Gospel as true standard and agree in general condemnation, and yet shirk particulaı application, hiding himself in crowd; but it has been well said, "There are no crowds in God's eyes" —

no, He deals in single souls;

(2) Man may never have realized guilt of own sin because he has never accepted truth of Gospel; but —

(3) To each who does God comes, laying finger on plague-spots; lowering measure into chamber of heart till it reveals depths of iniquity there; probing into wounds of spirit and showing need of healing; flashing His light into soul, revealing filth of unregenerate human nature.

Yes, God's arrow of conviction, shot with unerring precision by the power of His Holy Spirit, struck the sinful soul of Felix with all the mighty force of truth, and said, "Thou art the man!" No wonder "Felix trembled"! We watch him further. The shot has told. What will he do? On which side will he fall? We find —

2. *Procrastination* — "a convenient season" (v. 25)

Felix does not like this plain speaking — he is uncomfortable; In fact, he cannot bear sensation of terror that creeps stealthily over him, so cuts short interview. Well may God's Word warn that "the heart is deceitful above all things, and desperately wicked" (Jer. 17:9):

a. The deceitfulness of procrastination:

(1) Here was man steeped in vice and crime, terror-stricken, and yet unprepared to break off shackles of sin and do righteously;

(2) Here was man thoroughly aroused to realization of canker eating into the vitals of soul, yet deadened sense of pain as by opiate;

N.B. How different from jailor at Philippi who, also "trembling" (16:29) and equally aroused, did not rest till he had found cause of unrest and cured it!

(3) But here was man who did not intend to banish good altogether, who, self-deceived, intended at some future time to resume subject; doing, however, worse possible thing for himself, since canker still gnawing, though he was not so conscious of it.

b. The danger of procrastination:

(1) There are many like Felix, for postponement of consideration of eternal truths is Satan's own masterpiece to lure men to himself;
N.B. While atheism has slain its hundreds, and vice its thousands, procrastination has slain its hundreds of thousands; and just as men wishing to sleep will draw heavy curtains over windows to prevent light from waking them, so do they shut out light of conviction by curtain of procrastination;

(2) There are many who continually avoid any reference to right and wrong of own conduct because deep down there is uneasy feeling about answer.

Woe to that man who stifles his convictions! Such avoidance of eternal issues will assuredly lead to same end as in case of Felix —

3. *Indifference* — "but . . . left Paul bound" (v. 27)
   a. The hardness of indifference:
      (1) Opportunity — time after time during two years Felix had chance to hear and obey Gospel, but we know that was not main reason for his interview with Paul; on contrary, conviction had passed, and hardness had set in, for Felix actually thought Paul would bribe him for release (cf. v. 26);
      (2) Obscurity — after leaving Judaea Felix spent remainder of life in retirement and disgrace, to say nothing of future when he had to stand before his God; as any man who sets aside claims of known truth, Felix suffered for it; for, having heard truth, he knew it to be truth, but refused to act on it.
   b. The habit of indifference:
      (1) This habit is terribly powerful force — binds those who hear Gospel and yet set it and convictions of its truth aside — even though not entirely banished, merely deferred from youth to manhood, from manhood to old age;
      (2) Habitual indifference makes response harder and harder, for impressions received but not acted upon

are lost — when next they come they are fainter, and finally felt scarcely at all;

(3) Habit makes us familiar with evil and lessens our sense of its power — with Gospel and lessens sense of its urgency; thus we become both sin-hardened and Gospel-hardened;

Illus.: Upon entering badly ventilated room, one is at first nearly suffocated; let him stay there half an hour and he will be breathing more freely;

(4) Thus, law of habit causes means of salvation to lose their power over us, and outward difficulties multiply, until it is almost, if not quite, impossible to arouse soul; and every year makes it harder and harder to turn, because nature is gradually becoming deadened;

Illus.: Piece of sponge containing small particles of flint, if left to itself, will attract all surrounding particles of flint until softness is gone and whole mass is hard; thus do men by evil already in them attract fresh evil by continuing in sin, until they become rocks of adamant self-will and end in total disaster.

So the longer we yield to sin and put off claims of Christ, the more accustomed to sin we become and therefore the more impervious to appeal of Gospel. Character and consequence are inseparably linked together in God's order.

Conclusion

Such is life as seen by two men, Paul and Felix. Here are the two alternatives and only two— death and life:

1. *Spiritual Death*

A disordered nature, a wayward will, a wild imagination, perverted desires, vicious propensities, worldly lusts, low ambitions; sin darkening life, debasing tastes, weakening powers, soiling purity, and forever drawing veil between soul and God; no hope, no peace, increase of depravity, growth in hardness, and gathering clouds of judgment.

2. *Spiritual Life*

A nature renewed by power of Divine grace, penitent over

sin, accepted into sonship, its faculties working heavenward, its will subdued into happy obedience; heart loving what is lovely, looking up with fervent desire to Him who is foundation of life; and spirit enjoying favor, peace, joy in the Holy Ghost, comforts of pardoned sin, fellowship of redeemed, and anticipation of everlasting life.

Yes, these are the alternatives; as Moses said in Deut. 30:19, "I call heaven and earth to record this day against you, that I have set before you life and death, blessing and cursing; therefore choose life"!

Let others boast of heaps of gold—
Christ for me!
His riches never can be told—
Christ for me!
Your gold will waste and wear away,
Your honors perish in a day,
This portion never can decay—
Christ for me!

Study No. 116 — Paul's Appeal to Caesar

ACTS 25:1-27

AN ELDERLY Christian woman, very poor but noted for her constant activity, was laid aside by illness, and her neighbors asked her how she could bear it. She answered, "When I was well, the Lord said, 'Betty, go here,' and 'Betty, go there,' but now He says, 'Betty, lie still and cough'!" She had learned the lesson of life in relation to the will of God; and something like this must have been Paul's experience as he was cut off (and that unjustly) from his wonted activities for his Master. The two years of captivity at Caesarea, moreover, were followed by another attempt on the part of Paul's enemies to bring about his end.

I. The Conspiracy (vs. 1-9)

As in our Lord's case, there is here a coalition between Roman governor and Jewish authorities (cf. Mark 10:33):

1. *Fresh Effort* (vs. 1-5)
   - a. The Roman
     - (1) New governor, Porcius Festus (cf. 24:27), in office only short time — died after two or three years — said to have been of comparatively good character. but apparently typical Roman official, indifferent to religious ideas and disagreements of Jews;
     - (2) His "province" (v. 1) that of Syria, of which Judaea was part, and Caesarea political capital (cf. 8:40; 12:19; 23:23, 33) — on coast, 30 miles north of Joppa — rebuilt and enlarged by Herod the Great, who called it Caesarea Augusta in honor of Emperor; city became residence of procurator when Judaea passed directly under Roman rule;
     - (3) His policy (cf. v. 9), identical with that of prede-

cessors Pilate (cf. Mark 15:15) and Felix (cf. 24:27), being to get quickly on good terms with Jews, Festus lost no time ("after three days," v. 1) in going from Roman political center to Jewish national and religious one, Jerusalem.

b. The Jews
   (1) "Chief of the Jews" (v. 2) probably including chief priests (cf. 4:23) led by Ananias, "the high priest" (cf. 23:2), and Sadducean leaders as distinct from elders or Sanhedrin as a body (cf. Luke 19:47), soon approached new governor and kept on beseeching him (v. 3, Gr.) to grant them favor (not justice) of letting Paul come to Jerusalem, hoping thereby to kill him en route (cf. 23:12-22);
   (2) Fact that after two years they were still ready to murder Paul shows intensity of animosity to him and his message, and fanatical desire to strike deadly blow at new religion through its prominent leader; so far will human heart go in opposition to light and truth;
   (3) Would have been natural for new governor to grant favor for conciliation, which doubtless gave Paul's foes renewed hope; but Festus had sufficient sense of justice to refuse entreaties (cf. v. 16), though probably did not realize Paul's importance, and so he directed accusers to accompany him back to Caesarea.

2. *Further Examination* (vs. 6-12)
   a. The Arraignment (vs. 6-9)
      (1) Festus having returned to seat of government, and taken place as supreme judge, apparently accusers of Paul not only repeated old charges (cf. 24:5, 6), but added specific accusation of offenses against Caesar (cf. v. 8), significant point, if proved, against Roman citizen; but again (cf. 24:13) there was no evidence — nothing but bare statements;
      (2) So Paul once more protested innocence of alleged

crimes against Jewish law, temple, or state; and Festus saw at once that prisoner was guilty of no offenses against laws of empire, but that question was solely one of religion (cf. vs. 18, 19);

(3) Therefore, notwithstanding former refusal, proposed to refer matter to Sanhedrin in Jerusalem, with himself present because of Paul's Roman citizenship — weak, unjust, and partial suggestion for unworthy reason.

b. The Appeal (vs. 10, 11)

(1) Paul would not agree to this and, apparently realizing he was at turning-point of whole ministry, took momentous step — knew Festus would not release him, and going to Jerusalem would mean death, so made appeal to Caesar;

(2) Procurator was Emperor's representative (v. 10), and by law and citizenship his "judgment seat" was only proper place for trial; and since trouble due to prejudice and not illegality (cf. vs. 18, 19), Festus knowingly erred in not releasing Paul; and therefore Paul exercised right of every Roman to remove case from lower courts to highest, that of Emperor himself in Rome;

(3) Paul had been imprisoned in Caesarea two years, and at length saw way open for journey to Rome and realization, however different from expectation, of long-cherished hopes (cf. Rom. 1:10-15; 15:22-33); yet with fine spirit expressed readiness to die if proved guilty, but only by means of justice, not favor (v. 11).

c. The Assent (v. 12)

(1) Festus, doubtless puzzled by change in course of events, consulted with officials associated with him, and allowed Paul's appeal;

(2) Could do nothing else, without personal risk, because it was known words "I appeal" were "omnipotent in the Roman Empire"; and probably realized by this

time Paul was important person (cf. v. 24);

(3) Appeal seems to be evidence of remarkable progress of Christianity in empire; while formal permission proved to be God's way of leading Paul to witness in Rome (cf. 23:11).

II. The Consultation (vs. 13-27)

One more appearance — not trial — was to be Paul's lot, for Festus was desirous of advice on his case:

1. *The Ruler* (v. 13)
   a. Festus soon had state visit from King Agrippa II, great-grandson of Herod the Great (cf. Matt. 2), grandson of Herod Antipas (cf. Matt. 14:1-12; Luke 23:7-12), and son of Herod Agrippa (cf. chap. 12); his kingdom in north-east, with Caesarea Philippi (cf. Matt. 16:13) its capital; last of Herod's line to exercise sovereignty, and after fall of Jerusalem in A.D. 70 retired to Rome and died there about year 100.
   b. Visit doubtless one of polite greeting to new governor, and Agrippa brought with him half-sister Bernice — woman of notoriously bad character and sister of Drusilla (cf. 24:24) — who resided with him.
   c. Since Agrippa knew Palestine intimately and also had important Roman connections, it was natural for Festus to mention Paul to him and expect valuable advice; at that time Agrippa was in charge of temple and had power of appointing high priest.
2. *The Recapitulation* (vs. 14-22)
   a. Information given by Festus mainly repetition of events, though slightly modified in his own favor (v. 16); told how he had been wondering what wrong Paul could have done (v. 18), but found trouble merely religious and therefore of indifference to himself (v. 19);
   b. Again it is obvious that fundamental religious issue was resurrection (v. 19), and that one of governor's problems was solved by Paul's appeal, leaving another in its place — what reason to give for sending Paul to Rome. (cf. vs. 26, 27);

c. Agrippa interposed here, indicating he had for some time been desiring to hear Paul (v. 22, Gr.) — evidently knew of Apostle and Jewish hatred of him (cf. Luke 23:8) — and now opportunity had come.

3. *The Review* (vs. 23-27)
   a. Therefore with great display Agrippa and Bernice came next day into auditorium connected with palace, and prisoner appeared before them;
   b. Festus then repeated publicly substance of private statement, adding significant information that Jewish crowd had backed leaders in complaint against Paul (v. 24);
   c. Difficulty of Festus now in fact that it was usual to send to Rome explanation of charges against prisoner, and in this case there was nothing to send; hence investigation before Agrippa might prove of service (vs. 26, 27).

Conclusion

If, as Tennyson says, "solitude is the mother-country of the strong," we may be sure that Paul's captivity did not weaken his moral and spiritual fibre. The secret of this splendid Christian manhood is threefold:

1. *Fellowship with the Master*
   Like Christ before him (cf. Matt. 10:25; John 15:20, 21), treading pathway of suffering and wrong — not disheartened or sullen, but suffering long and being kind with it (cf. 1 Cor. 13:4); meanwhile, enforced quiet would enable Paul to ponder deeper truths about Christ's Gospel and produce maturer teaching (cf. remarkable differences between earlier Epistles and those written after this time — Ephesians, Colossians, and Philippians, containing some of his profoundest thoughts).
2. *Faithfulness to the Will of God*
   Paul had learned to wait as well as work — knew what "patience" was as well as "faith" (Heb. 6:12); many can trust who cannot wait, but Paul could do both (cf. Psa. 25:3, 5, 21; 37:7; Isa. 40:31); and this was because he had surrendered wholly to the will of God (cf. Eph. 1:5, 9, 11; 5:17; Col. 1:9; 1 John 2:17).

3. *Faith in God*

Deepest secret of all was Paul's trust and confidence in his God and in God's wisdom, love, and power; so, whether working or waiting, serving or suffering, all was well (cf. 2 Tim. 1:12).

Just where you stand in the conflict
There is your place!
Just where you think you are useless
Hide not your face;
God placed you there for a purpose
Whate'er it be;
Think He has chosen you for it,
Work loyally!

Gird on your armor, be faithful
At toil or rest,
Whiche'er it be, never doubting
God's way is best;
Out in the light or the darkness
Stand firm and true;
This is the work which your Master
Gives you to do.

Study No. 117 — Paul Before Agrippa

ACTS 26:1-32

A notable characteristic of our Lord's ministry is His wonderful way of turning to account the ordinary circumstances of His life for the furtherance of His kingdom, availing Himself of every opportunity to preach the Gospel of His grace. A request for a draught of water led up to the memorable words about the "well of living water springing up unto everlasting life" (John 4:14); and the feeding of five thousand hungry people led up to the still more memorable words about the "true bread from heaven" (John 6:32). We may discover instance after instance of how the conditions of every-day life that formed the foreground of the picture were deftly merged into a larger landscape of spiritual truth.

St. Paul had evidently drunk deeply of his Master's spirit, for he assuredly used every opportunity of proclaiming the Gospel of Christ. His own words to Timothy, "Be instant in season out of season" (2 Tim. 4:2), were eminently true of himself. Thus, each of the five defenses of Paul (chaps. 21-26) not only was appropriate to the occasion, but provided him with a fine opportunity of presenting the Gospel to persons who might not otherwise have heard it. They certainly would not have listened to Paul in the ordinary course of his ministry. In this fifth and last defense of which we have a record Paul reveals his intellectual and spiritual powers, laying himself out, as it were, to bear testimony to Christ while telling the story of his own career. It is of no wonder that this chapter is one of the most attractive in the New Testament for public reading. Here, then, is —

I. The Commencement of Paul's Testimony (vs. 1-8).

1. *Courtesy* (vs. 1-3)

a. Paul's attitude to Agrippa is noteworthy, returning courtesy (vs. 2, 3) for courtesy (v. 1) — glad to be able to tell story before one who was "expert" (v. 3) in political and ecclesiastic affairs of Palestine, as Festus, being both Roman and newcomer, could not be;
b. Paul had been accused by Jews, therefore Jewish characteristics noticeable throughout address (cf. vs. 3, 4, 7, 21);
c. Thus, with evident satisfaction, Apostle made his greatest *apologia* for life and work, pleading only for full and patient hearing.

2. *Conduct* (vs. 4, 5)
   a. From early days Paul's manner of life had been thoroughly Jewish and very well known because of enthusiasm for Judaism amounting to bigotry (cf. 22:3; 23:6; Phil. 3:5, 6);
   b. Paul now notes this familiarity, saying Jews, if only willing to testify truthfully, would be able to bear him out as to his membership in "most straitest sect" (v. 5) of Pharisees.

3. *Challenge* (vs. 6-8)
   a. This was associated with Jewish hopes of Messiah (cf. 13:23-29) found in O.T. and influencing all Jewish life; to Paul there was definite continuity, and no break, between Judaism and Christianity when properly understood (cf. 3:13; 24:14; Rom. 11:25-27);
   b. With emphasis he associates himself with Jews ("our religion," v. 5; "our fathers," v. 6; "our twelve tribes," v. 7); and then points out he is actually being accused of entertaining very hope of resurrection that they, like himself, were expecting, showing absurdity of Jews regarding him as "heretic," and inconsistency of charge;
   c. Then Apostle asks telling question (v. 8): Why should it be thought incredible for God, as in case of Christ, to raise dead? None but Sadducees could fairly deny it; and all through resurrection had been theme of apostolic preaching (cf. 3:15; 5:30; 10:40; 13:30; 17:31).

II. The Center of Paul's Testimony (vs. 9-18)

1. *Confession* (vs. 9-11)
   a. With frankness he told how at first, as Jewish enthusiast, he was opposed to Christianity, went to terrible extremes as persecutor, and had felt it all justified; note vigorous expressions: "I verily thought with myself that I ought to do" (v. 9); "which I also did . . . I shut up . . . I gave my vote" (v. 10, A.S.V.); "I punished . . . compelled . . . persecuted" (v. 11) — all showing extent to which he had carried hostility to new religion;
   b. This is reason he could say he had "lived in all good conscience" (23:1); but in spite of all efforts could not get Christians to blaspheme (v. 11, A.S.V.), showing at once his perseverance (Gr. suggests this), and their determination to be faithful.
2. *Conversion* (vs. 12-15)
   a. Then Paul recounted remarkable change — day when, on very errand of persecution, definite check and complete transformation occurred;
   b. This third account of conversion should be compared with others (chaps. 9 and 22), and fresh details noted, re-emphasizing Divine character of event;
   c. There is no doubt Paul actually saw objective, literal form of Risen Lord and no mere vision, for he bases apostleship on this fact (cf. 1 Cor. 9:1), and places appearance to himself on exact equality with appearances to other disciples before Ascension (cf. 1 Cor. 15:5-8);
   d. Furthermore, he was actually told he had come face to face with very One he had been persecuting in persons of followers of Christ — identity between Christ and Christians most significant;
   e. In particular, Paul refers more fully to voice of Lord saying it was "hard to kick against the goad" (v. 14, A.S.V.) — referring doubtless to some rebellion against God's will that Paul had felt from time to time as he went on persecuting Christians; for animal to kick against goad is only to cause deeper wounds and experience more pain

— Paul had evidently felt increasing compunction in proceeding with terrible task.

3. *Commission* (vs. 16-18)
   a. Conversion intended for distinct purpose, service for God, and Apostle states in important detail aspects of commission, given both direct and through Ananias of Damascus (cf. 9:15, 16);
   b. In these words (v. 18), almost whole Gospel is included:
      (1) Revelation — "to open their eyes";
      (2) Repentance — "to turn them from darkness to light";
      (3) Redemption — "from the power of Satan unto God";
      (4) Remission — "that they may receive remission of sins";
      (5) Riches — "inheritance among them which are sanctified";
      (6) Reliance — "by faith that is in Me."
   c. Work was to be that of "a minister and a witness" (v. 16), testifying of past, present, and future; and worker was to be protected both from his own people and from Gentiles to whom he was sent (cf. v. 17).

III. The Culmination of Paul's Testimony (vs. 19-23)

1. *Consecration* (vs. 19, 20)
   a. "Whereupon" (v. 19 — cf. v. 12) to hear was to heed, to receive was to respond — outcome of this revelation was immediate obedience, which according to teaching of N.T. is:
      (1) Recognition of God's claim (5:29);
      (2) Mark of conversion (Rom. 6:16);
      (3) Evidence of relationship to God (1 Pet. 1:14);
      (4) Characteristic of faith (Heb. 11:8);
      (5) Proof of love (John 14:15);
      (6) Condition of power (5:32);
      (7) Indication of grace (Phil. 2:12, 13).
   b. Summary of Apostle's work, briefly but forcefully given (v. 20) — wherever he went burden of message was threefold: repentance, faith, obedience.

2. *Capture* (v. 21)
   a. Yet for this very cause, born of his conversion and consecration, Jews had attacked him while worshipping in temple (cf. 21:27-30);
   b. They had even attempted to kill him (cf. 21:31, 32; 22:22; 23:12-22; 25:3, 24).
3. *Continuance* (vs. 22, 23)
   a. But God had protected him to that very day, fulfilling promise quoted in v. 17, and Paul had therefore continued to teach nothing else than that which Jewish Scriptures taught and implied about Messiah;
   b. In all this detail Paul is clearly thinking of Gospel rather than himself, of making Master known to Agrippa rather than effecting own release;
   c. He reiterates his creed — Christ's death, resurrection, and revelation to Jew and Gentile — and implies full belief in O. T. — "the prophets and Moses" (v. 22);
   d. Jewish refusal and loss, coloring much of N.T., emphatic here, and here also transfer of Gospel to Gentiles is implicit (cf. 28:17-29).

IV. The Consequence of Paul's Testimony (vs. 24-32)

1. *Criticism* (v. 24)
   a. Sudden interruption occurred at this point — Festus, cynical Gentile, could not grasp doctrine of resurrection (v. 23; cf. 17:32; 25:19, 20), and to him Paul appeared religious fanatic;
   b. With loud exclamation expressive at once of impatience, unbelief, and astonishment, told Paul he had reached some sort of insanity through much study and great learning in Scriptures — not that he was insane in modern sense, but so full of religious enthusiasm that it was form of mania.
2. *Calmness* (vs. 25, 26)
   a. To this Paul quickly replied with fine courtesy and restraint that, so far from being "mad" (vs. 24, 25), he was speaking with truth and sobriety, very opposite of frenzy;
   b. He then appealed to Jewish king, who would naturally

know more of Jewish religion than did Roman cynic and skeptic, and before whom Paul felt sense of freedom because Christianity had made such stir that Agrippa must have heard what had happened;

c. Thus did Paul emphasize that these things particularly resurrection, had not been without publicity (cf. Luke 24:18).

3. *Colloquy* (vs. 27-29)

a. Then followed striking and courageous personal appeal to king, perhaps prompted by something noticed on Agrippa's face — asked whether he believed prophets and, knowing king as Jew would at least have intellectual belief in sacred writings, answered his own question by expressing conviction that such was case;

b. Reply of Agrippa noteworthy though variously interpreted — does not mean king deeply convicted and near to becoming Christian, for Greek will not bear familiar translation "almost" (vs. 28, 29) and "altogether" (v. 29), but must be rendered "with little" and "with much" (A.S.V.); so that meaning quite contrary — either, ironically retorting, "You must think you can make me Christian very easily," idea of winning him, a king, over to contemptible sect and in such easy way being incredible; or, that he saw what Paul was aiming at, seeking to persuade him to be Christian, which he did not want to be, and therefore turned subject and avoided question;

c. Probably Agrippa really felt influence of Paul's great powers of persuasion (cf. 17:4, 34), for, with beautiful courtesy and genuine earnestness, Apostle replied that, whether with little persuasion or much, he wished with all his heart that king and rest of hearers were like himself, Christian, apart from bonds that held him prisoner; N.B. (1) Modern writer has said: "Paul was far more anxious to bring Agrippa face to face with his Master than he was to defend himself in the presence of Agrippa";

(2) It is usually thought that term "Christian" (found only here, 11:26, and 1 Pet. 4:16) was then used as nick-

name; but whether this was so or not it has become most honorable and universal term for followers of Jesus Christ (see Studies Nos. 55, under XII, page 218, and 56, page 226).

4. *Consultation* (vs. 30-32)
   a. This closed hearing, for now king and sister (cf. 25:23) arose and left auditorium, followed by retinue;
   b. If Josephus is correct, large number of Roman officers were present, and thus Paul had availed himself of splendid opportunity for witness;
   c. Even though Agrippa did not wait for more of Paul's appeals, it is not surprising that he, from Jewish standpoint, acknowledged belief in prisoner's innocence, concurring with Festus (cf. 25:25); and it is impressive that three Roman officials had in turn declared Paul guiltless (cf. Pilate in regard to Christ, Matt. 27:15-25; Mark 15:14; Luke 23:13-24; John 18:38);
   c. But appeal to Caesar was irrevocable and precluded settlement of case by any local tribunal.

Conclusion

In this chapter we have seen St. Paul in all the strength and glory of his Christian life, a "man of God," godly and manly.

The elements
So mixed in him that Nature might stand up
And say to all the world, "This was a man!"
—Wm. Shakespeare

His Christian manliness is seen all the more vividly when he is contrasted with the skeptical Festus, the politic Agrippa, and the unheeding retinue. In verse 19 his Christian experience is well summed up:

1. *The Heavenly Revelation* — "the heavenly vision"
   a. This was an unveiling of the Risen Christ as Saviour and Master; and, apart from the miraculous circumstances in the case of Paul, this is still the method of Christ with the soul;
   b. There is a personal revelation, a personal Redeemer, a personal redemption, and a personal claim on our allegiance.

2. *The Human Response* — "I was not disobedient"
   a. The immediate outcome was "the obedience of faith" (Rom. 1:5, A.S.V.; 16:26), that which springs always and inevitably from faith (cf. 6:7);
   b. Paul took Christ at His Word, believed what He said, accepted His salvation, recognized His Lordship, and did His will.

This, and this only, was to St. Paul the life that is Christ.

Study No. 118 — What Is Christianity?*

ACTS 26:1, 3

WHAT IS CHRISTIANITY? Not what is its irreducible minimum, not how little a man may accept and yet be a Christian, but what are the characteristic and distinctive elements of Christianity? What is its message, and what is its provision? These questions may be answered in a variety of ways, but one of the best is to take the life, or some focal point in the life, of a great Christian like St. Paul and seek to discover its true significance. In the remarkable story of his appearance before Agrippa we have a striking picture of him as a man and as a messenger.

As a man Paul is seen at his best, with no constraint or hesitation in his utterances; he is in his element. The subject suits him, and he yields himself to it, so that the result is this magnificent *apologia*. But as we listen to him we forget this first picture of Paul the man, and become wholly absorbed in a second and larger view of Paul the Apostle, going far beyond a mere defence of himself to plead for the Master whom he loved and served, and to proclaim his Master's everlasting Gospel. Thus we have not simply a prisoner defending and justifying himself, but chiefly an advocate proclaiming and defending another. The picture of Paul

---

* Appeared in full in *The Christian Life and How to Live It*, published by Moody Press, Chicago, and by The Church Book Room Press, London. Used by permission.

before Agrippa becomes merged into the far more heroic scene of Christianity at the bar of the world.

We read that Agrippa said to his prisoner, "Thou art permitted to speak for thyself," and that Paul answered with the plea, ". . . I beseech thee to hear me patiently." It is therefore evident that —

I. Christianity Has Something to say — "thou art permitted to speak" (v. 1)

If only the world will allow this opportunity, it will speak, for it has an urgent threefold message:

1. *Christianity has the Gospel of the Resurrection* — "God doth raise the dead" (v. 8, A.S.V.)
   a. Basis and burden of Apostolic message was "Jesus and the resurrection" (17:18); on this fact Apostles took stand and preached it everywhere, because of witness it bore to Godhead — not some distant Being unconcerned with world He created, but God who is near, approachable, available to every-day life (cf. 17:27, 28, 31);
   b. Cause of opposition, especially from Jewish authorities — "of the hope and resurrection of the dead . . . called in question" (23:6; 24:21) — because of implication, Godhead of Christ, for opposers knew well that to accept resurrection was to accept Christ as God, since thereby all His claims were substantiated.

   Yes, the Gospel of the Resurrection is a proclamation of the living Christ.
2. *Christianity has the Gospel of the Kingdom* — "the Lord said, I am Jesus" (v. 15, A.S.V.)
   a. Paul's wording both to and about Christ clearly shows acceptance of Him as God, and carries with it acceptance of Him as Lord and Master; and it implies acknowledgement of our position as servants;
   b. Since Christ is God He is supreme, King and Ruler, and we are His subjects;
   c. Consequently, through entire Book of Acts, we find references to Kingdom of God, e.g.:
      (1) Our Lord's conversations before Ascension concerned with it (cf. 1:3);

(2) Philip preached it in Samaria (cf. 8:12);
(3) Paul preached it at Ephesus (cf. 19:8); and —
(4) Last words of Book show him at Rome "preaching the kingdom of God" (28:31);

d. Thus Paul not afraid of logic of belief, practical outcome of fundamental doctrine, viz., "Since Christ is God, therefore I am His subject";
e. Both realized and preached Christ who, because He is God, claims men as His own and their lives to be ruled by Him, not only bestowing upon them great privileges, but calling for performance of duties of their heavenly citizenship (cf. Eph. 2:19; Phil. 3:20).

Yes, the Gospel of the Kingdom is a further revelation of the living Christ.

3. *Christianity has the Gospel of Pardon* — "that they may receive forgiveness of sins" (v. 18)
   a. This also integral part of apostolic preaching — men as rebels against God by reason of sin cannot become subjects of His Kingdom until, wills submitted and lives surrendered, they are pardoned;
   b. Unless rebellion of sin is quelled in man, not only can there be no entrance into God's Kingdom, but also no acceptance of Christ as God;
   c. Thus Paul preached everywhere forgiveness of sins (cf. 13:38; 16:31) — full, free, immediate, assured, everlasting pardon.

   Yes, the Gospel of Pardon is concerned with the conditions of entrance into the Kingdom of the living Christ.

II. Christianity Has Something to Say for Itself — "thou art permitted to speak for thyself" (v. 1)

This is what it desires and deserves, for —

1. *Hearsay evidence is often erroneous.*
   a. In this very Book we find glaring instances of danger of hearsay, e.g., Church regarded as obscure Jewish sect with peculiar ideas of "one Jesus" (cf. 17:7; 25:19) through smattering of knowledge at second hand;
   b. Unfortunately, we find same today — too much second-

hand religion gathered from common report, ordinary conversation, and literary tradition; Bible is condemned without being read, criticized without being studied, by many whose position and education warrant attitude vastly different; and often one church is condemned through false notions imbibed in another;

c. Same often sadly true of Gospel itself — error believed because of lack of real knowledge, and because hearsay evidence is indeed so often erroneous.

But we go further and say that even —

2. *Christian testimony is only partial.*
   a. No possible doubt that change in Paul's own life had great effect on hearers — fact they could not set aside;
   b. Yet, while Christians still retain "old Adam" (cf. 1 Cor. 15:22), there is always possibility of slips, failures, even sins, and he who takes his Christianity from Christians only is all too often to be pitied;
   c. No doubt we ought to show much more of Christ-life than we do — may God pardon us for so often being stumbling-blocks instead of stepping-stones; yet even when Christian testimony is real and true it is at best partial as far as others are concerned.

This leads us to realize that —

3. *Personal experience is always sure.*
   a. This was goal of Apostle — to this he tried to lead hearers and for it gave own testimony; desired Agrippa to test Christianity for himself — not only to hear of Paul's Christ, but to have Christ for his own;
   b. Prime necessity is to get our Christianity direct from Christ — not to ask this or that man, not to follow this or that book — but to go direct to Book of books and find Christ for ourselves;
   c. Cf. Philip, when Nathanael questioned whether any good thing could come out of Nazareth, did not preach, argue, or denounce — simply said, "Come and see" (John 1:46); this only safe test — to see who Christ is and what He asks;

d. Result of complying with His demands by surrender of life will be similar to that experienced by Samaritans who said, "Now we believe, . . . for we have heard Him ourselves" (John 4:42).

III. Christianity Has Something to Say for Itself Worth Hearing — "I beseech thee to hear me" (v. 3)

This is what Paul asked and what Christianity asks today; and why?

1. *The Gospel of the Resurrection explains the enigmas of life.*
   a. What world needs is God; without Him —
      (1) All is chaos and hopeless confusion;
      (2) There is no real life, no true happiness, no permanent satisfaction;
      (3) Past has no assurance, present no confidence, future no hope;
      (4) Man is creature lost in darkness and filth of sin, with nothing but gloom and despair at end of his days;
   b. But Resurrection of Christ, as seal of man's redemption, changes all this:
      (1) It reveals God, as Saviour, Guide, Strength, All;
      (2) It enables man to live abundantly in present and to hope steadfastly as to future;
      (3) It brings light of God's presence, joy, peace, power, preciousness of His salvation;
      (4) It solves riddle of life and provides pattern of immortality.
2. *The Gospel of the Kingdom meets the difficulties of life.*
   a. To find root of all man's troubles, we turn to Garden of Eden: man's desire to be independent, to set up self against God and instead of God, essence of all sin;
   b. Man will not have God's rule, will not acknowledge and obey God's law, but will have law of his own as guide of life; so, man attempts self-government — "local self-government" in very literal sense;
   c. Result is abject, absolute failure — e.g., in political life all through history, with several forms of government

tried, each incomplete, if not worse:
(1) Autocracy — found pernicious through tyranny;
(2) Aristocracy — found unsatisfactory through snobbery;
(3) Plutocracy — found dangerous through ignorance;
(4) Democracy — found inadequate through fallibility;

d. Form of human rule matters not — man never intended to be independent of God; and even democracy has in itself elements of failure and tyranny, along with elements of good;

e. Any system, therefore, should be guided and controlled by Theocracy, government by God;
N.B. De Tocqueville said: "Men never so much need to be theocratic as when they are most democratic."

f. What world needs, what each of us needs, is Absolute Monarchy of our Lord Jesus Christ, with laws, rules, sanctions of His Kingdom to settle permanently every problem of both individual and social life, and to satisfy human heart's yearnings for righteous kingship;
Illus.: Demonstrations in Trafalgar Square, London (c. 1888) settled by appeal to "Crown Rights," claim of monarch over that area; in like manner, any "demonstrations" of sin can be quickly settled by claiming and acknowledging "crown rights" of Christ;

g. Only let Him reign supreme in heart and life, and difficulties are met by Gospel of Kingdom.

3. *The Gospel of Pardon satisfies the needs of life.*

a. Chief need of man is forgiveness of sin, freedom from troubled conscience — old question oft recurring: "Canst thou not minister to a mind diseased?"

b. Unregenerate man has sense of —
(1) Guilt and unrest;
(2) Bondage and weakness;
(3) Defilement and separation;

c. So, only when Christ says, "Peace be still" (Mark 4:39) that man is at rest; only when He says, "Come out of the man" (Mark 5:8) that spirit of evil loses its power;

only when He reveals Himself that schism in our nature is healed, and needs of life satisfied by Gospel of Pardon.

These are reasons why Christianity is worth hearing.

IV. Christianity Has Something to Say for Itself Worth Hearing Patiently — "I beseech thee to hear me patiently" (v. 3)

This is what Paul said, and so says the Gospel today:

1. *It concerns our highest interests.*
   a. It has to do with life here and life hereafter;
   b. It claims to touch life at every point, to solve all its problems, to minister to its most important needs;
   c. It deserves and demands our most careful attention; if it is true at all, it is terribly true, and no one can reject it without peril.
2. *It speaks to our entire nature.*
   a. Christianity appeals —
      (1) Not to mind only, to interest it with mere speculation;
      (2) Not to heart only, to indulge it with mere sentiment;
      (3) Not to conscience only, to awaken and terrify it;
      (4) Not to imagination only, to entrance it with ephemeral visions;
      (5) Not to will only, to curb it and mold it;
      (6) But to whole nature of man, in every part, to guarantee real, complete, balanced character;
   b. But man may perversely close any part of his nature to Gospel of Christ —
      (1) Like Felix, allowing sin to hold him back; or —
      (2) Like Festus or Agrippa, cynically indifferent to it; *Illus.*: Charles Darwin sadly confessed, after long usage of faculties exclusively in direction of physical science, he had lost all taste for music and fine arts, becoming, to that extent, mentally atrophied;
   c. So, no man can with impunity close mind and heart against Christ; and he may indeed suffer moral atrophy and spiritual deadness by misuse or disuse of any faculty in relation to Gospel.
3. *It calls for the surrender of our whole life.*

Finally, the Gospel of Christ asks —

a. Openness of mind, which includes —

 (1) Putting away prejudice and preconception;

 (2) Listening carefully to its message;

 (3) Mastering its A B C first, and then passing on to higher, fuller knowledge;

 (4) Receiving its truth with that willingness to learn which forms basis of all wisdom;

b. Response of personality, so that truths accepted by mind shall be —

 (1) Yielded to in loving confidence by heart; and —

 (2) Lived out day by day in conduct.

Conclusion

This Gospel message comes to us now as it came to Agrippa, asking only a personal test. With courtesy it asks for candor, patience, and thoroughness of consideration. Given these, it will show us how all the demands of our complex life can be satisfied:

1. Our defilement cleansed by its salvation; our weakness made strong by its grace;
2. Our roughness made smooth by its power; our anxiety reassured by its reality;
3. Our doubt removed by its truth; our defencelessness surrounded by its protection;
4. Our tempest calmed by its peace; our darkness illuminated by its life;
5. Our sorrow alleviated by its comfort; our misery relieved by its joy;
6. Our coldness warmed by its love; our emptiness filled by its fulness.

Yes, the whole circumference of our need will be forever met and perfectly satisfied in the treasures of the Gospel of the living, present, Divine, glorious Christ; and, therefore, comes now to each one of us the simple message, the old familiar invitation: "O taste and see that the Lord is good: blessed is the man that trusteth in Him."

O make but trial of His love,
Experience will decide
How blest are they, and only they,
Who in His truth confide.
—Tate and Brady (1696)

Study No. 119 — The Resurrection of Christ*

ACTS 26:8

There is a point in the raising of every structure concerning which it may be said that if that point is soundly set, all is right with the foundation of the building. It would not be surprising if the same were true of Christianity, namely, that there be some alleged fact regarding it which, if proved to be beyond contradiction, would make secure the whole structure. A dispassionate study of the Book of Acts suggests that there is such a point of fact and that this is claimed to be the Resurrection of our Lord. There is scarcely an apostolic utterance that does not emphasize it, and it was "touching the resurrection" that Paul was "called in question" at each of his hearings (cf. 2:24, etc.; 23:6, etc.).

It is fitting for us to examine this foundation for, if it proves secure, there is no need to fear attacks on other points. Let us, then, call for a light, take the key of the vault, and descend to the foundations of this house of Christianity. Let us pass through the arches and examine especially this keystone of the central one. The result will surely be that we shall ascend from the foundations, put out the light, place the key in our pocket, and go quietly about our business, secure in the knowledge that, whatever alarms are raised, all is safe and secure.

---

* This is one of the author's dated sermons, preached first, in its original form, when he was 27 years of age. For a later and more complete presentation of the subject, see his volume, *Christianity Is Christ,* chap. 7 (Wm. B. Eerdmans Publishing Co., 1955).

We need make no apology for thus treating the subject of the Resurrection, for the Apostle's question in our text quite justifies the method. He appealed to Agrippa's reason and common sense when he asked, "Why is it judged incredible with you, if God doth raise the dead?" We may paraphrase this important question thus: Why should we regard it as incredible, impossible of belief, that Christ rose from the dead?

Here are four reasons that compel the belief that the Resurrection was a fact:

I. The Resurrection Involves the Life and Character of Christ Himself.

1. *His was perfect life, ending in shameful death.*
   a. Life and death alone, however, would not qualify Him as Divine Saviour and Lord;
   b. Resurrection necessary, for living faith cannot be placed in dead man;
   c. Christ is "alive for evermore," not only "he that liveth, and was dead" (Rev. 1:18);
2. *His character, like all others, included His words.*
   a. He spoke often of His coming resurrection as well as of His death:
      (1) In figurative language (cf. John 2:19-22);
      (2) More definitely (cf. Mark 8:31; 9:31);
      (3) In greater detail, while going up to Jerusalem (cf. Mark 10:32-34);
   b. He later revealed His resurrection as having taken place (cf. Luke 24:25-27);
   c. So His character would have suffered had He not risen.
3. *Both life and character showed Him to be no ordinary man who lived and died.*
   a. Had His death actually been close of His life, we could have had no Saviour — only human being of extraordinary character and heroic martyrdom;
   b. But resurrection was receipt, or seal, by which God showed Him to be truly Divine, "the Son of the Highest" (Luke 1:32; cf. 2 Cor. 4:14 with 5:5);

N.B. How strange disciples so soon forgot His many intimations of this! At empty tomb, angels rebuked them (cf. Luke 24:5-7), and only then "they remembered His words" (v. 8).

II. The Resurrection is Proved by the Disappearance of our Lord's Body.

A. *What became of our Lord's Body?*

1. *There can be no possible doubt that He really died;* those who crucified Him made quite sure of that — Pilate having body officially examined and its side pierced by soldier's spear (cf. John 19:31-37);
2. *Also, that body was taken down from cross,* buried in rock-hewn tomb at which huge stone placed and sealed, and Roman guard posted at entrance, are matters of simple fact (cf. Matt. 27:59-66);
3. *Yet on third day Christ's body disappeared;* so what became of it?

B. *It either was taken out by human hands or raised by supernatural power.*

1. *If taken by human agency it must have been by friends or by foes:*
   a. If by friends — allowing that they would, let us consider whether they could:
      (1) Openly? Disciples had shown themselves timorous and even cowardly, while women were physically weak; it is simply impossible that such a company could have overcome armed Roman guard;
      (2) Quietly, according to Jewish tale (cf. Matt. 28:11-15)? No, for —
         (a) Stones used for sepulchre of such huge size that noise must have been made in rolling one away;
         (b) For Roman soldiers to sleep while on duty was death (cf. 12:19; Matt. 28:14), and even if one slept it seems preposterous that whole guard did, being sometimes as many as 60 in number; and we are told by Matthew of heavy bribe just to lie about it;

(c) If they were asleep, how could they know disciples had taken body; and if they were awake, would they have permitted it?

(d) If disciples did do it, is it not remarkable that no account of it has ever leaked out, even under terrible persecutions and deaths which they suffered, largely for sake of belief in resurrection?

We may conclude, then, that Christ's friends did not take His body.

b. If taken by enemies — allowing that they could, let us consider whether they would:

(1) Because Jews recollected His word about rising on third day, placed guard before tomb (cf. Matt. 27:63, 64); surely, then, they would not do very thing that would spread report they were trying to prevent;

(2) And if they really did possess body they would have produced it to silence preaching of Peter when, 50 days later, he proclaimed resurrection (cf. 2:24-32) — would have been most damaging and complete answer to claim Jesus had risen;

Illus.: If, after death of Charles I, pretender had suddenly come forward saying he was Charles, most effective answer would have been to show tomb in St. George's, Windsor, with body in it.

2. *Theory, then, that our Lord's body was stolen from tomb is so full of absurdities and contradictions that no honest mind can accept it;*

a. Here is question that has never yet been answered: What became of body if Jesus did not rise from dead?

b. We are therefore compelled to fall back on only alternative: He rose from dead by supernatural power.

III. The Resurrection Bears the Blood-stained Testimony of Many Witnesses.

Again taking N.T. simply as ordinary history book, we examine carefully evidence of those who said they had seen Christ after His resurrection:

1. *The Witnesses*

Who were they?

a. The Women:

(1) If Easter message depended solely on assertion of those who may be thought of as weak, nervous, easily imposed upon, wishfully thinking, we might fairly ask, Is it true?

(2) Their testimony must be taken into account but, fortunately, we have host of other witnesses:

b. The Apostles:

(1) Peter, who 50 days later publicly announced it in Jerusalem (cf. 2:32);

(2) Remaining ten disciples at various times (cf. 1 Cor. 15:3);

(3) 500 brethren at once (cf. 1 Cor. 15:6);

(4) James, His brother, and "all the apostles" (cf. 1 Cor. 15:7); and —

(5) Last of all, Paul saw Him (cf. 9:17; 22:14; 26:13, 19; 1 Cor. 15:8).

2. *The Testimony*

Why was it remarkable?

a. Witnesses never expected resurrection, as can be seen from words of two going to Emmaus (cf. Luke 24:21, 22), and from fact of women coming on third day to embalm body (cf. Luke 24:1);

b. When Jesus had risen, disciples still doubted it (cf. Luke 24:11, 25, 37, 41; John 20:25);

c. When once convinced, however, never doubted again (cf. 1:3; 2:32, etc.; Luke 24:52, 53).

3. *The Validity*

a. Could witnesses have been deceived?

(1) Occasions whereon they became assured of fact of resurrection too numerous and varied: in dusk at Emmaus, in morning in Joseph's garden, near sea of Galilee, in closed room at Jerusalem, on mount of Olives, on road to Damascus at noon;

(2) Means whereby they became convinced of living Christ too intimate and personal: handled by them,

eating with them, talking to them, walking with them.

b. Could their testimony have been concocted? If so, —
   (1) Would Peter have dared to proclaim it seven weeks later, in very city near which Jesus was crucified (2:32)?
   (2) Would Paul have stood before Athenians as false witness saying God would judge world by "that man whom . . . he hath raised . . . from the dead" (17:31)?
   (3) Would John have invented such tissue of falsehood in his old age (cf. Rev. 1:5, 18)?
   (4) For whose good was such deception? Rather, witnesses received for proclaiming resurrection contempt, persecution, punishment, death by stoning, beheading, crucifixion, etc.

4. *The Fact*
   a. It is sealed with blood of "cloud of witnesses" (Heb. 12:1), so that we may challenge fearlessly any inquiry into nature and reality of their testimony;
   b. There is no single fact in history so well authenticated as resurrection of Christ;
      N.B. Dr. Arnold of Rugby, no mean judge of historical evidence, used to say no fact of ancient history so well attested and, but for its being miracle, no one would think of doubting it;
   c. No theory except theory of its truth will account for it; one by one, all other theories must be given up, and all reasonable men be compelled to return to undoubted fact of resurrection of Christ.

IV. The Resurrection is the Foundation of the Christian Church

A. *The Fact of the Church*
   1. *Its Composition*
      a. It is universal body of all those who profess and call themselves Christians;
      b. It is built on an empty grave.
   2. *Its Commencement*

a. First converts received tidings that Christ was risen, accepted it, and on its truth Church was founded; if that were not true, not one stone of building would have been placed in position;
b. Thus, throughout world today, we see Christian Church existing as fact: Here is stream; where is source? Here is effect; where is cause? No accounting for it except by acceptance of resurrection, and that belief would have been impossible unless fact were established;
c. Primitive Church's belief in resurrection not even founded on Gospel records, for it was believed, preached, and propagated, and had produced fruit long before any of Gospels written; not that this disparages written records, but is significant chronological fact;
d. But when Gospels appeared they afforded conclusive evidence to support oral testimony; and there were found to be two sets of post-resurrection appearances of Christ, one in Jerusalem, and other in Galilee.

B. *The History of the Church*

1. *Its Characteristics*
   a. Two chains of evidence may be cited, gradually forged, existing side by side for more than 19 centuries without gap of so much as single link:
      (1) The Lord's Supper
         (a) We look back to upper room in Jerusalem and see few friends breaking and eating bread together in remembrance of their Master and His death, until He comes again;
         (b) We note they do same thing week after week, and wherever they go — year after year, century after century, until this present day — as perpetual testimony to death of Christ;
      (2) The Lord's Day
         (a) We look back again at friends in upper room and note all are Jews, yet they gather on first day of week, not seventh;
         (b) We note Jewish sabbath, as such, has passed

away for Christians, and they keep first day, calling it the Lord's Day, because on it their Master rose from dead;

(c) We trace weekly observance in all places, through all centuries until today — as perpetual testimony to resurrection of Christ.

b. No accounting historically for observance of Lord's Supper except by admitting death of Christ as fact; and neither can we account historically for change of sabbath from seventh to first day of week except by admitting resurrection of Christ as fact.

c. We have Scriptural precepts and examples for our observances, but first Christians had no written N.T. until they wrote it out of own experiences, inspired by Holy Spirit; so they must have observed Lord's Supper and Lord's Day because convinced of their validity and appropriateness.

2. *Its Cornerstone*

a. We are told that this is Christ Himself (cf. Eph. 2:20; 1 Pet. 2:7), but it is quite evident that statement presupposes resurrection life — "a living stone" (1 Pet. 2:4);

b. Church would not have stood unshaken after nearly 2000 years of storm and stress if it had been founded on weak or crooked cornerstone or built on sand strewn by dozen enthusiasts or imposters;

c. Those who accept such a solution must be capable of excessive incredulity and mental, not to say moral, blindness; let them but honestly and candidly use God-given faculties and surely they cannot help admitting as foundation of Christian Church resurrection of her Lord and Master;

N.B. Archbishop Alexander of Armagh said: "As the Church is too holy for a foundation of rottenness, so she is too real for a foundation of mist."

V. The Resurrection is Attested by Christian Experience

This is different sort of proof, and to many it is strongest:

1. *Heart Experience*

a. It is possible to be convinced intellectually of truth of resurrection and yet lack personal, individual proof;
b. But every true Christian, from St. Paul down through the centuries to present day, testifies to indestructible presence of Christ in heart as he says, "Christ liveth in me" (Gal. 2:20); and —
   (1) Realizes His strength for daily need, as Risen Christ says, "I am with you alway" (Matt. 28:20);
   (2) Feels His comfort in sorrow, as He asks, "Why weepest thou?" (John 20:15);
   (3) Knows His presence when he has sinned, as Christ chides him, inquiring sadly, "Lovest thou Me?" (John 21:16);
   (4) Will feel and know Him if he comes to die, as he cries, "Abide with (me); for it is toward evening" (Luke 24:29), and "Lord Jesus, receive my spirit" (7:59).

This is but tithe of genuine experience of every true Christian, for there is also —

2. *Soul Experience*
   a. Some ridicule any expression of experience as unreliable; but, after making every possible allowance, we may aver that experience is real and due credit must be awarded it;
   b. Heart and mind must not be severed in Christian testimony; let heart testify from blessed experience, but let reason be convinced to utmost possibility, so that together man's whole personality may approve, and enjoy, and witness.

No, no one has right to denounce experience as unreliable who has not put test to his own life, and so it is also —

3. *Personal Experience*
   a. Daily, hourly, Christians can personally testify that Christ is risen;
   b. It is not dead Saviour to whom we pray;
   c. It is not empty doctrine that binds us together;
   d. It is personal experience of personal Christ, who was

dead, and is alive again, and who lives forevermore (cf. Rev. 1:18);

N.B. Greatest example of this is Saul of Tarsus, for how else account for his change of heart, his severed connections, his lost friends and prestige, his entrance into life of toil and shame — 25 years of service for Christ — and his recorded testimony?

Conclusion

Such, then, are the five proofs whereby we establish the fact of the Resurrection: the first from Divine evidence, the second, from common sense, the third, from contemporary testimony, the fourth, from universal history, the fifth, from individual experience. Taken separately, they are strong; taken together, they are cumulative and overwhelming. We have tried to use no special pleading, no arguments save those that will bear the hammer-blows of the sternest logic. Standing now, as it were, in the garden today, at the side of the open sepulchre, our eyes may trace the great mass of evidence for the Resurrection of Christ; and the hope mentioned by St. Paul (vs. 6, 7; 23:6) swells within us as the great mountain of facts rises higher and higher, until its peaks are lost in ineffable grandeur and glory. With these proofs in mind, let me ask:

1. Why should *you* think it incredible that Christ rose?
   Ah, I am persuaded you do not now think it so!
2. Do you not believe the Scriptures?
   I trust that you do; and so I beg of you to supplement and to seal the intellectual belief by the one that comes from your own experience.
3. Will you not, by surrendering yourself, spirit, soul, and body, to Christ as your Saviour and Lord, find what St. Paul meant when he spoke of "the power of His resurrection" (Phil. 3:10)?
   If you will, you shall know this power in —
   a. Forgiveness of sin;
   b. Deliverance from fear;
   c. Victory over temptation;

d. Continual holiness of life;
e. Noble character and true manhood or womanhood.

4. Will you not, therefore, enter fully into the glory of the Resurrection?
   By it —
   a. Christ was declared to be the Son of God and to have made sufficient sacrifice on Calvary for the sins of the whole world;
   b. We are assured of Christ as a living, personal Friend, having changed bodily presence for spiritual fellowship;
   c. We are assured of our own resurrection to immortality with Christ and reunion with our loved ones gone before.

"Therefore, my beloved brethren, be ye stedfast, unmoveable, always abounding in the work of the Lord, forasmuch as ye know that your labor is not in vain in the Lord" (1 Cor. 15:58).

Study No. 120 — The Christian Preacher (A Fragment)

ACTS 26:13-23

RUNNING through this experience of the Apostle may be traced the qualifications of any true preacher of the Gospel:

1. *His Contact* (vs. 13-15)
   a. With Christ through sight (v. 13);
   b. With Christ through hearing (v. 14);
   c. With Christ through speech (v. 15).
2. *His Commission* (vs. 16-18)
   a. As minister (v. 16);
   b. As missionary (v. 17);
   c. As evangelist (v. 18).
3. *His Compliance* (vs. 19-21)
   a. Practising obedience (v. 19);
   b. Preaching repentance, conversion, and newness of life (v. 20);
   c. Enduring persecution (v. 20).

4. *His Continuance* (vs. 22, 23)
   a. By Divine aid, making universal appeal, on Scriptural basis (v. 22);
   b. Preaching Christ suffering, risen, enlightening (v. 23).

Study No. 121 — "Called According to His Purpose"*

ACTS 26:15, 16

IN ALL THE ANNALS of Christian biography one fact is abundantly evident, namely, that while the modes of conversion were very diverse the purpose in each one has been exactly the same. In the conversion of, say, Augustine, John Newton, Baxter, Wesley, Moody, and very many more, God dealt in the way best fitted to the nature and temperament of the individual; yet in every case, the object of God is identical, whether the convert is later to serve Him as apostle, bishop, evangelist, pastor, or layman. We may best discover this plan of God by a study of one of the earliest and most notable of all conversions, that of St. Paul, for the Lord declared plainly, "I have appeared unto thee for this purpose . . ." (v. 16), and proceeded to tell what that purpose was.

In the Church year, it is interesting to note, of all the saints' days the one called "The Conversion of St. Paul" is the only one whereby a conversion is commemorated. The rest are concerned either generally with the life of the person or specifically with some episode in it subsequent to conversion. But St. Paul's conversion meant so much to him personally, and also as a pattern or type of God's dealings with others, that the Christian Church does well to emphasize it by reading the record of it and by praying for grace to follow "the holy doctrine which he taught" (see Collect on page opposite Editor's Preface).

* This is one of the author's dated sermons preached, in its original form, when he was 29 years of age.

In our text we have the purpose of God in calling Paul and also the particulars of God's purpose for us who also receive His call. By considering it we shall be enabled to realize more effectively the elements in that purpose in and for our Christian life. The first element is —

I. Salvation

Before Paul could know and do God's will he must have his nature transformed and his life altered, becoming personally fitted for his work, through —

1. *Revelation* — "I am Jesus whom thou persecutest" (v. 15)
   a. Paul's life had been like ship on wrong tack, and it was necessary to set it on straight course; this was possible only through giving it right direction;
   b. As Saul, he had thought this Jesus only a man, dead and buried; and lo, He is here, confronting His persecutor, and thus Saul meets Him face to face;
   c. This is great and absolute necessity, one and only foundation of all true Christian life and service — revelation of Christ; this is what every sinner needs;
   d. But there is something more; in seeing Christ Saul saw what sin was — "whom thou persecutest": I persecuted Thee? Nothing of the kind, I persecuted some fanatical and apostate Jews in Jerusalem and elsewhere. No, Saul, in persecuting them you persecuted Me!
   e. Sin is personal offense against God and painful thing to Christ, even though it be directed primarily against least of His creatures.

But there is another phase of Salvation. Had Paul been left with consciousness of sin, he might have despaired; to realize our sin and then to be left alone would be terrible. And so there is not only Revelation, there is —

2. *Restoration* — "I am Jesus" (v. 15)
   a. That to Jew would be full of meaning—from name Jeshua, or Joshua, in O.T. times, "Jehovah-Saviour," to given name of hated Nazarene — "Thou shalt call His Name Jesus; for He shall save His people from their sins" (Matt. 1:21);

b. Saul is being told Christ was exalted not only "to be a Prince . . . to give repentance," but also as "a Saviour" to bring "forgiveness of sins" (5:31); though thou hast persecuted Me, says the Lord, yet I am Jesus, the Saviour;
c. Thus we see salvation is simply personal revelation of Christ to soul, contact of soul with Christ — very simple, yet very real and precious; this is absolutely essential and prior to all else;
d. Christ is ready, willing, waiting to reveal Himself as our own personal Saviour if we, like Paul, will but yield ourselves to Him for His restoring grace.

Yes, revelation of sin brings also restoration of sinner.

The next element in God's purpose is —

II. Character

Christ saves in order, first, to form character, for sin has influenced inner self and must be dealt with; character makes the man, and in every true Christian character there are two elements:

1. *Integrity* — "But rise" (v. 16)
   a. There is nothing cringing in true character — nothing mean, or fawning, or crouching; it should be sincere, whole, not disabled or frightened, but able to rise because conscious of integrity, of probity;
   b. Man only able to rise if he has first been down, so, only when we come to end of ourselves, realizing what Christ is and can do, that we can rise in integrity of character;
   c. It was only when Jacob had come to end of himself, baffled, weakened, emptied, that God called him no longer Jacob — supplanter, sneak, liar — but Israel, prince of God (cf. Gen. 32:28);
   d. Integrity of character is possible only through Christ, for to rise without and apart from Him would be impertinence soon manifesting itself in utter failure;
   e. But when man has met Christ, has had his sin put away, he can and does rise, conscious of integrity and sincerity of character; he is Christ's freeman and He who calls him to rise gives him power to do so.

Another part of character is —

2. *Vigor* — "stand upon thy feet" (v. 16)
   a. Not only sincerity, but strength; there are many men sincere and true and yet as weak as water and as fragile as fading leaf;
   b. What Christ gives is not only inward holiness and purity, but force, courage, vigor; power to stand, as it were, foursquare to all winds that blow;
   c. Aye, and Paul did stand — there were three special times when he stood firm for God and His truth:
      (1) In that deadly conflict with powers of Rome under Nero, he stood and witnessed good confession;
      (2) In that deadlier conflict with weaknesses and temptations of his converts at Corinth, he stood and at all costs maintained purity and discipline of Christian community; and —
      (3) In that deadliest of all conflicts in Galatia, when through Jewish opposition and misrepresentations whole fabric of truth was in danger, and when integrity of Gospel depended principally on him, he stood firm, giving "place by subjection, no, not for an hour; that the truth of the Gospel might continue" (Gal. 2:5);
   d. Ah, there is nothing like Gospel of Christ to make man resolute, bold, firm, manly; for Christian is real man, whole man, man at his best;
   e. Man is not less man, but more manly when he belongs to Christ, who brings out his true self, his noblest powers, his highest possibilities; yes, true manhood — and womanhood — is possible only in Christ; in Him we are no drivelling sentimentalists, no poor, flabby species, no spineless jellyfish, but men and women — of integrity and vigor, of thoroughgoing action and life, of character.

Salvation and Character lead up to the topstone of the edifice of life —

III. Service

Here we see complete design of great Architect; it also is twofold:

1. *Work* — "to make thee a minister" (v. 16)
   a. This is God's purpose and object with us, for His ends are always practical and for benefit and blessing of others; He comes to men, not that they may have happiness, ease, comfort, success, though often included in His Providence, but not as chief and ultimate object, only means to end, which is service, work;
   b. Why was Abraham called by God from his far-off home? He would probably have lived contentedly at Ur of Chaldees; Why was Moses appointed leader of Israel? He would have been excellently well off at Pharaoh's court or at ease with Jethro's flock;
   c. Why was Jacob made recipient of birthright? He would have been more comfortable in many respects with younger son's portion; Why was Samuel appointed Eli's successor? It would have been easier for him to live at home with his family, playing as boy and growing up to quiet secular life;
   d. Soldier in war, sailor in storm, man in business do not think of ease, comfort, happiness; they think of duty, service, work;
   e. Same is true of nations: Why are Britain and America blessed today in way that is not true of Hottentots, for instance? Latter probably more comfortable, contented, and at ease;
   f. Object of all God's blessings is their use in blessing others and in doing His will, and is why life of ministry is noblest form (cf. Matt. 20:28; Mark 10:44); Paul's favorite designation of himself was that of servant or slave of Christ, for he knew there was nothing nobler, nothing higher than work;
   g. God help those who, like lilies of field, toil not, neither do they spin, whoever and wherever they may be; for greatest happiness is found in greatest unselfishness, in

blessing those near us, in doing at once duty close at hand, and in being in only true sense of word servant of Jesus Christ.

But another phase of God's service must also be noted:

2. *Testimony* — "to make thee . . . a witness" (v. 16)
   a. Not only is there to be actual work by which to bless others, but by means of that work and our life generally there is to be testimony on behalf of Christ;
   b. Our Lord's miracles were in themselves beneficient and helpful, and at same time were signs and testimonies to Himself as Saviour and Messiah; it is this to which He referred in familiar words of Matt. 5:16: "Let your light so shine before men" (there is the work) "that they may see your good works, and glorify your Father which is in heaven" (there is the testimony); and what is this testimony?
      (1) It is testimony to Christ and what He has been and is to us — "these things which thou hast seen";
         (a) It means that our life, having come into contact with Christ, will show influence of this in every possible way and at all times;
         (b) Christ is to be manifested and magnified in us, and our lives are to become living epistles of His (cf. 2 Cor. 3:3);
         (c) This testimony was to be part and parcel of Paul's character; when he testified he had seen Christ and Christ had changed him, and his hearers denied it, he could say, Deny my testimony and you deny my character; to say this is dream or invention on my part is to say I, Paul, lie and do not the truth;
         (d) Mark words "these things which thou hast seen" — not what imagined, not what invented, but what seen; yes, it has to do with fact;
         (e) Ah, this is sort of testimony that tells, that pledges whole character, and is what Christ calls His followers to bear; so to testify to reality and

fellowship, holiness and love of Christ that men dare not deny it without denying truth of one who testifies.

But this testimony goes further:

(2) It looks ahead — "those things in the which I will appear unto thee"

   (a) Christianity is a growing revelation; to every believer Christ says, "I have yet many things to say unto you, but ye cannot bear them now" (John 16:12);

   (b) Yes, Gospel is expanding future, enlarging experience, constant growth; and things yet to come will not be new in sense of unknown and unrevealed, but of progressive development and fruitfulness;

   (c) As every acorn contains germ of oak tree, yet in oak is nothing new that was not in germ in acorn, so is it with Christian — it is "this same Jesus" (1:11) but, growing in Him, learning more of Him, receiving more of Him, having fuller life, more wisdom, more love, more truth, more holiness;

   (d) He comes each day and imparts new grace and power and yet, at same time, He is always appearing to us and saying, "Thou shalt see greater things than these" (John 1:50).

Ah, there is positively nothing to compare with Christian life in power and in fulness. It starts with salvation through redemption wrought by a personal Christ; it goes on to character which it endows with truth and power; and then it leads to work, to testimony of life and lip, and to constant promise of increasing growth and enlarging capacity. Where shall we find another experience that can so minister to and supply every part of our complex nature, satisfy every craving, and equip us for every duty, every emergency?

Conclusion

1. *What was St. Paul's response to all this?*

"Wherefore," he said, "I was not disobedient unto the heavenly vision" (v. 19, A.S.V.):

a. There and then he yielded to God his whole life;
b. There and then he commenced that life of character and conduct, testimony and service, which stamps him as one of the world's greatest;
c. There and then he launched upon that experience which was to be no spasmodic effort, no interrupted flow, but a perpetually increasing and powerful stream of blessing for God and for man.

2. *And what is to be our response?*

God is asking every heart this question. "The Father seeketh such" (John 4:24); "The Son of man is come to seek and to save that which was lost" (Luke 19:10) in order to use our lives as He did St. Paul's:

a. He longs for each life, for He knows, if we do not, that He alone can use it to its utmost capacity;
b. And do we not long that our lives may be so used, that we may be all that we can be for God, and for good, and for the truth?

Then let us yield to Him now, and allow Him to enter our hearts and reveal Himself as our Saviour and our Lord. Then He will cleanse and energize, sustain and possess our whole life for Himself. This is what we want if we are to bear a testimony worth hearing and to lead a full-orbed Christian life with every faculty surrendered, with every avenue open towards God. And thus, with an enlarging capacity, an increasing strength, a growing wisdom, a widening sympathy, a deepening influence, and an abiding blessing, we shall go on from glory to glory until we reach the upper sphere for still further, untold possibilities through eternity, to the power and glory of God. So God give us all the fulness of life now for Christ's sake!

Study No. 122 — The Gospel in Paul's Commission

ACTS 26:18

FROM ALMOST the moment of his conversion Paul began to proclaim the truth of the Gospel; and at the close of his long life he urged Timothy to "preach the Word" (2 Tim. 4:2). In between, he used every opportunity, as here, quoting from his Divinely given commission. In these words lie the substance and purpose of it all; and they are a test for the ministry, for the Church, as to how far the Lord's people are true to their calling. Contained in this verse is practically the whole Gospel of Christ.

I. Illumination — "To open their eyes"

1. *Conviction of Sin*
   a. Sin leads to blindness as to spiritual condition;
   Illus.: Certain burrowing animals, such as moles, spend lives underground and therefore have very limited sight; other forms, such as crustacea in lakes in Mammoth Caves of Kentucky, apparently endowed with perfect eyes, but perfect in front only; behind is useless optic nerve — "eyes have they, but they see not" (Psa. 115:5, 8);
   b. Self-deception regarding sin another form of blindness;
   c. Thus, all need eyes opened as first part of work of repentance — cf. prophecy re John the Baptist (Isa. 40:5; 52:10; Luke 3:6);
   d. How? By Word (light — cf. Psa. 119:105, 130; Prov. 6:23); and by Holy Spirit (Revealer — cf. John 16:13-15; 1 Cor. 2:10-14).
2. *Revelation of Truth*
   a. Opening of eyes shows Gospel not superstition that tells adherents to close their eyes; Christianity says rather, Stand up! Open your eyes! Look around!

b. No blind Christians — or rather, in proportion as they are blind, they are not fully Christian;
Illus.: We read of churches with "dim, religious light" — no, if dim, not religious, and if truly religious, not dim!

c. Christian only true rationalist — in sense of superiority of reason and knowledge over sensory perceptions;
N.B. Contra, Renan, who said: "I dread for humanity the day when knowledge shall have penetrated all its strata" — i.e., humanity is happier ignorant!

d. Gospel not so — Christ opens eyes to ideas, visions, possessions; e.g., Bible new book to enlightened Christian — if "dry," eyes not opened, for "the secret of the Lord is with them that fear Him; and he will show them His covenant" (Psa. 25:14).

II. Conversion — "to turn them from darkness to light, and from the power of Satan unto God."

1. *Turning to New Element and Proper Sphere* — "from darkness to light"
   a. Without Christ, man in wrong place and direction;
   b. Intended to be in light as proper sphere — as bird in air, fish in sea, ship on water — in harmony with environment;
   c. But sin came, and turned man from light to darkness;
   d. Gospel restores: understanding to light of truth; heart to light of love; conscience to light of holiness; will to light of life — "for ye were sometimes darkness, but now are ye light in the Lord: walk as children of light . . . Christ shall give thee light" (Eph. 5:8, 14).

2. *Turning to True Master and New Government* — "from the power of Satan unto God"
   a. Sin brought bondage — not independence, as first man and woman hoped;
   b. Sin caused slavery — service of self and of Satan instead of service of God, "whose service is perfect freedom" (Prayer Book);
   c. Gospel delivers from power of Satan because Christ stronger than he (cf. Luke 11:20-22).

III. Redemption — "that they may receive forgiveness of sins, and inheritance among them which are sanctified."

1. *Forgiveness* — "receive forgiveness of sins"
   a. Not forgetfulness by man, lulling himself to sleep as to sin, but "forthgiving," or giving up by God of claim to requital (Webster) on grounds of Christ's sacrifice; then follows actual forgetfulness of sin by Him (cf. Isa. 43:25; Jer. 31:34; also Isa. 38:17; 43:22);
   b. Receiving indicates gift, free, full, personal, obtainable, eternal.

2. *Holiness* — "them which are sanctified"
   a. After forgiveness, or justification (cf. 13:39), comes holiness, or sanctification (cf. 1 Thess. 5:23);
   b. This means separation, dedication, and purification.

3. *Fellowship* — "among them"
   a. Then comes true brotherhood in Christ — not mere "Fatherhood of God and brotherhood of man," phrase so often misapplied;
   b. This the only true socialism — Christian sociableness and fellowship (cf. 2:42-47), because belonging to same family.

4. *Glory* — "inheritance"
   a. Present possession leading to future fulfilment;
   b. Word "heir" in Scripture always actual possessor (e.g., Gal. 4:7); cf. "inheritor" in Anglican Catechism.

Conclusion

Thus we see available a new heart, life, character, position, new privileges and hopes and, at the close, abundance of entrance into the Father's house. But how may these be made ours?

1. *"By Faith"*
   a. Faith is trust, confidence, acceptance;
   b. Eye which sees, will which turns, hand which receives, heart which hopes — all depend on faith.

2. *"In Me"*
   a. There is involved a Person, not things, or even truth;

b. So trust must also be personal — faith in the finished work of Christ.

Then will illumination, conversion, redemption be ours, now and forever.

Study No. 123 — What Is Sin? (A Word Study)

ACTS 26:18

Of the terrible fact of sin it may be truly said that familiarity breeds indifference. There is scarcely a lesson more definitely and constantly needed today than that of "the exceeding sinfulness of sin." How shall we be led to realize what sin is? By a constant recurrence to and use of the Divine standard, the Word of God. By it alone can we detect all kinds and degrees of deflection from righteousness. We may consider, then, a few of the Bible words for sin which reveal the manifold aspect of it, and through them see the nature and extent of its hideousness in the sight of God. The following study, based on eminent Greek authorities, may also awaken in us the desire for a better relationship with God and man, with ourselves and all creation.

1. *Sin is Failure.*
   a. As used by St. Paul in this verse, it means missing the true mark or aim of life, coming "short of the glory of God" (Rom. 3:23);
   b. This word is twofold in aspect, for failure characterizes both our inward state (cf. Rom. 6:1), and our outward act (cf. Mark 3:28);
   c. This thought of failure is most frequent of all references in N.T. to sin; in light of Gen. 2 and 3, it is not surprising.
2. *Sin is Ungodliness.*
   a. This is positive irreligion (cf. Rom. 1:18), refusal to render to God worship due Him;
   b. It also is in inward condition and outward conduct (latter form of word in Septuagint).

3. *Sin is Lawlessness.*
   a. This denotes being without law (cf. 1 John 3:4), and against law (cf. 2 Pet. 2:16), in sense of wilfully living contrary to known regulation; deliberate violation of law of our being;
   b. It also is twofold in aspect (as in Septuagint), affecting nature and action.
4. *Sin is Unrighteousness.*
   a. That which is not right, not just, violation of justice and equity, deflection from absolute standard;
   b. This is in heart (cf. Rom. 1:18), and in act (cf. 18:14).
5. *Sin is Heedlessness.*
   a. Hearing imperfectly or amiss, failing to hear at all, and all this wilfully and deliberately (cf. Rom. 5:19);
   b. Unwillingness to heed, resulting in disobedience.
6. *Sin is Transgression.*
   a. Crossing forbidden line, and trespassing on property not our own (cf. Rom. 2:23);
   b. Therefore, going beyond defined limits set by God's law.
7. *Sin is Lapse.*
   a. This is fall from way when we ought to be standing or walking thereon (cf. Matt. 6:14);
   b. Even willing fall, when we could remain upright on path of God's will.
8. *Sin is Ignorance.*
   a. This is want of knowledge when we might and should have known (cf. Heb. 9:7);
   b. Oversight that could have been avoided, therefore culpable.
9. *Sin is Loss.*
   a. This is diminishing of fulness due (cf. Rom. 11:12; 1 Cor. 6:7);
   b. Therefore, loss of that which is God's gift.
10. *Sin is Debt.*
   a. Because we owe God our whole life (cf. Matt. 6:12);
   b. As Peter said, "We ought to obey God" (5:29), obligation that makes sin debt which must be paid.

11. *Sin is Worthlessness.*
    a. Nothing whatever of value or use in it (cf. John 3:20);
    b. As Paul might ask, "What fruit had ye?" (Rom. 6:21) — i.e., by no possibility can sin be rendered truly profitable.
12. *Sin is Impurity.*
    a. It makes soul unclean with its polluting and defiling power (cf. Rom. 1:24);
    b. It renders both morally and spiritually impure (cf. 1 Tim. 1:9; 2 Tim. 3:2).
13. *Sin is Depravity.*
    a. There are three words with this connotation in one verse (cf. Rom. 1:29):
       (1) Wickedness of heart, or maliciousness;
       (2) Enmity of spirit, or malignity;
       (3) Baseness of deed, or malefaction;
    b. Last of these has root indicating man will not hesitate to toil uninterruptedly in evil — "with both hands earnestly" (Mic. 7:3).

Conclusion

These are only some of the "mournfully numerous" words, as Archbishop Trench called them, which reveal sin, but they emphasize the following important facts:

1. The more these words are studied the more evident will be the conviction that sin is indeed "this abominable thing" that God hates (Jer. 44:4);
2. It is a matter of common experience that superficial views of sin carry with them practical indifference to the atonement our Lord made for it (cf. Rom. 7:11; Heb. 9:26-29);
3. It is only as we realize the fact and extent of the plague of our own hearts (cf. 1 Kings 8:38) that we may not only be conscious of our deep need of salvation, but also gratefully and joyfully and humbly accept it (cf. Rom. 5:8-21).

Study No. 124 — Sanctification

ACTS 26:18

If we are asked the question, why did Jesus die, what is our answer? It may take various forms, such as, for us, for our sins, to atone for our sins, in our stead, for our justification. This is all true, but it is not all the truth. According to 2 Cor. 5:15, "He died . . . that they which live should . . . live . . . unto Him"; to Eph. 5:25, 26: "Christ . . . gave Himself . . . that He might sanctify"; to Tit. 2:13, 14: "Christ gave Himself . . . that He might . . . purify." These passages agree with what Paul is saying in our text, namely that Christ had sent him to the Gentiles that they might receive not only "forgiveness of sins," but also "inheritance among them which are sanctified." The blessed fact is that He died to bring us deliverance from three things: the penalty of sin (past); the power of sin (present); and the presence of sin (future). All three are found in such passages as Rom. 8:29, 30 and 1 Cor. 6:10, 11. They may be remembered by three prepositions: in Christ — for salvation; like Christ — for sanctification; with Christ — for eternity.

In 1 Thess. 4:3, Paul states that "this is the will of God, even your sanctification," and so, further on (5:23), he prays, "And the very God of peace sanctify you wholly." What, we may ask, constitutes this our "sanctified inheritance"?

I. The Meaning of Sanctification

It is familiar word — appears in Anglican Catechism: "I learn to believe . . . in God the Holy Ghost, who sanctifieth me, and all the elect people of God." It means two things:

1. *Consecration*
   - a. True relation to God — after pardon and redemption;

   b. Dedication to God — set apart as His possession — cf. priests of O.T.;
2. *Purification*
   a. True condition before God — ready for His use — cf. 2 Tim. 2:21 — "sanctified and meet";
   b. Indwelling presence of Christ by Holy Spirit — only way to influence fellow-men for God.

II. The Method of Sanctification

1. *The Divine Side*

   New nature is not achievement, but gift from Christ applied to our souls by Spirit of God:
   a. Christ made to us sanctification (cf. 1 Cor. 1:30);
   b. We are sanctified in Christ (cf. 1 Cor. 1:2).
2. *The Human Side*

   Gift comes to us —
   a. Through Word of God (cf. John 17:19; 2 Thess. 2:13);
   b. By faith in Christ (cf. 26:18):
      (1) Faith — act that receives justification;
      (2) Faith — attitude that accepts and maintains sanctification;

      N.B. Here, there often creeps in error: accepted by faith and maintained by fighting; pardoned by Saviour and purified by struggle. No! Christ has done it all — He both separates from evil and presents holy!

Conclusion

Thus, as there were four elements in conversion, so there are four elements in the Christian life: Christ — Spirit — Word — Faith. What is faith?

1. Faith is surrendering;
2. Faith is dedicating;
3. Faith is recognizing;
4. Faith is trusting;
5. Faith is claiming;
6. Faith is using;
7. Faith is obeying.

Study No. 125 — Resurrection Light

ACTS 26:23, A.S.V.

LONDON fogs are famous the world over for the suddenness with which they appear, enveloping all things and bringing danger and discomfort. But they disappear just as suddenly, and the morning after, everything is as usual.

On the first Good Friday, there was thick darkness, not only during the three hours while the Prince of Life hung on the cross, but also for all that day and the day after in the hearts of those who loved Him. Everything they had hoped for had come to an end, for His life on earth was over, and even the words He had spoken seemed vain. There was no hope — nothing but gloom — on the road to Emmaus, in the garden, and in the city, as Joseph, Nicodemus, the apostles and the women expected never to see their Master again. But after Christ's resurrection, what a different story! Suddenly there was light, there was joy, there was faith, and His followers never doubted again.

Today, there is often doubt, sorrow, uncertainty, with modern echoes of the Psalmist's quotation, "Who will show us any good?" (Psa. 4:6).

We have chosen to read our text in the American Standard Version because it is a more accurate translation: "Christ must suffer, and . . . first by the resurrection of the dead should proclaim light both to the people and to the Gentiles." In the light of the Resurrection three questions often asked in the gloom of present-day conditions are fully answered:

I. Can I Know God?

1. *Man has always needed to know God.*
   a. Job cried, "Oh that I knew where I might find Him!" (Job 3:23);

b. David declared, "As the hart panteth after the water brooks, so panteth my soul after Thee, O God" (Psa. 42:1);
c. Philip said, "Lord, shew us the Father, and it sufficeth us" (John 14:8).

2. *Man still needs to know God.*
a. All great thinkers admit Great First Cause, though not always calling Him God: e.g., Herbert Spencer, referring to Him as "the Infinite"; Matthew Arnold, with tendency to think of human life flowing, like stream, from its Source (God) to sea (Death);
b. But science has no comforting word for individual faced with problems of life;
c. Yet human heart craves Person — not, as in Christian Science, "Mind vs. Matter."

3. *Man can know God.*
a. Christ, His Son, and "image of the invisible God" (Col. 1:15), came making claim of Deity;
b. Claim established then by His resurrection — "declared to be the Son of God with power . . . by the resurrection from the dead" (Rom. 1:4);
c. Claim ratified now by Christian witness and fellowship (cf. 2:32);
Illus.: Every age needs Christ to reveal God; in India, Brahmin said, when he had first read Bible and admired contents, he wanted to know and serve God, but could not accept Christ; then tried to obey God's law, failed, and found, after all, he needed Christ.

Can I, then, know God? Yes, Christ reveals God in the light of the Resurrection.

II. Can I Get Rid of My Sin?

1. *Man has always needed to be rid of his sin.*
a. David prayed, "Wash me throughly from mine iniquity, and cleanse me from my sin" (Psa. 51:2);
b. Paul cried: "O wretched man that I am! who shall deliver me from the body of this death?" (Rom. 7:24).

2. *Man still needs to be rid of his sin.*

a. Guilt one thing that baffles, defeats, eludes;
b. There is no philosophy, no remedy for wicked heart: science, much-vaunted but weakest of all; in fiction, even imaginary hero such as George Eliot's Colonel Newcome is not completely perfect; poetry, even such as Kipling's "Recessional," can but plead:

For frantic boast and foolish word,
Thy mercy on Thy people, Lord!

3. *Man can be rid of his sin.*
   a. Christ came, speaking of His life as "a ransom for many" (Matt. 20:28) and of forgiveness (cf. Luke 5:24; 7:47), and Himself linked preaching of "repentance and remission of sins" with His rising "from the dead the third day" (Luke 24:46, 47);
   b. This was corroborated by St. Paul not only in our text, but in 13:37, 38: — "whom God raised again . . . through this man is preached unto you the forgiveness of sins"; in Rom. 4:25: — "raised again for our justification"; in Eph. 1:7: — "in whom we have redemption through his blood, the forgiveness of sins" and in v. 20, where we are told that God "raised him from the dead";
   c. Millions have received this forgiveness, with none lacking who asked for it.

Can I not, then, be rid of my sin? Yes, for Christ takes it away in the light of the Resurrection.

III. Can I Have Present Sufficiency and Future Security?

1. *Man has always longed for these.*
   a. Life staggers him — with its burdens (present) and fears (future);
   Illus.: Man in business, woman in home, young person in strange city;
   b. Death baffles him — when it takes loved ones, when it is his own turn; Job expressed eternal question — "If a man die, shall he live again?" (Job 14:14).
2. *Man still has these longings.*
   a. But he can get no outside help that will last, in spite of progress;

b. Science indicates only ruthlessness of nature and universality of death; society, because on his own level, will fail him.

3. *Man can find both sufficiency and security.*

a. Christ, "first begotten of the dead," said: "I am He that liveth . . . I am alive for evermore" (Rev. 1:5, 18); and He is Prophet, Priest, and King, whose resurrection illuminates past, present, and future, life and death;

b. Paul corroborates this by telling us "He ever liveth" (Heb. 7:25); so that Apostle can also state in Phil. 4:13, "I can do all things through Christ which strengtheneth me" (present); and, in (2 Tim. 1:12), "I . . . am persuaded that He is able to keep . . . against that day" (future); and urges us to "sorrow not, . . . if we believe that Jesus . . . rose again" (1 Thess. 4:13, 14).

Can I, then, know these truths experimentally? Yes, for Christ provides both sufficiency and security in the light of His Resurrection.

Conclusion

With these things in mind, we may be —

1. *Fearless against all opposition.*

A Christian need not be afraid — it is agnosticism that makes men cowardly and affords no permanent consolation.

2. *Satisfied in all circumstances.*

Are we longing, troubled, pressed, anxious? Hear the voice of Jesus: "I am the Resurrection and the Life" (John 11:28); "Go, and sin no more" (John 8:11).

Sursum corda! — Lift up your hearts! Yea, Lord, we lift them up unto Thee! And so, resting in the Reality of the Divine Presence, in the Redemption of the Atoning Sacrifice, in the Realization of Perpetual Power, in the Revelation of Future Glory, let us dwell in the light of Christ's Resurrection, until the day dawn and the shadows flee away!

Study No. 126 — The Voyage to Malta

ACTS 27:1-44

It is unknown how much time elapsed between the hearing before Agrippa (chap. 26) and the departure of Paul for Rome, but probably it was not long. The story of the voyage is unusually detailed and graphic, testifying to Luke's opinion of its importance in the Apostle's career. It is the most valuable document we of today possess concerning ancient seamanship; and it is also a striking illustration of the blend of natural and supernatural, Divine Providence and human struggle, that is so characteristic of life. This voyage was taken, of course, long before the invention of the compass or other recent instruments of navigation; and the vivid account of it, even though obviously written with the keenest interest in the sea, is the record of a landsman, not of a sailor, and is therefore popular, not technical. Yet its accuracy has been proven beyond question. The sparing use of the miraculous, and the necessity of taking ordinary precautions and deciding on ordinary procedures, add formidable weight to the truth of the story.

As a part of God's Word, this chapter is of special interest as showing how His promise that Paul should reach Rome (cf. 23:11) was fulfilled. There is here, as elsewhere, no warrant for supposing that the Scriptures recognize the element of chance, or luck. But there is a constant implication of what may rightly be called coincidence as part of the Providence of God. This is true even in passages like Luke 10:31 where the English word "chance" has been used in translating the original. Here there was a great crisis, and there was a great man to take full advantage of it, to the glory of God and to the furtherance of the Gospel.

This chapter, which brings the New Testament narrative well on its way westward into the modern European world, rewards detailed study with the aid of a map. The voyage it describes may be divided into five stages, with special attention given to the third, which has to do with the storm at sea:

I. The First Stage of the Voyage — The Start (vs. 1-8)

1. *From Caesarea to Sidon* (vs. 1-3)
   a. Resumption of "we" (v. 1), last seen in 21:18, shows Luke's presence (up to 28:16); and another companion was Aristarchus (cf. 19:23; 20:4; Col. 4:10; Philem. 10), a convert of Thessalonica whom Paul calls "fellow-laborer" and "fellow-prisoner";
   b. Centurion in charge was Julius, common name among Romans, and "Augustan band" (v. 1, A.S.V.), or cohort, probably refers to soldiers in some special relation to Emperor Augustus, like modern phrase, "King's Own Life Guards"; records of centurions in N. T. invariably refer to fine, upright men (cf. Mark 15:39; Luke 7:2-10; Acts 10:1-33), and Paul's influence on this one is evident;
   c. Adramyttium, seaport of Mysia (cf. 16:7), was important trading center near Troas (cf. 16:8, 11), and coastal ship from there was chosen so that party might find at some place of call vessel bound direct for Rome;
   d. Passage to Sidon (cf. Matt. 11:22; 15:21; Acts 12:30) would be about 80 miles, and Paul evidently found Christians there, as at Tyre nearby (cf. 21:3, 4); and Julius was courteous enough to give him permission to visit them though, of course, soldier would accompany him (cf. vs. 32, 42); it has been suggested that A.S.V. margin of v. 3 implies some special need of attention because of ill-health.
2. *From Sidon to Fair Havens* (vs. 4-8)
   a. Setting sail again, ship passed between island of Cyprus (cf. 13:4-12) and mainland "because the winds were contrary" (v. 4) — owing to opposing westerly winds they were dependent on currents and land breezes;
   b. At length they reached Myra in Lycia, from whence they

could get a ship sailing direct and carrying wheat (cf. v. 38), on which Italy depended, and centurion decided to take it;

c. With wind still contrary progress was slow and laborious, and it took "many days" (v. 7) to arrive opposite Cnidus, town at southwestern corner of Asia Minor;

d. Then, sheltered by coast of Crete (cf. 2:11), they reached island port of Fair Havens near Lasea, which still bears this name.

II. The Second Stage of the Journey — The Stay (vs. 9-12)

1. *The Right Advice* (vs. 9,10)

a. Owing to delay at Fair Havens, season dangerous to sailing (September to November) had commenced; fast mentioned was Day of Atonement (cf. Lev. 16:29-34), which fell towards end of September or beginning of October — perhaps Paul and fellow-travelers observed it on board, or else it is mentioned simply as note of time;

b. After about November 11 all navigation in open sea was suspended for five months, and Paul's observation and experience, obtained through his missionary journeyings and heightened by Divinely-given insight, suggested danger; so he told company of risks ahead for ship and crew, passengers and cargo.

2. *The Wrong Decision* (vs. 11, 12)

a. But it is not suprising that centurion favored counsel of trained sailors rather than that of Paul who, presumably, had no technical experience; and their advice was to leave less commodious Fair Havens for Phenice and "there to winter" (v. 11);

b. Phenice (or Phoenix, A.S.V.) now called Lutro, and said to be only safe harbor on south coast of Crete; faced north-east and south-east (cf. A.S.V. marg.), exact description of aspect of port today.

III. The Third Stage of the Voyage — The Storm (vs. 13-38)

1. *Extremity* (vs. 13-20)

a. Thinking all well because of gentle south wind, crew

weighed anchor and started west, again hugging coast of Crete (v. 13);

b. Had not gone far before tempestuous wind beat down from mountains of island: "Euroclydon" (v. 14), or "Euraquilo" (A.S.V.), comes from *euros,* east wind, and *aquilo,* northward, and indicates "nor'-easter";

c. Ship could not face it and sailors were soon utterly powerless before it, so "let her drive" (v. 15); and description of circumstances (vs. 16-20) is remarkably detailed;

d. Clauda was small island about 23 miles south of Phenice, and shelter of its coast enabled crew, with prisoners and others helping, to haul in boat, or dory, which, being towed, had become rapidly waterlogged; and then they had to pass ropes under ship to prevent boards bursting apart;

e. Syrtis (cf. v. 17, A.S.V.), was dangerous quicksand off north shore of Africa, and sailors were afraid wind would drive them onto it, so they lowered all sail except, doubtless, what was needed to keep ship's head to wind;

f. Thus they drifted (v. 17), and "labored exceedingly with the storm" (v. 18, A.S.V.), continuation of which necessitated sacrifice of "freight" (perhaps cargo on deck rather than in hold — cf. v. 38), and ship's furnishings — every heavy thing that could be spared (vs. 18, 19);

g. With no mariner's compass in existence, they had to depend entirely on observations of heavens; thus, it is no wonder that, with sun and stars hidden by clouds "for many days" (v. 20), crew lost all hope of gaining safety.

2. *Exhortation* (vs. 21-26)

a. Absence of food was doubtless due to difficulty of preparation during storm, with everyone occupied and anxious; but there was one passenger who, in spite of "long abstinence" (v. 21), had not lost heart or head;

b. Paul, standing forth, did not hesitate to remind crew of his rejected counsel, landsman though he was; and yet also bade them take courage, because he had been assured by God of protection, with no loss of life but only of the ship;

c. This was splendid confession of faith and fine testimony to the true God; Paul had been praying (vs. 23, 24), and had been granted as answer lives of all on board;

d. So they were to "be of good cheer" (v. 25) because Paul believed God would be true to His word; however, they were to be "cast upon a certain island" (v. 26) — prediction at once real and vague, for even Paul was told only what was necessary at moment and no more (cf. v. 39; 28:1).

3. *Effort* (vs. 27-32)

a. Storm was still raging and 14 days (v. 27) had passed since ship had left Fair Havens; it was drifting in Sea of Adria, that part of Mediterranean lying between Malta and Crete — not Adriatic Sea, or Gulf of Venice, as now understood; term Adria afterwards became applied to entire eastern part of Mediterranean; from Clauda to Malta is about 480 miles;

b. Now experience of sailors led them to surmise nearness of land and, for fear of shallow water, they let down sounding lead and found they were in about 120 feet (6 feet to 1 fathom) of water; then tried again and found 90 feet so, being afraid of rocks, threw out four anchors from stern, and waited and wished for daybreak;

c. Anchors usually let down from bow, but those from stern, in this case, helped keep vessel facing shoreward for landing; but some cowardly members of crew, hoping to save own lives and leave rest to take their chances, pretended to cast anchors fore as well as aft while they let boat down into sea;

d. But Paul recognizing real purpose, told centurion and his men that their preservation depended on sailors remaining on board, where they were greatly needed for action still to be taken; and it is significant that Paul was now believed, and soldiers thwarted cowardly sailors by letting boat go.

4. *Encouragement* (vs. 33-38)
   a. Once again it was Paul's turn, and he begged them all to take food after long ordeal; for, though doubtless they had had some food during the two weeks (cf. v. 27), there had been no proper meals, and physical health was involved (vs. 33:34);
   b. Suiting action to word, he himself took food, but not without having first testified again to God (v. 35); for, like every godly Jew, including his Lord (cf. Matt. 15:36; Luke 22:17, 19; 24:30), Paul asked blessing on food and thanked Giver of "every good gift" (Jas. 1:17); simple and unostentatious method of witness for all Christians, in public or private;
   c. His cheerfulness proved contagious to all in ship, and they were influenced to eat too (v. 36); total on board was 276 (v. 37), probably average number, since there is record of another ship about that time with 600 passengers and crew;
   d. After ample meal, they abandoned cargo of wheat to lighten ship and were ready for anticipated rescue (v. 38).

IV. The Fourth Stage of the Voyage — The Shipwreck (vs. 39-41)

1. *The Attempted Landing* (vs. 39, 40)
   a. Next morning, crew could see land not far away, but did not recognize it, though trying several times to identify it (vs. 39, Gr.); for even sailors who might have been at Malta before would be accustomed to landing at Valetta, some distance away;
   b. But as they continued to examine and test they perceived bay (now called St. Paul's Bay) with beach suitable for landing, and after careful deliberation they decided to make attempt there;
   c. So, loosening ropes that held anchors (cf. v. 29) to ship, they also unfastened bands of its rudders and hoisted its foresail in order to catch wind and get vessel as near as possible to land; ancient ships said to have had two paddle-rudders, one on either side — these had been

drawn in and fastened while vessel was at anchor; now they were loosened and put in proper place for steering (v. 40).

2. *The Unexpected Result* (v. 41)
   a. Suddenly they found themselves in place where "two seas met," probably narrow promontory with sea running on either side and meeting at tip — suitable place in calm weather on which to run ship aground;
   b. But now, as they did so and bow became fixed, stern, being loose, was exposed to "violence of the waves" and began to break up.

V. The Fifth Stage of the Voyage — The Safety (vs. 42-44)

1. *Death Thwarted* (vs. 42, 43)
   a. Band of soldiers responsible for prisoners (cf. 12:19; 16:27) wished to kill charges lest they should escape;
   b. But centurion prevented this and gave orders that all who could swim should jump overboard; Julius was under obligation to Paul, and this was great opportunity to acknowledge it.
2. *Life Assured* (v. 44)
   a. Swimmers landing first (vs. 43, A.S.V). would be able to help those who, not able to swim, reached shore on planks and other floating pieces from ship;
   b. Thus God's promise and Paul's twofold prediction (cf. vs. 22-26) were fulfilled; ship was wrecked, but with no loss of life, since all escaped safe to land.

Conclusion

This dramatic story is a splendid illustration of God's gracious attitude towards His servants resulting in mighty action on their behalf:

1. *God Protecting*
   a. In accordance with Divine assurance, all came safely to land;
   b. God always fulfills His Word — His promises are never broken (cf. Psa. 34:22).
2. *God Providing*

a. Shipwrecked people had all they needed in order to be saved, if they would but believe and obey;
b. God never fails to take care of His people — having saved their souls He supplies their needs (cf. Phil. 4:19).

Can we not, therefore, like St. Paul of old, declare: "I believe God!"?

Study No. 127 — Paul, Leader of Men

ACTS 27:1-44

There are times when a sudden change in circumstances, especially one involving danger, tends to throw men off balance. It was not so with St. Paul; he was always consistent and his life had a solidity that made him at all times true to God as the compass needle is true to the magnetic pole. The voyage to Rome was merely an epitome of his entire life. The Lord had told him that he should be a "witness" (23:11; 26:16), and certainly he fulfilled this prediction on that ship, for perhaps never did he bear a more remarkable testimony.

It has often been said that Paul was the real commander of the ship, for both sea-captain and centurion deferred to him as he first appealed directly to those on board and then dominated the scene of their operations.

I. What Paul Did

1. *He Exerted Direct Influence.*
   a. Confidence inspired (vs. 22, 25, 33-36) — ship was world in minature and his natural leadership came to fore;
   b. Effort made (vs. 19, 35) — doubtless Paul was listened to because he had helped with others in time of distress; when we practise what we preach our words are more likely to be heeded;
   c. Counsel given (vs. 10, 31-34) — physical, mental, moral, and spiritual needs all emphasized.

Equally striking was the way in which —

2. *He Exerted Indirect Influence.*
   a. Impressed centurion (vs. 3, 31, 43), for Roman officer showed distinct confidence in Paul's character;
   b. Influenced captain (v. 10), or would not, as prisoner, have dared to venture his advice;
   c. Preserved fellow-prisoners (vs. 42, 43), so that he was blessing to them as well as to crew.

II. What Paul Showed

1. *Calmness*
   a. Passive quality, as with self-control he did not "lose his head";
   b. Exerted courtesy, consideration, and tact towards all.
2. *Courage*
   a. Active quality, both in face of danger and before fellows;
   b. Stemmed from self-forgetfulness and faithfulness to God, and showed itself in cheerfulness and sympathy with others.
3. *Confidence*
   a. Both active and passive quality, for it came from complete trust in God and His pledge; and yet was —
   b. Revealed in alertness, insight, and foresight.

All of this indicated Paul's powerful personality.

III. What Paul Was

1. *Possessed by God* — "whose I am" (v. 23)
   a. Everything derived from his relationship to God;
   b. Had committed himself and his way to God.
2. *Prepared by God* — "whom I serve" (v. 23)
   a. Paul was servant as well as son;
   b. Gave testimony to God in all he said and did.
3. *Protected by God* — "no loss of life" (v. 22, A.S.V.)
   a. Had prayed to God and had been heard — "granted" (v. 24, A.S.V.);
   b. Having trusted God, he was certain rescue would be brought to pass, an so inward calm inspired cheerfulness in others.

Conclusion

This is the kind of Christian leader needed today; and the secret of Paul's life should be and may be the secret of ours. Can we say, "Whose I am"? We who are Christians belong to God —

1. *By Purchase* — Christ's death;
2. *By Conquest* — Christ's grace; and —
3. *By Self-surrender* — our consecration.

If, therefore, we can truthfully say, "I am the Lord's" (cf. Isa. 44:5), we shall find in the declaration the guarantee of pardon, peace, power, perception, progress, purity, and permanence in Christian experience.

Study No. 128 — Paul, Man of God

ACTS 27:22-25

The best description that can be given of any man of Christian character is to call him a "man of God." This is to say not only that he is "every inch a man" — in stature, intellect, feeling, bearing, conscience, will, character — but also that he is God's man, with every manly power His and for Him. The phrase is frequent in the Old Testament, where it is used of Moses and of all the prophets save Daniel, those who stood before God and spoke for Him — not foretelling primarily, but forth-telling, witnessing. In the New Testament the phrase is used of only one man, Timothy (cf. 1 Tim. 6:11; and by implication in 2 Tim. 3:17). This was a young man, apparently weak and nervous, and yet the grand title was given him by one who was himself the finest specimen of a "man of God." But Paul's own designation is at least implied in our text when he, speaking of God, adds "whose I am." Yes, Paul was God's man, a man of God if ever anyone was, and the circumstances in which he said these words are a grand illustration both of his right to the title and of the noble characteristics that support it.

I. His Position (v. 23)

1. *Owned by God* — "whose I am"
   This is primary; and how and why was Paul God's?
   a. He was purchased:
      (1) Once slave, in bondage to sin, he was set free (cf. Gal. 4:31; 5:1);
      (2) He was "bought with a price" (1 Cor. 6:20; 7:23), so he belonged to Christ who paid it;
   b. He was conquered:
      (1) Not only bought, but to be used, as shown by instant offer of himself (cf. 22:10);
      (2) On Damascus road, had met Master and been won by Him for His service;
   c. He was surrendered:
      (1) Possession by God realized — "I *am*" — present as well as future;
      (2) Knew it because he had freely yielded and acknowledged God's claim on his life.

   This, therefore, is first step to being "man of God": God's claim realized and accepted, with recognition that believer is trustee not owner, steward not master; and that no service is of any use otherwise.
2. *Accepted by God* — "whom I serve"
   Attitude not unwilling or mechanical, but voluntary and personal:
   a. Submission
      (1) As servant, as though with well-known motto, "*Ich dien*!" — "I serve!";
      (2) As son, who says "Even so" to all God's commands;
   b. Loyalty
      (1) One true to God, with heart right;
      (2) One to whom God's will is mainspring of life;
   c. Work
      (1) Paul did indeed work, early and late, with heart and soul;
      (2) This labor involved pure conscience, deep reverence, true humility.

Yes, service follows ownership as necessary consequence: never before, but certainly after.

II. His Privilege (vs. 23, 24)

1. *Preserved by God* — "there stood by me this night the angel of God" (v. 23)
   This manifestation was result of God's ownership of Paul:
   a. Safety:
      (1) Perfect, absolute;
      (2) Continual, eternal;
   b. Strength:
      (1) In difficulty, for overcoming;
      (2) In duty, for accomplishing;
   c. Support:
      (1) In sorrow, and in opposition;
      (2) Not free of trouble, but always to be ready for service.
   Angel of God may not be visible, yet preservation still real, for nothing can separate believing soul from God.
2. *Instructed by God* — "the angel of God . . . saying—" (vs. 23, 24)
   a. Courage — "fear not" — in time of need God always there;
   b. Guidance — "thou must be brought—" — experience like maze, but clue in God's hands (cf. Psa. 25:14);
   c. Blessing — "lo, God hath given—" — means of help to others, for believer's faithfulness always Divinely used.

III. His Power (vs. 22, 25)

1. *Used by God* — "wherefore—" (v. 25)
   a. Hope — "no loss of any man's life" (v. 22)
      (1) Ordinary landsman better silent on board ship in fair weather, but day may come when sailors thankful for cheering word; so Paul here, on subject other than his own;
      (2) So now — on vessel of life, in fair weather Christianity may be called fanatical piety; yet in dark days, with all hope lost, philosophers stand back and believing, praying man comes forward;

(3) So Paul in this scene — began as prisoner, but now master of situation; cf. our age — progress, yet no real hope or joy except through message about Christ entrusted to His followers.

b. Encouragement — "be of good cheer" (vs. 22, 25)

(1) Words uttered twice — Paul received good cheer first, and now passes it on;

(2) Some men seem naturally bright and happy, but only Christian really so, supernaturally so, for only Christianity says "Good cheer!"

c. Truth — "loss . . . of the ship" (v. 22)

(1) Paul faithfully reported dark side of message, and so must God's servants today;

(2) When he preached, men listened; and so they will to faithful witness today.

2. *Equipped by God*

a. Revelation

(1) Here was his strength — God had spoken — "I exhort you . . . for—" (v. 22);

(2) No uncertainty, nor mere inner voice, but definite message from Divine messenger — not "I suppose," but "I believe" (v. 25);

b. Faithfulness

(1) So real was God to Paul that he pledged Him to these men;

(2) "It shall be" (v. 25) — not may be or might be;

c. Trust

(1) "I believe God" (v. 25) was sheet anchor to his soul, as real as anchors holding ship;

(2) This is power of any true Christian, and men like Paul are greatly needed today.

Conclusion

What does it mean to be able to say, "I am the Lord's" (Isa. 44:5)?

1. It means surrender for pardon, peace, and power;
2. It means Holy Spirit filling (cf. Isa. 44:23);
3. It is the secret of joy, strength, wisdom, and satisfaction.

God must *own* before He can *use!* Do we admit His claim? Are we thus ready for His possession and His service? Can we in any sense lay claim to the transcendent title, "Man of God"?

Study No. 129 — Good Cheer

ACTS 27:25

If you have ever stood on a rocky seashore in windy weather you have probably noticed some outstanding rock or cliff against whose base the waves are dashing angrily. Its sides are enveloped in spray and its top is covered with mist. Yet every force of wind or water spends itself in vain; the rock stands undaunted and immovable amid the surrounding turmoil. It is a silent witness to the value of resistence to alien forces and, if it happens to have a lighthouse on its summit, it becomes as well a means of safe guidance to voyagers on the stormy sea.

Such a rock was St. Paul amid both tangible and intangible changes and chances of that memorable voyage to Rome. In the midst of an angry sea, and surrounded by fearful, despairing souls, he was all that a lighthouse means of stability, safety, and blessing. As we consider carefully his magnificent confidence and strength, it will be well for us and for our fellow-voyagers on the sea of life if we can find out his secret.

I. The Apostle's Attitude

We find herein three elements:

1. *Inward Calm Possessed*
   a. Chapter shows terrible conditions on board ship — for three days, storm-tossed, drifting; damp and cold from spray sweeping from stem to stern, perhaps no preparation of food possible — utensils probably swept away and some provisions sodden and spoiled; no wonder there was gloomy apathy, with hope growing less and less every

hour as those on board drifted to awful and, it seemed, certain death;

b. Yet, at least one passenger perfectly calm, one probably weakest in health and therefore greatest sufferer of all; in that darkness his soul was enlightened and in that upheaval of waters he was at peace; in spite of terrors of mind and heart around him, Paul was self-possessed, for no storm could affect that inward calm nor terrors daunt his trusting soul; and this led to —

2. *Invincible Courage Manifested*

a. To have peace was to show it in courage, and to possess calm was not to keep it selfishly hid but to share it, which he quickly did; he had entered ship as prisoner, now he ends voyage as virtual captain; he embarked humbly, he stands now foursquare in confidence;

b. While rest are abandoning themselves to despair, he steps forth and shows his wisdom and courage in spite of, nay, because of, all that seemed against him; and as storm proceeded and all hope was taken away Paul the Apostle was "strong and very courageous" (cf. Josh. 1:7). Then notice result —

3. *Inspiring Cheerfulness Urged*

a. Did he show this great courage to laugh others to scorn for their terror and to boast before them all? No, indeed, it was that he might stimulate rest to same courage; for effect of one glad soul will influence whole family, one life in right key will make it easier for others to join in song; and for this purpose Paul cheered disheartened shipmates;

b. Further, there is actual persuasion in strong conviction, and so amid misery and despair on that terrible day Paul the Apostle stands strong in the urging of inspiring cheerfulness, of "good cheer."

This, then, is our picture of Paul. May we not endeavor to show same attitude? We may not have to pass through same form of trial, but surely there are times of trouble that would be wonderfully brightened if only we were like St. Paul. So we may be, if we take to heart —

II. The Apostle's Secret

He gives us full explanation of his "good cheer," and may God enable us to enter fully into it:

1. *Clear Revelation from God*

   Paul says an angel of God stood by him that night:

   a. No inward hope or subjective experience, it was an outward, objective revelation that gave him that splendid spirit of courage and cheer — only ground of his confidence real manifestation from God to his soul, rock on which he rested; had had experience of voyages before, and doubtless reasoned from that in present case, but all this was of no real use as foundation for hope — had to be something outside himself, authentic revelation from God:

   b. And so it is always — our conscience, our experience, our reasoning are valuable in their place, but they are not rock on which to build; that rock must be certainty of God, and though we have not actual vision of angel we have clear revelation of God in Christ, who has indeed stood near us;

   c. His Word is basis of all life and confidence, voice from heaven, and we must be content with nothing less; man may say, I think, I expect, I have impression, I would make suggestion — but we say, Never mind your uncertainties — what saith the Lord?

   d. It is only in revelation of God that soul can keep courage and good cheer when in danger; there on that ship the one calm man was the man of God; for even if unbeliever does show mastery of self he cannot permanently cheer anyone else, for he has no objective truth, no definite hope, no Divine message, no true confidence; but Christian can not only be calm but reveal secret to others, and above storms of temptation and trouble see God and hear Him say all is well; yes, here is the rock — God *is,* and God has all power.

This is one part of secret of calm in every storm; but there is something else:

2. *Conscious Relationship to God*
   a. Not only had God spoken to Paul, but Apostle had realized there was tie between them that could not be severed, for it would endure through all storms of life:
      (1) "Whose I am" — he belonged to God, but to show this was not simply in general sense, that necessary sense in which all men belong to God, he added —
      (2) "Whom I serve" — he had freely and gladly given himself to service of his Master; all in that ship were God's by creation, but Paul was particularly His, having been born again (cf. 1 Cor. 15:8), and having become Christ's "slave" (cf. Phil. 1:1, Gr.); and so revelation was followed by redemption and consciousness of special relationship to God as His son and servant;
   b. Here is secret of confidence and courage — we belong to God and He belongs to us:
      (1) Not only by general revelation of God to man through His Word or through Nature, but by special revelation to us as His children by second birth and as His servants through redemption;
      (2) Because of this we are confident that "He which hath begun a good work" in us "will perform it" (Phil. 1:6) — complete it;
      (3) Not only so, but we are persuaded that relationship between us and God is such that He will indeed "perfect that which concerneth us" (Psa. 138:8) and fulfil in us all His purpose.

And so this is second secret of courage and cheer: God is; God has spoken; I am His child and servant; He owns me; He keeps me. Yet again see —

3. *Cordial Response to God*
   a. God had spoken, and Paul had replied, "I believe God" (v. 25); *there* was "the Apostle's Creed," short and to the point;

b. And mark circumstances — creed was professed not in church or schoolroom, but in darkness, in extremity when there appeared to be no God, so that Paul risked everything on it; this was indeed grand time to profess one's belief — with timbers creaking, waves dashing, ship drifting — and not merely when sun shines, sky clear, sea like glass, air balmy;
c. It was in storm Paul responded to God's revelation and pledged God to do all He had promised, for himself and the rest; and so he was able to "be of good cheer";
d. This is necessary consequence of all Divine revelation and only real, effective means of confidence — in our response to God to be able to say, "Amen" to all His providences, to say "I believe" to all His pronouncements;
e. It is easy to say it in lap of luxury, in atmosphere of peace, in comfort of civilization and culture; but quite another thing to say it in vortex of whirlpool, in tempest of sorrow, in dark fogs of doubt, in storm of temptation;
f. Our religion is not meant to be made into garden sunshade but should be to us as umbrella in rain, as shield in battle; for when we put up "shield of faith" (Eph. 6:16) declaring "God has spoken — I believe!" storm beats on us in vain.

Yes, the third part of Paul's secret was his response to both revelation and relationship.

Conclusion

Is Paul's "good cheer" ours? It may be if we are able to put together these blessed truths and find —

1. *Inward calm because of clear revelation;*
2. *Invincible courage because of conscious relationship;*
3. *Inspiring cheerfulness because of cordial response.*

Where else but in God can we have all this? Yes, that is the dominant message of this story: *"God,* whom I am, and whom I serve . . . *God* hath given . . . I believe *God"* (vs. 23, 24, 25); and, having made it our own, we shall also do as Paul did when he "gave thanks to *God"* (v. 35).

Study No. 130 — Paul Reaches Rome

ACTS 28:1-31

In this final chapter of the Book of Acts we may trace the last stage of St. Paul's pathway of progress from the capital of the Jewish world to that of the Gentile world. As has been truly said, here was a fitting climax. After the occupation of many outposts by Christian strategy — Antioch, Philippi, Corinth, Ephesus, and others —the very center of Empire, Rome itself, was to serve the Divine purpose of Paul's great Commander. This, it is said, would certainly throw light on the remarkable amount of space, proportionally, that is assigned to the steps by which the Apostle was brought to Rome, which to a Jew would be "the uttermost part of the earth" (1:8). To have reached this *ultima Thule* meant witnessing not only to those who held to a true religion though inadequately ("in Jerusalem"), nor to those who had a mixed religion, partly true and partly false ("in Samaria"), but to those who had no real, vital religion at all. These were "the Gentiles" mentioned at the close of this chapter (v. 28). To reach them Paul was marvelously led and kept en route to Rome and in that great city itself.

I. Preservation (vs. 1-6)

1. *Succor* (vs. 1, 2)
   a. When Paul and his companions in shipwreck got to land they found it was Melita (v. 1), Malta of today, island about 60 miles south of Sicily, 17 miles long and 9 broad at widest part; has belonged to British Empire for over 200 years, but in Paul's time was part of Roman province of Sicily;
   b. Name "barbarians" (v. 2, A.S.V.) for natives of island one always given by Greeks, of whom Luke was one, to

those outside own race, especially of mixed origin; but these were not barbaric in disposition, for they showed shipwrecked strangers "philanthropy" (Gr. here and in Tit. 3:4), i.e., love of man as man, or "man-lovingness," as Archbishop Benson once rendered it;
N.B. How much more should Christians be true "philanthropists," showing forth the "philanthropy," or man-lovingness, "of God our Saviour" (Tit. 3:4) in every possible way, by earnest love and constant prayer and zealous effort on behalf of all men!

c. These people welcomed Paul and his companions with warmth not only of heart, but of hearth, because of wet and cold; for it was middle of November, and perhaps Apostle was especially susceptible to damp and chill (cf. 2 Cor. 11:27).

2. *Surprise* (vs. 3-6)
   a. With characteristic energy and co-operation Paul was taking his part in gathering of brushwood for fire, when viper fastened on his hand; as it clung to him, onlookers in their superstition felt sure Paul must be murderer and that vengeance had thus overtaken him;
   N.B. Greeks personified Justice and worshipped her as goddess, and Maltese had evidently adopted similar idea;
   b. But Paul remained calm and, in short time after he had shaken off viper, they, having watched apprehensively, saw no harm had come to him; and so their superstition received salutory shock and, changing opinion radically in revulsion of feeling, thought Paul was a god;
   N.B. To pagan minds miracle suggested divinity (cf. 14:11, 12); perhaps Maltese knew of Greek myths representing certain gods as possessing power over snakes;
   c. Astonishment was great and Paul's experience, fulfilment of Christ's promise (cf. Mark 16:18a), so impressive as to help prepare way for Gospel.

II. Power (vs. 7-10)

1. *Salutation* (v. 7)
   a. Striking that prisoners should have been so courteously

received and entertained for "three days" by leading man of island.

b. Publius, local Roman governor, showed friendliness and generosity to Paul and his fellow-travellers;

2. *Service* (vs. 8-10)

a. Opportunity soon came for Apostle to do Master's work and return kindness in very definite way: father of Publius was ill with fever and dysentery (two Greek medical terms appropriate to Luke); and Paul, using his power of healing, was means of recovery and blessing (cf. Jas. 5:14-16);

b. This led to other similar cases of healing; and again Christ's words were fulfilled (cf. Mark 16:18c); and deep gratitude was shown;

N.B. Some think use of word "us" in v. 10 implies Luke's assistance as medical man; but it seems more likely that healings were all miraculous; in either case they were Divinely wrought to bear witness to Gospel (cf. Heb. 2:3, 4);

c. Luke tells us they stayed on Malta "three months" (v. 11), which would seem to bring them to February; or, as navigation did not usually open till beginning of March, term may be quite general; but we may be sure Paul was about his Master's business during this time of waiting.

III. Progress (vs. 11-16)

1. *Safety* (vs. 11-13)

a. With southerly wind to take them across to Sicily, party embarked in ship of Alexandria, perhaps another wheat cargo-boat (cf. 27:6, 38) which had been driven by gale to spend winter at usual Maltese port of Valetta, present capital of island;

N.B. "Sign" of ship (v. 11) would be figures painted or carved on prow according to custom, sometimes representing gods as well as name of vessel; "Twin Brothers" (v. 11, A.S.V., Gr. *dioscuri*) Castor and Pollux were two mythical sons of Jupiter, supposed to be protectors of navigation and guardian deities of sailors; said to have been taken up into sky, so that two stars in constellation Gemini (Twins) are called by their names;

b. Travelling without incident this time, first port of call was Syracuse (v. 12), chief town of Sicily, about 100 miles from starting-point; and stay of three days there perhaps due to need of favoring winds;

c. Thence proper course would have been northward through straits of Messina (where was severe earthquake in 1910), but as winds were evidently not favorable they had to tack, as sailors say; that is, go on in an indirect way, making slow progress — "made a circuit" (v. 13, A.S.V.);

d. They then arrived at Rhegium, modern Reggio, town on southwest tip of Italy, opposite Messina and about 80 miles direct from Syracuse;
N.B. Rhegium was famous for nearness of rock Scylla and whirlpool Charybdis, become proverbial for dangerous dilemma;

e. Finally, with south wind, such as they required, ship left next day and reached overnight Puteoli, modern Pozzuoli, on Bay of Naples; it was chief port of Rome, 140 miles away, and therefore great commercial center;

2. *Sympathy* (vs. 14-16)

a. Paul found Christians at Puteoli, interesting reminder of extent to which Christianity had spread during his lifetime, though we have no details of formation of such groups; but, as place was on main highway and had large Jewish population, fact of church there would not be surprising, and we know how widely report of Pentecost must have spread (cf. 2:5-11);

b. Stay of week at Puteoli may have been due to considerateness of Julius (cf. 27:3, 43), for as prisoner Paul could not have decided on it; but fellowship must have been great joy and cheer to him and to local group;

c. At length travellers approached imperial city, mistress of world, founded B.C. 753, and containing then about million and half people from all parts; road from Brundusium (modern Brindisi) to Rome called after great Roman official, Appius Claudius Caecus, who began its building in B.C. 312, the "Appian Way";

d. Christian brethren from city came 43 miles out to meet Paul at Market of Appius (v. 15, A.S.V.), where travellers rested and changed horses; another group, probably, met him 10 miles further on, at "The Three Taverns," inns or resting-places;

e. Seven days at Puteoli would have given time for these Christians to hear of Paul's coming; we know three years before there was important church at Rome (cf. Rom. 1:7-15; 15:14, 22-24, 28-33; 16:3-16), probably also founded from Pentecost (cf. 2:10);

f. Beautiful picture of Roman brethren coming to meet Apostle, and at sight of them he "thanked God, and took courage" (v. 15); this would seem to suggest some depression or even fear, for Paul was very human, and man of strong emotions who had been through much;

g. Thankfulness and trustfulness thus expressed themselves just as he was nearing goal; he would be reminded, as Bengel says, that "Christ was at Rome also," and would recall Master's "Be of good cheer" (23:11) and "Fear not" (27:24) looking toward this very time;

h. On arrival in Rome, Paul was granted special privilege of being "suffered to dwell by himself" (v. 16), striking testimony to his influence, and perhaps because of what he had done (cf. 27:21-36), to which Julius might well have borne witness; at any rate, "when a man's ways please the Lord He maketh even his enemies to be at peace with him" (Prov. 16:7);

i. Paul would, however, be bound to soldier guard by chain and, as man after man took his turn, Paul would be able to testify and so spread Gospel (cf. Eph. 6:20; Phil. 1:13; 4:22); and thus he was both physically fettered and spiritually free.

IV. Preaching (vs. 17-29)

1. *By Statement* (vs. 17-24)

a. With keen earnestness Paul allowed very little time to

elapse — "three days" (v. 17) — after tiring journey before summoning representatives of large and important body of Jews in Rome, where there were at this time not less than seven synagogues; for his intense desire was to prepare ground for Gospel by letting fellow-countrymen know truth concerning himself and something of what had happened;

b. In telling story he shows clearly he was true Jew and was accused, not accuser (vs. 17-26); he had invited them to hear his defense because it was through Messianic hope he was imprisoned (cf. 23:6; 24:15; 26:6-8);

c. Jews replied they had received no information by letter, probably because no letter could well have reached them so soon; and although some Roman or other Jews present must have heard of Paul they either were diplomatic and did not wish to report definitely against him, or else were anxious to show him courtesy of hearing;

d. All they knew — or said — was that Christianity was everywhere spoken against (v. 22); so day was fixed for careful consideration; and Jews assembled in great numbers;

e. Theme of Paul's message (v. 23) was Kingdom of God, Divine reign over Jewish nation to which Scriptures so often pointed forward (cf. Isa. 9 and 11; Dan. 7:13, 14, etc.); this was associated with Jesus as Messiah, king of David's line (cf. Isa. 9:7);

f. Manner of Paul's witness varied: he "expounded," or explained (cf. 11:4); he "testified," or gave his personal experience; thus kingdom (cf. 1:3; 8:12) and Jesus as Messiah (cf. 17:3; 18:5) were earnestly and definitely put before these Jews and based on own Scriptures (cf. 13:15; 24:14; 26:22);

g. Lovingly and clearly Paul "persuaded them" all day long, with result that some accepted his message and others continued in unbelief; Gospel always divides people (cf. 13:43-45; 14:1, 2; 17:4, 5).

2. *By Scripture* (vs. 25-29)

a. This want of harmony necessitated faithful, severe, final word; and, quoting from Isaiah (6:9, 10), Paul showed how remarkably Divine inspiration had foretold this very result;

b. Same passage had been used by Christ of disobedience in His day, when He was rejected by Israel (cf. Matt. 13:14, 15; Mark 4:12; Luke 8:10), and by John (12:40) at close of Christ's public ministry; and Paul's use of it here is especially significant since this seems to have been last offer of Gospel to Jewish nation as whole;

c. Door of Israel's national opportunity was closing, and that of Gentiles' was opening; so this action in relation to Jews is important, Paul having lived up to his own dictum, "to the Jew first" (Rom. 1:16; cf. 13:46);

d. His discussion had showed Messiahship of Jesus Christ according to O.T. (cf. v. 23); but when Jews refused to accept Him, Apostle used their own Scriptures against them, at same time separating himself very solemnly from their disobedience (cf. "your," v. 25, A.S.V., with "our," v. 17), and pressing home responsibility of rejecting his message;

e. Judicial hardening follows unbelief: first, we will not, then, we cannot; this is meaning of word "atrophied," condition of those who are "past feeling" (Eph. 4:19), with consciences seared, or branded (cf. 1 Tim. 4:2);

f. Offer of salvation then announced as being transferred to Gentiles (v. 28), and scenes of withdrawal from Jews in Antioch, Corinth, and Ephesus repeated with finality in Rome (cf. 13:46-48; 18:5-7; 19:8, 9); reluctantly, and yet without alternative, Paul turns from own kin to strangers, and Jews as nation are left outside fold.

V. Providence (vs. 30, 31)

1. *Sanction* (v. 30)

a. During two years in which Paul waited for his appeal to be heard, he was still permitted to "dwell by himself" v. 16); and he had "his own hired house";

b. He was also free to welcome all who came to see him; and we know from prison Epistles he was surrounded by loving friends who came and went as his messengers to churches (cf. Eph. 6:21; Phil. 2:19-30; Col. 4:10-14; Philem. 10-31, 23, 24).

2. *Summary* (v. 31)

a. Paul used prison experience as opportunity to herald Divine kingdom, with Jesus Christ as King, by means of "preaching . . . and teaching" — two aspects of Christian minister's work:

(1) Announcing Master to those outside fold; and —

(2) Instructing believers in their most holy faith;
N.B. Cf. Col. 1:28, A.S.V., written of himself at this very time: "admonishing" was warning, and "teaching" was instruction; God's representative must be both "salt" (cf. Matt. 5:13) and "light" (Matt. 5:14);

b. Part of "teaching" took form of Epistles written during period — Ephesians, Colossians, Philippians, Philemon; and they have to do with Gentile Church after Jewish rejection of Gospel (cf. Eph. 3:1-6);

c. Abruptness of book's close seems to suggest Paul was released, view supported by Epistles to Timothy and Titus; it is beautiful picture, last glimpse of Paul preaching in metropolis of world, "with all boldness, none forbidding him" (v. 31, A.S.V.; cf. Eph. 6:19; Phil. 1:12-14), for his prison had become his pulpit.

Conclusion

The story in this chapter is a striking illustration both of God's attitude towards His servants and of His action on their behalf:

1. *God Protecting*

In accordance with Divine assurance, all on shipboard had come safely to land, for God always fulfills His word and His promises are never broken; and this will He do for us also.

2. *God Providing*
   Shipwrecked company found not only safety, but sympathy, help, cheer, and all they needed (cf. Psa. 34:22; John 21:9; Phil. 4:19); and we shall find the same.
3. *God Preserving*
   Even poisonous reptile was not beyond power of God (cf. Mark 16:18), and He kept His servant alive in face of great danger; and thus He will keep us if it be His will.
4. *God Proving*
   Healings effected by Paul were fine testimony to grace of God in answer to prayer, and so definite a witness was not without permanent results; nor will ours be, though it may take different forms, according to God's will.
5. *God Planning*
   Completion of voyage to Rome and Paul's two years in prison there show every evidence of Divine direction, so that we may conclude with Bengel that when Paul is at Rome it is the proper ending of the Book of Acts; it is the climax of the Gospel; it is the victory of the Word of God.

Thus, once again, it was proved true that the Lord redeems, keeps, honors, uses, and blesses His servants. All that is necessary is that they should trust in Him and be surrendered to Him. That was what Paul did and what he ever proved himself to be. Shall we not follow his example even as he followed Christ's?

Study No. 131 — Gratitude and Fortitude

ACTS 28:15

THE APOSTLE had had more than one prison experience — those in Philippi, in Jerusalem, in Caesarea, for example. Now it was as a prisoner that he was nearing Rome. Three times God met His servant's special need as he endured the curtailment of his liberty. In 23:11, "the Lord stood by him"; in 27:23, "the angel of God" "stood by" him; but in our present text we read that it was "the brethren," Paul's fellow-Christians living in Rome, who were used to greet him in the Name of the Lord and to stand by him in sympathy and good cheer — "whom when Paul saw," we are told, "he thanked God, and took courage."

In these words are a summary of true Christian experience: gratitude, looking back over the past and seeing what God has done, and fortitude, looking forward trustfully into the unknown future because God is in it.

I. Thankfulness

1. *For Christian Fellowship*
   - a. It was timely — Paul had sent brethren in Rome Epistle from Corinth about three years before, but we do not know how they received it, nor how they heard time of his coming, unless through Christians at Puteoli, where he had spent week en route (cf. v. 14);
   - b. It was sacrificial — to reach meeting-places they had to walk 43 and 33 miles respectively, and they doubtless anticipated Apostle's needs by bringing necessities, as had Maltese in sending him on his way (cf. v. 10);
   - c. It was noble — he was prisoner in chains and perhaps they risked reputations or even safety in showing oneness in Christ.

2. *For God as Author of Christian Fellowship*
   a. Sight of brethren reminded Paul of God — nothing trivial or coincidental, but rather much that is invaluable and providential, in esteem of Christian friends;
   b. Paul recognized God in everything (cf. Rom. 10:12; 2 Tim. 3:11), and, like John on sea of Tiberias, was quick to declare at such times, "It is the Lord" (John 21:7);
   c. Paul proved Providence of God promotes thankfulness in all circumstances of life.

II. Trustfulness

1. *Reason* — Paul, 60 years old by now, after strenuous life of service for Christ, and much persecution and hardship, could well have become permanently discouraged; but no, as he later wrote (2 Tim. 1:12), though he suffered, he was not ashamed, for he knew whom he had believed and was persuaded that God was able;
2. *Meaning* — trust may be summed up as faith fixed upon God's presence, purpose, promise, and power;
3. *Result* — courage, which includes renewed strength and revived gladness.

Conclusion

1. Discouragement may come to all, but consideration of God's grace will bring encouragement: thankfulness and trustfulness, gratitude and fortitude;
2. Then there will be no relaxation of purpose, no reason for despondency, no fear of failure, no doubt of sufficiency:
   "It is better to have courage to face difficulties than to have no difficulties to face: the one is a leaping, sparkling river; the other is a stagnant pool."
   Let us, also, thank God and take courage!

Study No. 132 — The Apostle in Captivity

ACTS 28:15-31

ST. PAUL and Rome! The Apostle to the Gentiles and the metropolis of the Gentiles! What a striking combination! "I must also see Rome," said he (19:21), thus early purposing to go there. "I long to see you," he wrote to Christians there (Rom. 1:11), "I trust to see you" (Rom. 15:24). "So must thou bear witness also at Rome" (23:11) — so spake the Divine promise. Now we read, "And when we came to Rome" (v. 16); at last Paul's hopes were fulfilled, but with what a difference! He had little thought in earlier days of the precise circumstances of his actual arrival in the great city of his dreams.

I. The Prisoner

1. *Physically Fettered*
   a. Nothing new to Paul in chains — "in prisons more frequent" (2 Cor. 11:23);
   b. But he had also written: "I will glory of the things which concern my infirmities" (2 Cor. 11:30); for he was —
2. *Spiritually Free*
   a. Rejoicing in fellowship (v. 15), in answer to prayer (cf. Rom. 1:12);
   b. Revealing courage (v. 15), because of that fellowship;
   c. Receiving privilege (v. 16), perhaps through his services during shipwreck, but certainly because of his outstanding character;
   d. Realizing duty (v. 17), prisoner though he was, and after only three days set to work to witness to his Master.

II. The Preacher

1. *Where He Preached*
   a. Prison was Paul's pulpit;
   b. Cf. difficulties mentioned in "Prison Epistles" (e.g., Eph. 3:1; 4:1; 6:19, 20; Phil. 1:7, 12-17; 2:19-30; 4:11, 12; Col. 1:24; 2:5; 4:10, 18).
2. *What He Preached*
   a. Had definite plan and unmistakeable message;
   b. Observe terms used:
      (1) "Hope of Israel" (v. 20);
      (2) "Kingdom of God" (vs. 23, 31);
      (3) "Salvation of God" (v. 28);
      (4) "Concerning Jesus" (v. 23) and "those things which concern the Lord Jesus Christ" (v. 31).
3. *Why He Preached*
   a. Paul could not but witness to great realities of Christian faith;
   b. For years they had dominated his life, and nothing, not even physical circumstances of most untoward nature, could prevent him from declaring those things that possessed his very soul.
4. *How He Preached*
   a. Lovingly (vs. 17-20) — nothing could be finer than spirit in which he approached Jewish leaders;
   b. Clearly (v. 23) — "expounded" message from Scriptures as basis of all he had to say;
   c. Earnestly (v. 23) — "testified" — of his own experience; "persuading" hearers to experience Christ for themsleves;
   d. Faithfully (vs. 25-28) — when message refused, Apostle showed Jews alternative by quoting from own Scriptures solemn description of hardness of heart (cf. Isa. 6:9, 10);
   e. Confidently (v. 31) — "with all boldness" (A.S.V.) — message of salvation (cf. v. 28) given fearlessly, for Paul knew well value and power of Divine grace (cf. Rom. 1:15,16).
5. *When He Preached*
   a. Promptly — "after three days" (v. 17);

b. Tirelessly — "from morning till evening" (v. 23);
c. Incessantly — "two whole years" (v. 30) — never wearied of his theme.

III. The Prophet

This prison ministry of St. Paul was much wider, fuller, and deeper service for God than Apostle could conceivably have imagined beforehand; he here takes his place in noble succession of prophets, not only echoing words of Isaiah, but assuming prophet's dual responsibility:

1. *Foretelling*
   a. Saw occasion for prophesying wider ministries for Gospel (cf. v. 28);
   b. Foresaw that Jewish refusals would lead to Gentile acceptances;
2. *Forth-telling*
   a. "Preaching" kingdom of God and "teaching" about Christ, there "in his own hired house" (vs. 30, 31);
   b. Instructing contemporary churches by sending friends to minister to them, and also by writing some of choicest Epistles (Philippians, Colossians, Ephesians, Philemon);
   c. Influencing Church of Christ down through centuries — his life and work much more widely known today, and far more powerful, than could have been apart from such an opportunity for meditation and writing.

IV. The Plan

Situation was so wholly different from all reasonable expectations, and yet advantages were many and marvellous:

1. *For the Man*
   a. Paul was safe from Jews; no plots or opposition could touch him (cf. 21:30, 31; 23:12-15; 25:1-3, etc.);
   b. He was free from burden of churches; no longer worn and torn by anxieties or physical strain (cf. 2 Cor. 11:28-31), he was enabled to recuperate spiritually and bodily after years of heavy pressure;
   c. He was in close touch with friends of various churches through whom his influence could still be strongly felt

(cf. Phil. 2:21; 4:18; Col. 4:7, 8, etc.).

2. *For the Message*
   a. Messenger became conspicuous to all (cf. Phil. 1:12-14; 4:22);
   b. Must have witnessed to many a soldier guarding him (cf. v. 16), who was relieved frequently; thus message of Gospel would be carried far and wide to different divisions of Roman army;
   c. Christian message, humanly speaking, might never have been written into Epistles but for this enforced seclusion of St. Paul.

Conclusion

1. *The Mystery of God's Goodness*
   Paul's experience was striking illustration of movement of God's Providence as seen in Rom. 8:28:
   a. It is active — "work"
   b. It is inclusive — "all things work"
   c. It is harmonious — "all things work together"
   d. It is beneficent —"all things work together for good"
   e. It is specific — "all things work together for good to them that love God, to them who are the called according to His purpose"
   Does this wonderful statement apply to us? Are we called, and do we love Him?
2. *The Might of God's Grace*
   Here is illustration of Divine power:
   a. What one man, though in prison, can do if only he is filled with Holy Spirit;
   b. What one servant of God can accomplish anywhere if only he is faithful.
   "Not I," said Paul, "but Christ" (Gal. 2:20); "not I, but the grace of God" (1 Cor. 15:10); "I can do all things through Christ which strengtheneth me" (Phil. 4:13). Can we say this from our hearts?

Study No. 133 — God's Plan for Paul

ACTS 28:31

"EVERY MAN'S LIFE A PLAN OF GOD" is the suggestive title of one of Horace Bushnell's masterly sermons. We can readily see its appropriateness to the career of St. Paul. The circumstances of his life were very different from his expectation, and yet how remarkably he was blessed. Most assuredly his life was "a plan of God," and nowhere is this more clearly shown than during the two years of his imprisonment in Rome.

I. Influence

1. *Paul's First Circle of Influence*
   a. Testimony to soldiers who "kept him" (v. 16);
   b. Through them to guard and palace (cf. Phil. 1:12, 13).
2. *Paul's Second Circle of Influence*
   a. Witness to personalities in far-off places; cf. Onesimus and Philemon (Col. 4:19; Philem.);
   b. Through them and many others to churches and individuals otherwise, perhaps, untouched.
3. *Paul's Third Circle of Influence*
   a. Writing of "Epistles of First Captivity" — Ephesians, Colossians, Philippians, Philemon — in which Christ is seen preeminently as Lord;
   b. Through them to countless millions in all Church history, all over world.

II. Instruction

1. *On God's Providence*
   a. We today may learn, as his followers doubtless did then, from Paul's experience that where God sets us there is work to do for Him;

b. We do not need change of surroundings, but change of attitude — if man is willing God is able.

2. *On Untoward Circumstances*
   a. We shall do well to remember apparent hindrances often prove real help;
   b. Cf. Biblical examples of Divine over-ruling, e.g. —
      (1) Joseph and his brethren — "God meant it unto good" (Gen. 50:20);
      (2) Balak and Balaam — "God turned the curse into a blessing" (Neh. 13:2);
      (3) Pilate and Herod — "Thy counsel determined before to be done" (4:27, 28);
   c. As Paul wrote Epistles in prison, so have other servants of God devoted waiting time to profitable writing that has blessed many: e.g., John Bunyan imprisoned in Bedford Gaol wrote major portion of *Pilgrim's Progress;* Martin Luther shut up in Castle of Wartburg translated Bible into German;

   N.B. Mackay of Uganda said: "Times of persecution are always busy printing times."

Conclusion

If we would exercise Paul's influence and profit from his instruction, we must emulate his character. When he said, "Whose I am —" he was declaring that God's ownership of him was the basis of his ministry; and in Rom. 1:14-16 he reveals his strong feeling about his message by means of three positive assertions:

1. *"I am debtor"* (v. 14); he realized his obligation to the souls of men;
2. *"I am ready"* (vs. 15); he declared his preparedness to witness in Rome;
3. *"I am not ashamed"* (v. 16); he expressed his unfaltering courage and unshakeable conviction in relation to the Gospel.

Oh, that we might follow Paul as he followed Christ!

Summary

The Book of Acts is marked by three great features:

1. **The predominance of the Divine element in the Christian Church.**

   This is seen in the prominence given to the Risen Lord and the Holy Spirit as the very existence of the Church is explained. That "blessed company of all faithful people" was supernatural in its beginning, and supernatural in its course. No compulsion led to membership in this Church, for every worldly advantage was against it. Men could persecute it and devastate it; but they could not destroy it. This supernatural manifestation is one of the greatest evidences of Christianity itself. In the Book of Acts, therefore, a new dispensation of God's grace is being experienced.

2. **The universality of the Gospel.**

   The keynote of this is struck in 1:8, followed by gradual preparation, development, and realization, until the scope of the Book has included Rome, the center of the then known world (chapter 28). Thus, a world-wide commission is being fulfilled.

3. **The hostility of the world towards Christianity.**

   This is encountered very early in the Book (chap. 3), and is prominent throughout, taking various forms. The Jewish religion is being fulfilled and thereby abrogated, while Gentile idolatry is being opposed and destroyed, with resulting deadly enmity from both Jews and non-Jews. This is met primarily by the instrumentality of Paul, as "persecutor becomes propagator." Doubtless the Acts was written very largely to record the fading of Israel's glory and the coming of Christianity into clear light. Thus a great revolution is being carried out.

These three great principles also characterize present-day Christianity when it is truly understood and fully proclaimed. We as Christians are experiencing the dispensation of grace; we are continuing to fulfil the Master's world-wide commission; and a great spiritual revolution is being carried on. At the same time, however, we cannot but note that the Book of Acts ends as it began, with "the kingdom of God" (1:3; 28:31), that consummation which is yet to be realized, when Christ comes again and not before. We pray, "Thy kingdom come" (Matt. 6:10), thereby implying that it has not yet arrived. The Church is here, but the Kingdom is yet to be. Acts is not only the Book of the Church, then, but also the Book of the Kingdom, and this was appropriately the theme of St. Paul in relation to the Jews. Today, we preach the Gospel of Divine grace, as did he, to both Jew and Gentile, but the time will come when the Kingdom of Christ will be set up and He will reign as King. "Even so, come, Lord Jesus!"